The Encyclopedia of Furniture

By Joseph Aronson

THE ENCYCLOPEDIA OF FURNITURE

THE BOOK OF FURNITURE AND DECORATION: PERIOD
AND MODERN

The Encyclopedia of Furniture

THIRD EDITION—COMPLETELY REVISED

Joseph Aronson

CROWN PUBLISHERS, INC., NEW YORK

CONTENTS

FOREWORD TO THE FIRST EDITION

It has long seemed to me that the art and industry of furniture sorely needed a convenient encyclopedia. Everyone who buys or uses furniture, who makes, designs, or sells it, collectors, architects, decorators and students must feel frequently the singular lack of a handy reference work for the checking of details, the verification of periods, the inspiration of designs, the nature of materials, and so on.

In preparing this work I have kept that need before me. Of course, a balanced condensation of the vast body of furniture history and technique could not be achieved without the sacrifice of an infinity of detail, all interesting and pertinent to the critic and the specialist. That sacrifice seemed justified in the cause of compactness. If accuracy, accessibility and thoroughness could compensate for brevity and limited details, it seemed that a handy one-volume encyclopedia could prove useful and valuable for most needs. I have sought therefore to provide dependable *initial* information. The seeker after more detailed knowledge has available a vast library from which the bibliography (page 476) is selected as having been of most assistance to the writer.

One picture, say the Chinese, is worth ten thousand words. This numerical ratio based on the quantity of photographs offered in this volume would probably satisfy the writer and the reader in their joint temptation to delve into the endlessly fascinating details of furniture lore. The major part of this book consists of monographs of the important items of furniture knowledge, supplemented by some 2,500 separate definitions and descriptions. The larger subjects or classifications — America, Chair, Construction, France, Gothic, Modern, Wood, and so on — are treated at some length and are related to the arrangements of pictures. More than half of the book is devoted to photographs, in the hope of effecting the economies suggested by the aforementioned Chinese proverb. Thus Number 170, a Gothic cupboard of Flamboyant style, is grouped with CABI-NETS but is also listed by number under FLAMBOYANT. The sequence of types pictured in these groups is roughly based on the chronological development from the basis or prototype; it also seeks to demonstrate the flow of influences over national boundaries, and the bridge of time as well as locale in these developments.

That omissions of more or less importance exist is a foregone conclusion, their importance depending on the point of view. The accuracy of material presented is often a matter of choosing between conflicting sources; for more palpable errors, I beg the reader's indulgence in advance. In this connection it is interesting to observe that actual furniture relics of older days are sometimes less dependable as sources of knowledge than are the old documents, engravings, and paintings.

JOSEPH ARONSON

New York, N.Y.
October 10, 1938

FOREWORD TO THE THIRD REVISED EDITION

The Enjoyment of Furniture, in common with other arts of cultivated living, has in a generation achieved the status of an art itself. There is useful and philosophic pleasure in recognizing, in the evolution of utilitarian design from artifact to art, a key to the manners, mores, and means of other times and places.

The simple fact that a vade mecum to this art survived over a quarter of a century is significant. During this period I have received a stream of generous and constructive criticism, resulting in: the format of this edition, which intends primarily to offer a quicker correlation between pictures and text; addition of material on the 19th century; substitutions and relocations to emphasize particular points; and the review of illustrations as pertinent to the broad subject in style and provenance.

The format, with its continuous dictionary style, endeavors to bring illustrations into close sequence with the text, to minimize page turning, to visualize and verbalize simultaneously. The ideal balance is of course never achieved, since illustrations simply do not occur in such neat sequence. Let us confess that most evolutionary steps are theoretical—traceable only after the fact; one can hardly say that form A actually inspired form B. Chronologically, the reverse may often be true. This merely proves that style development is never the work of an individual; rather, the large maturing of style is the product of a whole society, homogeneous and one-purposeful.

The enlarged view of 19th-century furniture is a bow to the passage of time and widening horizons. As the century recedes into perspective, its Industrial Revolution gains significance as the springboard for all 20th-century philosophy of design. Grandparents become ancestors, and the young no longer try to hide the shame of ancestral esthetic indiscretions, but are charmed by the naïveté, the philosophic gropings, and the inept grapplings with technical innovations and discoveries.

Whether or not late-19th-century furniture may legitimately be called antique is a question for antiquarians. It *is* furniture; and for better or worse it sums up emotions and capabilities and perceptions of its makers, the sentiments of a wide range of impulses reflecting a whole milieu. This book offers no esthetic judgments. It seeks only to illustrate those forms and styles that in their time gave satisfaction to their makers and users.

Parenthetically, I make no claim for the authenticity of any piece pictured in this volume. A piece whose origins and history must be reconstructed from the physical evidence of its material leaves much to the imagination and veracity of the "expert." Expertise is an occupation beyond the province of the student of the art of furniture. Before mass production, virtually every piece was unique, the concept and creation of an individual working whimsically and often capriciously. We can identify some motives and manners; finally we are compelled to say that if this or that detail is not demonstrably true, it ought to be so by deduction. Dates, most of all, are a snare and a delusion. They are used here less for historical certification than to try to place a feature of a style within a historical framework. The collector will do well to precede every date with a good broad "circa."

One group of suggestions came from those who felt that artificially narrow limits had been placed on the geography of furniture design. I am convinced that the mainstream flowed from Italy to France with the spreading Renaissance; thence all over Europe to merge with or to obliterate the native arts peculiar to isolated locales. With the end of isolation usually came the end of native art. Every country absorbed what it wanted of outside influences, and reissued its version of what it accepted. Thus all of Europe and Europe's colonies developed styles tributary to the mainstream. These are generally too parallel to the source, too little varied in essence, to justify extensive differentiation in a volume dedicated to conciseness.

England merits disproportionate attention because the domestic scale in furniture, the felicity of everyday living, as we know it, and the prototypes of most American furniture developed there. And, of course, there is substantial representation of American furniture, for all its provincial derivation from English furniture.

The question of nomenclature was solved arbitrarily in favor of conciseness. This removes "stylish" names, trade jargon, and the faintly precious use of foreign terms. The French have good, precise terms for many articles of furniture, but liberal usage here would weight the book too heavily with bilingual redundancies. Similarly, the fashionable names beloved of the merchandising world tend to be too ephemeral, and were sacrificed to brevity.

JOSEPH ARONSON

New York, N.Y.
November 1, 1965

ACKNOWLEDGMENTS

Without a world of assistance, advice, and cooperation of many individuals and institutions, this work would have been impossible; and whatever merit it may prove to have is largely due to their generous aid. Among the collectors and dealers who provided photographs as well as advice, I am pleased to list:

Mrs. Faith Andrews; Bergdorf Goodman Antiques; Brunovan, Inc.; Dalva Brothers, Inc.; Di Salvo Galleries; Dover Publications; Duveen Brothers, Inc.; French & Company, Inc.; Ginsburg & Levy, Inc.; Charles R. Gracie & Sons, Inc.; Knoll Associates, Inc.; Liebhold-Wallach, Inc.; Frederick Lunning; Lo Mejor de España; Herman Miller Furniture Co.; P. Nathan, Inc.; Needhams Antiques, Inc.; R. Olivieri; Frank Partridge, Inc.; Putting Antiques Corp.; Jens Risom Inc.; Don Ruseau, Inc.; Israel Sack, Inc.; Mrs. Samuel Schwartz; Stair & Co., Inc.; Swedish News Agency; Symons Galleries, Inc.; Thonet Industries, Inc.; Arthur S. Vernay, Inc.; John S. Walton, Inc.; Wood and Hogan, Inc.

* * *

The major source of photographs has of course been the magnificent collections of many libraries and museums. I am happy to voice my gratitude to their staff members who so courteously and resourcefully put so much material into my hands.

Albany Institute of History & Art, Albany, N.Y.; Avery Library, Columbia University, New York; The Brooklyn Museum, Brooklyn, N.Y.; Calhoun Mansion, Clemson College, Clemson, S.C.; Colonial Williamsburg, Williamsburg, Va.; Cooper Union Museum, New York; The Henry Ford Museum, Dearborn, Mich.; The Frick Collection, New York; The Newark Museum, Newark, N.J.; The Grand Rapids Public Library, Grand Rapids, Mich.; Grand Rapids Public Museum, Grand Rapids, Mich.; The Hispanic Society of America, New York; The Maryland Historical Society, Baltimore, Md.; The Metropolitan Museum of Art, New York; The Montreal Museum of Fine Arts, Montreal, Canada; Munson-Williams-Proctor Institute, Utica, N.Y.; The Museum of Modern Art, New York; Museum of The City of New York, New York; Museum of New Mexico, Santa Fe, N.M.; Musée de la Province, Quebec, Canada; William Rockhill Nelson Gallery of Art, Kansas City, Mo.; The Newark Museum, Newark, N.J.; New-York Historical Society, New York; New York Public Library, New York; The Atheneum of Philadelphia, Pa.; Philadelphia Museum of Art, Pa.; Museum of Art, Rhode Island School of Design, Providence, R.I.; Royal Ontario Museum, Toronto, Ont., Canada; Sleepy Hollow Restorations, Tarrytown, N.Y.; University of California, Los Angeles, Calif.; United States Department of the Interior, National Park Service, Washington, D.C.; Victoria & Albert Museum, South Kensington, London; Wadsworth Atheneum, Hartford, Conn,, Yale University Art Gallery, New Haven, Conn.; American Walnut Manufacturers Association; Henry Francis du Pont Winterthur Museum, Winterthur, Del.

The Encyclopedia of Furniture

THE ENCYCLOPEDIA OF FURNITURE

ABACUS. The topmost member of the capital of a column. See ORDERS.

ACACIA. A group of trees similar to the locust. Some varieties from Australia and the Sandwich Islands yield beautiful veneers ranging in color from yellow-brown to red and green. In England the name is given to the American locust, the wood of which is tough and durable and similar in texture to oak.

ACAJOU. French word for mahogany.

ACANTHUS. Conventionalized leaf of a plant growing in Asia Minor. It is found as the basis of all foliage ornament in classic Greek and Roman decoration. Romanesque and Byzantine acanthus were stiff and spiny. The Renaissance revived its use in graceful designs for every purpose. Every succeeding style has used the acanthus in exuberant or restrained manner, according to its type. See also ORNAMENT.

ACANTHUS SCROLL · LEAF · MOLDING

ACORN. Turned ornament resembling an acorn; common in Jacobean furniture as finials on chair posts and bedposts, as pendants, and as the profile of leg turnings in Jacobean tables. See also TURNING. [737.]

ACROTERIUM. Originally an ornament on the roof corners of Greek temples. In classical furniture, similar ornaments applied to the top corners of secretaries, bookcases, highboys, and other important furniture.

ADAM, The Brothers. Robert, 1728-1792; James 1730-1794. Robert, elder son of a Scottish architect, began practicing his art in London in 1758 after four years in Italy. There he had been fascinated with the excavations at Herculaneum to such an extent that the "Herculaneum" style became his, and through his influence, England's basis of decoration for half a century. This classical influence displaced the Rococo forms exploited by Chippendale and his school, and led to an excessively refined, often inappropriate delicacy of structure and ornament.

The Adams practiced as architects, employing cabinetmakers, painters, sculptors, etc., to execute their designs. Thus we find a mixture of names around some designs, such as Hepplewhite, Angelica Kauffmann, Pergolesi, Flaxman, and others, presumably in the association of designer and craftsman. They believed that every detail of the house and its furnishing must grow from the same mind, and carried this out in all the minutiae of decoration; witness their designs for carpets, lighting fixtures, sedan chairs, table service, snuffboxes, and whatnot. The fundamentals of all this they state in their book, *The Works in Architecture of Robert and James Adam* (1773). "We have been able to make use of . . . the beautiful spirit of antiquity, and to transfuse it with novelty and variety. . . ." While there exists in their work the delicate splendor of the style of Louis XVI, it derives not from the French but directly from the Roman remains. This classicism is in the earlier work imposed upon the accepted forms and proportions of Georgian furniture; later, it demanded lighter lines, in style and delicacy far removed from the mid-Georgian solidity.

The Adams fostered the transition from the Age of Mahogany to the Age of Satinwood. Their choice of woods covers just this span; beginning with the accepted mahogany, they later employed whole sur-

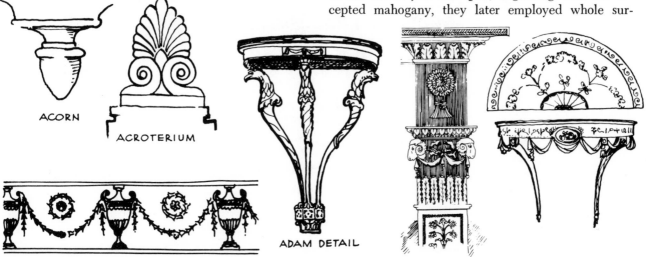

ACORN

ACROTERIUM

ADAM DETAIL

1 Page from *The Works in Architecture of Robert and James Adam* (1778).

2 DINING ROOM, LANSDOWNE HOUSE, BERKELEY SQUARE, LONDON. Designed by Robert Adam, 1765-1768.
Metropolitan Museum of Art, Rogers Fund, 1932

faces of satinwood, harewood (sycamore dyed gray), and much painted decoration. Sycamore or satinwood had delicate designs painted over in outline, or with plaques and medallions; whole pieces were likewise painted and exquisitely decorated by or in the manner of Angelica Kauffmann and her followers. Gilding over a base of white or green paint was extensively employed, particularly for mirrors, consoles, etc.

Because the architectural picture was of first importance, Adam rooms possessed a unity of design previously found only in French palaces. Most of the furniture was designed for special places. Consoles, mirrors, couches, buffets, etc., were as integral a part of the room designs as the mantels and doors. Ceilings were exquisitely ornamented with classical plaques and rinceaux; walls, generally painted light gray or jasper, were a foil for the gilt, painted, or light wood furniture. Their decoration was after the antique models of Pompeii and Herculaneum; rich ornamentation of great delicacy was painted or executed in raised plaster (composition), with medallions of classical figures, architectural motifs as pilasters, arches, niches, etc., generously distributed. Floors were patterned to reflect the ceiling design, either in carpet or in stone.

Their distinguishing details are: a preference for straight lines or square outlines; swags, festoons, rinceaux, in fact, all ornaments freely drawn but exceedingly fine in scale and painstakingly executed; mythological figures, rams' heads, lions' heads and claws, centaurs, griffins, sphinxes, caryatids, etc., with plant forms and vases on most surfaces in paint, low-relief carving, composition, and inlay.

The style has great charm and beauty, and an academic spirit of architectural correctness. Yet its very perfection brought it the criticism, in its own day as now, of being excessively polite, lacking in human warmth and the quality of livability. See also ENGLAND. [145, 471, 587, 1113, 1115, 1352.]

ADELPHI, THE. Signature or trade name of the Brothers Adam.

AFFLECK, THOMAS. Philadelphia cabinetmaker, came from London 1763, died 1795. Worked in Chippendale style. [33, 1269.]

AGE OF OAK, WALNUT, MAHOGANY, SATIN-WOOD. Easy division of the prime English periods by the woods employed in furniture, as defined by MacQuoid. Though the use of the woods may overlap, the general separations are:

Age of Oak, 1500-1660
Age of Walnut, 1660-1720
Age of Mahogany, 1720-1765
Age of Satinwood, 1765-1800

ALCOVE. Recessed part of a room. Bed alcoves exist in Pompeiian rooms, and such placing of the sleeping quarters was common in northern Europe through the Middle Ages and later. In the 18th century special beds were designed to fit such recesses. Alcoves are also used for bookcases and cabinets, dining groups, etc. [116, 668.]

ALMERY; ALMONRY. See AMBRY.

ALPINE. The mountainous sections between Germany and Italy were meeting places of the northern and southern styles. In lands like Switzerland and the Tyrol mixed styles developed, too individual to be associated definitely with either source. [104, 114, 343.]

AMARANTH. Purplish wood used for veneering since the 18th century; also called "violetwood" and "purpleheart."

AMBOYNA. An East Indian wood, used as veneer and inlay. The burls are light reddish brown, highly mottled and curled. Known and used in furniture since Roman times.

AMBRY. In medieval churches a recess for the storage of goods. The addition of doors gave it the cupboard form. The English equivalent became a large cupboard with doors; the interiors were fitted with shelves for storage. See also ARMOIRE. [169, 458, 545.]

AMBULANTE (French). Small portable table, used for serving tea, etc. Period Louis XV and after. [1251.]

AMERICA. The furniture of early America, far from being a single consistent style, is the furniture of many lands, periods, and castes. Each colony imported its furniture or its way of making furniture. Englishmen, Swedes, Hollanders, Frenchmen, Spaniards, and Germans brought to their isolated seaboard settlements the crafts of their homelands. There was virtually no intercommunication that might have amalgamated their various talents; most communication was with the home country, from which the changing styles slowly came. Consequently, the basic theme of Colonial American furniture is a laggard echo of the simpler European styles of the day.

The English colonies were predominant. Two distinct strains appear: the Puritan colonies in New England, and the royal-grant plantations in the South. The Dutch colonized the Hudson Valley, but yielded to the British merchant class. Swedes brought to the Delaware Valley their own arts, and later German colonists established their culture in the Pennsylvania forests. The French and Spanish colonies, less permanent, bore little fruit. In the Canadian Maritime Provinces and the American Southwest, respectively, there are relics of provincial improvisations on themes of the mother cultures. [1170.]

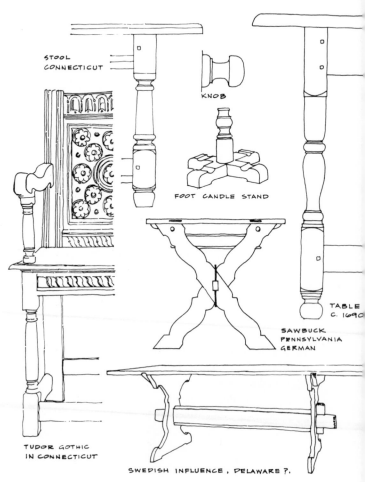

STOOL CONNECTICUT

KNOB

FOOT CANDLE STAND

TABLE C. 1690

SAWBUCK PENNSYLVANIA GERMAN

TUDOR GOTHIC IN CONNECTICUT

SWEDISH INFLUENCE, DELAWARE?

AMERICAN DETAILS

AMBRY

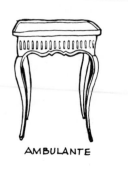

AMBULANTE

EARLY COLONIAL PERIOD—17TH CENTURY

The New England colonists were provincial middle class. Possessed by the religious zeal that later precipitated the Civil War in England, they left their homes shortly after Elizabeth's death. Inevitably, the homes they built in the New World were direct reminiscences of the Late Gothic-Tudor tradition. Novelty of a decorative nature was excluded for reasons of religious principle, economy, and possibly a lack of skill. New England furniture of the period 1620-1720 is largely distinguished by its directness and the persistence of English Jacobean characteristics. Pictures 221 and 227 show chairs of clear Gothic lineage. Chests and cupboards bore the distinctive rectangular paneled construction, as illustrated in pictures 352 and 357.

Tables of trestle type were supplemented by box styles and simple drop-leaf types, as in 1194. Desk boxes, Bible boxes, forms or stools, and a few crude beds probably complete the meager inventory of the period. The materials were usually those closest at hand and, for expediency, those most easily worked. Pine was available in tremendous widths; oak, birch, and maple were also largely used, with later work in walnut, poplar, and all at-hand woods. The wood was generally left raw, acquiring color and depth and polish through simple friction and natural darkening.

Virginia and most southern colonies were settled by a wealthier, more secular group. Their earliest furniture probably comprised the more elaborate Jacobean efforts, and it is likely that they actually imported more English furniture than did the New Englanders.

Medieval European furniture also appears in the Pennsylvania settlements of Germans and Swiss, in the Swedish colonies in the Delaware Valley after 1636, and in the Dutch communities on the Hudson. Straightforward peasant workmanship and inspiration appear in the typical chests and cupboards, tables and chairs. A naïve type of painting embellishes much of this work and indicates its descent from the Germanic peasant decoration. The older influences followed the pioneers, and pushed away from the coast to the frontiers, while the coastal settlements advanced closer to the current European model. By 1680, there was a well-established merchant class on the seaboard. Wealth and fine houses begat fine furniture. Europe was in a fine rash of commercial development, and the process of style exchanging and communication was immeasurably accelerated. French and Flemish versions of the Italian Baroque style were rapidly translated in England into the styles of the Restoration and William and Mary. There were modifying influences by way of Spain and Holland, and the Chinese urge was never altogether absent after the formation of the various trading companies.

This later 17th-century phase is identified in American furniture by the use of walnut, by turnings of bold trumpet or inverted-cup shapes, spiral turnings, elementary forms of cabriole legs, carved shells and pendants, and the appearance of highboys, lowboys,

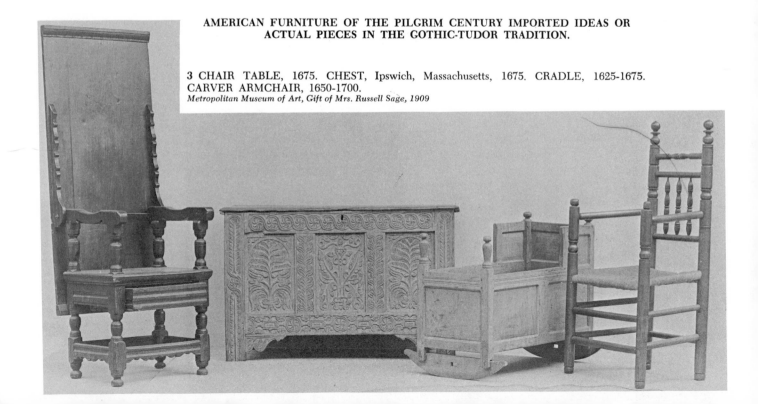

AMERICAN FURNITURE OF THE PILGRIM CENTURY IMPORTED IDEAS OR ACTUAL PIECES IN THE GOTHIC-TUDOR TRADITION.

3 CHAIR TABLE, 1675. CHEST, Ipswich, Massachusetts, 1675. CRADLE, 1625-1675. CARVER ARMCHAIR, 1650-1700.
Metropolitan Museum of Art, Gift of Mrs. Russell Sage, 1909

**AMERICAN FURNITURE IN THE 17TH CENTURY SIMPLIFIED THE
DECORATION DETAILS OF THE MOTHER COUNTRIES.**

4 COURT CUPBOARD, oak, carving of early style.
Metropolitan Museum of Art

5 PRESS CUPBOARD c. 1700. Pine of simplified
Jacobean style.
*Metropolitan Museum of Art,
Gift of Mrs. Russell Sage, 1909*

6 PILGRIM TYPE c. 1660.

7 BREWSTER CHAIR.

8 WAINSCOT CHAIR, 1648.

9 WAINSCOT CHAIR,
tape loom back.

Chairs courtesy Wadsworth Atheneum, Hartford

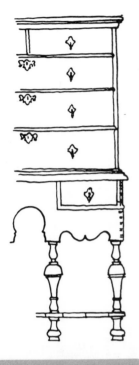

10 TRESTLE TABLE, Massachusetts, c. 1650. **11** SUN-
FLOWER CHEST, Connecticut, c. 1680. **12** MINIATURE
SPICE CABINET, Pennsylvania. Model of William and Mary
highboy.

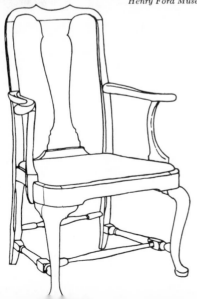

AMERICAN FURNITURE OF THE EARLY 18TH CENTURY IMPORTED MOTIFS
OF ENGLISH RESTORATION, WILLIAM AND MARY, AND CONTINENTAL STYLES.

13 BANISTER-BACK ARMCHAIR, ram's-horn arms, c. 1690. GATELEG TABLE, 1730-1740, reveals early use of mahogany. FLEMISH-STYLE ARMCHAIR, belonged to Colonel Peter Schuyler, Albany.
Henry Ford Museum, Dearborn, Mich.

15 WALL CUPBOARD, Pennsylvania. Gothic reminiscence in hardware and joining.
Metropolitan Museum of Art

16 STRETCHER TABLE, Pennsylvania type, 1725-1750.
Henry Ford Museum, Dearborn, Mich.

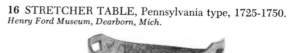

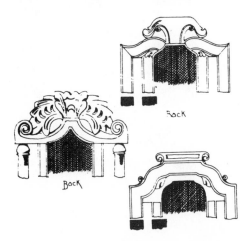

CHAIR DETAILS—FLEMISH STYLE

Front Stretcher

14 HIGHBOY, Boston, 1680-1700. William and Mary style, trumpet turnings, decorated lacquer.
Ginsburg and Levy

Scale 0   6   12   24 Inches

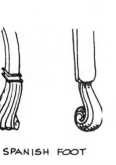

SPANISH FOOT

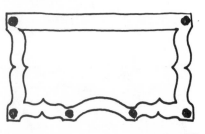

PLAN OF HIGHBOY STRETCHER

AT THE OPENING OF THE 18TH CENTURY THE ENGLISH CHARACTER
YIELDED TO A DISTINCTIVELY AMERICAN STYLE. THIS BECAME THE TYPICAL
COLONIAL OR PROVINCIAL STYLE THAT PERSISTED IN COUNTRY
FURNITURE FOR TWO CENTURIES. SEE 77-84.

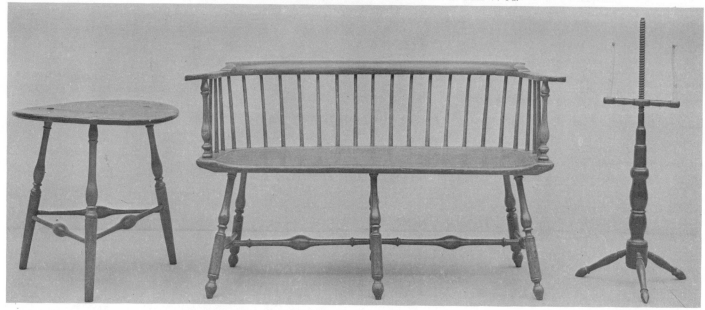

17 WINDSOR TABLE, PENNSYLVANIA SETTEE, CANDLESTAND.
Metropolitan Museum of Art, Gift of Mrs. J. Wesley Blair, 1947

19 SLANT-TOP DESK ON FRAME, New England, 1680-1700.
Pine and maple.
Museum of Art, Rhode Island School of Design, Providence

18 QUEEN ANNE ARMCHAIR, black,
New England, c. 1730.
Israel Sack, Inc.

20 WILLIAM AND MARY SIDE CHAIR,
painted black, New York, c. 1710.
Israel Sack, Inc.

22 DECORATED CHEST, Connecticut, c. 1690; oak and tulipwood.
Wadsworth Atheneum, Hartford, Conn.

21 QUEEN ANNE SIDE CHAIR, maple, Spanish
foot. Attributed to John Gaines, Portsmouth, New
Hampshire, c. 1720.
Israel Sack, Inc.

23 ROUNDABOUT CHAIR.   **24** WAGON SEAT, New England, 18th century.

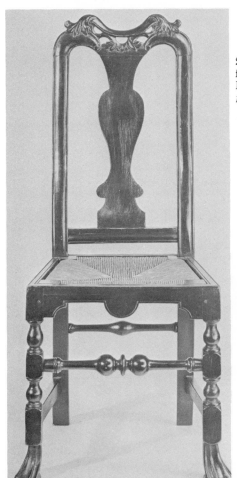

Metropolitan Museum of Art, Gift of Mrs. Russell Sage, 1909

25 LOWBOY, New England, early 18th century, is matched with **26** HIGHBOY, *below.*

Israel Sack, Inc.

Israel Sack, Inc.

27A A MIRROR IN QUEEN ANNE STYLE. Early date indicated by glass in two pieces.

27 DETAIL, NEW HAMPSHIRE CHEST, 1775-1790, attributed to Samuel Dunlop. *Wadsworth Atheneum, Hartford*

THE MID-18TH CENTURY
SHOWS EMERGING AMERICAN CHARACTERISTICS.

chests, upholstered chairs, etc.—in fact, the roots of the entire furniture program of the 18th century.

LATER COLONIAL—18TH CENTURY

With the 18th century came mahogany, the development of separate style centers in various cities, the Rococo influence, and the wealth and culture to employ them. The Queen Anne style is a generalization for the use of cabriole legs with shell carvings, pad or animal feet, and a consistent refinement of style and finish. The Georgian styles were sometimes executed in walnut, but mahogany ultimately came to the fore. By 1750, there were distinct styles of cabinetmaking in Boston, Newport, New York, and Philadelphia. Goddard in Newport, Savery, Randolph, Gostelowe, and Gillingham in Philadelphia produced furniture comparable to the better English work. Their styles were individual, employing architectural details, intricate Rococo curves, claw feet, and most of the ornament vocabulary current in England.

28 CHEST, curly maple, drake foot, mid-18th century.
Israel Sack, Inc.

Henry Ford Museum, Dearborn, Mich.

29 SECRETARY in three parts, 1730-1750. Connecticut ornament, cherry.

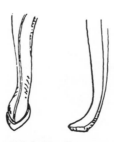

SNAKE FOOT

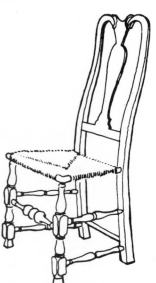

MATURE 18TH-CENTURY BAROQUE.

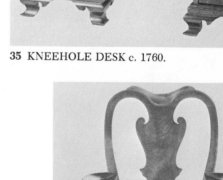

35 KNEEHOLE DESK c. 1760.   *Israel Sack, Inc.*

30 MIRROR, Dutch style.
Wadsworth Atheneum, Hartford, Conn.

31 BLOCKFRONT DESK, 1760-1770.   *Israel Sack, Inc.*

32 QUEEN ANNE WALNUT ARMCHAIR,
drake foot, attributed to William Savery,
c. 1750.   *Israel Sack, Inc.*

34 CORNER CHAIR with fluted column,
Massachusetts, c. 1760.   *Israel Sack, Inc.*

33 CHIPPENDALE-STYLE CHAIR attributed to Thomas Affleck.　*Wadsworth Atheneum, Hartford*

36 "THE ADAMS SECRETARY."　　　*Ginsburg and Levy*

37 CAMELBACK SOFA, Philadelphia, c. 1760.　*Israel Sack, Inc.*

38 CHEST-ON-CHEST, Massachusetts, 1770-1780. Transition of the base shape from serpentine to block form, then to the flat upper plane, is unusual and most ingenious. *Henry Ford Museum, Dearborn, Mich.*

39 LATE-18TH-CENTURY BED. *John S. Walton, Inc.*

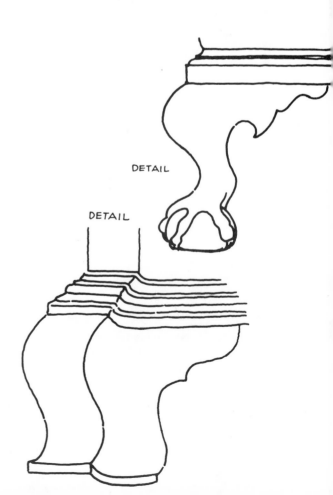

DETAIL

DETAIL

40 SERPENTINE-FRONT BUREAU, ogee bracket feet,
Massachusetts, c. 1750.   *Israel Sack, Inc.*

41 BOMBÉ CHEST, Massachusetts, c. 1760.
Henry Ford Museum, Dearborn, Mich.

42 TALL CLOCK, second quarter of
the 18th century.
Albany Institute of History and Art

TRANSITION FROM BAROQUE-LATE COLONIAL TO
CLASSIC FEDERAL STYLE IS MARKED BY GENERAL
LIGHTENING OF ORNAMENTAL DETAIL AS
WELL AS OF BULK.

44 CHEST, Sheraton style, 1820-1830. *Israel Sack, Inc.*

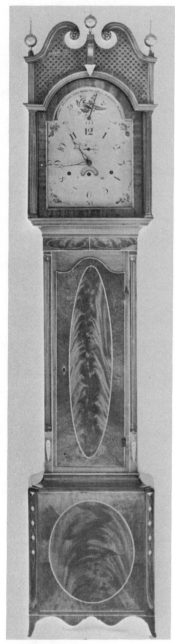

43 PENNSYLVANIA CLOCK,
c. 1810.
Henry Ford Museum, Dearborn, Mich.

FEDERAL PERIOD

The Colonial period may be considered ended by
the Revolution. When the war was over, there was
enough resentment of English things to promote the
French influence; since English style of the period
was strongly classical, however, it is difficult to isolate
the direct Italian influence through Thomas Jefferson,
the French imports, or the English classicism of Adam,
Hepplewhite, Shearer, and Sheraton. Of the latter,
there remain excellent interpretations by the Salem
carver Samuel McIntire, by Charles Bulfinch, and by
Robert Wellford of Philadelphia. The pinnacle of
American classicism was attained by Duncan Phyfe
[962] with his superb designs after Sheraton and the
French Directoire manner.

The houses into which this furniture found its way
had by this time established their own idioms, dif-

45 EXTENSION TABLE in three drop-leaf units, Hepplewhite style, late 18th century.   *Israel Sack, Inc.*

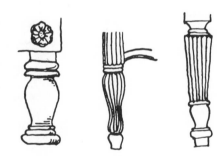

FEDERAL
TURNING

AMERICAN SHERATON CHAIR BACK

fering from the European sources and from each other, according to climate. In the South the rich plantations supported great Italian villa forms more naturally than either Italy or England. More compact houses of stone and brick developed with local variations in all seaboard cities. New England produced a superb type of wooden house, beautifully adapted to the climate and the materials. Sound craftsmanship flourished. A discreet classicism embellished architecture and furniture alike. Exterior corner boards became pilasters; flat cornice boards were molded into classically dentiled friezes; gables became pediments. Interior parts affected the same architectural costuming: fireplaces, doors and windows, dadoes and cornices were fine-scaled after Palladio and Vignola. The furniture of the period 1780-1810, whether imported from France or England or of domestic manufacture, was notably free of architectural excesses.

CHAIRS OF AMERICAN FEDERAL STYLE WERE LARGELY AFTER SHERATON.

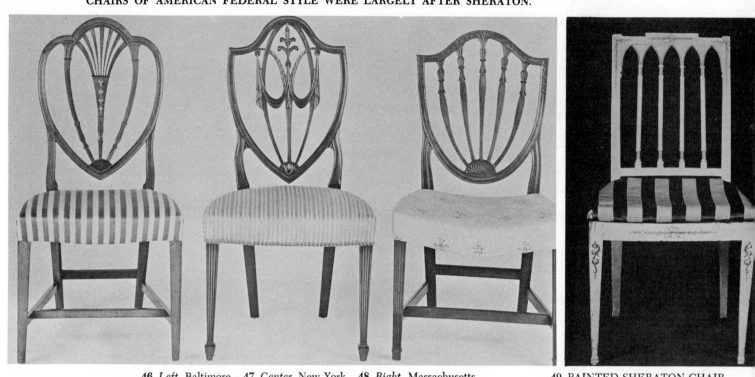

46 *Left,* Baltimore.   47 *Center,* New York.   48 *Right,* Massachusetts.

49 PAINTED SHERATON CHAIR.

50 CABINET, Sheraton style.

51 CLOCK.

All photos Israel Sack, Inc.

54 Attributed to McIntire.   **55** Maryland.   **56** Newburyport, Massachusetts.   **57** Philadelphia.

52 TAMBOUR DESK, New York.

**INLAYS AND FINE VENEERS
ARE STRESSED
IN EARLY-19TH-CENTURY
CABINETWORK.**

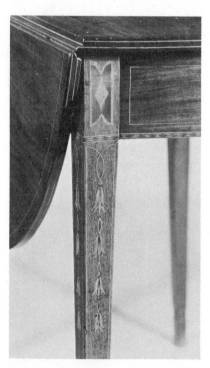

51A INLAY DETAIL, New England,
end of 18th century.   *Israel Sack, Inc.*

53 SERPENTINE-FRONT SIDEBOARD, Hepplewhite style, c. 1790.

Israel Sack, Inc.

58 BEDPOSTS, Salem, Massachusetts. **59 MAHOGANY FOUR-POSTER** in the Sheraton tradition, New York, c. 1820.

Yale University Art Gallery, Mabel Brady Garvan Collection

60 TERRY MANTEL CLOCK c. 1817.
Henry Ford Museum, Dearborn, Mich.

61 CARD TABLE, New York, attributed to Michael Allison.
Henry Ford Museum, Dearborn, Mich.

Israel Sack, Inc.

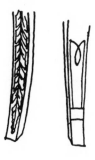

62 SIDEBOARD, reeded legs.
Ginsburg and Levy

63 CHAIR, style of Phyfe, Albany, N.Y.,
1815-1820. *Albany Institute of History and Art*

64 TRIPOD TABLE, 1810-1820.
New-York Historical Society, New York City

65 DETAIL OF CARVING,
table c. 1800.
Museum of the City of New York

66 SOFA TABLE.   *Israel Sack, Inc.*

67 NEW ENGLAND TAMBOUR DESK.

71 MIRROR, 86 inches high.
Albany Institute of History and Art

Photographs Henry Ford Museum, Dearborn, Mich.

68 SEWING TABLE, Massachusetts, c. 1800.
The stretcher is rare.

69 HEPPLEWHITE ARMCHAIR, Massachusetts, c. 1790. **70**
SHERATON-STYLE "MARTHA WASHINGTON" ARM-
CHAIR, Massachusetts, 1790-1800.

72 GIRANDOLE MIRROR.
Albany Institute of History and Art

73 SIDEBOARD, Sheraton style, Boston, 1800-1810.
Henry Ford Museum, Dearborn, Mich.

74 FALL-FRONT DESK.
Israel Sack, Inc.

75 BOW-BACK SOFA, Massachusetts, c. 1800.   *Israel Sack, Inc.*

76 SEWING TABLE, New York, c. 1810.
Henry Ford Museum, Dearborn, Mich.

77 LIVING ROOM, LUTHER BURBANK BIRTHPLACE.

All photographs except No. 82 from Henry Ford Museum, Dearborn, Mich.

AMERICAN COUNTRY FURNITURE

The country or village styles of Colonial American furniture developed many utilitarian types absent or scarce in city life. Chief of these is the Windsor chair, with its innumerable local variations. Stools, chairs, benches, chests, cabinets, etc., of unique types made in pine, maple, hickory, oak, apple, or cherry wood exhibit the tremendous vitality of a people dependent on their own resources. Beds with short posts, ladder-back chairs, wagon seats, rocking chairs, writing chairs, etc., are uniquely American. By far the greatest independence of design and technique is found in these robust folk arts that declined only with the Machine Age. [*77 et seq.*]

78 HITCHCOCK CHAIR, 1825-1828. 79 SHERATON "FANCY" CHAIR, New York, 1820. 80 FIVE-SIDED TABLE c. 1785. 81 ARROWBACK ARMCHAIR, Massachusetts, 1820-1830.

PENNSYLVANIA
"LEPPELBORTIE"

82 PINE DRESSER, mid-18th century.   *Anderson Galleries*

83 PAINTED ROCKING SETTEE, c. 1830.

84 NEW ENGLAND
BOW-BACK WINDSOR
c. 1800, with concave
stretcher.

AMERICAN EMPIRE

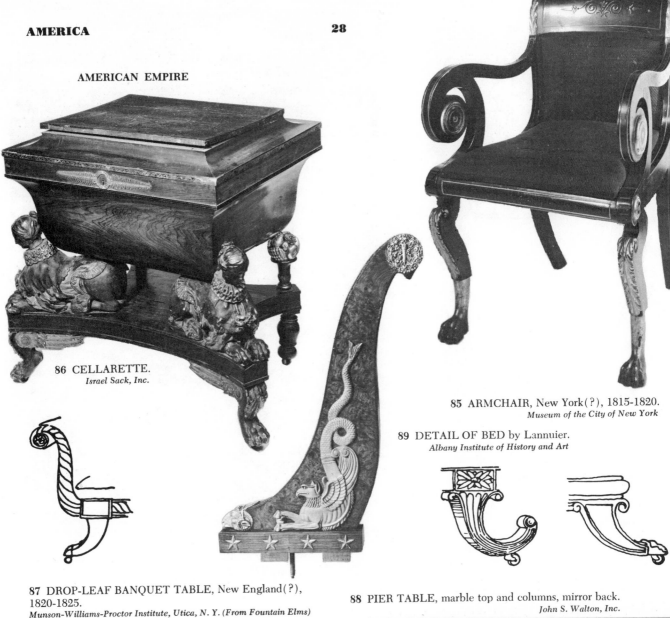

86 CELLARETTE.
Israel Sack, Inc.

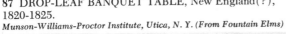

85 ARMCHAIR, New York(?), 1815-1820.
Museum of the City of New York

89 DETAIL OF BED by Lannuier.
Albany Institute of History and Art

87 DROP-LEAF BANQUET TABLE, New England(?), 1820-1825.
Munson-Williams-Proctor Institute, Utica, N. Y. (From Fountain Elms)

88 PIER TABLE, marble top and columns, mirror back.
John S. Walton, Inc.

90 MAHOGANY SIDEBOARD c. 1820.

Museum of the City of New York

EMPIRE

Napoleon's Empire style was not long in arriving. It added to furniture a forced architectural heaviness that symbolizes the decline of pure line. Even Phyfe's work after 1825 took on the thick, graceless quality that earned the title "Butcher's Furniture." Closely following the Regency mannerisms in England, the Pompeiian-Roman delicacy yielded to Greek-Egyptian solidity. A mistaken archaeology interpreted the solid stonework of the latter into wood furniture of massive plainness. Curved brackets, legs, etc., were thick and heavily ornamented. Sleigh beds, massive bureaus, scroll sofas, heavy pedestal tables, etc., were decorated with coarse carving, sometimes gilded, suggested by the bronze appliqués used in France. [210, 423, 495.]

Phyfe, Lannuier, and other outstanding designers moved from Directoire inspiration to Empire; then, together with the craft as a whole they coarsened, debased the Empire, crossed it with neo-Gothic, neo-Classic, neo-Rococo, and every other whim that crossed the Atlantic. Expanding markets created a far-flung industry based on the machine and on mass production. Sheraton's chair gave rise to the "fancy" chair, for which there was an insatiable appetite. (Carl Deppard estimates that in 1830 there were more than 8,100 chairmakers for fewer than 13 million people.) The Hitchcock chair is a good example. In 1818, Lambert Hitchcock devised a mass-production chair, shipped and exported—in parts—by the many thousands every year.

The style setters (custom makers with rich clienteles in the large cities) kept fashion turnover lively. The classicism of the thirties was lost in the voluptuous curves of a pudgy Rococo, inspired by the 1851 Crystal Palace. By the end of the Civil War, this Rococo revival had assumed the forms and manners of a full style, commonly called Victorian. Belter

represents the flowering of this mood that ran through the seventies. [124.]

About 1874, a reform wave, drawing on ideas propounded earlier by Charles Eastlake, synthesized a return to neo-Gothic simplicity, but in structural principle rather than in mere detail. The style of the 1880's lived only to yield to a revived classicism after the Columbian Exposition in 1893. On the most fashionable levels this looked back to the Italian Renaissance, the French Renaissance, to Louis XV, and an effort at total recall, not excluding a resuscitated Colonial. Laissez-faire eclecticism or stylishness has been the American leitmotif ever since. As this situation is not limited to the United States, the subject is considered more thoroughly under the heading NINETEENTH CENTURY. See also EASTLAKE; HITCHCOCK; PHYFE.

AMORINI

AMORINI (Italian). Cupids, painted or carved in decoration. Sometimes only the winged head is used. Profuse in Baroque work, especially under direct Italian influence.

ANCIENT FURNITURE. Our knowledge of the furniture of the ancient civilizations is gleaned from two sources: (*a*) actual remains or remaining models, and (*b*) pictorial, sculptural, or written descriptions. Thanks to the Egyptian custom of providing the dead with objects of daily use, we find in their tombs a key to the earliest furniture forms. Of the furniture of Assyria and nearer Asia there remains only the record of stone sculptures. Greece and Rome also left picture records in carving and vase ornaments and wall paintings, as well as some relics in stone and metal. These point to a highly developed art of woodworking in keeping with the architectural superiority of these peoples, but actual forms and styles are conjectural.

Egypt may be regarded as the source of the most ancient furniture ideas, some vestiges of such development being attributed to the era prior to 1800 B.C. In this remote time, tables and chairs, couches, stools, and chests of recognizable form were in use, indicating skill in turning, carving, joining, inlay, and painting. These talents and their products were exported to the then known world—Crete, Assyria, Babylonia, Phoenicia, and, later, Persia and Greece. More or less similar motives were reworked to the local taste and materials, and descended to the present day.

See also ANTIQUE; EGYPT; GREEK; POMPEIIAN; ROMAN.

ANGEL BED. Bedstead with a canopy, but with no pillars in front. The curtains are drawn back at the sides next to the head of the bed. Usually the canopy extends over only a part of the bed, while the counterpane goes right down over the foot. Chiefly French, 18th century. See BED. [113.]

ANIMAL-COUCHANT FOOT. Furniture leg ending in the form of a reclining animal. [1035.]

ANIMAL COUCHANT FOOT

ANTHEMION

ANTHEMION. The Greek honeysuckle pattern conventionalized to radiating cluster.

ANTIMACASSAR. 19th-century doily or cloth used to protect chairbacks from soiling by hair, which at that time was dressed with macassar oil.

ANTIQUE, THE. Reference to the classic Greek and Roman styles.

ANTIQUES. In current use the description "antique furniture" implies something more than "old furniture." The something more is relative, depending on local attitudes and values, particularly as to age and cultural worth.

Antique furniture is prized for age, rarity, unique beauty, association, or documentary interest or personal sentiment. Though the United States Customs rules that antiques must be "before 1830," age alone is too relative and includes too much. In the young West a piece of Civil War date that might earn reverence as an antique could be regarded as mere junk in three-century-old New England. In the South the same piece might evoke a nostalgia for a departed and glorious past, the sentiment overcoming possible aesthetic deficiencies. Original worth or style is of prime importance, yet many crude or rough styles are valued. The market for antiques is therefore one of specialties.

The cult of antique collectors comprises a complete industry, with values and standards and ethics. The genuineness of antiques is almost as relative as age. Excluding deliberate counterfeiting or outright deception, the dealer has rarely more than his judg-

ment to offer as evidence of age or authenticity. Thus there is a premium on reliability. This is turn must invite a degree of reticence on the part of reliable dealers. The signs by which authenticity is recognized are too precarious for the average collector.

Antique furniture may be described as repaired, restored, or copied. The last frankly admits to being newly made, but more or less painstakingly after an old model, often employing old wood and old processes. Restorations are a pitfall, since the restored sections may represent the greater bulk; an old tabletop mounted on a new base, no matter how well studied and matched, should not be represented as an antique, although such representations are occasionally detected. Repairs are often necessary for the continued existence of the piece. The extent of these and the care with which they are effected will be the determining factors in the valuation of the piece. See also ANTIQUING; FAKES AND FAKING; REPLICA; REPRODUCTION .

ANTIQUING. The process of treating wood or finish on furniture to make it look old. Wood may be simply worn off at the edges and corners; it is sometimes scratched, gouged, planed, etc. (called "distressed" finishes). Even fine bird shot and nails are used to simulate wormholes and other ravages of time. Wood is also subjected to various acid treatments, bleaches, and stains to suggest age. Paint finishes are glazed with washes of dirt colors to reduce the brilliance and to provide an uneven surface.

APPLE. The wood of the apple tree is very hard, of a brown-pink color, polishes well, and can be used for small parts in furniture. It is ideal for turning, and as such is found in many American 18th-century pieces. Like all fruitwoods, it has been extensively used in provincial furniture throughout Europe.

APPLIQUÉ. Applied ornament. See ORNAMENT.

APRON. A structural part of furniture. In tables, the piece connecting the legs, just under the top; in chairs, beneath the seat; in cabinets, etc., along the base. Sometimes called "skirt." See also CONSTRUCTION.

ARABESQUE. Painted, inlaid, or flat carved designs, composed of floral and geometrical scrolls, human or animal and mythological forms, etc. Usually framed within a simple shape such as a rectangle.

ARCA. Chest for storing treasures, chiefly in the Middle Ages and Early Renaissance in Spain and Italy. See also COFFER; CUPBOARD.

ARCADE. In furniture, a carved decoration representing a series of arches; also, a chairback in this form. [345, 443, 546, 1017.]

ARCADED BACK. Chair or bed back with top rail cut to resemble one or more arches with pillars. [118.]

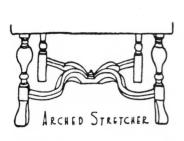

ARCADED PANEL. Typical English Renaissance panel decoration consisting of two stubby columns with arch in low relief. [226.]

ARCHED STRETCHER. Arched or hoop-shaped stretcher in chairs, tables, and cabinets of the English Restoration period. [267, 1032, 1235, 1276.]

ARCHITECTS' FURNITURE. Specifically, English furniture of the 18th century, designed by architects and exhibiting architectural features, such as arches, columns, etc.

ARCHITECT'S TABLE. Desk with drawing board in a drawer or otherwise attached, with other drawers for supplies. Made in England in the late 18th century for the then fashionable interest in architecture. Similar to DAVENPORT DESK.

ARCHITRAVE. Lowest member of a cornice. Also a door molding. See ORDERS.

ARKWRIGHT. Early English name for cabinet-maker. From "ark," the old name for cabinet, and "wright," mechanic or maker. Arkwright furniture refers to Late Gothic types in England in which the construction resembles carpentry rather than cabinet-work.

ARM PAD. The upholstered part of a chair arm.

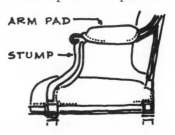

ARM STUMP. The front vertical support of the arm of a chair. See also CHAIR; CONSTRUCTION.

ARMCHAIR. See CHAIR.

ARMOIRE. A tall cupboard or wardrobe, with doors. The Gothic types are massive and are decorated chiefly with elaborate iron hinges and locks. [173.] The earliest armoires were probably painted, and were used for the storage of arms and armor. Later they were carved with elaborate pictorial panels or simple linenfold patterns. In France the Renaissance

91 FRENCH RÉGENCE, early 18th century.
Metropolitan Museum of Art, Rogers Fund, 1919

92 CANADIAN, early-19th-century Provincial Louis XV.
Montreal Museum of Fine Arts

93 AUSTRIAN OR BAVARIAN, painted, dated 1819.
Liebhold-Wallach

influence endowed the armoire with a wealth of columns, pilasters, canopied niches, and panels carved with mythological pictures. [695, 1335, 1336.]

ARRAS. Tapestry, particularly as used to drape beds and walls after the 14th century. Derives from the city Arras, where the weaving of tapestries was a major industry in the Middle Ages.

ARRIS. Sharp or salient edge formed by the meeting of two surfaces. Particularly the ridge between the channels of a Doric column. See also ORDERS.

ARROW. Decorative theme used in revivals of classic styles; Renaissance and later, especially Directoire, Empire, and Biedermeier.

ARROW SPINDLE. Flattened spindle with one end resembling an arrow. Found on some Sheraton chairs, and on derivative forms in American chairs of the Federal period. [79.]

ART MODERNE. French term for the various schools of contemporary design, affectedly used in America during the 1920's to label the earliest modern work. See also MODERN.

ART MODERNE

ART NOUVEAU. A revived interest in the decorative arts flowed over Europe about 1875, giving rise to a concerted rebellion against the stale eclecticism of the time. A conscious effort to create along new lines inspired this "New Art." It drew on various motives— Gothic and Japanese principally—and established an ornamental vocabulary based on natural growing forms. The typical line is long and slightly curved, ending abruptly in a whiplike sharp curve.

Henri Van de Velde is the outstanding name of the style. His exhibitions in Brussels and Paris in 1894 and 1895 demonstrated his personal style. The

94 DETAIL OF SIDE TABLE designed
by Hector Guimard c. 1908.
Museum of Modern Art, New York
Gift of Mrs. Hector Guimard

copyists were numerous but less successful. His manner particularly influenced French design for about a decade, while the Arts and Crafts Movement in England was a contemporary expression, as were developments like the *Jugendstil* (Youth Style) and *Secession* in Germany and Austria.

Generally, the results of these rebellions were more successful in the minor arts, such as silver and jewelry work, than in furniture or architecture. Most vital is the impetus toward a clearer, more rational expression. See also MODERN; NINETEENTH CENTURY.

95 ART NOUVEAU CABINET, Paris, c. 1900.

ARTS AND CRAFTS MOVEMENT. A revival of interest in decorative art in England began about 1875. By 1884, it grew to a definite revolt against tasteless overmechanization; and it inspired groups like the Art-Workers Guild to seek to reestablish the individual quality in the crafts. The ideal was the personal craftsmanship of the Middle Ages. Neo-Gothic architects, such as the Pugins, Henry Shaw, and Philip Webb, and the Pre-Raphaelite group of painters, led by Dante Gabriel Rossetti and Edward Burne-Jones, and such strong personalities as William Morris and John Ruskin all contributed to this ideal. Their efforts created new interest and new expression in furniture and architecture, pottery, jewelry, textile, and book design. A deliberately amateur quality, glorifying handwork, was too violently in opposition to all but the most intellectual trends, and the movement failed to elicit a popular response. In America it materialized in a parallel movement; Elbert Hubbard and his Roycroft crystallizing the ideal, while various degrees of success attended the efforts of commercial manufacturers who accepted the outward forms for machine-made products. The Mission style is one of the offshoots. The furniture forms of the Arts and Crafts Movement are essentially simple and crude; in their joinery concepts, rudimentary. They consciously lack grace, lightness, and charm. The value of the intellectual movement cannot be overestimated. It clearly set a track for later thought. Schools of design and individuals were moved to examine the forces at work, and the result is only now materializing. See also EASTLAKE; MODERN; MORRIS; NINETEENTH CENTURY.

ASH. A family of trees, the woods of many of which are used for furniture. The European ash belongs to a group that also includes olive, lilac, privet, and jasmine. The olive ash burls of both England and France are exquisitely figured, and capable of beautiful veneer matching. The color varies from a light honey color to a medium brown. The American ashes are used principally as lumber where great strength is required, as in upholstery frames. The wood is a very light creamy color, heavy and dense, with a prominent grain resembling oak. It was used for some turnings and bent work in very early Windsor chairs.

ASPEN. Species of poplar; the wood is light in weight and color, satiny in texture; poor structurally, but decorative as veneer.

ASSYRIAN. Assyrian decorative art was approximately contemporaneous with the Egyptian. Ornamental motives were borrowed, the lotus and other natural forms being adapted. Animal forms were more distinctive, featuring the winged bull, lion, and eagle.

Bronze, ivory, and gold ornaments remain; the wood has disappeared, so that the forms of Assyrian furniture are conjectural.

ASTER CARVING. On Connecticut chests, three flowers on a central panel; also sunflower carving. See also CONNECTICUT CHEST.

ASTRAGAL. Small half-round or convex bead molding; molding on overlapping doors. [173.]

ATHENIENNE. Round tripod table or stand, adapted in Louis XVI and Empire periods to washstands, etc. [1338.]

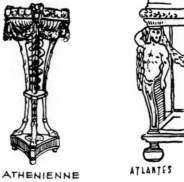

ATHENIENNE   ATLANTES

ATLANTES. Supporting columns in the shape of male figures. See CARYATID. [1035.]

AUBUSSON. Fine handwoven tapestries or carpets originating in the French village of that name. [1132.]

AUSTRIA. Austrian furniture is essentially German, following the Gothic phase with the Renaissance influences of Italian origins. Proximity to Italy brought the Italian manners, but the German character is basic. The Alpine variants of these styles are found in Austrian furniture of the 16th and 17th centuries; oak, pine, and fir in paneling, chests, and beds recall the Swiss types. Cabinets are in the South German manner. Occasionally, there were periods when the High Renaissance Italian types dominated, but Austria must be considered aesthetically a German province. There are no distinct types or schools; the local variations, while highly characteristic and individualistic, may be considered uniformly German in character. See also GERMANY. [457, 466.]

AVODIRE. African wood of medium density and strength, light-yellow color and satin-smooth texture. Extensively used in decorative veneering in modern cabinetwork.

AYOUS. Light-colored wood similar in color and markings to primavera, but softer in texture.

BACHELOR CHEST. Modern name for small chest of drawers in typically early-18th-century English style. [568.]

BACK STOOL. Early form of chair without arms, such as the *sgabelli* of Italy and similar forms in Alpine countries. [217, 707.]

BACKGAMMON BOARD AND TABLE. The game goes back to the Middle Ages, and furniture for its play appeared as soon as specialized tables appeared in the 17th century. Fine examples occur in French and English work. [1278.]

BAG TABLE. Small work or sewing table, with one or two drawers, the lower having a cloth bag attached. Common in 18th and early 19th century, England and America. See also TABLE. [68, 96, 1260.]

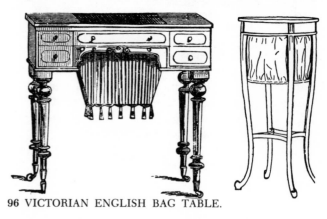

96 VICTORIAN ENGLISH BAG TABLE.

BAHUT (French). In the Middle Ages, a portable coffer or chest used for personal luggage. It usually had a rounded top, and was covered with leather and studded with nails. It developed into a chest permanently mounted on feet, and was used for storing household goods. The current form in France is a decorative high cabinet.

BAIL. Metal loop or ring forming a handle. See also HARDWARE.

BALDACHIN. A free-standing canopy supported on columns.

BALL AND CLAW. See CLAW AND BALL. [27, 183.]

BALL AND RING. A turning of a ball and narrow member, found in 17th-century work.

BALL FOOT. Round turning used as foot on chests, etc., chiefly in 17th-century furniture. Same as bun foot in England. [798, 1034.]

97, 98 ENGLISH BALLOON-BACK CHAIRS, 1850-1870.

BALLOON BACK. Chairback style developed by Hepplewhite, extensively used in Victorian work. [97, 897.]

BALUSTER. Small column, turned, square, or flat, supporting a rail: it also formed chairbacks in architectural forms. [635.]

BAMBINO. Representation of the infant Jesus, used as a decorative feature in Early Italian Renaissance work, and subsequently.

BAMBOO. The wood of the bamboo tree is used for furniture in the East, and came to the Occident with the various waves of Chinese influences. In the 18th century this was so important that the characteristic appearance of the bamboo was simulated in wood turnings in England and America, and the type is known as the "bamboo turning." [1087.] In the last quarter of the 19th century, a literary and artistic enthusiasm for things Japanese produced a unique style in minor or cottage furniture, worked in actual bamboo as well as in turned-wood simulations painted ochre yellow.

BANDEROLE. Painted or carved ribbon decoration, often with an inscription or other device. See also RIBAND.

BANDING. A narrow edging or border of veneer around the fronts of drawers; a contrasting band of inlay. [389.]

BALL FEET

BAMBOO SETTEE ENGLISH 19TH CENTURY

BANDY LEG. Cabriole leg.

BANISTER. Baluster.

BANISTER BACK. Chairback with spindles or similar upright members. In 17th-century English and American work, it was common as split turnings. [242.]

BANJO CLOCK. 19th-century American wall clock in the form of a banjo. [101.]

99 BAROMETER, England, 1793. **100** BAROMETER, New York, 1820. **101** BANJO CLOCK, Willard, 1801.

BANK. A long seat or form, of the Middle Ages (England).

BANQUETTE (French). An upholstered bench.

BANTAM WORK. Type of lacquering in late-17th-century Dutch and English work, derived from Bantam in Dutch Java. Design usually incised in black ground.

BAROMETER CASE. Barometers, with other scientific instruments, were objects of great interest in the 18th century. Handsome cases were designed for them, particularly in England, France, and Italy, in the various Rococo and classical styles. [99, 100.]

BAROQUE. The whole tendency of European design in the 17th century was toward exaggeration, over-emphasized brilliance. The movement was a natural consequence of the increasingly ornamental Renaissance style; its extremes resulted from the Jesuit Counter Reformation, the effort of the militant Catholic order to recapture the imagination of the masses through overawing splendor. Italian art had exhausted the simpler vocabulary by 1550. The need for new types opened a path for unrestrained virtuosity. The spreading Renaissance carried this free manner everywhere, and for two centuries most European art was Baroque.

Motion is the essence of the Baroque, as distinguished from the repose of the classic ideal. Large curves, fantastic and irregular, are explosively interpreted, reversed, ornamented. Twisted columns, distorted and broken pediments, and oversized moldings sacrificed the structural sense to a tremendous theatrical effect. Scale and proportion had new meaning, everything being calculated to strike the eye, to excite rather than to suggest quiet and harmony. [172.]

In furniture the earlier Baroque tendencies were merely exaggeration of scale. Fantastically overloaded ornament was added later; the earlier work was actually freer of plastic decoration than the preceding Late Renaissance types [192, 464]. Cabinets whose midsections were simply, if insistently, paneled, were carried on excessively carved bases and bore great pediments, usually broken and capped with towering finials. Chairs were elaborately scrolled and carved [559]. Tables had bases of rich sculpture, fancifully shaped stretchers; others had twisted columns or complex scrolls as legs. Beds, particularly in France and England, were colossal structures of draped textiles. [107.]

BAROQUE PEDIMENT

Surface treatment became more splendid after 1650. Earlier solid wood surfaces were then painted, gilded, polychromed; inlays and marquetry reached their ultimate heights in the work of Boulle and the imitative scrollwork of seaweed marquetry. Marble and imitation stone, vivid textiles, cane and metals all contributed to this unrestrained decorative orgy. [159.]

The Baroque is withal a masculine style, virile and

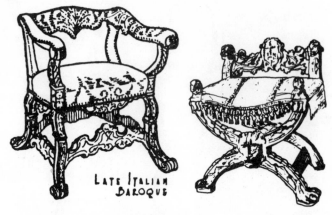

LATE ITALIAN BAROQUE

blustering and bold. Its feminine counterpart, the Rococo, came in the 18th century, substituting prettiness and charm for Baroque magnificence.

BARREL CHAIR. Easy chair with a fully rounded back, developed in England after the *gondole* of the Louis XV period. [289.]

BASE. The lowest member of a piece of furniture or of a column. As "basses" the word designated the lower part of 17th-century English beds.

BASIN STAND. Washstand; light table on which basins were set. Common in 18th-century English work, it was sometimes spelled "bason-stand." [1339.]

BAS-RELIEF. Sculpture in which the carving projects only slightly from the background. See also CARVING.

BASSET TABLE. Card table, Queen Anne period.

BASSINET. Bed for a baby. Originally basket shaped, and sometimes made of wicker.

BASSWOOD. American wood of light color and weight, soft texture, slight figure, and medium strength. Works well and does not warp or check readily. Used for inexpensive painted flatwork, but chiefly valuable as core stock for plywood panels.

BATIK. Figured fabric produced with wax resist and successive dyeings or paintings, after an ancient Javanese process.

BATTEN. Strips of wood used as a brace or cleat across one or more boards.

BAYWOOD. Honduras mahogany.

BEAD. Half-round molding, usually small. See also MOLDING.

BEAD AND REEL. Bead mold in which are carved alternate round and oval forms. See also MOLDING.

BEADED DRAWER: Fine molded half-round or quarter-round profile on four edges of a drawer, typically 18th-century English. [476.]

BEARING RAIL. Member in table or cabinetwork that carries the drawer. See also CONSTRUCTION.

BEAU BRUMMEL. Late-18th-century English dressing table with complex arrangements of adjustable mirrors, candle brackets, shelves, and drawers. Designed for men's use, they became increasingly complicated after Early Georgian types, as male dandyism spread. The name was acquired during the George IV period. [520.]

BEAUFAIT, BEAUFATT, BEAUFET. Early spellings of "buffet."

BEAUVAIS: Tapestry from French city of that name. Looms started in 1664. [1125.]

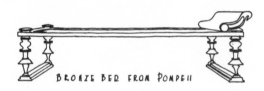

BRONZE BED FROM POMPEII

BED. Ancient drawings portray well-developed bed types in Egypt, Assyria, Persia, Greece, and Rome. Over basic structures of stone, wood, or metal were thrown animal skins and textile for softness and warmth. The framework was often well designed and adorned with inlays or appliqués of metal, ivory, etc.

Egyptian tomb remains show typical couches, wood frames with lacing of hide or rope, often made to fold. Turned or animal-shaped legs of good design are common. Bedding consisted of manifold layers of linen sheets. The pillow was a wooden stand curved to fit the head, and more comfortable than it looks; it was cool in the hot summer nights and prevented the elaborate headdress from becoming disarranged.

Greek sculptures show high frames, with turned legs, probably of wood. Roman beds were even higher, with a raised head section and inlays of gold and ivory in fine woods. Bronze and even silver were also used. The fabric parts were elaborate and costly. Some Pompeiian houses had curtained alcoves for beds.

The first beds in northern Europe were piles of leaves upon the floor covered with skins, followed at an early date by a shallow box or chest filled with

DUTCH
BOX BED
NEW YORK C. 1650

leaves and moss. Mattresses, stuffed with feathers, wool, or hair were invented early in the Middle Ages. These were piled upon benches against the wall or into the low boxlike structures that persisted in provincial sections through the 18th century. Probably the Crusades yielded the idea of the canopy or curtain, for after the 12th century beds are always pictured with draperies that could enclose the bed. These grew in elegance and size; in the north the addition of wood panels made a complete room-within-a-room. After the 14th century fabrics were richer and thicker. One type of free-standing bed had suspended tester or canopy and several layers of draperies; this form grew in importance through the 17th century when it attained tremendous size and splendor and extremes of costliness. In northern Europe the wooden-enclosure idea was favored, utilizing the two walls of a corner. Picture 102 shows a North German example with curtains forming the enclosure. The step in the foreground is a chest for bedding, etc. In the northern French provinces a similar type lasted through the early 19th century, often with sliding wood panels in place of curtains. Pictures 103–104 show free-standing German structures of wood embodying the same idea, smaller in scale and freer for ventilation. In the English example, 105, it is significant that the bed stock is a separate frame.

The wooden superstructure and enclosure reached its zenith in England in Elizabeth's reign [549]. By that date the Continental tendency toward multiplication of fabric parts had spread to England. The period saw the bed grow, like the dinosaur, to the exaggeration that predicted its doom. In France the state bed was a composition of over thirty textile parts, with yardage of embroidered satin and bullion fringe and cloth of gold enough to run the cost into fair fortunes.

102 NORTH GERMAN RENAISSANCE, 1568. Corner of room enclosed by wood canopy and curtains.

103 SOUTH GERMAN, early 17th century. Free-standing wood canopy.

104 LATE GOTHIC ALPINE c. 1500. Detached boxlike enclosure.

No wood was visible. There was a multiplicity of fabric members—*pentes, basses, cantonniers,* and *bonnegrâces* covering everything, and topped off by clusters of plumes or swags. In England, too, the bed remained a colossal symbol of wealth and position up to the reign of Queen Anne. Measuring 7 by 8 feet and 11 feet high, the cost often ran up to many thousands of pounds. [105.]

The 18th century scaled down room and furniture. Beds became lighter and simpler in woodwork and drapery. In France many variations appeared: the small separate bed frame in an alcove, draperies covering the open front; the baldaquin bed, or crown bed; the angel bed, with suspended canopy and curtains looped back; the duchess bed, and others. In England the general type was a simpler four-poster bearing canopy and draw curtains. Beds by Chippendale, Hepplewhite, the Adams, and Sheraton were important and highly decorative structures but the draperies are less voluminous and the whole scale finer. The "field bed" appeared as a smaller canopy type that became popular in America. Beds of the Empire period were low, chunky blocks, usually undraped, and sometimes set on a dais, often with the typical heavy scroll. In America this was known as the "sleigh" bed. Most significant about all 19th-century beds is the low, solid quality. American four-posters with abnormally heavy posts, richly carved,

105 THE "GREAT BED OF WARE," late 16th century. Carved oak, inlaid and painted, 10 feet 9 inches square.

106 ENGLISH, period of Henry VIII.

105A CHINESE, MING DYNASTY, 1368-1628. Light enclosed framework is described in documents of the era.

From Chinese Household Furniture, *by George Kates, courtesy Dover Publications, New York.*

107 THE GREAT STATE BED OF THE 17TH CENTURY, from Rushbrooke Hall, England, c. 1685. In size and cost of decoration, beds of the Restoration period in England and of the era of Louis XIV in France reached a peak. All exposed parts are of fabric and needlework.

108 The 18th century saw the diminution of size and of fabric parts, and increasing emphasis on decorative woodwork. Black and gold lacquer, made by Chippendale c. 1755. Drapery missing.

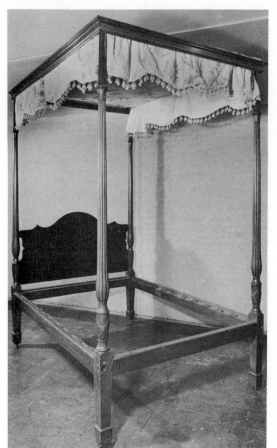

109 AMERICAN, mid-18th century. *John S. Walton, Inc.*

110 PHYFE, 1800-1810.   *Museum of the City of New York*

111 FRENCH, late 18th century.   *Don Ruseau*

112 WOOD CANOPY, DIRECTOIRE.   *Don Ruseau*

THE CANOPY BECAME MERELY DECORATIVE AT DIFFERENT TIMES AND PLACES ACCORDING TO THE CHANGE IN VENTILATING CONDITIONS OF ROOMS.

are still common. The current styles of beds are chiefly based on these designs, scaled still smaller, and ornamented with period forms rather than copied literally from the larger prototypes.

The perfection of modern springs and mattresses has removed the necessity for the heavy wood framing that was required by the laced-rope floor of 19th-century beds. The minimum framing, just enough to raise the bedding from the floor, with a panel for the head, is favored in much contemporary designing.

Metal frames, usually iron or brass tubing and/or bars, became popular about mid-18th century, and have more or less held favor since. Wrought-iron headboards had been familiar in Mediterranean countries earlier, but utilitarian production and sanitary aspects appealed to 19th-century logic. Cast-iron appeared in decorative designs in Spain, France, and America or wherever casting was practiced. It gave way to assemblies of bars and tubes fabricated with cast-iron ornaments in the later 1800's and culminated in the tubular brass bed. [1095a, 1312.]

113 "ANGEL" BED, France, c. 1780. The canopy is on the wall. 114 BEDSTEAD, pine, Tyrol, 16th century. 115 COLONIAL AMERICAN c. 1725. The partial canopy and curtains are purely decorative.

Don Ruseau

Metropolitan Museum of Art

THE ALCOVE AS BASIS OF THE BED DESIGN EXPRESSED THE ULTIMATE LUXURIOUSNESS OF THE 18TH CENTURY.

116 BED ALCOVE in the Palazzo Segrado, Venice, c. 1718. Harmony of architectural elements and accessory furniture makes the whole composition more significant than the bed alone.

Now in Metropolitan Museum of Art

117 BED ALCOVE, period of Louis XVI, from the Hôtel de Gaulin, Dijon, 1772.

Now in Metropolitan Museum of Art

118 ITALIAN RENAISSANCE, 16th century.

Di Salvo

IN WARMER CLIMATES THE CANOPIES DISAPPEARED ENTIRELY, AND POSTS BECAME DECORATIVE ONLY.

120 FLEMISH c. 1625. Free-standing bedstead with stump footboard. *Ginsburg and Levy*

119 ITALIAN, 17th century.

French and Co., Inc.

BEDSTEPS
ENGLISH
18TH CENTURY

EARLY-19TH-CENTURY EMPIRE INFLUENCE.

121 AMERICAN EMPIRE STYLE, mahogany with ormolu decoration, c. 1810-1820. Probably the bed referred to in Duncan Phyfe's bill. (See PHYFE.)

122 MAHOGANY "FRENCH BED" OR "SLEIGH BED" with square plinth feet in the style of the Restóration, New York or Newark, 1835-1845.

123 FRENCH, designed by Percier and Fontaine, executed 1815 by Desmalter. State bed of Alexander I. Mahogany, with ormolu mounts. Statues at foot are "Conquering Love" and "Apollo Conquering a Lion." Medallions of Day, Night, Signs of the Zodiac, etc.

BED BOLT. Covered bolt and sunken nut used in some styles of bed to fasten the rail to the headboard and footboard. Decorative brass cover plates occur in Federal American beds. See also HARDWARE.

BED MOLDING. Small mold under the corona or large molding of a cornice.

BED STEPS. Low steps made for climbing into high beds; 18th-century English and American work.

BEDSTOCK. In Elizabethan and some Continental types the posts of the bed often stood clear of the bed proper. In this type the bedstock was the framework that actually supported the bedding. [105.]

BEECH. Northern hardwood, Europe and America; dense texture and light color. Used chiefly in middle-quality work, country style in England, etc., since the 17th century; found in good French provincial furniture. Adapted to turning, polishes well to light-brown color.

BELL SEAT. Round seat, Queen Anne period.

BELLFLOWER. Ornamental detail, carved or painted, resembling bell-shaped flowers arranged vertically. See also HUSK; ORNAMENT.

BELTER, JOHN H. American cabinetmaker; he had a shop in New York after 1840, and made rosewood, walnut, and oak furniture in the style of the Second, or late, Empire, generally referred to as Victorian. Highly carved sinuous framework lines with heavy roll moldings and fine naturalistic flower carving; upholstery in brocades and damasks. The craftsmanship was excellent, and much of his work survives.

125 CONSOLE WITH WHATNOT. Rosewood and maple "parlor suite," by John Belter.
Metropolitan Museum of Art,
Gift of Mr. and Mrs. Lowell Ross Burch and Miss Jean McLean Morron, 1951

Belter is credited with developing a form of lamination for chairbacks, which were later pierced and carved in complex designs that would have been impossible in solid wood. [125, 912.]

Brooklyn Museum

124A CHAISE LONGUE by Belter, c. 1860. Rosewood.

124 CENTER TABLE.

126 PRIMITIVE TYPE. *Don Ruseau*

130 SPANISH, 17th century. Chestnut. *Hispanic Society of America*

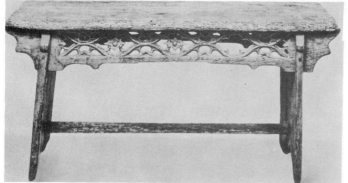

127 FLEMISH, 15th-century Gothic. *Philadelphia Museum of Art*

BENCH. Seat without a back, usually a long oval or oblong. In England the word sometimes refers to seat with a back or ends, or a settee. See also CASSAPANCA; SETTEE; WAGON SEAT. [126 *et seq.*, 1160.]

BENCH–Workman's, joiner's, etc. Heavy worktable, usually fitted with vise, tool racks, etc. "Bench made" implies handwork, as distinguished from machine or quantity-assembled work.

131 SPANISH. *Lo Mejor de España*

132 FRENCH, RUSTIC. *Don Ruseau*

128 FRENCH BANQUETTE, 17th century.

129 SPANISH. *Lo Mejor de España*

133 ITALIAN, 16th century. *Metropolitan Museum of Art, Gift of George Blumenthal, 1941*

BENEMAN, GUILLAUME. Outstanding cabinet-maker-designer of the earlier Empire style in France; noted for monumental mahogany cupboards and commodes of architectural character.

BENTWOOD. Bending of wet wood into chair parts —legs, bows, arms, etc.—was practiced by country woodworkers (probably originally wheelwrights) from earliest times. Windsors in England and America show skill with certain woods. About 1840 Michael Thonet in Vienna began to bend all parts of chairs designed so as to utilize the special strength of such parts scientifically joined together. This was one of the earliest mass-production enterprises, and millions of chairs, tables, etc., made by this technique were produced, are still being produced, and are in general use. Bentwood must not be confused with molded plywood. See also NINETEENTH CENTURY. [913, 1006.]

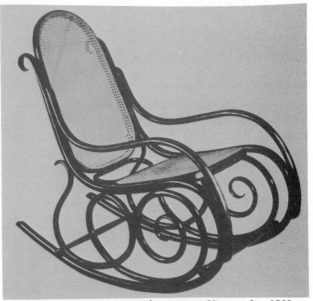

134, 135, 136 BENTWOOD by THONET, Vienna after 1860.

BERAIN. French family of designers and craftsmen. Jean, 1640-1711, published books that spread the style of Louis XIV; he designed arabesques, etc., for Boulle. Claude, brother of Jean; Jean (the younger), 1678-1726. See also BOULLE; FRANCE. [1125.]

137 BIBLE BOX c. 1690 on chest dated 1693. New England, oak. Typical half turnings and small panels.

Wadsworth Atheneum, Hartford, Conn.

BERGÈRE. Upholstered armchair with closed upholstered sides. Specifically, chairs of French style, copied in England and Germany. Also spelled *"birjair," "barjair."* [284.]

BEVEL. A sloping edge, of various angles, applied to any material—wood, glass, metal, etc. Similar to CHAMFER.

BIBELOT. Small objets d'art; knickknacks. Stands like whatnots, étagères, etc., made for collections.

BIBLE BOX. Small slant-top table or desk, used to hold the Bible. [1016.]

BIBLIOTHÈQUE. French term for large architectural bookcase. See also BOOKCASE. [143.]

BIEDERMEIER. German style, first half of the 19th century, chiefly based on French Empire forms. It is essentially a style of the lesser nobility and the bourgeoisie, imitating the Paris Empire *meubles de luxe* of the grander houses. These adaptations, the products of local materials and skill, are odd mixtures in varying degrees of sophisticated motives, with naïve proportions and techniques. Architectural themes and classic ornaments are given homely interpretation. Carved details are represented in paint, black or gold; the classic flora are sometimes rendered as more familiar vegetable forms. Simplified surfaces and details recall Empire outlines. The woods are largely local—pear and other fruitwoods, walnut, maple, birch, beech—but much mahogany furniture remains. The name derives from a comic-paper character, Papa Biedermeier, symbol of homely substantial comfort and well-being—*Gemütlichkeit*. Later, it also connoted "old fashioned," "stodgy." In either case the style, imitative and awkward as it may be, is an interesting example of the process of copying and adapting a foreign style *in toto*. See also BIEDERMEIER; GERMANY. [138, 151, 164, 331, 337, 391, 901, 1056.]

BILBOA. Mirror with frame of marble or of marble and wood. Popular late 18th century, named after the usual port of origin. Also spelled "bilbao."

BIRCH. Wood family of many varieties found in temperate zones. White and sap birches are soft; red, black, and yellow are hard. Used everywhere for furniture, usually inexpensive. Harder varieties have great strength, work well and polish well, often as imitations of mahogany and walnut. Most extensively used for structural work, next to gumwood.

BIRDCAGE. Openwork box of wire, wood, wicker, etc., used for caging birds. Occurs decoratively in many styles, and sometimes forms an important feature in the decoration of rooms.

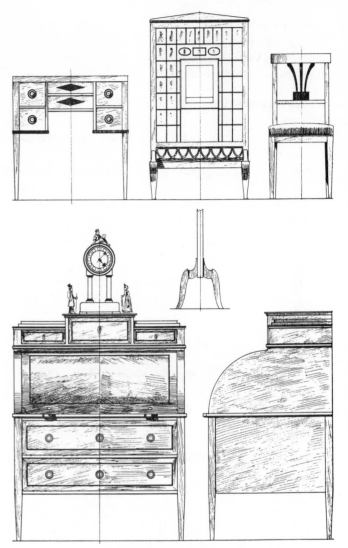

BIEDERMEIER

BIRDCAGE
ENGLISH · 18TH CENTURY

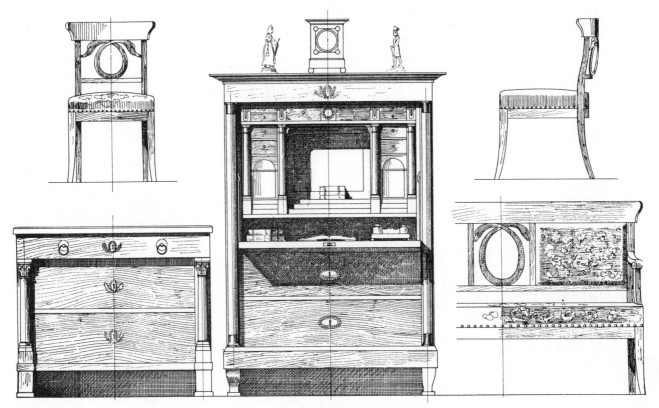

BIEDERMEIER

BIRDCAGE CLOCK. English brass clock with open pendulum and weights, chiefly late 17th century.

BIRD'S-BEAK. Rounded V cut on molded corners: English and Early American.

BIRD'S-EYE. Small figure in wood grain resembling a bird's eye. Principally in maple but occasionally in other woods. It is produced by cutting tangentially through the indentations that sometimes appear in the annual rings. [801, 928.]

BISELLIUM. Roman seat for two persons.

BLACK WALNUT. See WALNUT.

BLACKAMOOR. Negro figure used as table base in Baroque Continental furniture, early 18th century and again in Victorian work, 1850-1870, England and America.

BLANKET CHEST. Any chest for the storage of blankets. Now, particularly, chests with a hinged top section with drawer in or near the base.

BLISTER. Figure in some woods, such as maple, mahogany, cedar, poplar, and pine.

BLOCK FOOT. Square end of an untapered leg, as in Chippendale work. [409.]

BLOCK FOOT

BLACKAMOOR

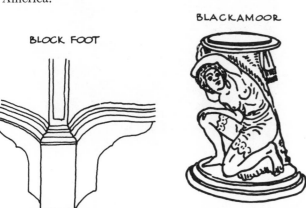

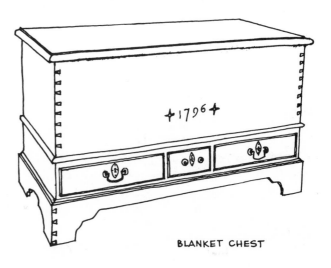

BLANKET CHEST

BLOCKFRONT. Front of chest, desk, etc., divided vertically into three panels, the center concave, the end panels convex. The best types are mainly flat, curving only near the panel edges. The tops end in flat arches, or, better, with a carved shell. The type seems to be peculiarly American, a Baroque expression dating from the period of 1760-1780, and is associated with the work of John Goddard and the Newport School. [367, 489.]

BLOCK FRONT –GODDARD

BLOND WOODS, FINISHES. A vogue for light wood tones has brought forward many of the lighter woods such as holly, primavera, avodire, aspen, birch, and maple. In poorer work these are given a cloudy whitish finish, tending to obscure the irregularities of grain and color. Other devices include bleaching, successful to a degree in mahogany and walnut; pigmentation, in which the open grain is filled with light opaque fillers; pickling, using plaster on soft woods.

BOARD. Table, prior to the 16th century. Early dining tables were loose boards borne on trestles. Later, refers to sideboard.

BOASTING. Rough or preliminary carving.

BOAT BED. Low heavy bed of Empire period, chiefly American, like the gondola or sleigh bed. [122.]

BOBBIN-TURNED. The bulging or swelled part of the turned stretchers of Windsor chairs. [473.]

BODYING-IN. The operation of filling the grain of a coarse wood in the process of finishing.

BOISERIE. French term for woodwork; used specifically for 18th-century carved panels.

BOMBÉ COMMODE · GERMAN

BOLECTION. Important projecting molding, used to frame a fireplace, large panel, etc. Generally with outward roll and ogee shape in section.

BOMBÉ. Swelling or convex surface; bulging fronts and sides, as found in furniture of period of Louis XV, late-18th-century Italian and other Baroque work. [41, 365, 370, 1036.]

BOISERIE · 18ᵀᴴ CENTURY FRENCH

BONHEUR DU JOUR. French desk consisting of a flat cabinet with fall front, carried on legs. Developed for the use of ladies in the era of letter and diary, period of Louis XVI and afterward. [141, 494.]

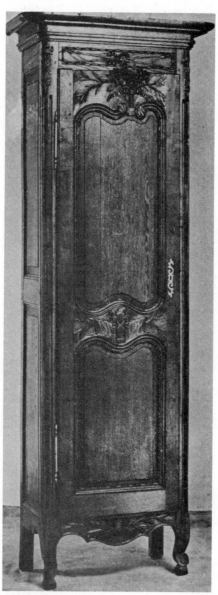

Dalva Brothers, Inc.

141 BONHEUR DU JOUR, Louis XVI, Sèvres plaque in face.

French & Co., Inc.

142 BONNETIÈRE, France, end of 18th century. Normandy type of traditional Louis XV design but with Revolutionary symbols.

BONNEGRÂCE. Bed curtain, 17th century.

BONNET TOP. An unbroken pediment or top section of a highboy, secretary, and the like; also "hooded top." Typical late-17th, early-18th-century English design.

BONNETIÈRE. French cabinet, tall and narrow, and deep enough to accommodate the elaborate bonnets peculiar to Normandy and Brittany in the 18th century. [142.]

BOOK BOX. Same as BIBLE BOX.

BOOKCASE. The earliest bound books were stored in shelved closets, and the architectural bookcase was the only type known until the 17th century. About the middle of that century detached bookcases appeared, retaining their architectural relationship to the room. About 1700, smaller cases were known in France. Detached bookcases of oak and walnut appeared in England during the Restoration; and in the first half of the 18th century they were of prime interest to architectural designers like Kent and the

Metropolitan Museum of Art

143 BIBLIOTHÈQUE, painted white and gold, from the Hôtel de Gaulin, Dijon, 1772. Though not detached from the wall paneling, this shape is essentially that of the breakfront type developed contemporaneously in England.

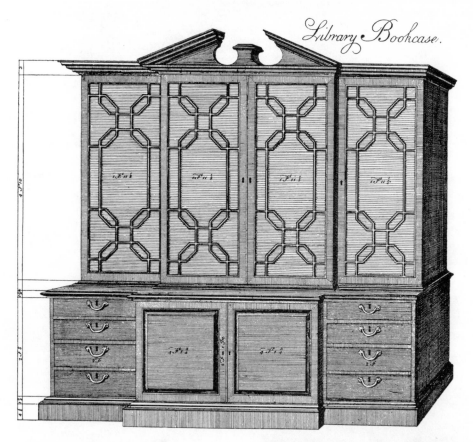

Library Bookcase.

Langleys. Bookcases by the latter were simply detailed and beautifully proportioned. Kent applied nonarchitectural ornament in the form of columns, consoles, and rich carving. By mid-18th century, Chippendale had developed his masterful designs to a level that has remained a standard ever since. [144, 727, 1322.]

The architectural character remained throughout the 18th century, in which the bookcase form developed. The three-part breakfront form was most popular in France and England. The best examples, from the point of contemporary usage, were made in England. These were usually conceived as the permanent decorative features of a given wall, in which respect they developed from the architectural idea. [Cf. 143 with 146.] Chippendale, the Adams, Hepplewhite, etc., valued the bookcase as a wall feature, and their bookcases are among the best of their designs.

The small bookcase [bookshelf, 155] seems to have originated in France, but its superior development took place in England toward the close of the 18th century. The Regency period shows the best of this size, with numerous variations, such as alcove and recess cabinets, smaller stands, combinations with worktables, shelves for display of biblelots, curios. Nineteenth-century bookcases were too often an excuse for an excessively architectural composition of too many unrelated parts. Small bookcases were devices accessory to easy chairs. They often had revolving racks. See also CABINET; SECRETAIRE; SHELVES; WHATNOT.

146 ENGLISH c. 1800.

147 ENGLISH, late 18th century.   **148** AMERICAN BREAKFRONT, Gothic tracery.

149 BOOKCASE-CONSOLE,
English Regency.   *Symons Galleries, Inc.*

150 WRITING TABLE WITH   *Symons Galleries, Inc.*
BOOKRACK, Regency.

151 BIEDERMEIER c. 1810.

152 ENGLISH REGENCY c. 1820.
            Symons Galleries, Inc.

153 ENGLISH REGENCY TABLE WITH BOOK CARRIER. **154** REVOLVING BOOK-STAND, English c. 1800. **155** BOOKSHELF, English c. 1780. **156** REVOLVING BOOK TABLE, French c. 1880.

BOOKREST. Slanting framework, sometimes adjustable, on which to rest a book. See also READING STAND.

BOOKSHELF. See BOOKCASE; STANDING SHELF.

BOOTJACK. Hinged or solid board with V cut to fit the heel, used to help pull off boots; in Early American work, a V cut in the end board of a chest, for the same purpose.

BORAX. Colloquial for cheap, showy furniture, particularly intended for the installment trade. The origin of the word in this sense is speculative. One guess attributes it to the premiums formerly given with a well-known cleaning compound of borax; others identify it as corrupted foreign-language slang.

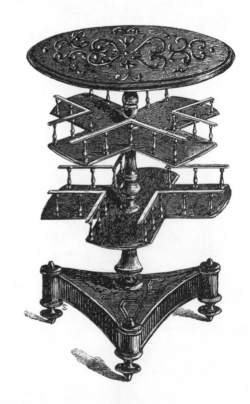

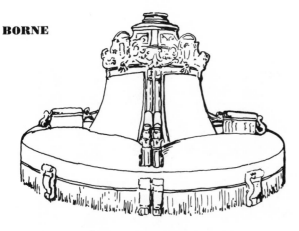

BORNE · FRANCE C. 1850

BORNE. French type of sofa, oval or round, with a pillar in the center. [910, 1307].

BOSS. Round or oval ornament after Gothic sources, common in 17th-century English and American work, particularly on chests. Usually half-turning painted black. [11, 352.]

BOSTON ROCKER. Rocking chair, American 19th century, with wood seat curved upward, wide scrolled top rail, and delicate spindles. Usually painted with fine ornamental detail. [77, 157.]

157 BOSTON ROCKER c. 1835. Stenciled gilt flowers on seat and top rail.

Henry Ford Museum, Dearborn, Mich.

BOTTLE-END GLAZING. The bull's-eye forms, or bottle bottoms, were leaded together and used to glaze the doors of cupboards in England and on the Continent, 16th and 17th centuries.

BOTTLE TURNING. William and Mary leg turning reminiscent of the shape of a bottle. Originally Dutch. [1194.]

BOUILLOTTE TABLE. Small round table originally made for the game of that name, French, 18th century. [158.]

158 BOUILLOTTE TABLE, Louis XVI. Marble top, parquetry.   *Dalva Brothers, Inc.*

BOULLE. André-Charles Boulle, 1642-1732, French cabinetmaker under the patronage of Louis XIV. He designed and executed the mirrored walls, "wood mosaic" floors, inlaid paneling, and pieces of marquetry of the Palace of Versailles. He advanced the art of marquetry and introduced the practice of inlaying brass into wood or tortoiseshell. This distinctive style has come to be known by his name, often spelled "Boull" or "Buhl" work. [179, 502, 636, 1039, 1375.]

159 BOULLE "SECRÉTAIRE A ABATTANT" inlaid with pewter, brass, mother-of-pearl, ivory, mounted *bronze-doré*.

BOX BED
SVEDEN · 18ᵗʰ C.

BOURBON RESTORATION. After Napoleon I, the French restored the Bourbon monarchy, which lasted through Louis XVIII and Charles X (1824-1830). Design in this period took no initiative but followed the eclectic Late Empire trends current throughout Europe. See also NINETEENTH CENTURY; RESTORATION.

BOW BACK. Windsor chairback in which the bow or hoop is continuous either down to the arms or to the seat. [1349.]

BOW TOP. Continuously curved top rail of a chair.

BOWFRONT. Convex-shaped front of a chest, buffet, etc., characteristic of 18th-century work.

BOWL STAND. Same as BASIN STAND; WASHSTAND.

BOX. One of the most primitive pieces of furniture, boxes are used as receptacles for every conceivable object. They lend themselves to the widest variety of decoration, and so are more easily described by their special uses. See also CHEST; COFFER; DESK BOX; PIPE BOXES.

BOX BED. Early beds of northern Europe were more or less boxlike enclosures, an open side having wood panels (in France) or curtains. Later, a folding type was common in Scotland.

BOX SETTLE. Low chest used as a seat, with back formed by a hinged lid. Early development from coffer. [3.]

BOX STOOL. Stool with hinged lid over box section; chiefly Early Renaissance. [879.]

BOXWOOD. Dense, light yellow wood of genus *Buxus*. Its uniform close grain is excellent for carving and for small articles, such as turned parts, handles, rules, inlays, etc.

BRACED BACK. See FIDDLE BRACE BACK. [318.]

Wadsworth Athenenum, Hartford, Conn.
160 CARVED WALNUT CASKET, Dutch, c. 1600.

Museum of the City of New York
162 SEWING BOX, American, 1800-1820.

Metropolitan Museum of Art
161 PAINTED BOX, Italian (Ligurian), 15th century.

Museum of the City of New York
163 DUELING BOX, London, c. 1830.

BRACKET. A small ornamental shelf. Also, any wall lighting fixture. A supporting member between the leg and seat of a chair or table, or the leg and body of a case. Pierced brackets of many designs are characteristic of Chippendale work.

BRACKET CLOCK. English clock intended to stand on a bracket or shelf. See also CLOCK; SHELF CLOCK. [421.]

BRACKET CORNICE. Cornice supported by brackets or modillions at regular intervals. [102.]

BRACKET FOOT. Simple base on chests and case furniture of the 18th century. The foot runs two ways from the corner, in more or less simple shapes. The type was highly ornamented by Chippendale in England, by Goddard and others in America. [262, 442, 565, 710.]

CHIPPENDALE
FRETWORK
BRACKETS

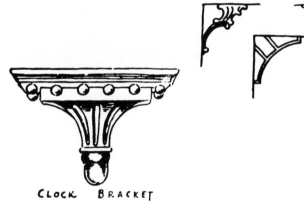

CLOCK BRACKET

BRASSES. Handles.

BRAZIER. Metal receptacle for holding burning coals, commonly used in the Orient and the Mediterranean countries for heating; they are often beautifully designed and decorated. [1156.]

BREAK. Marked projection on a cabinet.

BREAKFRONT. Front formed on two or more planes. Specifically, the word is now used to describe a bookcase or cabinet in which a center section projects forward from the two end sections. [95, 146, 578, 1322.]

164 BIEDERMEIER BREAKFRONT BOOKCASE, first quarter 19th century.

165 "SALEM" SECRETARY, American Breakfront, c. 1800. *Henry Ford Museum, Dearborn, Mich.*

166 BREAKFRONT BOOKCASE, English, Early Victorian.

BRETON. French provincial style of Brittany.

BREWSTER CHAIR. Early New England type either originated by the Pilgrims or brought over by them. It has heavy turned posts, many turned spindles, and a wood seat. Provincial Jacobean in type, its general characteristics are common in earlier chairs from the Continent. [7, 227.]

BRIDAL CHEST. Same as DOWER CHEST or HOPE CHEST. A decorated box for the accumulation of household and personal goods. The romantic implications led to its becoming the object of considerable decoration, particularly in New England, Germany, and Sweden. See also CONNECTICUT CHEST.

BRITISH COLONIAL. Style in architecture and furniture developed by British settlers and officials in colonies such as the West Indies (Bahamas, Bermuda, etc.), South Africa, India, etc., in late 18th and early 19th centuries. Consistently simple and reminiscent of Late Georgian work, it exhibits local influences in appropriate planning and materials.

BROADCLOTH. Plain woven fabric; mentioned as a material for bed curtains and draperies.

BROCADE. Textile woven with a pattern of raised figures resembling embroidery. Originally in gold or silver, in later use any fabric richly wrought or flow-ered with a raised pattern. An important upholstery and drapery fabric originating in India and extensively used in the Renaissance and other ornate styles. [287.]

BROCATELLE. Heavy fabric, chiefly silk, woven usually in large patterns that appear to be embossed.

BROKEN ARCH; BROKEN PEDIMENT. Referring to a pediment whether straight, swan-neck, or gooseneck, the side lines or scrolls of which do not meet or come to a point. [91, 738.]

BROKEN FRONT. Breakfront.

BROKEN PEDIMENT. Pediment of any shape that is interrupted at the apex. [36, 444, 1041, 1045.]

BRONZE. Extensively used for furniture in the ancient world, its strength permitted an extreme lightness of design that is accepted as typically Greco-Roman, and was so copied in the classic revivals of the 18th century. ORMOLU, process of gilding bronze, became very popular in 18th-century France. Louis XV and subsequent work is noted for its superb bronze chasing and modeling. [1296, 1338.]

BUBINGA. African hardwood of even stripe with mottled figure, medium red-brown. Very hard and durable, and polishes well.

BUFFET. Sideboard; dining-room dresser, of almost any description, used as a receptacle for articles not immediately wanted at the table. Originally Italian, the buffet was highly developed in France and in England in the Stuart period, and later in many forms throughout the Georgian Era. See also COURT CUPBOARD; SERVER; SIDEBOARD; TABLE (SIDE).

BUHL. Spelling used in England for Boulle work.

BUILT-IN FURNITURE. Chests, cabinets, corner cupboards, bookcases, etc., treated as integral parts of the structure have been known since the earliest times. In the Far East, particularly Japan, the practice is universal in the case of receptacle furniture. In Europe the upper classes in the Middle Ages lived a nomadic existence, necessitating portable chests, etc., but the lower classes developed built-in beds and benches, chests and cupboards. Recent styles have favored such built-in equipment as cupboards, closets, and bookcases. The contemporary functional style utilizes the economy and efficiency of built-in furniture, including even seatings to an unprecedented degree. [1094.]

167 BUILT-IN FURNITURE originated in treatment of storage utilities as part of woodwork. Recessed sideboard of Gothic elements.

BULBOUS. Turning resembling a bulb, common to most European styles from the Renaissance on. The Dutch passed it on to the English, who made it an outstanding characteristic of their furniture in the 16th and 17th centuries. [555, 1194.]

BULLION FRINGE. Fringe of heavy twisted cords. Originally these had metal strands.

BULL'S-EYE MIRROR. Round ornamental mirror, often with convex or concave glass. See also GIRANDOLE. [72, 866.]

BUN FOOT. English term for "ball foot," usually somewhat flattened. [356.]

BUREAU. Originally a cloth cover for a table, used when writing. In France, a desk derived from a chest set upon a table, and pushed back to afford the writer an armrest (Louis XIII). [1033.]

Sheraton defined the bureau as a "common desk with drawers," and this was the name given in England to the entire family of desk-and-drawer combinations known in America as "secretary." In America the word came to refer to a chest of drawers, generally for the bedroom, and was highly developed during the early 19th century.

BUREAU BOOKCASE. Chippendale's term for a piece of furniture of which the lower part was a desk, the upper a bookcase.

BUREAU TABLE. Goddard's name for his kneehole table.

BURJAR. Chippendale's name for a large upholstered chair like the French bergère.

BURL. Excrescences or abnormal or diseased growths appearing on trees, often from an injury to the bark. When sliced into fine cross sections for veneer, they produce beautifully figured mottled or speckled patterns. These are used for the most decorative veneering. As the usable portions are often small, they are matched in symmetrical panels. Walnut, maple and ash are the commonest American burls, but many fine burls occur all over the world. [567, 573, 737.]

BURR. Burl.

BUTT. The stump end of the log. The root spreads away from the trunk, and sections through the juncture possess a unique grain, desirable for decorative veneering.

BUTT HINGE. Common type of hinge for hanging doors. See also HARDWARE.

BUTT JOINT. Joining, either of solid wood or of veneer, at the ends of the grains. See also CONSTRUCTION.

BUTTER CUPBOARD. Ventilated cabinet used in Europe for the storage of bread. [459.]

BUTTERFLY TABLE. Small drop-leaf table whose leaves are supported by a swinging bracket resembling a butterfly wing or rudder. Chiefly American, after 1700, the earliest examples are of maple. [168.]

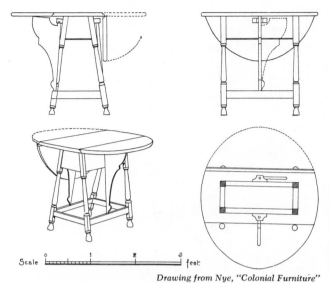

Scale [0 1 2 3 feet]

Drawing from Nye, "Colonial Furniture"

168 BUTTERFLY TABLE.

BUTTERFLY WEDGE. Butterfly-shaped cleat inserted into adjoining boards to hold them together.

BUTTERNUT. Hardwood similar to black walnut. Its importance increases with the demand for black walnut. Also known as white walnut, its grain is similar to that of black walnut, but its color is lighter and texture softer.

BYZANTINE. From Byzantium, Roman Empire of the East, centering in Constantinople, 476-1200. Byzantine furniture, entirely royal or ecclesiastical, was debased Roman with profuse ornamentation in Near Eastern style. Rich carving, with inlays of gold, glass, stones, in motives of ritual significance. Interlacing bands, stiff animal forms, sharply cut foliage, etc., remain in later Russian and South European as well as Italian work.

BYZANTINE. Specifically, a three-cornered chair believed to have originated in Scandinavia, and popularized in England in the Middle Ages. [239.]

BYZANTINE THRONE

CABINET. Almost any type of receptacle furniture may be termed a cabinet, though it generally implies drawers or shelves.

The cabinet, or cupboard, form has a mixed ancestry in the coffer or chest, and the closetlike armoire [91] or ambry. It is primarily a receptacle; as such its variety must be infinite. It was early realized in Italy and France that the top of a coffer could be used as a seat or table; this suggested the front opening instead of the top, the first stage in the cabinet. The form was complete when the cabinet was mounted on legs high enough to eliminate stooping to see the interior [170]. This type is the sideboard-credence type. The parallel type, the boxlike cupboard, whatever its source, came to resemble the chest-on-legs as soon as it was found expedient in the latter to make use of the lower section by closing in the open space. The convergence of these elementary types is shown in the evolution of French cabinets from the simple Gothic box [714] to the Burgundian cabinet [175] with vertical emphasis, or from the horizontal cabinet of earliest Renaissance style to the mature style of Louis XIII [177]. In this period, the early 17th century, the cabinet was the dominant article of furniture, embellished by every decorative resource. Carving and painting, inlaying, marquetry, and encrustation with stones of beauty and value, with mirrors or metals, paneling and moldings, were lavished on the monumental cabinets of Italy and France. Their height and physical importance made them focal points in the room, and their association with articles of value and beauty justified the lavish decoration. The cabinetmaker was therefore the head of the woodworking craftsmen, and the name persisted.

Another structural point caused this name to stand out. Earliest coffers were solid wood planks. Sometime in the Middle Ages the carpenters who specialized in furniture hit on the framed panel (a thin panel fixed in grooves in a stout frame). For lightness and strength this was far superior to the solid board. It also reduced the risk of cracking and of warping from shrinkage. The paneling itself provided some decorative character. The guild of *huchiers-menuisiers* broke away from the guild of simple *charpentiers*. Ever since, the *huchier*—hutch maker, cabinetmaker—has isolated his craft from that of the mere carpenter.

The ornate cabinet passed its zenith in France but did not deteriorate in the provinces for two centuries. The bold pointed panels of this style are characteristic [633]; these passed to England, and characterize Jacobean work. German cabinets favored twisted turnings, applied at corners [172]. The Augsburg style was famous. Another development was the desk cabinet.

169   *Metropolitan Museum of Art, Gift of J. Pierpont Morgan, 1916*

170   *Symons Galleries, Inc.*

EARLY CABINETS DEVELOPED FROM THE CHEST OR CUPBOARD, RAISED OFF THE FLOOR AND FITTED WITH PAIRED DOORS FOR ACCESS FROM THE FRONT AT EYE LEVEL.

169 CUPBOARD developed from chest; Flemish, late-15th-century Gothic.

170 CHEST-ON-STAND; flamboyant Gothic-Early Renaissance, France.

Hispanic Society of America

171 INDO-PORTUGUESE, 17th century. Redwood with ivory, ebony, and mother-of-pearl inlay.

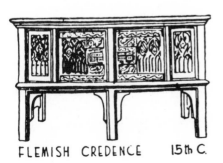

FLEMISH CREDENCE   15th C.

Since money and papers had been stored in coffers, the specialized cabinet providing many small compartments, and drawers persisted. [1037, 1056.]

Charles II brought back to England the craze for cabinets. Styles are largely exemplified by cabinets after that: the William and Mary highboys with their turned bases and marquetry top sections, the Chinese lacquered cabinets [392] of Queen Anne and Georgian times, the richly carved and gilded bases of late-17th-century cabinets, and the important cabinets of Chippendale and the Georgian designers testify to their vitality.

Specialization in the 18th century led to so many types that they can scarcely be listed—the use is part of the name, as in jewel cabinet, sewing cabinet, etc. Cabinets were less imposing as they became smaller, so that today the usual implication is a box or case for a particular use. Many cabinets are built in, or so designed as to form part of the plan of the room, such as corner cupboards, recess cupboards, etc.

Small cabinet stands appeared in the 18th century as accents in architectural decoration, and for the housing and display of collections of objets d'art, and curios. See also BUFFET; CHEST; DESK; HIGHBOY; HUTCH.

172 DUTCH, 17th-century Baroque. Rosewood and ebony.
Metropolitan Museum of Art, Rogers Fund, 1912

173 GOTHIC OAK CABINET, late-15th-century French. Post-and-panel construction with linenfold panel decoration. The carved astragal and wrought-iron lock and hinges are superior features.

174 CHINESE INLAID WOOD CABINET, Late Ming Dynasty, 1368-1628.

175 FRENCH, Henry IV, early 17th century. *Armoire à deux corps.* Style of Jean Goujon.

176 ITALIAN, 16th century.

177 FRENCH, Louis XIII c. 1620-1625; Italian influence, ebony.

THE CABINET REACHED ITS HEIGHT AS A SHOW-
PIECE AFTER 1600 IN ALL ADVANCED CENTERS
OF EUROPE.

William Rockhill Nelson Gallery of Art (Nelson Fund), Kansas City, Mo.

Symons Galleries, Inc.

Metropolitan Museum of Art, Gift of Mrs. A. H. Wiggin, 1951

Di Salvo

178 GERMAN JEWEL CABINET, 17th century.

Wadsworth Atheneum, Hartford, Conn.

179 CABINET in the style of Boulle, Louis XVI. *Frick Collection*

180 ENGLISH c. 1771. Rosewood and satinwood veneer with inlays of marble mosaic.

181 REGENCE "VITRINE."

CHARLES II CABINET

182 ENGLISH c. 1700. Walnut and marquetry.

CABINET STAND. Decorative stands for cabinets, chests, etc., appeared as soon as life in Europe ceased to be nomadic. The handsome chests and, later, Oriental cabinets were mounted on elaborately carved and gilt frames. Planned for use against a wall, only the fronts were ornamented. There was often a rim to hold the cabinet in place. The shape either evolved into a side-table form, or combined with the cabinet to form the highboy and the tall cabinet.

CABINETMAKER. General term for joiners or case-furniture makers. Joiners make rigid box forms in which the parts are articulated by means of specially shaped interlocking parts, such as dovetails, secured by adhesives, not nails, or adhesives helped by screws as well as by the cut joint. This distinguishes the cabinetmaker from the carpenter, who makes structures mostly held together by nails.

Specialization within this field began early. The European guilds defined ranks of achievement, rising to the *ébéniste*. Incidental specialists became turners, chairmakers, etc. See also CABINET; CONSTRUCTION; JOINERY.

CABINETWORK. The finer classification of interior woodwork and furniture, as distinguished from carpentry.

CABLE. Rope molding. [810.]

CABLE FLUTING. Fluting whose lower ends are filled in with a convex molding.

CABOCHON. Carved ornament resembling a gem or polished stone, common in French Rococo work and English derivatives.

CABRIOLE. Furniture leg shaped in a double curve, the upper part swelling out, the curve swinging in toward the foot, which again flares out. Its use in European furniture began late in the 17th century with the many efforts at varying the familiar turned and square legs. Baroque virtuosity sought new complexities for this member, having exhausted all manner of decorated and spiral turnings. First it added scroll forms to the feet; then double and reversed scrolls. In time the sharp break was smoothed out and the whole leg made into a sinuous line. Elaboration appeared at the knee, the top outcurve, and at the foot. In the method of articulating the vertical leg to the horizontal apron came the development of flowing lines that distinguish the Rococo style.

The foregoing development is particularly exemplified in the Dutch, Flemish, and English schools of the late 17th century, but illustrates only one phase of the general trend toward curvilinear forms. In France the transition from Baroque Louis XIV to Rococo Louis XV through the Régence is illustrated in the growing importance of the curved leg. Here the type evolved through the fancy of the animal foot—*pied-de-biche*—being carved from the square block in a slight curve ending in a carved animal's foot—doe, goat, ram, horse, etc. In time the curve became richer, the shoulder or knee (upper part) being more continuously joined to the curve of the horizontal structure. In later Rococo work the animal resemblance was abandoned and became an abstract sinuous line ending in a scroll.

Another source of the cabriole form may be in the Far East, whence the Dutch navigators brought the dragon foot, clasping a jewel. This general form is heavily echoed in some work of the middle 17th century.

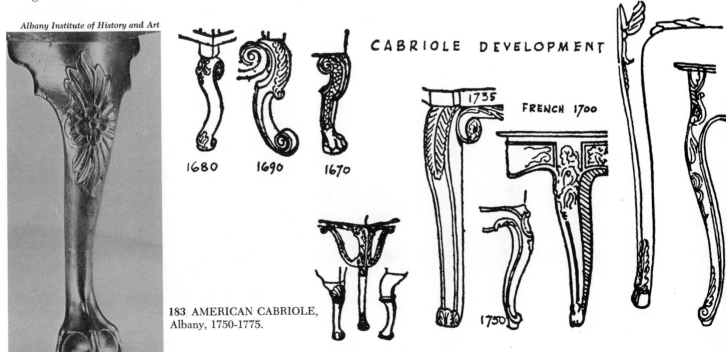

Albany Institute of History and Art

CABRIOLE DEVELOPMENT

1680 1690 1670

1735 FRENCH 1700 1750

183 AMERICAN CABRIOLE, Albany, 1750-1775.

The name springs from the root *capra*—goat—through the Spanish *cabriole,* suggesting its resemblance to the bent leg of an animal.

In all styles in which it appears, the excellence of the cabriole leg is an index of the quality of the whole design. A good flowing line that nevertheless retains an unbroken center line in conformity with the grain of the wood is more pleasing to the eye than an excessive curve that cuts the vertical quality. [262, 314, 479, 528.]

CAFFIERI, JACQUES, 1678-1755; PHILIPPE, 1714-1774. French bronze workers; made important metal decorations for furniture, period of Louis XV.

CAMBER. Hollowed or slightly convex surface, to correct the illusion of sagging in unsupported horizontal lines.

CAMELBACK. Double curved chairback, shield-shaped; characteristic Hepplewhite type. [37.]

CAMEO. Raised carving, usually delicate, on stone or imitations of stone. Used as furniture ornaments by Sheraton, the Adams, and in the Empire style. [141, 204.]

CAMPAIGN FURNITURE. Primarily military; portable utilities such as chairs, tables, beds, chests, desks. Often folding or collapsible or separable into parts, fitted with handles and lugs, and with minimum protuberances, to facilitate carrying and stowing. [359.]

CANADA. Scant surviving furniture of the early settlements indicates little more than the most functional French and British mannerisms, with a minimum of imports. At the turn of the 18th and 19th centuries, a fairly definite trend emerges in the French-speaking areas, typically rustic-provincial with a remembered French accent, gay and independent. Separately, the English colonists continued their Late Georgian tradition with imports and adaptations. [248, 435, 451, 971, 972.]

CANAPE. Sofa or couch, originally curtained. [1126.]

CANDLE BOARD. Small sliding shelf beneath a tabletop, used to hold a candlestick. Principally English 18th century.

CANDLE BOX. Tall hanging box of tin or wood in which candles are kept. [964.]

CANDLE SLIDE. Sliding shelf just over the desk section of secretaries, on which candlesticks were placed. [1069, 1387.]

CANDLESTAND. Small table, usually tripod, pedestal or with four legs, for candlestick or small objects. [17, 1243.]

CANE. Flexible rattan woven in open patterns for chair seats, backs, etc. First occurring in English furniture about the time of the Restoration, it was favored by furniture makers of the periods of Charles II, William and Mary, and Queen Anne; during the revivals of the Chinese taste in the late 18th century, and in the classic work of the Adams brothers; also in French furniture of the corresponding periods, particularly the Louis XV and Louis XVI styles. [256, 279, 646, 902.]

CANNELLATED. Fluted.

CHAIR CANADA
17TH CENTURY (?)

184 CANADIAN PINE COFFER, 18th century.   *Musée de la Province, Quebec*

CAQUETEUSE

185 CANTERBURY, English c. 1800.   *Needham's Antiques, Inc.*

CANOPY. Covering or hood over bed or throne, suspended from wall or ceiling or carried on posts. Architecturally, an ornamental projection. See also TESTER. [102, 1311.]

CANT. Bevel or chamfer, as on an edge.

CANTEEN. Small box or case, partitioned for cutlery or bottles.

CANTERBURY. In current use, a magazine rack; originally a portable stand with partitions for sheet music, etc., also used to carry supper tray, cutlery and plates. Named for the cleric who first ordered such a piece. [823.]

CANTONNIERE, also CANTOINE, CANTONEER. Narrow embroidered band forming part of the drapery of a canopy bed.

CAPITAL. The head of a column or pilaster. The various orders of architecture are easily distinguished by their capitals. All types are used in furniture ornament. See also ORDERS.

CAPPING. A turned or square ornament.

CAQUETEUSE; CAQUETOIRE. French chair with high narrow back and curved arms. Late 16th century. [220.]

CARCASS; CARCASE. Body or framework of a piece of cabinet furniture.

CARD CUT. Latticework ornament in low relief (not pierced) in the Chinese manner. Favored by Chippendale. [413.]

CARD TABLE. Appearing in the later 17th century, card tables reached their zenith in 18th-century England. From Queen Anne through the Regency every style has fine examples. Leisure and a passion for gambling universal among the upper classes made the card table an outstanding necessity. Card tables were almost always made to fold. Earlier types featured scooped-out "guinea holes." Finely ornamented cabriole legs are typical. The style spread to the Continent, and fine types are found in Late Italian work, especially in the Directoire style. The fixed type, or permanent, bridge table and the completely collapsible utilitarian table are the chief types today. See also GAME TABLE; TABLE. [61, 962.]

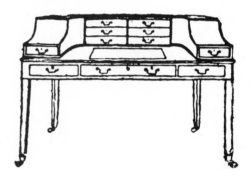

CARLTON HOUSE DESK

CARLTON TABLE; CARLTON HOUSE DESK. English writing table, end of 18th and early 19th century. In Sheraton's Drawing Book it appears as a "Lady's Drawing and Writing Table," with a bank of small drawers and compartments placed upon a table. The central part of the tabletop pulls out or is adjustable to an angle, and beneath this leaf are wide drawers for drawing paper. Usually mahogany or satinwood, with brass gallery. [1382.]

CAROLEAN. Referring to the period of Charles II, King of England 1660-1685. See also ENGLAND; RESTORATION.

CARTEL CLOCK. 18th-century hanging clock, often bronze. [416.]

CARTON-PIERRE. Composition substitute used to simulate wood carving, introduced by Robert Adam.

CARTONNIER (French). Ornamented box for holding papers. [1378.]

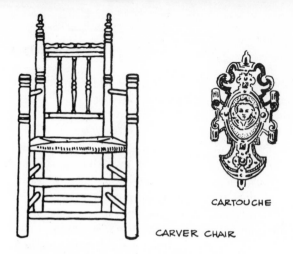

CARTOUCHE

CARVER CHAIR

CARVING. Carving applied to furniture includes every type of relief from simple scratching, gouging, and chipping, using conventional patterns largely in one plane, to full relief in plastic or sculptural form. Semisavage decoration includes the carving of geo-

William Rockhill Nelson Gallery of Art (Nelson Fund), Kansas City, Mo.
186 COPTIC CARVING, stone, 5th century. Vigorous space-filling flat relief.

CARTOUCHE. Ornamental feature in the form of an unrolled scroll or oval table with the edges curled or rolled over; originally a card partly unrolled or turned over at the corners, often emblazoned with arms, initials, etc., as a central decoration in architecture and furniture. Derived from Italian Renaissance architectural forms, it occurs extensively in Italian furniture after the 15th century, and in French work from Francis I on. Chippendale employed cartouches as the central motive on high cabinets. [191, 198.]

CARVER CHAIR. Early American chair of turned wood parts, named after a chair owned by Governor Carver of Plymouth. Earlier models are ash, later of maple, usually with rush seats. [3.]

Henry Ford Museum, Dearborn, Mich.
188 NEW ENGLAND CHAIRBACK c. 1690. Coarsely simplified detail is due to hardness of curly maple.

Albany Institute of History and Art
189 PHYFE CHAIR SPLAT, 1815-1820.

190 LOUIS XVI CHAPEL CHAIR by I. Jacob. Overall surface pattern of rinceaux.
Dalva Brothers, Inc.

187 SHALLOW FLAT SURFACE CARVING in pine-board face of New Mexican chest; Spanish influence, early 19th century.
Museum of New Mexico

191 ITALIAN RENAISSANCE, 16th century; late naturalistic figure modeling.

Frick Collection

metric spaces in flat relief. Relics of the most ancient civilizations show the application of this decorative technique to articles of everyday utility such as stools, boxes, etc. Egyptian furniture was carved with religious symbols and representations of animals done with meticulous craftsmanship. There is every reason to believe that the Greeks, Assyrians, Romans, and other ancients used plastic forms in wood furniture as well as in stone. Byzantine and Romanesque carving of the Early Middle Ages show classic vestiges, together with the Near Eastern or Mohammedan influences, which include sharp geometric forms in low relief. During this era the Far East enjoyed the labors of superlative craftsmen using highly conventionalized motives and methods. China, Japan, and India exploited carving beyond most other arts; these were largely in wood, and partake of the wood quality. [472, 934.]

European Gothic wood carving is in the greatest tradition. Its style was perfected in oak and superbly adapted to the hard, brittle, coarse texture. Renaissance carving, largely in walnut, is finer and subtler, in the classic contrast of thin detail against smooth surface, but the drawing and architectural outline are uniformly firm. As the Renaissance waxed, carving grew more bold, approaching the great plastic compositions, with much freestanding relief, by which Baroque art is distinguished. [837.] This robust high relief also typifies the Late Renaissance in France. In particular, the Burgundian school of Hugues Sambin

192 BAROQUE, EARLY GEORGIAN. Full relief naturalistic sculpture as table support. (See 574.) *Stair & Company, Inc.*

spread carving over everything, to the obliteration of architectural outlines. [175, 632, 640.]

In the north countries, the Early Gothic tradition clung; indeed, Romanesque-Celtic influence in the form of complex convolutions persisted in cruder work, while the Gothic and earlier Renaissance styles dominated the upper classes. Scandinavian, German, Celtic, and even English carving of the 15th and early 16th centuries show such qualities. On them and their Gothic mixtures was imposed the classical Renaissance formula. England carved in oak for another century before accepting the walnut prevalent on the Continent. The Renaissance forms of fruit and flowers, angels and instruments, carved throughout Europe, inspired Grinling Gibbons and a great art in England. [798.]

Eighteenth-century carving throughout Europe follows the trend from free naturalism to stiff classic decoration. In England the Grinling Gibbons school, full formed and robust, persisted through the period of Chippendale influence, and some authorities estab-

French & Co., Inc.

Metropolitan Museum of Art, Michael Friedsam Collection

193 LOUIS XVI. Strong, deep modeling.

194 *Left center.* NEW ENGLAND c. 1770. Shell carving into the block.

195 BAVARIAN BED HEADBOARD, early 19th century, style of Louis XVI in Provincial simplicity.

196 FRENCH RENAISSANCE, 16th century.

Israel Sack, Inc.

Liebhold-Wallach, Inc.

CORNUCOPIA
BIEDERMEIER
SOFA · C · 1820

lish 18th-century chronology by types of carving: lion mask, satyr mask, etc. In Continental carving the Baroque was lush, large, and full. The Rococo tended toward lightness and grace, replacing mythological figures and large-scale classic motives with rocks and shells, flowers, swags, and ribbons in unclassical asymmetry, graceful and rambling. Much plastic or modeled decoration of this style was executed in bronze, cast and chased, and overlaid upon fine wood veneers. [159, 559, 574, 582, 649.]

The classic revivals of the later 18th century minimized carved ornamentation. The Adams and the Louis XVI styles used the thin classical carvings of Herculaneum; scrolls and mythological figures were always attenuated, as were acanthus and water leaves and other formal band moldings. Paterae, medallions, swags, vases, etc., were contained within severe outlines, differing from the loosely composed Rococo compositions. The Empire style used carving more sparingly than any other, but later 19th-century developments employed coarsened classic forms. Modern styles have almost completely eliminated carving on furniture. See also ORNAMENT. [641, 646.]

CARYATID. Greek architectural ornament in the form of female figures used as supporting columns. Male figures of the same character are called Atlantes. Adapted to form legs of tables, chairs, stands of cabinets, etc., and as pilasters for beds, cabinets, mantels, paneling, etc., they are found in the classic revivals and in all the more decorative architectural styles of furniture, such as the later Italian Renaissance, Jacobean, Francis I, Louis XIV, Empire, etc. [640.]

CASE. General term for any receptacle, cabinet, or box used for holding things. In cabinetwork, "case" refers to the boxlike structure that forms the shell of a chest of drawers, cabinet, etc.

CASKET. Small box or chest, often of value and beauty, made of precious woods and metals; inlaid, carved, or painted, they were used to hold money, jewels, papers, and other valuables. See also CHEST; COFFER. [160, 178.]

CASSAPANCA. Italian settee formed by adding arms and back to a chest—literally *cassone* plus *banca*. Chiefly Middle Renaissance Florentine; prototype of English box settle, etc. [198, 1073, 1077.]

CARYATIDS

197 CASSONE, Italian, 16th century, walnut.

Frick Collection

198 CASSAPANCA, Italian, 16th century, walnut.

CASSOLETTE. Box or vase with perforated cover for incense or perfume; also called "essence vases." England, last half of the 18th century.

CASSONE. Italian chest or box with painted, carved, or inlaid decoration. See also CHEST; ITALY. [191.]

CAST IRON. Iron casting figures extensively in 19th-century decorative work. By midcentury there was a large list of outdoor furniture. The ease of duplicating different carved effects appealed to the Victorian love both for factory methods and for ornate surfaces, and it could be done cheaply. In interiors it found use mostly in utilitarian things such as sewing-machine stands, reading stands, table bases, brackets, boxes, etc. These were often beautifully modeled, with irrelevant ornament. Stoves, as scientific devices, beginning early in the century, were designed architecturally or with decorative cast-iron elements of naïve charm if not of appropriateness. Beds were fitted with cast-iron ornaments applied to wrought-iron or tubing frames, although there are some all-cast examples. See also IRON; METAL FURNITURE. [199, 1299.]

CASTELLATED. Architecturally a regularly pierced cornice, from the parapets of fortified castles. The motive was copied in some Gothic furniture.

CASTOR. Small roller attached to the feet or base of a piece of furniture, for ease in moving around without lifting. Castor making was a distinct trade in England by the end of the 17th century. Early castors were of wood; later superseded by leather and brass, they are now principally made of rubber and synthetic materials. At the height of their use in the 18th and 19th centuries, they were used as a definite part of the design. This commendable practice died in the 19th century, and even now for the most part castors are merely applied after the piece is completed, with the result that they often mar a good design.

CATHEDRAL SHAPE. Pointed arch in bookcase tracery, late 18th and 19th centuries (Gothic revivals) in England and America; also on the backs of some Sheraton chairs, and in the shaping of the bases of some simple chests of drawers. [446, 1089.]

CAUSEUSE. Upholstered armchair with open sides.

CAVETTO. Concave molding usually found as the important member of a cornice. In English walnut furniture this was often veneered crosswise.

CEDAR. The *Juniperus virginiana* of North America and the *Cedrela odorata* of the West Indies are the fragrant red cedar familiarly used for protection against moths. It first appears in 18th-century English furniture for drawer linings, boxes, and traveling chests, a use that is still current.

CEDAR CHEST. The current American household chest for storage of woolens, etc., for protection against moths.

CELLARETTE. Deep drawer for bottles in a sideboard; also a separate cabinet for liquors, glasses, etc. See also CISTERN; WINE COOLER; WINE SIDEBOARD. [86, 1351.]

Henry Ford Museum, Dearborn, Mich.

199 STOVE, Troy, New York, 1843. Four-column dolphin design.

200 CAST-IRON GARDEN CHAIR, Philadelphia, 1804.
Israel Sack, Inc.

America has long been noted for the luxurious easiness of its chairs, which combine in themselves all the means of gratification a Sybarite could wish. The AMERICAN CHAIR COMPANY, of New York, exhibit some novelties, which even

increase the luxury and convenience of this necessary article of furniture; instead of the ordinary legs conjoined to each angle of the seat, they combine to support a stem, as in ordinary

music-stools, between which and the seat the SPRING is inserted; this we exhibit in our first cut. It will allow of the greatest weight and freest motion on all sides; the seat is also made

to revolve on its axis. The design and fittings of these chairs are equally good and elegant, and certainly we have never tested a more easy and commodious article of household furniture.

From "Industry of All Nations; the Crystal Palace Exhibition, 1851."
201 CHAIRS OF CAST IRON with steel springs c. 1850.

CENTER DRAWER GUIDE. Wooden track under the center of a drawer as a guide for its operation when drawn. See also CONSTRUCTION.

CENTER TABLE. Round, oblong, oval, square, or any other shaped table finished on all sides so that it may be used in the center of a room for any purpose. [125, 135, 543, 952.]

CERAMIC. Seen in furniture as tile tabletops in the Near East, Spain, Italy, and the Netherlands, and in modern work. Decorative inserts in cabinets and tables appear in 18th-century work in France (Sèvres) [202] and England (Wedgwood) [204], and in Oriental screens and cabinets. China made whole ceramic pieces as stools and tabourets. Picture and mirror frames and accessory furniture articles were made in the great experimental potteries in Italy and Germany (Capo di Monte and Meissen) and in Scandinavia. Decorative and ingenious ceramic stoves and fireplaces were made in the Baltic lands in the 18th and 19th centuries. [708.]

CERTOSINA. Style of inlay employing bone or ivory on a dark wood ground. Usually small geometric patterns—stars, triangles, crescents, etc., suggesting Mohammedan origin. Appears in Venetian work in the 14th century; also in Spanish work of Moorish type, and in subsequent derivations. [215, 1145.]

Dalva Brothers, Inc.

203 DIRECTOIRE CONSOLE, ceramic panels in top. Aprons and legs framed with *bronze d'oré*. France c. 1800.

202 LOUIS XVI GUERIDON, gilt bronze with Sèvres plates.   *Frick Collection*

204 WEDGWOOD PLAQUES inserted in cylinder desk, c. 1780, by Saunier.   *French & Co., Inc.*

CHAIR. The chair, a single movable seat, is most ancient. Most familiar types were known in ancient Egypt, Greece, and Rome; significantly, the names for special types are ancient. [205 *et seq.*]

Egyptian remains indicate the use of wooden chairs as well as of ivory and metal. The folding, or X, type is found in tombs; it was often carved with animal forms and covered with whole skins. Fixed four-legged chairs were significantly carved and painted, animal feet, as of the bull and lion, being common. Greek chairs, evidenced by sculptured reliefs, were of gracefully curved form; the grand type was called *thronos*. From Rome there are relics of light turned chairs of metal, wood, and ivory elaborately wrought and cushioned with silk pillows. In Rome the X-chair had some significance of caste; it seems to have been reserved for magistrates and nobles on public occasions. The *cathedra* was a chair with a back used by women.

The Early Middle Ages left little evidence of a common use of chairs; the curule type, developed as a folding form, persisted for the use of dignitaries. Later medieval chairs were entirely a prerogative of high estate; they traveled about with the lord, and when set up were mounted on a dais and capped with a tester or canopy. A more permanent type of chair evolved in Late Gothic times by the addition of a seat to the wall paneling—the wainscot chair that with a solid panel back is found as late as the 17th century in New England. Elsewhere the panel became posts, the whole structure lighter and more comfortably proportioned; but the connotation of caste remained.

In Italy the Renaissance brought forward (besides the development of the curule chair into Dantesca and Savonarola types) the simple chair structure of four posts with arms, less architectural than the wainscot or paneled chair, though scarcely more comfortable. Comfort came with the addition of upholstery, at first loose cushions; later, attached pads with fine fabric or leather covering. The development of ornamentally carved members as seats and stretchers was rapid and significant. Lesser chairs were usually a narrow board or frame; early domestic types of turned frameworks with rush seats were known. Spanish chairs followed the Italian in most respects; the rustic types of crude workmanship probably became common in the 17th century.

France produced the earliest comfortable chairs and the widest variety. The *chaire* always has had special significance. Under Francis I it begat scaled-down versions with modifications, always toward lightness, producing a simple armchair type at first called *chaises à femmes*, and finally a simple portable framework dubbed *caquetoire*, or gossip chairs. The *chaises à*

vertugadin, like the farthingale chairs of England, were made necessary by the women's extravagant skirts. Later, the *fauteuil*, a comfortable chair with arms, developed, utilizing the newly invented upholstered seat. Louis XIV saw the development of magnificent, luxurious chairs, scaled from thrones to simple styles—and by 1700 most of the familiar forms had appeared: fauteuils, bergères, wing chairs, confessionals. During the Régence the lines became flowing, curved; stretchers disappeared; chairs of the Louis XV period are delicate, exceedingly graceful, masterpieces of fluid line. About this time springs were invented, changing the upholstery principle.

In England progress followed the French example, with local variations. Jacobean chairs were still basically Gothic, and the Renaissance appeared slowly, adding details from Italy, Spain, Flanders. Heavy oak was universal in square box constructions through the Commonwealth, with nothing but sausage turnings to modify the angularity. With the Restoration came Baroque details, spiral turnings, boisterously carved stretchers and crestings; these were imposing but rarely comfortable. The X-chair fairly disappeared at this time, but the elementary overstuffed chair came soon after. The Dutch William and Mary established the cabriole leg; and Queen Anne's style shows a wholly new type, Baroque in its wholesale curvature, yet distinctly English. Seat plan, back posts and front legs, splats and cresting were all curved, yet the curvature was entirely different from the contemporary French chair. For some years the development of the English chair followed this decorated Queen Anne style. Chippendale developed pierced slats, new top-rail shapes, and finally the square front-foot after Chinese lines in place of the ubiquitous claw-and-ball cabriole leg. Chippendale chairs are notably wider, lower, more comfortable.

The French influence again became dominant after 1750. Hepplewhite and others literally reproduced the exquisite Rococo shapes. Even the Classic Revival accepted the whole proportion and silhouette, substituting for the sinuous lines a set of sharply rectilinear shapes that we identify as Adam, Louis XVI, etc. This angularity invited new forms; and Sheraton and the other end-of-18th-century designers produced them without limit, borrowing, adapting, distorting every motive from classical times. In their extreme variety early-19th-century chairs show clearly the frenzied search for novelty. Probably the most significant type was the graceful chair form associated with Duncan Phyfe in Federal American work.

Of course, chair forms were multiplied everywhere in Europe. The *sgabelle* type appeared in all provincial work, most ornate and uncomfortable in the excessively carved Swiss and German forms. The northern versions of Régence and Rococo bergères, etc., were almost new types in themselves. The old chairs of turned parts persisted in outlying districts into the 19th century, even the triangular type. The ladder back developed both into a crude rush-seated affair and into beautifully proportioned slat backs, best of all in America. The exquisite straw-seated chairs of France also grew out of these turned-post forms.

The Windsor chair, utilizing turnings and bent parts, developed in America into a triumph of lightness, comfort, strength, and economy.

The nineteenth century began with a proliferation of chair styles and sheer quantity as a result of the Industrial Revolution. Sheraton and the Empire dominated England and the Continent and the colonies. From these came infinite variations, some creditable, but more on the path of debasement that ran right through the century. Most characteristic types on historic models are the balloon-back Victorian Rococo shapes in England and America and France; the semiclassic, such as the Biedermeier in northern Europe and the Directoire derivatives in Italy. The last quarter of the century saw the whole gamut of eclectically inspired innovation, approached from every fashion angle. Upholstery saw the most intensive development in history.

Collaterally, the chair presented a new challenge to those who perceived the scope of the new mechanics and materials as well as of the new society. Adventurous experiments in mechanical seating devices seldom went beyond the Patent Office, but there was fruitful groping with mediums. Though iron, cast and wrought, was handled with imagination, it was not pursued far enough. Some of its line quality passed into Thonet's bentwood. Plasticity was recognized in the techniques of lamination.

The chair, being insistently a functional engineering object, challenged the reformers from the start. The Morris chair met a demand squarely, whereas the *avant-garde* three decades later—men such as Charles Mackintosh, Frank Lloyd Wright, Gerrit Rietveld—strained theory to achieve art. A truer rationale in the 1920's culminated in Marcel Breuer's steel tubing chair and its derivatives; in Mies van der Rohe's Barcelona chair; Alvar Aalto's molded plywood; Charles Eames's Fiberglas; Eero Saarinen's shells; Harry Bertoia's wire frames; Hans Wegner's wood craftsmanship; the engineered logic of George Nelson. In the United States this idiom has had the benefit of commercialization by architecturally oriented firms such as Knoll, Risom, and Miller.

205 GREEK TOMBSTONE showing chair, 5th century B.C.

206 207 EGYPTIAN, 2nd century B.C.

208 ROMAN, stone, 1st century C.E.

209 ROMAN, stone, 2nd century C.E.

210   *Maryland Historical Society*

211   *Metropolitan Museum of Art*

212

THE FURNITURE OUTLINES OF CLASSICAL
ANTIQUITY REAPPEAR IN SPONTANEOUS REVIVALS,
SUCH AS THE RENAISSANCE AND THE EMPIRE
STYLE OF THE EARLY NINETEENTH CENTURY.

210 REVIVAL OF CLASSIC MOTIVES. American, c. 1815,
by Lannuier, New York. **211** ITALIAN EMPIRE. **212**
FRENCH, period of the Consulate, 1799-1804, painted and
gilded.

*Metropolitan Museum of Art, Gift of Captain and Mrs. W. G. Fitch,
1910, in memory of Clyde Hill*

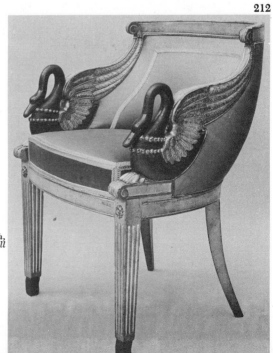

Metropolitan Museum of Art, Rogers Fund, 1927

213 ITALIAN, early 16th century, primitive folding chair, nail-studded walnut with stretched leather.

214 ITALIAN, 16th century, "Dante" folding chair, luxuriously detailed.

214   *Metropolitan Museum of Art*

Metropolitan Museum of Art, Gift of William H. Riggs, 1913

215 ITALIAN, "Savonarola" folding chair, inlaid certosina work of ivory and metal.

Metropolitan Museum of Art, Rogers Fund, 1913

216 ENGLISH c. 1570. "Faldstool," Late Gothic carving with lozenges of French Renaissance type.

Metropolitan Museum of Art,
Bequest of Annie C. Kane, 1926

217

Metropolitan Museum of Art,
Fletcher Fund, 1930

218

Metropolitan Museum of Art,
Rogers Fund, 1908

219

220

THE SGABELLE TYPE

SOME CHAIR FORMS GREW OUT OF THE ADDITION OF A BACK TO A STOOL. THIS PERSISTED IN RUSTIC WORK, AND HAS SOME IDENTIFICATION WITH THE WINDSOR CHAIR IDEA.

217 ITALIAN (Urbino?), early 16th century. **218** ITALIAN, 1490. From the Strozzi Palace, Florence. **219** SWISS, 17th-century peasant chair. **220** CAQUETEUSE, French, 16th century. **221** AMERICAN (Ohio) c. 1850. German peasant tradition. **222** ENGLISH, 18th century. **223** GERMAN, 18th century. **224** SWISS, 19th century.

221   *Henry Ford Museum,*
Dearborn, Mich.

222   *Arthur S. Vernay, Inc.*

223   *Metropolitan Museum of Art,*
Rogers Fund, 1908

224

THE WAINSCOT CHAIR GREW OUT OF THE ADDITION OF A SEAT TO THE WOODEN WALL PANELING. DETACHED, IT GREW LIGHTER AND LESS THRONELIKE.

225

Metropolitan Museum of Art, Gift of George Blumenthal, 1941

226   *Metropolitan Museum of Art, Rogers Fund, 1907*

Metropolitan Museum of Art, Sylmaris Collection, Gift of George Coe Graves, 1923

227

225 FRENCH GOTHIC c. 1500. **226** FRENCH (Lyon), 1550-1580. Italian Renaissance detail. **227** THE "BREWSTER" CHAIR, brought to America in 1623.

228 AMERICAN, early 17th century. **229-30** ENGLISH c. 1635-1650, lighter and smaller; Gothic influence in carving.

228   229-30

Israel Sack, Inc.

Arthur S. Vernay, Inc.

231

232

233   *Hispanic Society of America*

BASIC BOX FRAMES EVOLVED OUT OF THE WAINSCOT-CHAIR FORM.

231 ROMANESQUE FORM, Norway.   **232** NORTHERN EUROPEAN, Gothic Era.
233 SPANISH, 17th century.   **234** ITALIAN, late 16th century, Venice or Brescia.   **235**
FRENCH, Louis XIII.   **236-237** ENGLISH, c. 1630, "Yorkshire" chairs.

234
Metropolitan Museum of Art,
Gift of J. Pierpont Morgan, 1916

236-237

235

Stair & Company, Inc.

Don Ruseau

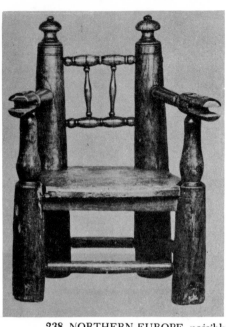

238 NORTHERN EUROPE, possibly before 16th century.

Metropolitan Museum of Art, Rogers Fund, 1909
239 ENGLISH, late 16th century.

Henry Ford Museum, Dearborn, Mich.
240 AMERICAN, late 17th century.

CHAIRS MADE OF TURNED OR "THROWNE" PARTS
ORIGINATED WITH THE ART OF WOOD TURNING, AND APPEARED EVERYWHERE
AS A PRIMITIVE FORM. THE DEVELOPED FORM USED DECORATIVE VARIATIONS,
SUCH AS FACE TURNINGS IN BACKS, AND OFF-CENTER TURNINGS FOR THE
SPOON-FOOT IDEA, AS WELL AS SPLIT TURNINGS FOR SMOOTH BACKS.

241 PENNSYLVANIA, 1700-1725,
half-turned back splats; flat members. Walnut.
Metropolitan Museum of Art,
Gift of Mrs. Robert W. de Forest, 1933

242 NEW ENGLAND, 1700-1720.
Turnings used decoratively.

Israel Sack, Inc.

243 ENGLISH, 18th century. Turnings
suggest Indo-Portuguese influence.

Stair & Company, Inc.

244 SWISS, 1679. Turnings treated with decorative variations.

245 AMERICAN ROUNDABOUT CHAIR, Spanish foot.

246 FRENCH PROVINCIAL, late 18th century.

VARIATIONS IN TURNINGS AND THE ADDITION OF FLAT AND SHAPED PARTS CREATED ENDLESS VARIETY.

249 FLANDERS, 17th Century. Spiral or twist turnings.

248 CANADIAN, 17th century. Fully turned Provincial French forms, splint seat.

247 ENGLISH, 18th century. Rush seat, ladder back.

250 *Metropolitan Museum of Art,*
Gift of George Blumenthal, 1941

251 *Metropolitan Museum of Art, Gift of J. Pierpont Morgan, 1916* 252 *Frick Collection*

250 SPANISH 16th-century folding chair with stretched leather. **251** FLEMISH, 17th century. Spanish influence in carving. **252** FRENCH, 16th century. Early Italianate.

**THE SIMPLEST CHAIR FRAMEWORKS WERE OF A SCALE TO SIGNIFY
IMPORTANCE RATHER THAN COMFORT, BUT THE BEGINNINGS OF
UPHOLSTERY ALLOWED FOR SOME COMFORT AS WELL
AS THE DISPLAY OF RICH FABRICS.**

253 ITALIAN, 16th century. **254** PORTUGUESE, second half of the 17th century, embossed leather. **255** ENGLISH, 1660-1685. Charles II style.

253 *Metropolitan Museum of Art,*
Gift of Mrs. Henry S. Redmond, 1947

Metropolitan Museum of Art, Rogers Fund, 1911
254

255 *Metropolitan Museum of Art, Rogers Fund, 1932*

256 *Metropolitan Museum of Art,*
Gift of Mrs. Russell Sage, 1909

258 *Wadsworth Atheneum, Hartford, Conn.*

256 ENGLISH, 1660-1680. Charles II style. Caned walnut.

258 AMERICAN c. 1700, Flemish influence.

BY 1700 THE GREAT DECORATIVE CHAIRS HAD BECOME
LIGHT, GRACEFUL, AND MORE COMFORTABLE.

Metropolitan Museum of Art, Gift of J. Pierpont Morgan, 1917

257 FRENCH, Late Louis XIV style.

261 FRENCH "CONFESSIONAL." The stretchers
show early Louis XV date.

259 AMERICAN c. 1700.

260 FRENCH c. 1700. Transitional Régence leg.

FLEMISH FOOT

Metropolitan Museum of Art, Gift of J. Pierpont Morgan, 1906

260

259 *Israel Sack, Inc.*

Metropolitan Museum of Art, Bequest of Benjamin Altman, 1913

262 *Frick Collection*	**263** *Wadsworth Atheneum, Hartford, Conn.*	**264** *French & Co., Inc.*

262 ENGLISH, early 18th century. Straight front legs with animal foot suggest cabriole. **263** AMERICAN c. 1700. Spanish foot with novel leg shape. **264** ENGLISH, Early Georgian. Decorated cabriole form, advanced style.

EVOLUTION OF THE CABRIOLE LEG MARKS THE DEVELOPMENT OF THE SIDE CHAIR IN THE EARLY 18TH CENTURY.

265 ENGLISH. Queen Anne. Early form without stretchers. **266** EARLY GEORGIAN, 1720-1730. Carved gesso, gilt. **267** COLONIAL (Eastern) version of Georgian English design.

265
Metropolitan Museum of Art, Rogers Fund, 1910

266
Metropolitan Museum of Art, Rogers Fund, 1931

267 *French & Co., Inc.*

269

268

270

268 NEW ENGLAND c. 1740. Queen Anne corner chair. 269 AMERICAN, Dutch influence, 1740-1760. 270 NEW ENGLAND c. 1740, Queen Anne type.

BAROQUE EXUBERANCE BECAME DOMESTICATED WITH THE BEGINNING OF THE GEORGIAN EPOCH.

271 ENGLISH c. 1750. 272 PHILADELPHIA c. 1750, balloon-shaped seat, intaglio carved knee. 273 ENGLISH c. 1710.

Drake foot.
Shell on knee.

SCROLL   HOOF

272

271   273

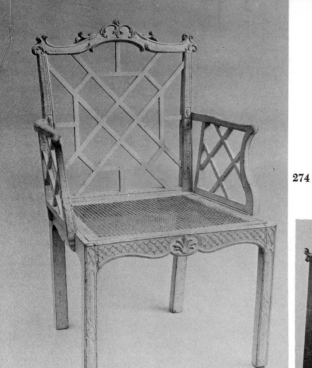

Metropolitan Museum of Art,
Rogers Fund, 1931

FANCIFUL ECLECTICISM MARKS THE SCHOOL OF CHIPPENDALE—ENGLISH, PROVINCIAL AND COLONIAL.

274 CHINESE STYLE, 1755-1766. Painted white, gilt decoration. **275** GOTHIC, a style widely revived at intervals in the 19th century. **276** COUNTRY TYPE, English.

274

275

276   *Arthur S. Vernay, Inc.*

Arthur S. Vernay, Inc.

277 COCKFIGHT CHAIR,
Queen Anne, walnut.   *Wood and Hogan*

278 PHILADELPHIA c. 1770.   *Israel Sack, Inc.*

Metropolitan Museum of Art, Rogers Fund, 1926

Metropolitan Museum of Art, Gift of J. Pierpont Morgan, 1906

279 SIGNED G. SENÉ (1724-1792), carved molding; painted white with flowers and leaves in natural colors and molding in red.

280 DESK CHAIR, Louis XV, roundabout form, carved beechwood with cane.

IN THE ERA OF LOUIS XV, CURVES FLOWED OVER EVERY SURFACE AND LINE. THE CURVILINEAR SHAPE REACHED PERFECTION IN THE MID-18TH CENTURY, AND WAS A BASIS FOR CHAIR DESIGN IN EUROPE FOR THE NEXT CENTURY.

281 PROVINCIAL FRENCH. *Don Ruseau*

282 VENETIAN, mid-18th century. *Brunovan, Inc.*

283 LOUIS XV, height of Rococo style. *French & Co., Inc.*

Metropolitan Museum of Art, Gift of J. Pierpont Morgan, 1906

284 RÉGENCE. Square plan with slow curving
ornamentation, painted gray.

Metropolitan Museum of Art, Rogers Fund, 1922

285 ITALIAN, mid-18th century.
Lacquered and silvered wood.

**FRENCH CHAIRS REACHED THE HEIGHT OF THE STYLE BY BECOMING LIGHTER,
MORE GRACEFUL, AND MORE COMFORTABLE THROUGH SHAPE,
PROPORTION, AND SOFT UPHOLSTERING.**

286 "GONDOLA," Louis XV c. 1750.
Metropolitan Museum of Art, Gift of J. Pierpont Morgan, 1906

287 CLASSIC, period of Louis XVI. Signed G. IACOB.
Metropolitan Museum of Art, Gift of J. Pierpont Morgan, 1906

Arthur S. Vernay, Inc.

288 EARLY-18TH-CENTURY TYPE.

289 BARREL CHAIR c. 1765,   *Needham's Antiques, Inc.*
Chippendale style, mahogany.

ENGLISH UPHOLSTERED CHAIRS STRESSED COMFORT AND SOLIDITY OF OUTLINE.

290 ENGLISH, 1735-1750.

Arthur S. Vernay, Inc.

291 WING CHAIR, George I, c. 1725. Walnut.

Needham's Antiques, Inc.

CHAIR

294   *Metropolitan Museum of Art,*
Fletcher Fund, 1945

295   *Metropolitan Museum of Art,*
Rogers Fund, 1923

292 ARMCHAIR, 1770-1780, signed G. IACOB, shows inclination to angular lines with Greco-Roman detail. 293 HEIGHT OF LOUIS XVI STYLE, signed P. BRIZARD. 294 FRENCH c. 1786. 295 Signed I B LELARGE. 296 Appearance of the LYRE MOTIF. 297 HEPPLEWHITE c. 1785.

292

Metropolitan Museum of Art, Purchase, 1928

293   *Metropolitan Museum of Art, Rogers Fund, 1926*

CLASSIC REVIVAL, BEGINNING WITH LOUIS XVI, REPLACED CURVES WITH STRAIGHT LINES, AND ENDED THE BAROQUE-ROCOCO ASYMMETRY. THIS SUITED THE TASTE OF THE ENGLISH TO THE EXTENT THAT THEY PERFECTED THE FORM AND SPREAD IT THROUGHOUT THE WESTERN WORLD.

296
Metropolitan Museum of Art,
Gift of J. Pierpont Morgan, 1906

297   *Arthur S. Vernay, Inc.*

298   *Arthur S. Vernay, Inc.*

Arthur S. Vernay, Inc.   299

Metropolitan Museum of Art, Bequest of Annie C. Kane, 1926   300

298 PAINTED SATINWOOD c. 1790.   **299** HEPPLEWHITE, 1780-1790.
300 VENETIAN, 18th century, carved and polychromed.   **301-302** SPAN-
ISH, 19th-century interpretation of Louis XVI and Hepplewhite.   **303**
SHERATON STYLE, painted and gilded.

Metropolitan Museum of Art, Gift of Mrs. Russell Sage, 1910   303

301-302   *Lo Mejor de España*

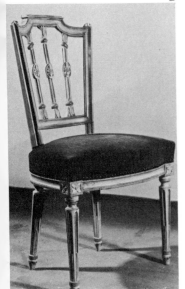

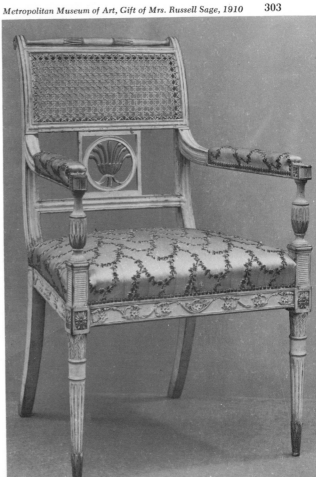

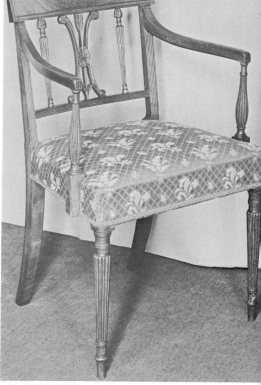

Ginsburg and Levy
304 NEW YORK SHERATON c. 1795.

Philadelphia Museum of Art, Photograph A. J. Wyatt
305 PHILADELPHIA c. 1820. Klismos
form with painted Greco-Roman decoration.

**SHERATON'S STYLE DOMINATES THE END OF THE
18TH CENTURY. TRANSITIONAL WORK BEGINNING
SOON AFTER 1800 SHOWS A MIXTURE OF CLASSICAL
INFLUENCES.**

306 ENGLISH c. 1800.   *Arthur S. Vernay, Inc.*

307 FRENCH EMPIRE c. 1810.   *French & Co., Inc.*
Bronze mounts on mahogany.

P. Nathan
308 LATE REGENCY, English c. 1825.

309   *Munson-Williams-Proctor Institute, Utica, N.Y.*

310   *Collection Bergdorf Goodman Antiques*

309 DUNCAN PHYFE, 1815-1820. Klismos form with water-leaf carved legs, paw feet. **310** ENGLISH REGENCY c. 1815. Painted decoration, gold on black. **311** FRENCH EMPIRE c. 1810. Classical angularity after Percier and Fontaine. **312** NEW YORK, 1810-1820, after Thomas Hope. **313** FRANCE, RESTORATION MAHOGANY CHAIR.

311   *Don Ruseau*   312   *Museum of the City of New York*   *Metropolitan Museum of Art, Rogers Fund, 1926*   313

SPLAYED LEGS PEGGED INTO A WOOD SEAT, AND A BOW BACK BRACED WITH LIGHT SPINDLES ARE THE ESSENTIAL INGREDIENTS OF THE WINDSOR CHAIR.

Symons Galleries, Inc.

315 ENGLISH c. 1800, Elm and yew wood.

Victoria and Albert Museum, Crown Copyright

314 ENGLISH, probably mid-18th century, with splat back, good cabriole leg, and curved stretcher.

THREE NEW ENGLAND WINDSORS IN THE HENRY FORD MUSEUM, DEARBORN, MICHIGAN.

316 The classic-type form, 1775-1800. **317** Rare X-stretcher c. 1800. **318** The seat was probably originally upholstered; c. 1775-1800.

319

Israel Sack, Inc.

320

*Metropolitan Museum of Art,
Gift of Mrs. Russell Sage, 1909*

319 COMB-BACK WRITING CHAIR, fitted with drawer and candle slide. The comb is off center, indicating a comfortable writing angle for the sitter. **320 TURNINGS, SEAT SHAPE, AND COMB WIDTH** are peculiar to Pennsylvania. Spruce and oak, 1750-1775. **321-322 ENGLISH WINDSORS. 323 OHIO,** 1830-1870, painted and grained.

321-322

Stair & Company, Inc.

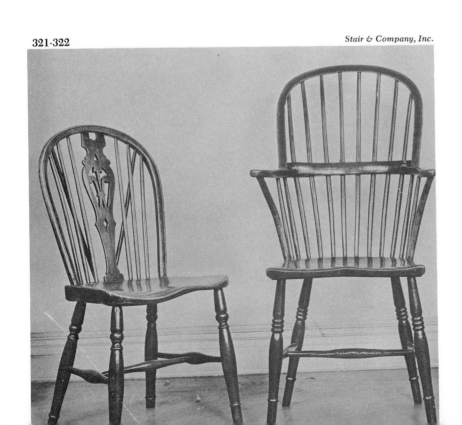

323   *Henry Ford Museum, Dearborn, Mich.*

324 *John S. Walton, Inc.*

325 *Ginsburg and Levy*

326 *Metropolitan Museum of Art, Bequest of Mrs. Maria P. James, 1911*

324 AMERICAN "FANCY" CHAIR after Sheraton school. **325** HITCHCOCK STYLE, Boston, 1820-1825. "Fancy"-chair type with unusual arms and eagle splat. **326** BENT FOOT, "cheesebox" rush seat edging. Stenciled. **327** LATER HITCHCOCK TYPE, 1829-1843, cane seat. **328** ENGLISH, mid-19th century. Papier-mâché, gilt decoration on black. **329** ITALIAN NEO-CLASSIC.

Symons Galleries, Inc.

329 *Lavezzo.*

327 *Henry Ford Museum, Dearborn, Mich.*

328

330   331   332   333

330 NEO-GOTHIC, German c. 1820.

331 GERMAN CLASSICISM, early 19th century.

332 MID-VICTORIAN AMERICAN c. 1860 (Buttfield).

333 SWEDISH, c. 1925, by Karl Malmsten.

CONTEMPORARY VARIATIONS ON THE WINDSOR CHAIR.

334 SWEDISH, 1947, ash and teak,
designed by Hans Wegner.   *Frederick Lunning, Inc.*

335 JAPANESE, 1961.   *Japan Trade Center*

CHAIR-BED. Chair that can be extended to form a bed. Common in 18th-century England. [994.]

CHAIR TABLE. Chair with a hinged back that forms a tabletop when tipped down, a chairback when up. See also MONK'S BENCH. [3.]

CHAISE LONGUE. A long chair; a form of sofa or daybed with upholstered back, for reclining. French 18th-century types were often made in two or three parts; the two-part type consisted of a deep bergère and a large stool; the three-part style had two armchairs and a stool between. [336 *et seq.*] See also DAY-BEDS; REST BEDS.

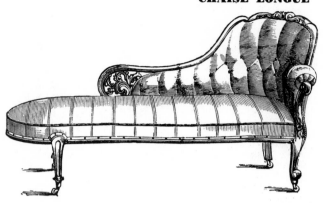

338 MID-19TH CENTURY, suggests Louis XV; tight upholstery.

336 LOUIS XV STYLE.
Don Ruseau

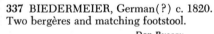

337 BIEDERMEIER, German(?) c. 1820.
Two bergères and matching footstool.
Don Ruseau

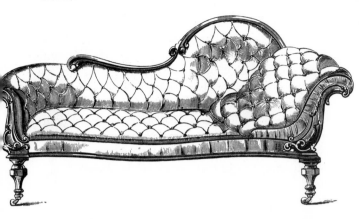

339 ENGLISH VICTORIAN c. 1870, heavily tufted upholstery.

CHAMBER HORSE. Exercising chair, English late 18th century.

CHAMBERS, SIR WILLIAM, 1726-1796. English architect. After traveling in China, he published in 1757 his *Designs of Chinese Buildings, Furniture, etc.,* strongly influential in developing the fad for chinoiserie.

CHAMFER. Groove, splayed, or beveled-off corner of a post or a molding. [710.]

CHANNEL. Groove or fluting cut into a surface as a decorative accent; sometimes filled with reed-shaped convex mold.

CHARLES I. King of England, 1625-1649. Furniture style classified as Early Jacobean. See also ENGLAND.

CHARLES II. King of England, 1660-1685. Furniture style referred to as Carolean, Restoration, Late Jacobean, Late Stuart. See also CAROLEAN; ENGLAND.

CHARLES X. King of France, 1824-1830. Period of Bourbon Restoration, furniture of late Empire, Louis XVI, and eclectic Rococo and Renaissance detail. See also NINETEENTH CENTURY.

CHASING. Ornamentation of metal by etching, engraving, or incising. See also ORMOLU.

CHAUFFEUSE. Small French fireside chair with low seat. [675.]

CHECKER, CHEQUER. Decorative use of alternately colored squares, as in a checkerboard.

CHEESEBOX SEAT. Chair seat, usually rush, and round or bell shaped with thin rim of wood bent around the edge. American, early 19th century. [324.]

CHENILLE. A kind of velvety cord with short thread ends standing out, used in trimming and banding upholstered furniture. It is also used in rug weaving, and in fabrics for upholstery and drapery fabrics.

CHERRY. American wild-cherry wood is a hard compact fine-grained, red-brown wood, usually light. It is highly suitable for cabinetmaking, is beautiful and strong both for structural and for decorative uses; it resists warping and takes a fine polish. It was favored by the colonists wherever it was found, and much old American furniture of cherry remains from the entire period of colonization as well as from the 19th century. The European cherry is similar but lighter in color; it appears in much country furniture, and extensively in Biedermeier and similar 19th-century styles.

CHERUB

CHERUB. Winged child figure used in decoration from the Renaissance and afterward; also called *amorini*. In Italian and French work the whole figure is usual, but after Charles II the English carvers, such as Grinling Gibbons, often used the winged head alone.

CHESSBOARD; CHESS TABLE. See GAME TABLE. [1275, 1319.]

LOUIS XVI

LOUIS XIV

CHEST. Originally a large box with hinged lid, the coffer, or chest, is the primary form of all receptacle furniture. In ancient Egypt and Rome they assumed artistic form, and developed variations for special purposes. In the Middle Ages, the instability of life made the portable chest the most vital piece of furniture. As conditions settled and life became more sedentary, chests became larger and produced the deviations recognized as chests of drawers, credences, cabinets, buffets and sideboards, bureaus, and all receptacle types; also traceable to it are bed forms, from the retainers' habit of sleeping on the chest; as well as several seating forms. [396.]

Early chests everywhere were small and sturdily constructed, often with iron bands. Gothic chests generally were larger and more ornately carved and painted. Renaissance chests were made with a clear architectural profile and classic ornament. In the same century the French Gothic chest began its evolution into a credence. In the 16th century the Italian chest had begun to yield to the variety of credenzas, sideboards, etc.; the influence in England produced court cupboards, and modification of the chest by means of drawers and door compartments, which gradually raised the total height and produced, finally, the chest of drawers. For special purposes the chest with hinged lid has survived, as the marriage or dower chest in Germanic communities, including the Pennsylvania Dutch; the blanket chest and ceremonial or decorative types.

340 FLORENTINE MARRIAGE CHEST, early 15th century.

Victoria and Albert Museum, Crown Copyright

341 ITALIAN c. 1500. WOODEN CASSONE; painted gesso with iron mounts.

Metropolitan Museum of Art, Rogers Fund, 1918

342 VENETIAN VELVET COFFER, 16th century.

From "Chinese Household Furniture" by George Kates, courtesy Dover Publications, N.Y.

344 CHINESE, undated. Style may be from 14th century to contemporary.

Liebhold-Wallach

343 ALPINE, dated 1766. German-Gothic vestiges in shape and ornamentation.

345 WOOD CHEST with linenfold and Late Gothic carving, dovetailed corners. Berne, Switzerland, 16th century.

Metropolitan Museum of Art, Rogers Fund, 1907

346 *Center, left,* GERMAN BAROQUE, 17th century. Oak and ebony inlay.

Philadelphia Museum of Art

347 PENNSYLVANIA GERMAN c. 1720. Stenciled decoration; architectural theme recalls Baroque work.

Ginsburg and Levy

348 VENETIAN, 16th century. Climax of decorative carved chest.

Duveen Brothers, Inc.

349 UMBRIAN, early 17th century.
Early appearance of drawers.

350 SPANISH "PAPELERA," 17th century.
Renaissance architecture with Moorish sentiment.

Hispanic Society of America

351 CONNECTICUT c. 1700. Painted "Guil-
ford" chest; hinged top with drawer, raised
feet.

Henry Ford Museum, Dearborn, Mich.

CHEST

THE DRAWER DISTINGUISHES THE AD-
VANCED CHEST FROM THE ELEMEN-
TARY PORTABLE CHEST. IN GENERAL
IT WAS ADDED TENTATIVELY TO THE
BASIC LIFT-LID DESIGN. HOWEVER, THE
FULLY DRAWERED CABINET APPEARED
EARLY IN REGIONS WHERE JOINERY
HAD ADVANCED.

354

Henry Ford Museum, Dearborn, Mich.

353   *Philadelphia Museum of Art*

352   *Ginsburg and Levy*

352 CONNECTICUT (Hartford) c. 1700. Sunflower
chest; hinged lid and drawer, carved ornament Tudor
style. **353** PENNSYLVANIA GERMAN DOWER
CHEST, 1803. Painted in late style. **354** HADLEY
CHEST, Connecticut, c. 1690. Shallow all-over carving in flower motif.

355 FRENCH CHEST OF DRAWERS, 15th century,
made for church vestments.
*Metropolitan Museum of Art,
Cloisters Collection, Purchase, 1947*

356 ENGLISH c. 1700. Oak chest with burl walnut drawers.

357 MASSACHUSETTS c. 1690. Jacobean geometric panels, grained walnut surface.

358 PENNSYLVANIA c. 1830. Blue-green paint with thumb-print decorations.

359 ENGLISH c. 1830. Naval captain's chest with two portable elements; similar to "campaign" chests.

360 ENGLISH c. 1685. Oystered top, ornate marquetry. *Anderson Galleries*

**BAROQUE FORMS OFTEN USED FANCIFUL SURFACE TREATMENT
AS A FOIL AGAINST FLAT, SIMPLE FORMS.**

CHIPPENDALE

361 FRENCH COMMODE, end of the 17th century. Rich hardware over rosewood veneers complements extravagant modeling of bombé shape. Forerunner of the sinuous lines of Régence and Louis XV Rococo.

362 ENGLISH c. 1765. Carved bracket feet, pull-out leaf.

Needham's Antiques, Inc.

363 ENGLISH c. 1765. Serpentine, with canted console corners, ogee bracket feet.

Ginsburg and Levy

Metropolitan Museum of Art, Rogers Fund, 1908

364 DUTCH(?), mid-18th century, "in the French taste."

Ginsburg and Levy

365 BOSTON c. 1760. Kettle base with lift handles. Made for Hancock family.

366 CONNECTICUT c. 1770. Serpentine bureau with fitted top drawer (see also 523).

Israel Sack, Inc.

367 NEW ENGLAND, 1770-1780. Blockfront style.

Israel Sack, Inc.

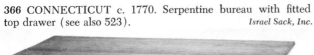

368 RÉGENCE, LOUIS XV, attributed to Charles Cressent, bronzes by Caffieri from Meissonier design. *Dalva Brothers, Inc.*

369 LOUIS XV MARQUETRY.
Dalva Brothers, Inc.

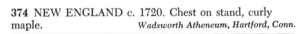

370 LOUIS XV MARQUETRY BOMBÉ CHEST ON STAND.

374 NEW ENGLAND c. 1720. Chest on stand, curly maple. *Wadsworth Atheneum, Hartford, Conn.*

372-373 PROVINCIAL FRENCH, late 18th century. *Don Ruseau*

375 TRANSITIONAL TO RECTILINEAR STYLE OF LOUIS XVI. Stamped SAUNIER (JME 1752).

TRANSITION TO RECTILINEAR STYLE OF LOUIS XVI.

376 LOUIS XVI c. 1785. Bronze with cipher *MA* (Marie Antoinette?).

377 COMMODE by Jean-Henri Riesener. Height of Louis XVI style. *Frick Collection*

378 DIRECTOIRE, attributed to Bernard Molitor (JME 1787) c. 1795. *French & Co., Inc.*

379 ITALIAN, Directoire.   *Don Ruseau*

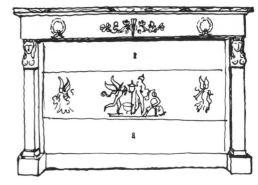

FRENCH EMPIRE CHEST c 1800

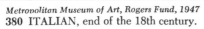

Metropolitan Museum of Art, Rogers Fund, 1947
380 ITALIAN, end of the 18th century.

381 FRENCH, Late Louis XVI.
Don Ruseau

382 FRENCH DIRECTOIRE. *Don Ruseau*

383 GERMAN BIEDERMEIER c. 1820.

384 FRENCH EMPIRE. *Don Ruseau*

387 AMERICAN c. 1810.   *Israel Sack, Inc*

Anderson Galleries

385 DRESSING CHEST, New England, c. 1800.
Hepplewhite bowfront with French foot.

386 NEW YORK c. 1830. Empire dressing bureau, mahogany
with gilt stencils.

Munson-Williams-Proctor Institute, Utica, N.Y.
(From Fountain Elms)

388 NEW YORK, 1820-1825. Silver chest. Mahogany, ormolu
mounts.

Cooper Union Museum

CHEST OF DRAWERS. Case fitted with drawers, for storage, usually of clothing. The drawer chest, or commode, completely superseded the coffer chest, by reason of its greater convenience, by the end of the 17th century. France and England led in the development of the drawer chest. Once the type was established, it remained to the present as the favorite piece of storage furniture; various styles have only changed the detail and ornamental aspects. "Highboys," "tallboys," "chest-on-chests" are merely one chest on top of another, or on a tablelike base. Other chests are used as desks, dressing tables, etc., by slight changes in profile or drawer arrangements.

CHEST-ON-CHEST. Chests of drawers in two sections, one placed upon the other. Surmounted by elaborate cornices or pediments, they were often imposing pieces of furniture. They are chiefly English and American, 18th and 19th centuries. See also HIGHBOY. [38, 739.]

CHESTERFIELD. Overstuffed couch or sofa with upholstered ends. [1304.]

CHESTNUT. Moderately soft grayish-brown wood with coarse open grain, resembling oak but lacking the large rays. Rather weak structurally, its principal use now is for veneer cores.

391 CHEVAL GLASS, Biedermeier.

389 CHIFFONIER, French, Louis XVI marquetry. Six- or seven-drawer type called "semainier."
Dalva Brothers, Inc.

CHEVAL GLASS. Large mirror, usually full figure length, swinging from vertical posts mounted on trestles. Best examples occur in French and English work of the second half of the 18th century. A small form, often with a drawer between the posts, is made to be placed upon chests or tables. [874.]

CHEVAL SCREEN. Fire screen mounted upon two feet. See also SCREEN.

CHEVRON. V-shaped design for inlay and other decoration.

CHIFFONIER. Tall narrow bureau or chest of drawers. From the French *chiffonier*, ragpicker. See also SEMAINIER, a seven-drawered chest for daily linen change. [389.]

CHILDREN'S FURNITURE. Small-scaled furniture for children, such as tables and chairs, is found in every style. Cradles and beds have always been made as distinct designs rather than merely smaller models. This tendency is observed today in the design of most articles for children: that is, the child's needs are not merely those of a physically small adult, but are highly specialized. Modern children's furniture, comprising beds and cribs, tables, bookcases, chairs, and chests, is planned to facilitate learning, self-help, etc.; and colors and decoration are less quaint, less fancifully pictorial or fairy tale than formerly. See also CRADLE; HIGH CHAIR. [743, 955.]

CHIMERA; CHIMAERA. Mythical fire-breathing monster, used as a motive in ornament.

CHIMNEY FURNITURE. The accessories of a fireplace: andirons, chimney boards, coal bin or scuttle, fenders, bellows, firebacks, forks and shovels, hob grates, cranes, trivets, pothooks, and other utensils.

CHIMNEYPIECE. Mantel shelf. Ornamental structure, usually of stone or marble, with molding, carving, etc., over and around the open recess of a fireplace. Also a picture, piece of sculpture, or tapestry placed as an ornament over a fireplace.

CHINA. The normal furniture of rich homes in Chinese cities traditionally has been largely of fine simple design, made of choice hardwoods, beautifully finished, unornamented except for careful moldings and important hardware. The origins of the designs are hidden in ancient Chinese history. Japanese treasure houses contain examples of the 7th and 8th centuries. Drawings and documents show designs of early Sung dynasties, but of actual relics, none are known to date prior to the Ming Dynasty, 1368-1644. Of the latter, however, there is an appreciable body of well-preserved examples exhibiting a continuous or static trend in design quite unlike the heavily ornamented examples apparently made for the 19th-century export trade. [105a, 174, 344, 1381.]

The range of objects includes chairs and couches, chests, cupboards, tables of many uses and sizes, and a variety of functional objects, indicating the activities and pursuits of a cultivated, stable people. The woods, chiefly imported, resemble purple sandalwood, rosewood, blackwood, various burls, all used with finesse, taste, and a unique joinery. Metals—pewter, brass and copper—are worked into tasteful mounts and working hardware. The design and disposition of these parts is exceptionally sophisticated. Lacquer is less extensively employed than is generally inferred

French & Co., Inc.

390 CHINA CABINET, English, end of the 18th century. Sheraton.

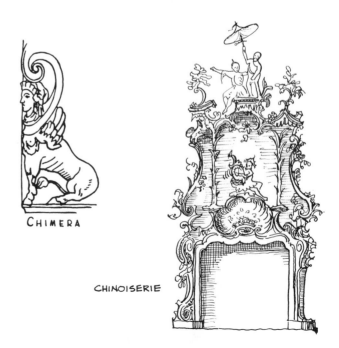

CHIMERA

CHINOISERIE

from the European concept of chinoiserie. To a degree there are inlays of metals and stones, faience and marble, contrasting woods and ivory, and the whole gamut of accessory materials. It is significant that the furniture maker is an artisan, not an artist; there is no name or family or school to identify with any furniture, which remains anonymous in place and origin as well as in time. See also ORIENTAL. [1108.]

CHINA CABINET; CHINA CLOSET. Important cabinet, often with glass front and sides, for the storage and display of fine china.

CHINESE CHIPPENDALE. 18th-century adaptation of Chinese motives to English furniture, chiefly after Chambers's drawings. Chippendale used these suggestions freely, and the typically amalgamated style is now associated with his name. The simple rectilinear outlines have suggested their use in some phases of modern design.

CHINESE FOOT. Bracket foot.

CHINESE TASTE. Europe became fantastically aware of the Far East in the 17th century, a result of the commercial exploitation following exploration and colonization. Dutch, English, and French trading companies brought over silks and lacquers, paintings and utilitarian objects, and their curious decoration stirred a mad craze for "chinoiserie." In varying degree this lasted for almost two centuries. Rarely analyzed or understood, it embraced designs from Persia, China, India, Japan without discrimination, mixing pagodas, monkeys, foliage, landscapes, mandarins, and abstract designs with the greatest freedom. The result is often quite charming. It undoubtedly inspired a large part of Rococo design, although in the earlier Louis XIV work it had had great popularity. The English styles after William and Mary had constant recourse to the Chinese, and after the publication of Chambers's drawings the Chinese manner of Chippendale formed a definite style. The tendency toward the Chinese taste disappeared with the Classic revivals.

Metropolitan Museum of Art, Rogers Fund, 1909
392 CHINESE CABINET, 17th to 18th century. Teakwood decorated with jade, mother-of-pearl, lapis lazuli.

18TH CENT CHINESE

CHINESE TABLE

CHEST

CHINESE CHIPPENDALE

Photographs from Chinese Household Furniture, *by George Kates,*
courtesy Dover Publications, New York

394 PAIR OF CUPBOARDS, 39 inches high.

399

398

395 K'ANG. A heated platform-couch device, with incidental furniture like tables, stools, and chests, was the dominant article of furniture. This example is 10 feet long.

396 SMALL CABINET, often used by tradesmen; 32 inches long.

397 K'ANG CUPBOARD, 45 inches long.

402 SEMICIRCULAR
SIDE TABLE, 3 feet long.

404 GAME TABLE with removable
chessboard.

393 TABLE, 33 inches high.

400

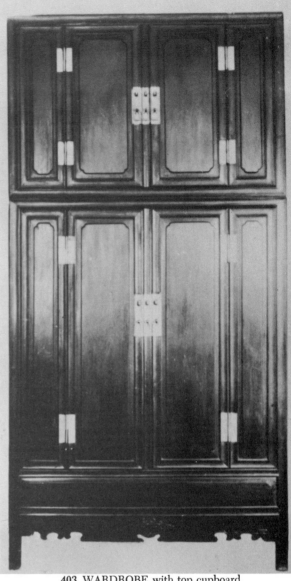

403 WARDROBE with top cupboard,
9 feet high.

406 K'ANG CUPBOARD, for bedding storage, 4½ feet long.

405 FORMAL SIDE TABLE, 86
inches long.

401 ICE CHEST with pewter lining,
brass and copper bands.

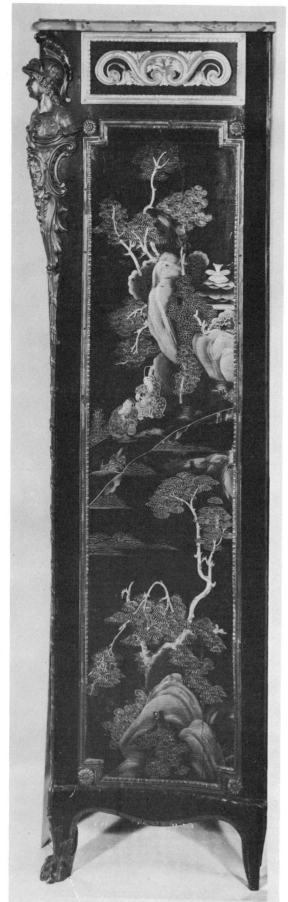

407 CHINOISERIE: black lacquer decorated to imitate Chinese work. French, transitional Louis XVI.

French & Co., Inc.

CHINOISERIE (French). Referring to things Chinese, the Chinese taste or manner. [14, 108, 409, 444, 582, 1038.]

CHINTZ. Inexpensive thin cotton cloth, fast printed with designs of flowers, etc., in a number of columns, and usually glazed. It is useful for minor draping and slip covers.

CHIP CARVING. Simple carved ornament executed with chisel or gouge in medieval furniture.

CHIPPENDALE, THOMAS, 1718-1779. Chippendale published *The Gentleman and Cabinet-Maker's Director* in 1754. Other editions followed in 1759 and 1762. Europe had seen publications on design for two hundred years, but never before one so specialized on furniture, so thorough a catalogue of the prevailing types and styles. Its influence spread everywhere; the Continent and the colonies used it as a guide to style, design, and construction. Hence the freedom with which so much furniture of this school is labeled Chippendale. Chippendale himself executed few of these designs. Most were in the Late Baroque-Rococo manner, adaptions of Louis XV and Georgian shapes with bits of Chinese and Gothic detail. [33, 37, 108, 144, 274, 275, 290, 581, 1086.]

Chippendale's shop was relatively small, at a time when there existed much greater establishments. He appears never to have worked for royalty, but his productions for noble and wealthy patrons commanded high prices. Much of his work was executed from designs by architects, chiefly Robert Adam, but he was a master designer in his own right, and his understanding and attention to detail and construction were masterful.

As a designer Chippendale was open to every changing whim or influence; with little personal conviction he adapted, amalgamated, modified every caprice of style. But he did this with such mastery that almost uniformly his designs hold together, artistically and

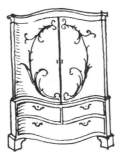

CHIPPENDALE

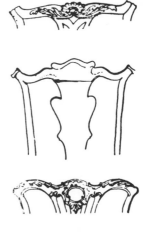

structurally. He added style and distinction to whatever he borrowed. His furniture is solid yet graceful; it looks and is firm, at no sacrifice of grace or refinement.

Chippendale's early work shows a refinement of the solid Georgian style, richly decorated and rather heavy, using a rich claw-and-ball foot, complex Rococo scrolls with the typical natural forms. He later borrowed freely from Chambers's Chinese designs and also took over literally the prevailing French shapes. Chairs of Chippendale design are most characteristic, particularly the types in which the solid splat is made lighter by being pierced into graceful openwork convolutions of ribbons and scrolls. Bookcases and cabinets are remarkably well proportioned; sideboards and chests, cabinets, tables show the same mastery. Chippendale died in 1779. His son succeeded to the partnership with Thomas Haig, which lasted until 1822. See also ENGLAND.

CHISEL. Cutting tool, usually with flat edge, but also made in curves and shapes for carving, cutting moldings, etc.

CHOP INLAY. Primitive form of inlaying by fitting pieces into a solid surface.

CHURN MOLDING. Zigzag molding occurring in Norman architecture.

CHURRIGUERESQUE. Spanish Baroque style, 17th century, so called after the architect Churriguera. See also SPAIN.

408 PLATE XX FROM CHIPPENDALE'S "DIRECTOR," showing "French chairs." None of the legs is alike, in the manner of pattern books suggesting alternatives.

French Chairs.

Metropolitan Museum of Art, Kennedy Fund, 1918.

Metropolitan Museum of Art, Bequest of John L. Cadwalader, 1914

409 THE "CHINESE MANNER," 1750-1770. English example with pagoda top rail, fretted back posts, splayed arms, and clustered legs.

410 CHIPPENDALE'S "GOTHIC TASTE," hoop back, scoop seat; the arms have a fine Rococo sweep. Back legs chamfered.

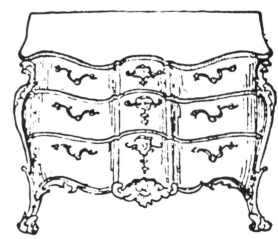

CHIPPENDALE "THE FRENCH MANNER"

412 *Left.* SQUARE BACK WITH MIXED DETAILS. Openwork vase-shaped splat with Gothic, Chinese, and acanthus carving; Chinese cresting and fretwork on posts; dolphin feet. C. 1755.

Arthur S. Vernay, Inc.

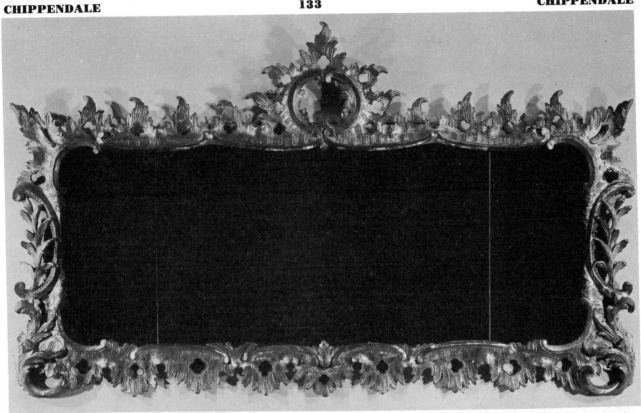

411 OVERMANTEL MIRROR in Chippendale Rococo manner.

Needham's Antiques, Inc.

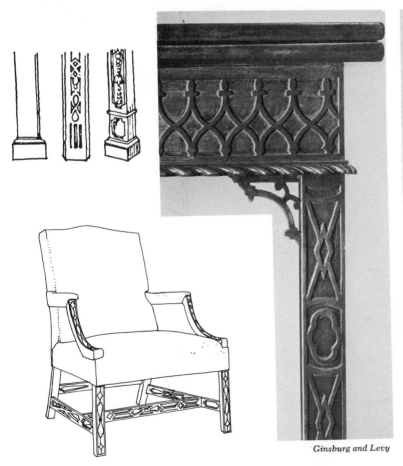

Ginsburg and Levy

413 DETAIL OF PHILADELPHIA CARD TABLE by Thomas Affleck. Gothic and Chinese fretwork.

Henry Ford Museum, Dearborn, Mich.

414 NEW YORK CHIPPENDALE, inscription under seat reads "1757 Philena Barnes." Gadrooned square apron in laggard style. Carved tassel and ruffle in pierced vase-shaped splat, somewhat crude.

CINNAMON WOOD. Camphorwood.

CINQUECENTO. Italian period 1500-1600. The High Renaissance. See also ITALY.

CINQUEFOIL. Gothic foliated ornament of five points, used in some furniture of the Gothic revivals.

CIPRIANI, GIOVANNI, 1727-1785. Florentine artist who worked in England, painting the decoration of many houses and public buildings. His style inspired much of the painted decoration of furniture of the period.

CIRCASSIAN WALNUT. Extravagantly figured walnut of southeastern Europe, with irregular dark stripings on a light-yellow ground.

CISELEUR (French). Engraver or maker of metal ornaments.

CISTERN. See WINE COOLER.

CLASSIC. The ancient styles of Greece and Rome, called Classic or Classic Antiquity, were the inspiration of the Renaissance. The Middle Ages had descended so low in the scale of culture that the early humanists, looking backward over twenty centuries, saw in ancient history a Golden Age of art, literature, philosophy, and government. The antique, often confused and misunderstood, inspired all the arts; classicism alone was beautiful. The Romanesque and Gothic of the prior six centuries were regarded as crude, barbaric. The ancient ruins were excavated and studied for the secrets of classic beauty. Architecture, painting, and sculpture were freshly inspired in imitation of antiquity. Furniture followed; the shapes and ornaments were taken directly from ancient architecture, since no furniture remained from of old. This mistaken use of architectural details identifies Renaissance furniture, and all subsequent styles in which architectural sources are so used are called "classic revivals." Such are the great periods of the late 18th and early 19th centuries. The classic style of Louis XVI was principally derived from the archaeological studies of Herculaneum and Pompeii. This inspired the style of the Brothers Adam in England, and it became the fashionable gentleman's duty to extend the researches into antiquity. Italy and the Mediterranean islands, northern Africa and Greece were dug over for ruins. The publication of splendid folios produced source books for furniture designers. After the Adam and the Louis XVI styles came Hepplewhite, Sheraton, and the Directoire, animated by the Greco-Roman discoveries. About the turn of the 19th century research into antiquity extended to Egypt and Greece. These inspired the Empire style and its many offshoots—Regency, Biedermeier, and the local Empire versions of Italy, Spain, Sweden, Russia, and America. See also ADAM; ENGLAND; FRANCE; ITALY; ORDERS; ORNAMENT.

CLAVICHORD. Early keyboard musical instrument, forerunner of the modern piano.

CLAW AND BALL. Foot carved in the form of a bird's foot gripping a ball. Its earliest form in Chinese bronze shows a dragon claw holding a jewel; the cabriole leg terminating in the ball and claw was a favorite motive in Chippendale's earlier work, but it ceased to be fashionable after 1765. [27, 183, 1282.]

CLEAT. Strip of wood fastened to a flat surface to brace or strengthen or to prevent warping.

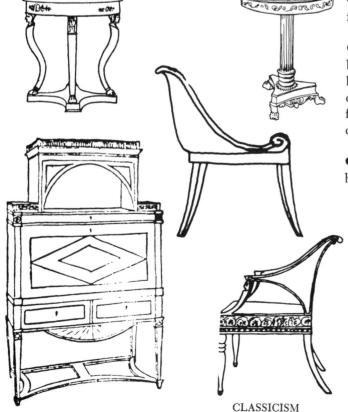

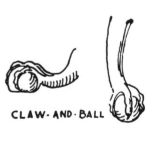

CLAW-AND-BALL

CLASSICISM
NORTHERN EUROPE—EARLY 19TH CENTURY

CLOCK; CLOCK CASE. Wood cases for clocks appeared late in the 17th century, earlier clocks being encased in brass or metal. [415.] The tall clock, now called "grandfather," was a development of the Louis XIV style, where it attained great magnificence. Carolean English oak cases remain from about 1680; walnut soon took the lead, and in the Queen Anne style the chinoiserie-lacquered cabinet is common. [573.] Clock cases in England tended toward narrowness and smaller size [42]; on the Continent, clocks in Rococo style had bombé cases, often monumental in size and heavily ornamented [636, 644]. Decoratively carved and painted clock cases are found in most peasant styles—German, French, and Swiss styles being most familiar.

Wooden clock cases flourished in America. Fine mahogany tall cases were made in Boston about 1725 by Bagnell. The Willards helped New England maintain leadership in clock production for most of the 18th century. About 1800, Simon Willard designed the banjo clock. Shelf clocks of Sheraton character were made by Eli Terry. These types were developed by Seth Thomas and other New Englanders to the extent that clockmaking was a major industry, with many makers known for decorative cases. [42, 51, 60.]

415 SHELF CLOCK, German, 16th century. Gilt, brass.
Metropolitan Museum of Art, Gift of Mrs. Simon Guggenheim, 1929

416 ROCOCO, by Robin. *Dalva Brothers, Inc.*

417 CHIPPENDALE c. 1770. *Needham's Antiques, Inc.*

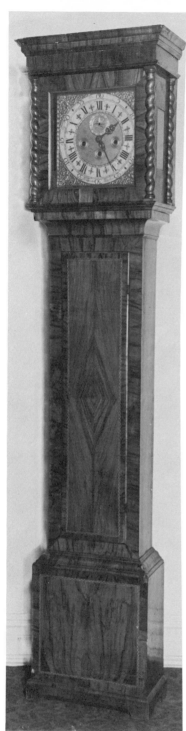

418 QUEEN ANNE, walnut, c. 1705.
By Sawtell.

419 CHIPPENDALE c. 1775.

420 RÉGENCE STYLE, 1740-1750, in
Palais de Versailles. Ebony and brass. By
LaLoutre.

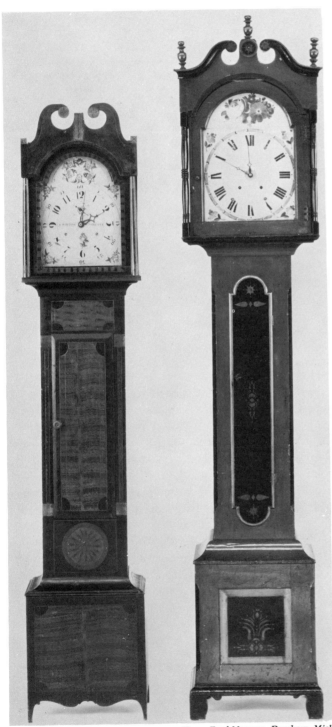

Henry Ford Museum, Dearborn, Mich.   *Israel Sack, Inc.*   *Dalva Brothers, Inc.*

424-425 AMERICAN c. 1830.   **426 AMERICAN c. 1780. 427 EMPIRE REGULATOR, France, c. 1815.**

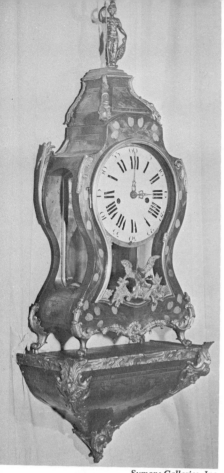

Symons Galleries, Inc.
421 LOUIS XV c. 1770. Marquetry clock and bracket.

422 NEW YORK c. 1775. By Charles Geddes.
Henry Ford Museum, Dearborn, Mich.

Henry Ford Museum, Dearborn, Mich.
423 AMERICAN c. 1844. Gothic steeple clock.

CLOTH OF ESTATE. Medieval decorative cloth draped over the throne or chair of persons of exalted rank.

CLOTHESPRESS. Wardrobe; cabinet for storing clothes, with or without drawers. [804, 1335.]

CLOTHS OF GOLD, SILVER. Textile consisting of threads of gold or silver interwoven with silk or wool. Used for tapestry and upholstery, and draped in ornate styles.

CLOVEN FOOT. Table leg or chair leg ending in the form of an animal's cleft foot, English and Continental work, chiefly 18th century.

CLUB FOOT. Stubby foot of a furniture leg resembling the head of a club, the leg swelling out to a knot with a thick flat base; 18th century.

CLUSTERED COLUMNS. Three or more small wooden columns clustered together to form a single support used as bedposts, table legs, chair legs, etc., in 18th-century work, particularly by Chippendale and Ince, showing Gothic influence in their work. [409.]

COASTER. English tray fitted with small rollers, used for circulating food and bottles on a dining table, 18th century. They took many fanciful forms, such as cannon or kegs, but the later ones were simple cylindrical shapes handsomely chased or engraved.

COCK BEAD; COCKED BEADING. Small half-round projecting molding applied to the edges of drawers. First appears in English work after 1730, and American work somewhat later. Sheraton and many French designers sometimes used strips of brass for this purpose.

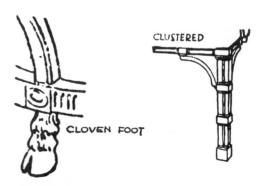

CLUSTERED

CLOVEN FOOT

COCKFIGHT CHAIR. Special chair having a narrow back with wings, shaped seat. English, 18th century. At cockfights the gentleman straddled the seat, facing the narrow back, and kept his score on an adjustable easel. [277.]

COCKLESHELL. See SHELL MOTIF.

COCK'S-HEAD HINGE. Hinges with the leaves cut to resemble the shape of a cock's head. They occur in wide variety in English cabinets of the 16th, 17th, and 18th centuries, and are generally made of brass. See also HARDWARE.

COCOBOLO. Dark purple-brown wood from Bengal and Burma, very dense and heavy.

COFFEE TABLE. Low, wide table now used before a sofa or couch. There is no historical precedent, but the shape permits the adaptation of low tables or bench forms of every style.

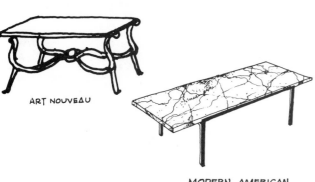

ART NOUVEAU

MODERN AMERICAN
MARBLE AND IRON

COFFER. Chest that served as seat, table, trunk, or for storage of valuables; one of the earliest forms of furniture in Europe, when unsettled conditions made it imperative that furniture and contents be readily transported together.

COFFERED PANEL. Deeply sunk panel.

COIN. Eighteenth-century English corner cupboard. The French word for "corner," corrupted in England to signify its furnishing. See also ENCOIGNURE.

COIN CABINET. (French, *médaillier*). Collector's cabinet with shallow trays or drawers, late 18th, 19th centuries. [539.]

COLLAR. Horizontal molding on a leg.

COLLARED TOE. Foot with a wide band.

COLONIAL. American period from the earliest settlements to the Revolution. Improperly applied to most American furniture up to 1850. See also AMERICA.

Other Colonial types developed from current styles in the mother countries wherever explorers and colonists extended the spheres of England, France, Spain, Germany, Holland, and Scandinavia. For examples, South Africa has a distinct English style; the Spanish roots in South and Central America produced a brilliant provincial churriguerresque.

COLONNETTE. Miniature columns used ornamentally on furniture. [1061, 1336.]

COLUMN. In architecture, a pillar or post, usually round and associated with pedestal, base, capital, and entablature to form an "order" or conventional style. (See ORDERS.) Its use in furniture consists of the ornamental treatment, to simulate an accepted style of a pedestal or supporting member, or as a purely ornamental feature applied to a case or similar structure to suggest support. [1162.]

AMERICAN
COLONIAL

COMB BACK. Windsor chairback in which several spindles extend above the main back, resembling an old-fashioned high comb. American, 18th century. [319.]

COMMODE. The commode is a loosely defined type of chest or cabinet, usually low, and used against a wall as a receptacle, bureau, chest, console, etc. It may have doors or drawers; on the Continent the word applies generally to the English chest or chest of drawers. It evolved out of the earliest coffers or chests, mounted on legs, but the name appears only about 1708, connected with a Régence type by Berain. Its development was rapid in the early 18th century, and it became a favorite ornament for drawing rooms. Some references mention them as "tables with deep drawers," but the more common type, the

COMB BACK CHAIR

CLOSE STOOL

commode en tombeau, describes Boulle's sarcophagus-like idea. The English borrowed the idea; early Georgian commodes, especially by Kent, were lavishly decorated but lacked the unity of the French designs. Chippendale produced many fine designs and probably was the first to plan the commode for the bedroom and clothing storage. Bombé and other shapes were common; Chinese motives were favored, and no resource of cabinetmaking and decorations was overlooked. German console-commodes were elaborately carved and metal-trimmed.

The Classic Revival brought to the commode a consistent architectural form, pilasters or colonnettes forming the corners. In the Empire style this was exaggerated, the actual casework being subordinated to the architectural frame. [428-438, 791, 1337.]

COMMODE, BEDROOM. Enclosed "chamber boxes" or "close stools" of the 17th and 18th centuries were developed into decorative pieces of furniture, later being combined with washstands. The term "nightstand" was applied to them after Chippendale. See also POT TABLE.

428 FRENCH "POT TABLE," bedroom commode, early 19th century.   *Don Ruseau*

429 "CLOSESTOOL," or bedroom commode. Italianate Tudor, 17th century.   *Cavallo*

COMMODE FORM

430 CABINET TABLE, Tuscan, 16th century. Prototype of commode form.

Metropolitan Museum of Art, Fletcher Fund, 1929

431 COMMODE, English, 1760-1770, in the French manner. Inlaid satinwood.

432 COMMODE, English, 1770-1780, in the French manner of the Hepplewhite school.

433 COMMODE, English, late 18th century; Italian influence in inlaid decoration.

THE CHEST WITH DOORS DEVELOPED SIMULTANE-
OUSLY WITH THE DRAWER CHEST. THE NAME "COM-
MODE" IS NOT DEFINITIVE. ACCORDING TO SIZE,
USE, AND LOCALE THE SAME TYPE MAY BE CALLED
A CHEST, CABINET, SIDEBOARD, ETC. IN THE 18TH
CENTURY IT BECAME CHIEFLY AN IMPORTANT
ORNAMENT.

434 DEMILUNE COMMODE,
tulipwood with marble top.
English(?) c. 1800.
Anderson Galleries

435 QUEBEC, 1800-1850. Sacristy cupboard in provincial
style of Louis XV. Doors simulate drawers.

Musée de la Province, Quebec

436 FRENCH PROVINCIAL,
late 18th century, style of
Louis XV.

Don Ruseau

437 FRANCE, NAPOLEONIC ERA. Commode by Jacob and Louis, believed to have been made for Lucien Bonaparte.

438 FRANCE, late 18th century. Burl panels with ormolu mounts.

FARTHINGALE CHAIR

COMMONWEALTH OR CROMWELLIAN
TABLE · CHAIR · BED · RUSH LIGHT HOLDER

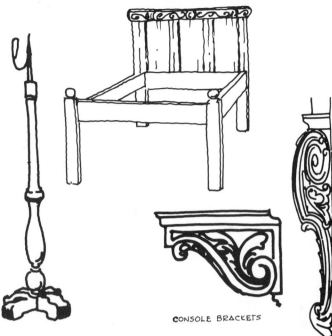

CONSOLE BRACKETS

COMMONWEALTH. Puritan or Cromwellian period in English history (1649-1660). Austere forms replaced the ornate Stuart styles. See also CROMWELLIAN; ENGLAND.

COMPO; COMPOSITION (carton-pierre). Molded substitute for wood carving. Whiting, resin, and size are kneaded and molded in carved shapes, which are then attached to wood furniture for decoration.

COMPOSITE. Architectural order of columns combining the Corinthian and Ionic capitals. See also ORDERS.

CONCERTINA MOVEMENT. Folding mechanism used in card tables and dining tables for expansion. The back half of the frame or apron is cut and hinged two or more times under the extended top leaf, to fold in upon itself. [1213.]

CONFESSIONAL. Large, high, upholstered easy chair with wings. French, 18th century. [261, 634.]

chests and oak chests with various decorative motives survive to illustrate the artistic abilities of the colonists. [11.]

CONSOLE. Architectural term for a bracket of any kind used to support cornices or shelves. The bracket is usually of scroll form. The word "console" is also applied, incorrectly, to tables fixed to the wall and supported only at the front by legs, a carved eagle, or other figure. Currently, almost any type of wall table. [88, 124, 649, 755, 1232, 1279 *et seq.*]

CONSTITUTION MIRROR. American mirror of about the period of the adoption of the Constitution, 1791 or after. The head or cornice of the frame usually has a series of balls as decoration. [869.]

CONFIDENTE

CONFIDANTE; CONFIDENTE. Sofa or settee with separate seats at each end.

CONNECTICUT CHEST. New England chest, 17th or 18th century, ornamented by three carved panels and split spindles. They were extensively used throughout the northern colonies as dower chests and for storage generally, and many fine examples remain. Sunflower

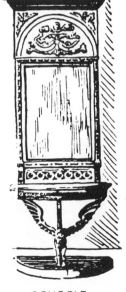

CONSOLE

CONSTITUTION MIRROR

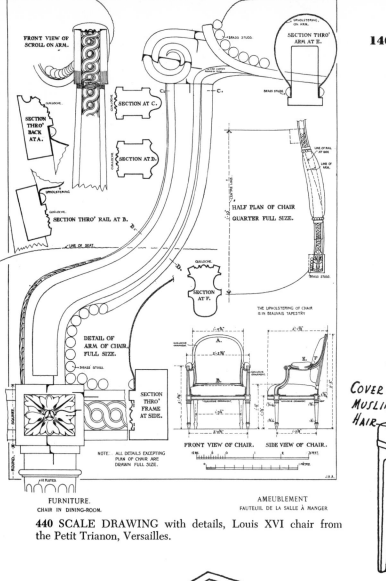

CONSTRUCTION. In the making of wood furniture the commercial factory process still follows the basic steps of the hand process, but at every stage the quantity-production procedure depends on machines and scientific equipment for economy and quality control. From the cutting and seasoning of timber, the conversion into dimension stock, veneers and plywoods; the machining of moldings, rabbet, and dadoes, shaping, turning, carving, boring, etc.; the assembly of machined parts; and the final finishing and assembling, all possible handwork is eliminated for precision as well as for economy. Nevertheless, the succession of steps still follows the handicraft sequence.

FURNITURE.
CHAIR IN DINING-ROOM.

AMEUBLEMENT
FAUTEUIL DE LA SALLE À MANGER.

440 SCALE DRAWING with details, Louis XVI chair from the Petit Trianon, Versailles.

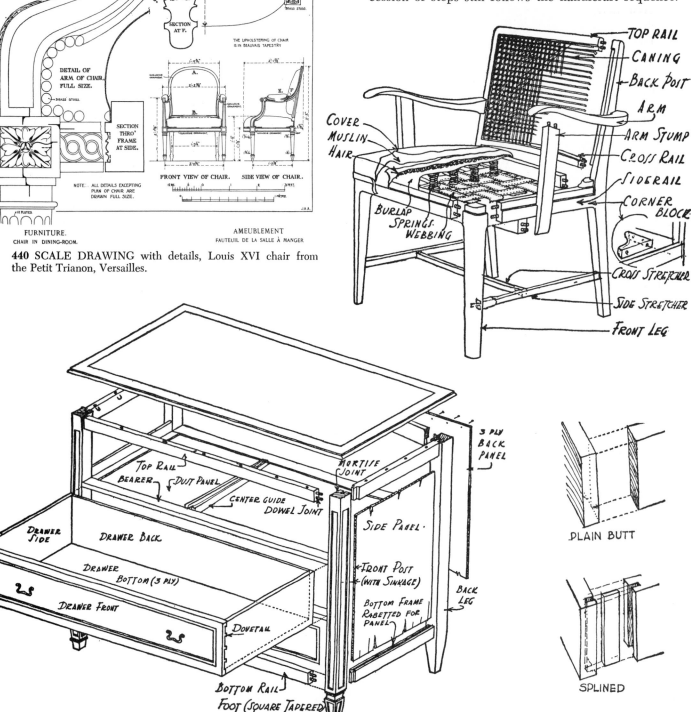

1. The pictorial sketch of the designer is projected into working-scale drawings. From this the "full-size detail" or pattern is made and usually transferred to wooden full-size sections called the "rod." From this is taken the "stock list," or schedule of dimensioned parts.

2. PREPARATION OF WOOD. Air- and kiln-drying are highly technical procedures. Similarly, the cutting of veneers and making of plywoods rely on scientific techniques and apparatus, many of which are separate productions outside the furniture factory, which receives such laboratory specification products as its raw material.

3. ASSEMBLY. The handmade, or custom, product is largely put together by one man working at a bench. The factory product may move down a production line with many hands, each applying his specialized operation. This is the part that occasions the greatest cost variation. Skilled handwork is scarce and costly and can *almost* be replaced by intelligently disciplined assembly-line procedures.

4. FINISH. Production methods in finishing have advanced tremendously with the advent of new synthetic materials, replacing traditional shellac, varnish, and paint, and with the advent of processes involving heat, chemistry, spraying, electronics, etc. (See also FINISH.) Again, the result of a completely mechanical process never quite looks like that of a hand-finished process. Efforts to synthesize patinas and to achieve the effects of great age or skilled individual labor are usually obvious.

The construction of framework furniture (like chairs) and of case furniture falls into different categories that were specialized trades in much of furniture history. Material and skills vary widely. Chairs are frameworks designed primarily to withstand such stress as weight and twisting. They basically follow an arbitrary shape in which the articulation of members is as important as the proportions, which are governed by the human body and by a particular manner of sitting. Thus, styles of design and construction of chairs continually revert to factors of strength,

Wadsworth Atheneum, Hartford, Conn.
441 DOVETAILED DRAWER, 18th-century American chest.

Ginsburg and Levy
442 DRAWER SLIDE, English chest c. 1755-1760.

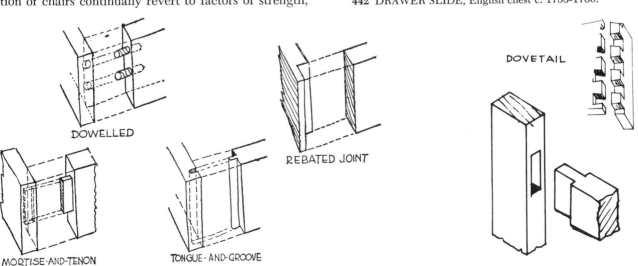

DOWELLED

MORTISE-AND-TENON

TONGUE-AND-GROOVE

REBATED JOINT

DOVETAIL

SKETCH SHOWING CONSTRUCTION

lightness in handling, and body comfort for sitting. The simple stool, legs attached to a board, was given a back, and the final products are as varied as Chippendale chairs and the Windsor. In both cases the excellence of construction grew out of artistic perceptions of the strength of materials and the possible ways of making the assembly rigid and capable of resisting stress. By the strategic arrangement of the parts, the members brace one another. Adhesives at the joints prevent the parts from moving and allowing the framework to dissolve. A good chair is a great engineering achievement.

The molded chair models a matrix-form for the body. Beginning with a shaped wooden seat, it evolves into a single shell comprising back, arms, and seat. The effect was originally obtained through upholstering. Modern materials and techniques achieve such forms in plastics, molded plywood, etc. These may be surface-softened, as was the original framework chair, with upholstery materials.

A table is essentially an engineering problem. It is a flat plane that carries weight, and the framework is designed to resist this stress, as well as the strain of lateral and lifting movements.

Casework furniture includes receptacles or storage devices such as chests-of-drawers and cabinets. The drawer is essentially a mechanical device. Its invention after the Gothic period really marks the beginning of modern furniture. The box idea began with a hollowed-out log; then came the joining of planks. Its first breakthrough came with the framed panel, achieving relative lightness, dimensional stability and rigidity necessary for the movable box-in-a-box or drawer. Methods of fastening together the various flat parts progressed from simple butt-joining, braced strategically, to complicated dovetailing, both of carcass and drawer. Nothing in Western work approaches the complex jointing of Chinese cabinetry, but their casework is independent of glue, and therefore never attains the rigidity and tight fitting of modern Western work.

The heavier posts and crossrails were grooved to hold the lighter inner panel (later of plywood), the feet being part of the posts. In late-18th-century work there was a recurrence of flush sides, both in solid and in veneered panels. With the advent of plywood it became more feasible to use flush sides. Drawer cases are held together by horizontal partitions, or dust panels, between the drawers. Flush doors in cabinets are best made with framed cores.

JOINERY, better known as cabinetmaking, differs from carpentry in that it requires greater precision and a different understanding of strains and materials. Carpentry is concerned with weight and strains and

their balance by the form and position of structural parts; joinery is concerned with the strength of joints. There are a number of primary joints: (1) plain butt, (2) rabbeted, (3) doweled, (4) mortise-and-tenoned, (5) splined, (6) dovetailed. There are also infinite variations of these joints, developed for special purposes or through the joiners' ingenuity.

Rabbeted joints are known as dadoed, housed, or grooved, with many combinations. Doweled joints, the most generally used today, are in effect secured butt joints. Splined joints are known as tongue-and-grooved when the edges of the boards are shaped to go together, instead of a strip being inserted in identical meeting grooves. Dovetailing, now used to join drawer sides, occurs in older casework at the meeting of sides and top.

All rules for joinery are qualified by position and material.

Virtually all joints require glue, or would be improved by it. Glueing is an art and science in itself. See also GLUE.

Nails are rarely used, except for temporary setting until glue takes hold. Screws or clip fasteners are often used to allow movement of the wood in some planes.

Frameworks, such as chairs, tables, etc., depend for rigidity on the strength of the joint, plus scientific cross bracing. Doweled joints are most commonly used, with braces arranged to distribute the strains into other planes. Such are stretchers, which, being visible, may not be used in some styles; corner blocks are universally used in the concealed structure of upholstered chairs and under the tops of tables.

See also FINISH; UPHOLSTERY.

CONSULATE. Napoleon's term as First Consul, 1799-1804. The style continued the Directoire manner up to the development of the Empire. See also FRANCE. [212.]

CONTEMPORARY. Current style, presently specific to modern eclectic work, more or less adapted from historical styles, with modern overtones.

CONTRE-PARTIE. Boulle work in which the brass predominates.

CONVERSATION CHAIR. Loose term for comfortable chairs, not quite so low or so deep as lounge chairs, but more comfortable than straight chairs.

CONVOLUTE. In the form of a scroll.

COPY. Reproduction, replica. Furniture copies are usually made of old pieces having historic or antiquarian interest, with more or less fidelity. The patina of old pieces, with their wear marks, are sometimes so skillfully duplicated that they are carelessly or intentionally sold as originals. See also ANTIQUES.

COQUILLAGE. Shell motive in ornamental design for frames and other carved surfaces, after the French *coquille*, a shell. It is Rococo, and occurs in French work of the early 18th century and in French-influenced English work. Chippendale's school used it extensively as the central ornament surrounding a cabochon on seat rails of chairs.

CORBEL. Bracket or brace to carry weight, deriving from the architectural term "to corbel out," in which one or more bricks or stones project to carry a weight. Common decorative theme in 17th- and 18th-century furniture.

CORDOVA LEATHER. Leatherworking in Europe derived most of its inspiration from the technique of decorating leather evolved in Cordova, Spain, during the Middle Ages. By the time the Renaissance spread over Europe, all leatherwork came to be known as Cordova leather. Flanders inherited the method from the conquerors of the Lowlands, whence it was popularized in French and English decoration. Much of the leather was stamped with ornate, rather Oriental, designs, gilt and polished. [1151.]

CORE. Internal part of plywood, usually poplar, chestnut, or similar porous woods, upon which the crossed layers of veneer are applied. See also PLYWOOD.

CORINTHIAN. Architectural order of column, with scrolls growing out of acanthus leaves. The most ornate Greek form, it was adapted and highly developed by the Romans. See also ORDERS.

CORINTHIAN CAPITAL

CORNER ARMCHAIR. Armchair with the back on two sides based on three legs, the fourth leg being in the middle of the front. See also ROUNDABOUT CHAIR. [268.]

CORNER BLOCK. Triangular blocks set in the corners of chair frames, etc., as reinforcement. See also CONSTRUCTION.

CORNER CUPBOARD. Cupboard designed to fit a corner, the front being diagonal or curved. Smaller ones were made to hang; very important ones were built integral with the room. Paneling lines often carry through in the architectural forms. They were common throughout the 18th century in England and America, and in France as ENCOIGNURE. [443 *et seq.*]

446 CORNER CUPBOARD, New England c. 1810.
Henry Ford Museum, Dearborn, Mich.

443   *Metropolitan Museum of Art,*
Rogers Fund, 1925

445

Metropolitan Museum of Art,
Rogers Fund, 1918

443 AMERICAN, walnut, c. 1745.

444 ENGLISH, 1725-1730. Black lacquer with Chinese decoration.

445 CONNECTICUT VALLEY, 1730-1750.

444

Metropolitan Museum of Art,
Bequest of John L. Cadwalader, 1914

448 GENOA, parquetry in Louis XIV style.   *Dalva Brothers, Inc.*

449 FRANCE, Early Provincial style of Louis XV.   *Don Ruseau*

452 CORNER GATELEG TABLE,
English, early 18th century.
         Symons Galleries, Inc.

Israel Sack, Inc.

453 BALTIMORE c. 1780. Mahogany corner table,
marble top.

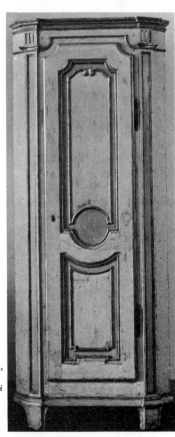

447 ITALIAN, painted,
late 18th century.
     Olivieri

450 PENNSYLVANIA GERMAN, mid-18th-century corner hanging cupboard, pine.

451 QUEBEC, 19th century. Pine corner cupboard in two parts.

CORNICE (CORNISH). Horizontal top or finish molding or group of moldings of a piece of furniture or architectural unit. Detached boxes or frames from which curtains hung were also so called in the 18th century. See also MOLDING; ORDERS.

CORNUCOPIA. The horn of plenty, overflowing with fruits and flowers. A motif in decoration of many styles, from the Renaissance to the present. Favorite stencil motif, American 19th century.

CORNUCOPIA SOFA. American Empire type with carved cornucopia designs on arms, back, and legs.

COROMANDEL. Bombay ebony from the Coromandel coast; blackish rosewood in texture, with light stripes. [647.]

COSTUMER. Stand or frame with pegs or hooks, for hanging clothing. (Recent.) [1095a.]

COT. Light, portable bedstead.

COTTAGE FURNITURE. Specifically English simplified types originating in functional demands rather than in display. Corresponds to provincial styles generally in superimposing echoes of fashionable details on basic functional articles. Good 18th- and 19th-century work is scantily ornamented, unlike provincial work of France. Late-19th-century English reform movements worked largely with country models. [1324.]

COTTONWOOD. Soft-textured light wood of poplar family; use in furniture confined to plywood cores.

COUCH. Sofa that has a half-back and head end only. See also REST BEDS; SOFA.

COUNTER-BOULLE. Brass groundwork with tortoise-shell inlay. See also CONTRE-PARTIE.

COUNTERPANE. Coverlet for a bed, originally woven in squares or figures. From the French *contre-point*, a fabric woven on both sides. Mentioned in most early furnishings inventories.

COUNTERS. Originally tables or chests whose top surfaces are marked off for either measuring or counting. They originated in Flanders in the 15th century.

COUNTERSINK. Conical boring in wood to receive a screwhead so that the surface of the screw is lower than the wood surface.

454 COURT CUPBOARD, Jacobean, melon-bulb turnings, Italianate carving.

Stair & Company, Inc.

COURT CUPBOARD. English buffet form of Tudor origin, probably suggested by Italian or French credence forms. Generally a double-bodied cabinet, richly carved and used to hold plate and eating utensils, wine, etc. Highest development in Early Jacobean times. Similar forms appear in American work of the same period. [4, 461, 548.]

COURTING CHAIR. Two-chair-back settee or sofa.

COURTING MIRROR. Small wood-framed mirror, usually pine, with a picture over the glass; a conventional courting gift. American, 18th century. [838.]

COVE. Large concave or hollow molding.

COVED CUPBOARD. Early American cupboard whose top is swept forward like a hood.

COX, JOSEPH. Upholsterer and cabinetmaker, had a shop in Dock Street, New York, in mid-18th century. Settee with his label now in the Metropolitan Museum of Art.

COZY CORNER. Mid-19th-century interest in the Near East led to draped, cushioned constructions; by the 1880's these were reduced by lower-class commercial interpretation to a species of hooded corner settee compositions with fancy frameworks; middle class in England and America.

CRADLE. Child's bed of ancient type, mounted on rockers or some swinging arrangement. Every style has produced a variety of types, from simple boxes to the great draped state cradles of 18th-century France. Renaissance forms are unbridled imaginative designs; similar complex forms appear in Sheraton's drawings; and a notably elaborate cradle is that of Napoleon's son, in the Empire style. Peasant styles bear much painted and carved ornament, especially in rural Germany, Switzerland, and France. The cradle is now almost obsolete in favor of the more functional crib. [3, 455, 888, 956.]

455 CRADLE, American 17th century. Panels recall Late Gothic-Jacobean influence.

Wadsworth Atheneum, Hartford, Conn.

456 AMERICAN PINE, early 18th century.   *Israel Sack, Inc.*

CREDENCE. Important side table of Gothic style, usually oak. Origin probably religious, from *credere*, to believe. Later used as sideboard for carving meat, displaying plate, etc. Prevalent in northern Europe, it evolved into the buffet-sideboard type. [719, 723.]

CREDENZA. Credence, Italian form. An important production of the 15th and 16th centuries. See also ITALY. [719.]

CRESCENT STRETCHER. Bowed or concave stretcher on Windsor chair, American, English, 18th century.

CRESSENT, CHARLES, 1685-1768. French furniture maker and *ciseleur*, pupil of Boulle and leading figure in Régence and Rococo design. [653.]

CRESTING. Carved decoration on top rail of chairs, daybeds, mirrors, etc.

CREWELWORK. Embroidery of fine worsted on linen. English, 16th and 17th centuries.

CRIB. Child's bed with enclosed sides.

CRICKET. Old English wooden footstool, usually low. Also, simple versions in American work.

CRICKET TABLE. Small Jacobean three-legged table, generally round. [17.]

CRINOLINE STRETCHER. Stretcher on Windsor chairs, the two front legs joined by a semicircular curve, with short stretchers to the back legs. See also CRESCENT STRETCHER.

CRISSCROSSED WORK. Latticework.

CROCKET. Gothic architectural ornament consisting of moldings terminating in a curve or roll. Used on medieval woodwork, and again in work of the 18th century.

CROMWELLIAN. The brief period, 1649-1660, of Puritan domination in England is named after its central figure, Oliver Cromwell. The furniture of this time is a severe, undecorated version of the Jacobean, out of which it grew. These Puritan influences were naturally those carried across the sea by the Puritan settlers of the New England colonies; consequently, the early gateleg tables, Welsh dressers, square-backed chairs, and other furniture of the colonies exhibit the same qualities. The wood was chiefly oak; turnings

of simple ball profiles are the chief ornament. See also ENGLAND. [473.]

CROSS FIRE. Regular mottled figure across the grain of wood, yielding a brilliant transparency, particularly in some mahogany, walnut, satinwood, and other tropical woods. See WOODS.

CROSS STRETCHER. Intersecting X-stretcher, straight or curved, on tables, lowboys, and chairs. Baroque Italian inspiration developed by the French Renaissance designers and employed in England in the William and Mary productions and later. [1196.]

CROSSBANDING. Border bands of veneer in which the grain runs across the band. Treatment is characteristic of walnut furniture after Charles II, and follows throughout the 18th century in England and on the Continent.

CROSSRAIL. Horizontal bar or rail in a chairback.

457 CUPBOARD GABLE-ROOFED ROMANESQUE FORM, Austrian, 15th century. Cabinet, of pine, is 76 inches high, 45 inches wide.

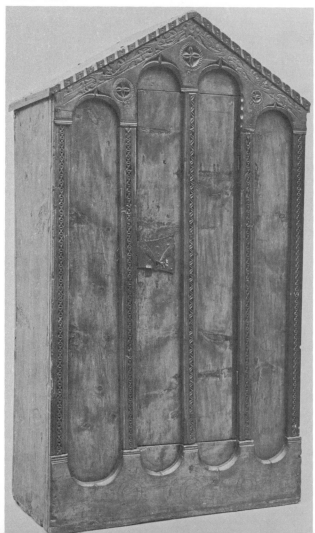

CROTCH. The wood from the intersection of a branch with the trunk of the tree has an unusual V-shaped figure when cut into veneers. The matching of these veneers produces striking patterns much favored by cabinetmakers. See also WOODS.

CRUSHED BALL FOOT. Furniture foot similar to club foot.

CROWN. Motive in decoration. In carving it is found in Italian, French, Flemish, and English work after Charles II. It occurs also as painting, as in medieval wall decorations. Its use as a motif in weaving dates from the Early Saracenic textiles and the Sicilian weavers of the 12th century. [470.]

CUP-AND-COVER TURNING. Turned ornament consisting of a bulb, topped by a lid or cover. Jacobean and later. See also TURNING.

C-SCROLL

C-SCROLL. Carved C-shaped design found in much late-16th- and 17th-century French and Flemish work and later in England.

CUP-TURNING. Cup-shaped bulge in turned legs.

CUPBOARD. Cabinet or box with doors, for storage. The special types and names are numerous, springing from special uses and locations. Sometimes a cupboard is considered an architectural feature only, the free-standing equivalent being a cabinet. See also CABINET; CHEST; CORNER CUPBOARD; COURT CUPBOARD. [457 *et seq.*]

EARLY CUPBOARDS WERE KNOWN IN ENGLAND UNDER VARIOUS NAMES SUGGESTING USE FOR FOOD STORAGE: ALMONER, AMBRY, DOLE, LIVERY (FOR DELIVERY). THE EARLY FORMS HAD ONLY ONE DOOR AND USUALLY SOME DEVICE FOR VENTILATION. THE CABINET FORMS DEVELOPED SIMULTANEOUSLY FOR ALL OTHER STORAGE USES, FINALLY REACHING A CLIMAX IN THE GREAT DECORATIVE CABINETS OF THE 17TH CENTURY.

Metropolitan Museum of Art, Rogers Fund, 1910
458 OAK AMBRY, English c. 1475.

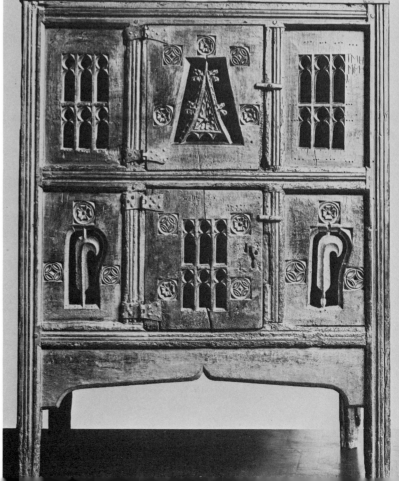

459 ENGLISH LIVERY CUPBOARD c. 1500.
Victoria and Albert Museum,
Crown Copyright

"CUP-BOARD" LITERALLY WAS ANOTHER SOURCE OF THE CUPBOARD-CABINET IDEA. FILLING IN THE OPEN SECTION PRODUCED THE COURT-CUPBOARD TYPE.

GOTHIC MOLDING DETAIL

460 ENGLISH, early 17th century.

Arthur S. Vernay, Inc.

461 ENGLISH COURT CUPBOARD, mixed Gothic-Italianate ornamentation, 1630-1640.

Stair & Company, Inc.

Metropolitan Museum of Art, Gift of Mrs. Russell Sage, 1909

462 ENGLISH, mid-17th century.
Court-cupboard shape with simplified Italianate detail.

STRAPWORK

ELIZABETHAN CABINETWORK DETAILS

463 ENGLISH c. 1620. *Stair & Company, Inc.*

Anderson Galleries

465 MASSACHUSETTS, early 18th century. Fluted decoration reminiscent of linenfold paneling.

466 BAVARIA or Austria, dated 1811. High painted cupboard.

Liebold Wallach

464 SWISS, early 18th century. *Metropolitan Museum of Art, Rogers Fund, 1907*

CUPID'S BOW. Double ogee curve, bow shaped, such as favored by Chippendale for top rails of chairs.

CURLED FIGURE. Feathered appearance in the grain of some woods when cut across the grain. Maple, birch, walnut, and others show distinct cross-grain markings in parts of some logs. This figure is prized for special veneerings, inlays, etc. See also WOODS. [374.]

CURLED HAIR. Upholstery filling made principally from the mane and tail hair of horses, valued for its resiliency and long staple. Less valuable is the curled hair of cattle and hogs.

CURLY BIRCH, MAPLE, etc. Occasional variants in grain markings in some woods show strong parallel waves or curls. Curly maple was favored in Early American work. See also WOODS. [374.]

CURRICULE CHAIR. Sheraton's term for a classical type having semicircular back and elongated seat. See also CURULE CHAIR.

CURULE CHAIR. X-shaped chair, the *sella curule* of the Romans. [788.]

CUSP. Gothic ornamental knob or point projecting from the intersections of two curves. [622, 1017, 1144.]

CUSPED ARCH. Gothic detail of pointed arch with pointed break into the curve. [1144.]

CUTWORK. Fretwork.

CYLINDER FRONT. Quarter-round fall front of a desk. Also the name of the desks having such rolltops, made during the late 18th century in France and England. [483.]

CYMA. From the Greek for wave—a simple double curve.

CYMA RECTA. The ogee molding.

CYMA REVERSA. The cyma recta reversed.

CYPRESS (Cupressus semperoneus). Dark reddish wood of very hard texture, valued for its durability. Cypress chests were made as early as the 14th century.

DAIS. Raised platform at one end of medieval rooms, upon which was the table for the master, while the retainers sat below. Also occurs in Empire style for use with beds.

DAMASK. Silk figured fabric used for draperies and upholstery, named after Damascus, where it appears to have been made before the 12th century. The manufacture of damask began in Italy very early, and until the end of the 17th century Venice and Genoa supplied most of Europe. The French weavers took over the process with the Renaissance, while Dutch and Flemish weavers carried it to England about 1570.

DANISH. See SCANDINAVIA.

DANTE CHAIR (Dantesca). X-chair of the Italian Renaissance, having four heavy legs curving up to arms, with leather or fabric seat. Spanish type rather top-heavy; French, English, and Teutonic versions more ornate. See also CHAIR; CURULE CHAIR. [214.]

DARBY AND JOAN SETTEE. Two-chairback settee, English. [1078.]

DARLY, MATTHIAS. 18th-century English designer and engraver, published books on design.

DAVENPORT. Small writing desk. In current American use, an upholstered sofa.

DAVENPORT BED. Couch that may be unfolded to form a bed.

DAVENPORT DESK. Small writing desk, chiefly mid-19th-century English. Characteristically, there are drawers that pull out sideways, and a lift lid, with or without gallery. [467.]

CUSPED ARCH IN WOODWORK

CYMA CURVE

467

DAVENPORT TABLE. Long narrow table used behind a sofa when placed in the center of a room.

DAVID (David Roentgen). French designer and cabinetmaker, 1743-1807. See also ROENTGEN.

DAYBEDS. Rest beds, chaise longues, and other elongated seating forms may be called daybeds; these usually have a raised pillowlike end. They are pictured in ancient Greek and Roman remains, and occur in France after the Louis XIV era. They appear in England with the Restoration. The commoner reference in America is to a true bed form with both ends the same height and placed lengthwise to the wall. This form grew from the alcove bed of 18th-century France, which evolved through the Louis XVI and Empire styles into the familiar shape of the current style. See also CHAISE LONGUE; REST BEDS. [468, 471, 506, 598.]

GREEK SCULPTURE 1st century.   **468**

Anderson Galleries

470 DAYBED c. 1680. Charles II, walnut and cane, scroll leg and stretcher with crown.

469 AMERICAN QUEEN ANNE.   *Israel Sack, Inc.*

471 DAYBED, English, 1780-1790. Late style of the Adams.   *Metropolitan Museum of Art, Rogers Fund, 1910*

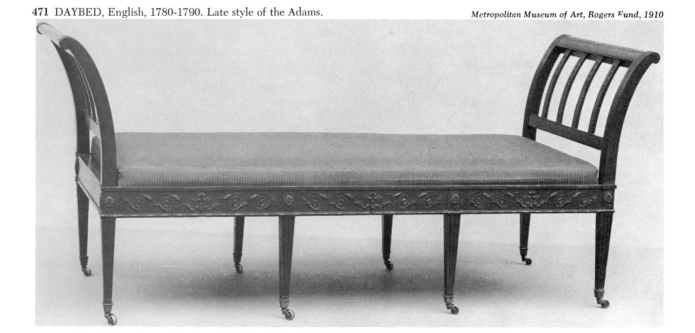

DEAL. English term for pine, particularly the Scotch pine. Sheraton explains the name as the Dutch term for "a part," signifying the division of boards when used as the core for veneering.

DECALCOMANIA. Picture applied in reverse to paper, then transferred to furniture by sticking and removing the paper. As a substitute for painted decoration, it appeared in the late 18th century, but became popular only in the early 1800's, chiefly in America. Hitchcock and similar chairs were sometimes decorated with such transfer patterns.

DECANTER STANDS. See COASTER.

DECORATED QUEEN ANNE. English style, approximately 1710-1730; Early Georgian. Such essential details of Queen Anne style as cabriole legs, round-back chairs with fiddle splats, claw-and-ball feet, and generally curved forms were enriched in scale and heavily adorned with carving. [266.]

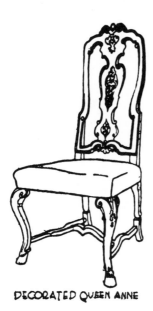

DECORATED QUEEN ANNE

DEMI-DOME. Half dome, such as the shell-top niche in a cupboard.

DEMILUNE. Half round in plan, as in a console or commode. [434, 1066.]

DEMOISELLE. Early French pedestal table fitted with the form of a woman's head, and used to hold headdresses.

DENTILS. Equally spaced rectangular blocks in a cornice molding, resembling teeth.

DERBYSHIRE CHAIR. English country chair. Jacobean period.

DESK. The original desk was a writing box, a small chest with sloping lid. Inside were kept writing materials and valuables. This form was known in ancient China and Egypt; it is the monastic *scriptorium* of the Middle Ages. These Gothic forms, growing larger, came to be mounted on stands [474], and presently the hinging of the lid was reversed so that the inner side formed a writing surface when opened [476]. Hence the slant-front and fall-front types that are known today. The desk box survived into the 18th century. From the French practice of covering it with a woolen cloth (French *bure*) comes the word "bureau," later signifying any desk compartment, and corrupted in America to mean chest of drawers.

The filling in of the desk frame with drawers to the floor came in the late 17th century with the appearance of the chest of drawers [485]. In England and later in America this type became a leading article of furniture. The addition of the bookcase top made the tall secretary. The name is derived from *scrutoire* or *scriptoire*. Italy, Austria, and Germany produced elaborate secretaries in Baroque complexity. The late-18th-century types of England and America are superb architectural compositions. In the Empire period the slant front almost disappeared, and the straight fall-front cabinet, in one front plane, was a rectangular mass of superimposed architectural motives.

Biedermeier secretaries carried this even further; tall compositions, sometimes of three architectural façades, complete with columns and cornices and pediments, were made in light woods. American desks of the same period favored a debased Sheraton form with slightly slanted fold-over leaf and turned legs. In the Victorian era the tall slant front came back; it was very large, with softened contours.

Smaller desks, the type known as "ladies' desks," appeared about 1680 in England. An epidemic of letter writing and memoirs raged in France during Louis XV's reign and, with its counterpart in England, made desks essential in every room. These were dainty tablelike affairs with small enclosed top sections, closing with lids, doors, tambours, or cylinders that rolled back. From the cylinder type came many important variations; through the Empire they were popular, and begat the 19th-century rolltop, the "Carlton desk," and numerous other table forms flourishing in England.

Table desks developed naturally from the simple writing table; banks of drawers were added below, and often a small block of drawers sat loosely on top. A form of kneehole arrangement occurs frequently, often identical with dressing-table forms. In American work a practical workdesk, sometimes called "George Washington," set precedent for modern utilitarian pieces. These types are called "library tables" in England. See also LIBRARY TABLE; WRITING DESK. [437 *et seq.*, 1095, 1374 *et seq.*]

ONE ROOT IS IN THE PORTABLE DESK BOX SET ON A TABLE OR FRAME. ANOTHER IS IN THE READING STAND OR LECTERN, FILLED IN UNDER THE SLANTING TOP.

Henry Ford Museum, Dearborn, Mich.
473 MASSACHUSETTS, Jacobean, 1680-1700.

Wadsworth Atheneum, Hartford, Conn.
472 DESK BOX, probably Pennsylvania, 18th century.

DESK BOX. Portable box for writing materials and valuable papers; usually with hinged slant top for writing. In earliest furniture history they were small; as they grew larger they were equipped with stands, to which they finally became attached and so were the ancestor of the modern desk. See also DESK. [472.]

474 SCANDINAVIAN, 17th century.

475 ITALIAN, 16th century, ironbound olivewood.

**THE DESK-ON-FRAME EVOLVED INTO THE
GRACEFUL DESIGN KNOWN IN LATER PERIODS
AS "LADIES' DESKS."**

Wadsworth Atheneum, Hartford, Conn.
476 AMERICAN, 1690-1700, walnut, cross stretcher.

477 PENNSYLVANIA c. 1710. Box stretcher desk-on-frame.

479 LOUIS XV, height of Rococo.   *French & Co., Inc.*

478 ENGLISH c. 1700. Queen Anne, walnut.
Fully developed type, cabriole leg.

Metropolitan Museum of Art

480 AMERICAN, 1710-1725, Queen Anne influence. Detachable desk box on lowboy.

481 FRENCH, Directoire, with Revolutionary emblems.

EIGHTEENTH-CENTURY MASTERPIECES REPLACED
THE FALL FRONT WITH A ROTATING CYLINDER
THAT ROLLED BACK. A FLAT WRITING BED COULD
THEN BE DRAWN FORWARD. COMPLICATED MECHAN-
ICAL CONTRIVANCES CAME FROM ROENTGEN, SHER-
ATON, ETC.

484 LOUIS XVI MAHOGANY ROLLTOP DESK by David Roentgen, Gautier *bronze-doré*
plaque.

French & Co., Inc.

Victoria and Albert Museum, Crown Copyright

482 FRENCH ROCOCO, elaborate marquetry.

Needham's Antiques, Inc.

483 ENGLISH, late 18th century.

THE ADDITION OF THE SLANT-FRONT DESK BOX TO A CHEST OR
CABINET FOLLOWED LOGICALLY AFTER 1650. THE FORM CONTINUES
TO DEVELOP THROUGH CURRENT STYLES.

Anderson Galleries

485 ITALIAN (Florence), mid-17th century. Walnut desk
with closed-in base section.

Needham's Antiques, Inc.

486 ENGLISH c. 1710. Queen Anne, walnut, slope front.

487 DUTCH(?), beginning 18th century. Voluted corners are hinged and conceal four small drawers.

489 BLOCKFRONT, 1765-1780.

488 VIRGINIA, 1700-1710. Walnut slant top.

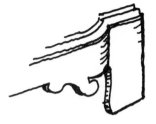

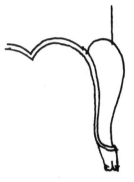

Henry Ford Museum, Dearborn, Mich.

490 CONNECTICUT c. 1780; the use of mahogany is unusual.

Don Ruseau

492 FRENCH, Provincial style of Louis XV, probably late 18th century. Hoof foot.

491 GEORGE I, WALNUT KNEEHOLE DESK. *Needham's Antiques, Inc.*

493 ENGLISH c. 1795. Directoire influence.

Needham's Antiques, Inc.

494 FRENCH, Louis XVI, stamped Saunier. Wedgwood plaques in satinwood panels, brass ornamentation.

French & Co., Inc.

495 AMERICAN, 1810-1820. Mahogany bureau desk, fall front.

New-York Historical Society, New York City

496 FRENCH c. 1785. Stamped N Lannuier. Drop-front secretary, satinwood, Sèvres plaque, marble top.

French & Co., Inc.

Metropolitan Museum of Art,
Gift of Mr. and Mrs. Andrew Varick Stout, 1935

497 AMERICAN, Sheraton style made in New York about 1800.

Israel Sack, Inc.

498 AMERICAN, 1790-1800. Tambour front, fold-over writing bed.

499 LOUIS XVI, signed PIRET, 1785. *Bronze-doré* by Gautier, drop front.

French & Co., Inc.

500 MASSACHUSETTS c. 1800. Figured mahogany.

Metropolitan Museum of Art,
Kennedy Fund, 1918

501 FRENCH c. 1925. Macassar ebony. Designed by Ruhlmann.

Metropolitan Museum of Art,
Edward C. Moore, Jr., Gift Fund, 1932

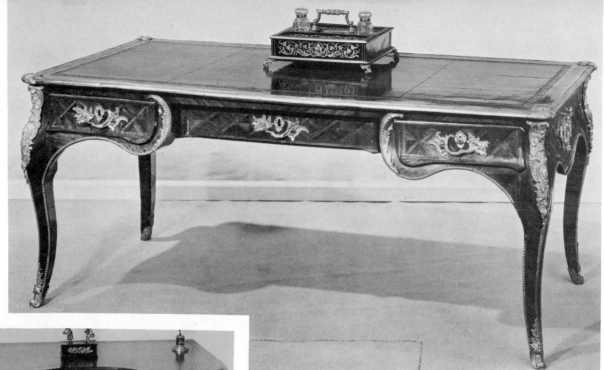

502 BUREAU PLAT, Régence parquetry, Boulle inkstand.

503 ENGLISH c. 1835. Georgian style, leather top.

504 DESK DRAWER in campaign chest, English c. 1830.

LATE GEORGIAN DECORATED

EARLY VICTORIAN
CLOSED DESKS.

505 DESK BOX, Salem, Massachusetts, c. 1730, walnut.

LADIES' DESK, SWEDISH ROCOCO

DIAMOND-POINT
PANELS (LOUIS XIII)

DIAPER PATTERN

Don Ruseau
510 DIRECTOIRE PEDESTAL
with bronze candelabrum.

DIAMOND-MATCHED VENEER. Straight-grained woods cut diagonally and put together in quarters so as to produce a diamond pattern. See also woods.

DIAMOND POINT. Lozenge; a geometric-shaped panel in casework, typical of early-17th-century work in France, Flanders, and England. [466, 633.]

DIAPER. Design in regular repeats, usually small, spaced to form a diagonal pattern. Probably first woven in Ypres in the 16th century, it took its name from d'Ypre. Also, a basic pattern in conventional wall painting, wallpapers, inlays, etc. [377, 516.]

DINING TABLES. See TABLE.

SAWBUCK TABLE NORTHERN EUROPE, 17th-18th c.

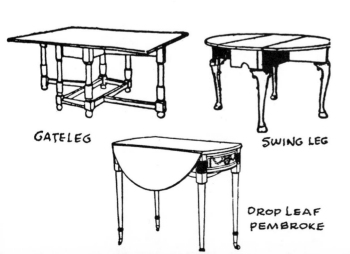

GATELEG

SWING LEG

DROP LEAF
PEMBROKE

DIRECTOIRE. The French Revolution ended the reign of Louis XVI, but his classic style adjusted well to Republicanism. The new government of the Directory encouraged most of the great craftsmen to discard the sumptuous regality, to reduce scale and ostentation of materials, and to emphasize Greco-Roman forms. Percier and Fontaine emerged in this brief period, and the artist David was effective. Napoleon extinguished the Directory in November, 1799, and in his Consulate laid the foundation for the Empire, coinciding with the transition to full autocracy in 1804. The hasty transition in style was less marked in other countries, where the *retardataire* Louis XVI-Directoire style created the Early Regency manner in England, the elegance of Duncan Phyfe and Lannuier in America, a capricious Directoire in Italy, and a coldly sober classicism in Scandinavia. See also EMPIRE; FRANCE. [378, 481, 662 *et seq.*, 789.]

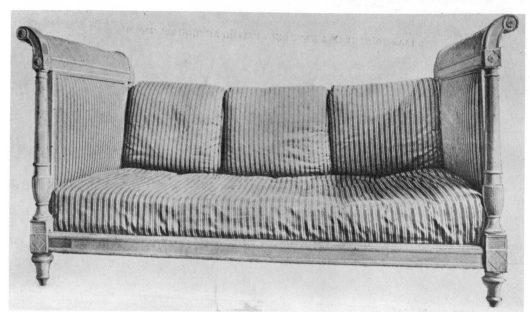

506 DAYBED, Early Directoire. Basically Louis XVI with reeding, insert diamonds, typical of Revolution.

Don Ruseau

508 TRANSITION LOUIS XVI TO DIRECTOIRE. Commode c. 1795. Matched mahogany veneers presage Empire flat surfaces. **509** DETAIL, DIRECTOIRE CHEST POST.

512 DIRECTOIRE DAYBED c. 1805.

Don Ruseau

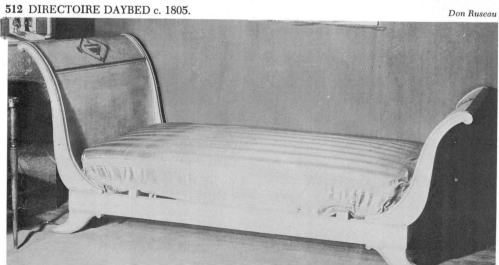

507 ITALIAN DIRECTOIRE *Don Ruseau*
CHEST AND MIRROR.

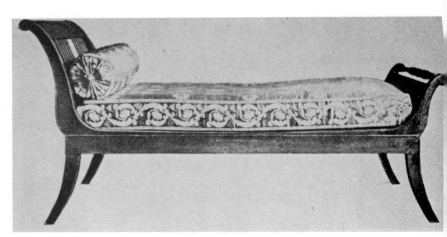

513 FRENCH DIRECTOIRE c. 1800. Daybed of simple style.

ITALIAN DIRECTOIRE

Don Ruseau
511 DETAIL, FOOTBOARD.
Provincial Directoire.

514 ITALIAN DIRECTOIRE COMMODE c. 1810. Inlaid walnut. *Anderson Galleries*

DISC FOOT. Flat, rounded foot in Queen Anne work.

DISHED. Hollowed out, often by turning.

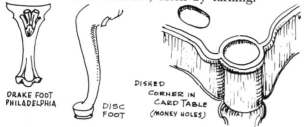

DRAKE FOOT PHILADELPHIA

DISC FOOT

DISHED CORNER IN CARD TABLE (MONEY HOLES)

DISHED CORNER. In card tables, a hollowed-out space in each corner for holding money. [1267.]

DIVAN. Upholstered couch without arms or back, originating in Turkish form of pile of rugs for reclining. See also UPHOLSTERY. [506.]

DOCUMENT DRAWER. In desk cabinets, the small vertical drawers, usually found one on each side of the central compartment in the interior or writing section. Often ornamented with carved colonnettes, etc. [477.]

DOCUMENT DRAWERS

DOG-EAR. Projecting rectangular ornament at the head of a door frame or paneling, found in Early Georgian work.

DOGTOOTH. Ornamental detail, chiefly Gothic, in the form of repeated cones, like pyramidal dentils.

DOLE CUPBOARD. Ecclesiastical cupboard for food for the poor; disappeared after the Middle Ages. See also AMBRY; ENGLAND; LIVERY CUPBOARD. [545.]

DOLPHIN. Sea animal used more or less realistically in carving and painting on furniture, bronze and stone in architecture. [192, 199.]

DOLPHIN FOOT ENGLISH REGENCY

DOLPHIN HINGE. English hardware used in secretaries, name suggested by its dolphin-like shape. See also HARDWARE.

DOME BED. Canopy bed with tester in either full dome or arched shape.

DOME TOP. Half-round pediments of cabinets, etc., especially Queen Anne period; similar to hooded top. [1060.]

DORIC. The primary Greek order of architecture. Heavy arrissed columns with simple details yield a sense of structural value. Roman Doric, lighter and more refined, retains much of Greek simplicity. See also ORDERS.

DOSSER. Prior to the 15th century, a fabric cover or hanging on walls or behind the seats.

DOUBLE CHEST. Two sets of drawers, the lower usually slightly larger than the upper; chest-on-chest; tallboy.

DOVETAIL. Method of joining boards at the ends, as in a drawer or a case, made of interlocking tenons suggesting the form of a dovetail. Also, a butterfly-shaped inset used to join boards lengthwise in table-tops, floors, etc. See CONSTRUCTION. [441, 476, 1169.]

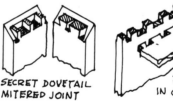

SECRET DOVETAIL MITERED JOINT

DOVETAIL IN CARCASE

BOARDS JOINED BY FLUSH DOVETAIL

DOWEL. Round wooden pin or peg fitted into holes in two adjacent pieces of wood, with glue to hold them together. See also CONSTRUCTION.

DOWER CHEST. The custom of providing a chest for the plenishing of a prospective bride, a hope chest, appears universally in most civilizations. The romantic aspects have inspired fanciful efforts in every style, but in some the production carries special interest. In the Italian work it is not easy to distinguish between the ordinary chest and those planned as dower. In later styles the intention as a bride's chest is plainly deduced from the initials, the inscription, or the forms of ornamentation. Two distinct types are found in America—the Connecticut chest, and the marriage chest of Pennsylvania. [353.]

DOWN. The underplumage of fowl, used in upholstering for the filling of soft cushions.

DRAFT CHAIR. Large English wing-backed chair; wholly wood in Tudor, upholstered in later styles.

DRAGON. Legendary beast used in more or less detail in furniture. Scaly feet and claws, fierce heads, serpentine coils, etc., are motives drawn from the dragon, being generally derived from Oriental art. Free renderings occur in Baroque carvings in Italy, France, and Germany.

DRAKE FOOT. Three-toed foot occurring in 18th-century furniture. [28, 32.]

DRAPERY. In all historic styles the hanging of fabrics has been a prime device in decoration. Originating in utilitarian need, the technique has invariably run away with the object, making drapery an end in itself. The draping of cold stone walls by means of *arras* or tapestries fostered the triumph of European weaving of the 15th, 16th, and 17th centuries. Windows and doorways, thrones, canopies, beds, and chairs likewise inspired weaving and tailoring that too often subordinated the object to the form. Yet the manipulation of rich folds of handsome fabrics does produce effects of luxury not attainable by other means. Like good structural architecture reduced to ornament, this has led to the simulation of the effect of drapery in painting and wallpaper, carving and plasterwork. Witness linenfold paneling; the painting of swags and festoons, and the painting of textile forms and styles as wall decoration.

DRAW RUNNER; DRAW SLIP. Small piece of wood freely inserted into a slot just under a fall front, drop lid, or slant flap, as on a desk or secretary. When the lid is dropped, the draw slip is pulled forward to support it.

DRAW TABLE; Drawer, Drawing, Draw-out, or Draw-top Table. Refectory-type table with a double top, the lower of which is in two sections which pull out at the ends to increase the length of the table. The original base must therefore be quite heavy to balance the extended table. First appears in Italy, France, and England in the sixteenth century; its highest development is in the Jacobean oak refectory tables of the 17th century. [627, 1201, 1209.]

DRESSER. 1. A low chest of drawers, with a mirror over it, for clothing, storage, and dressing (American usage). See also COMMODE.

2. Sideboard or buffet chiefly for the storage and display of eating utensils. European usage derived from *dressoir*.

DRESSING MIRROR. Small mirror on standards, used in connection with table, lowboy, or chest for dressing. Also, CHEVAL GLASS. [874.]

DRESSING TABLE. Almost any form of table may be used as a dressing table when it is equipped with the customary mirror, drawers, etc. The use of types has varied considerably with the mode, eras of greater luxury producing more complex solutions for this function. Dressing tables appeared commonly about the end of the 17th century. The luxury of the period in England and France encouraged their development in many varieties. Men made much of dressing tables in England and France, and for over a century much ingenuity was expended on arrangements of mirrors, lighting, etc. The "Beau Brummels" of England and the *poudreuses* of France are outstanding types. See also BEAU BRUMMEL; POWDER TABLE; TABLE. [515 *et seq.*]

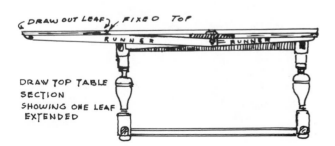

DRAW OUT LEAF   FIXED TOP

RUNNER   RUNNER

DRAW TOP TABLE SECTION SHOWING ONE LEAF EXTENDED

Israel Sack, Inc.

515 AMERICAN DRESSING TABLE, Queen Anne style c. 1750.

516 *Frick Collection*

517 *Dalva Brothers, Inc.*

519 *Symons Galleries, Inc.*

518 *Don Ruseau*

520 *Symons Galleries, Inc.*

516 POUDREUSE, Louis XVI. 517 LOUIS XV MARQUE-
TRY. 518 LOUIS XV PARQUETRY. 519 LATE-18TH-
CENTURY ENGLISH. 520 BEAU BRUMMEL TAMBOUR
CUPBOARD, English c. 1790.

521

Metropolitan Museum of Art, Gift of John L. Cadwalader, 1911

522

521 DRESSING TABLE folds into simple rectangle. Style of Sheraton c. 1780. **522** ENGLISH c. 1780. Style of Sheraton. **523** CONNECTICUT c. 1770. Fitted dressing drawer in serpentine chest. **524** OPEN AND CLOSED DRESSING TABLE, satinwood, English c. 1800.

523

Israel Sack, Inc.

524

Symons Galleries, Inc.

525 MASSACHUSETTS
c. 1800. Bird's-eye maple and mahogany.

526 ENGLISH, Victorian c. 1870.

DRESSING TABLES
19TH CENTURY

527 AFTER EASTLAKE c. 1880.
Japanese influence in panels.

DRESSOIR. Buffet-cupboard-sideboard, usually with open shelves or racks for china. Late Gothic development of credence in France, Flanders, and Germanic countries. The type became chiefly rural in England in the 18th century. Now identified as dresser. [1109.]

DRINKING TABLE. See WINE TABLE. [1239.]

DROP. Pendant ornament, either turned and hanging free, half turned and applied, inlaid, or carved into the surface, as the husk ornament in 18th-century classical work.

DROP FRONT. Desk front or leaf that falls forward for use.

DROP HANDLES. Handles that hang in pendant fashion. See also HARDWARE. [393 *et seq.*]

DROP LEAF. Hinged flap or leaf on a table that when raised enlarges the top. [87, 1212.]

DROPPED SEAT. Concave seat, in which the sides are slightly higher than the middle of the front and back. Also called SCOOP SEAT.

DRUM TABLE; DRUM TOP. Round library or center table with a deep apron, sometimes with drawers. The shape suggests a drum. See RENT TABLE. [606, 1384.]

DRUNKARD'S CHAIR. Deep, rather low armchair; 18th-century England. [528.]

528 DRUNKARD'S CHAIR. English Windsor, mid-18th century. *Stair & Company, Inc.*

DRY SINK. Cabinet with open tray top, usually zinc lined; cupboard below. American, 19th century. See also RUSTIC FURNITURE; WATER BENCH.

DUCHESSE. French chaise longue, or large upholstered chair and stool designed together to form a couch. Hepplewhite's version had two armchairs facing each other, with a stool or ottoman of the same level between.

DUCHESSE BED. French canopy bed with full tester, fixed to the wall instead of to posts, the drapery hanging down to the bedding and floor.

DUCKFOOT. Incorrectly used term for Dutch foot; sometimes a three-toed foot or webfoot.

DUMBWAITER. Generally three or four circular trays graduated in size from the largest at the bottom, revolving about a central shaft; originated in England in the early 18th century; spread to France and Germany. They were generally placed near the hostess' end of the table, and carried additional plates and silver, dessert and cheese and, later, liquor bottles and glasses. An American version for use *upon* the table developed as the "lazy Susan," a revolving tray for condiments, etc. [154, 529, 1255, 1342.]

DUMMY BOARD FIGURES. Boards cut out with the silhouette and painted figure of humans, animals, and objects of furniture. They appear throughout the 17th and 18th centuries in England and the Low Countries. Since no use seems plausibly ascribable to them, it is assumed that they were made and used merely as whimsical decoration.

DUNLAP, SAMUEL, 2nd. New Hampshire joiner, made furniture in the late 18th century; notably deep carved shells. [27.]

DUST BOARD, DUST BOTTOM, DUST PROOFING. Thin wood panel used between drawers to exclude dust and hinder access. See also CONSTRUCTION.

DUTCH COLONIAL. Period of Dutch colonization in North America, 17th century. Long Island, New York, and the Hudson Valley up to Albany were occupied by the Dutch long enough to leave a permanent character in houses and furniture. This is simplified Baroque; massive, stolid, unpretentious. Local woods were used almost exclusively; turning is common, usually deeply cut and with feet often eccentrically turned to produce a rudimentary cabriole foot called Dutch foot, spoon foot, pad foot, or duckfoot. There was

Symons Galleries, Inc.
529 DUMBWAITER, Chippendale c. 1760.

some rude carving, but paint was a more common decorative medium. Distinctive are large cupboards called "Kas," usually painted. [799.]

DUTCH CUPBOARD. Large cabinet or buffet with open shelves above for display of plates, etc. [82.]

DUTCH FOOT. Generally, a club foot. Variations are the angular foot, the elongated foot (forming a point), and the grooved foot.

DUTCH FURNITURE. See NETHERLANDS.

DUTCH INFLUENCE. In English furniture, the influence of the Dutch was so apparent as to give its name to the work of the William and Mary and Queen Anne periods; in fact, to most of the walnut styles between 1690 and 1735. The Dutch settlements in New York and the Hudson Valley established a persistent strain modifying Colonial and Federal work. [269, 364.]

DUTCH SETTLE. 18th- to 19th-century settle with back pivoted to form a table. See also BOX SETTLE.

EARLY GOTHIC—SOLID BOARDS AND SIMPLE PANELING, PRIMITIVE HARDWARE AND CARPENTER ORNAMENT—REPRESENTED TO CHARLES EASTLAKE THE RETURN TO BASIC CRAFTSMANSHIP, LOST TO THE MACHINE. THE WINDSOR CHAIR, PRETTIFIED, SHOWS AN "APPRECIATION OF THE COUNTRY CARTWRIGHT, UNCONTAMINATED. . . ."

530 WINDSOR CHAIR—"country craftsman." *Drawings from* Hints on Household Taste, *1872.*

531 UPHOLSTERED CHAIR, model for much American and English work after 1870.

533 DRAWING-ROOM CHIFFONIER.

534 IRON BEDSTEAD.

535 LIBRARY BOOKCASE.

532 PLANK CONSTRUCTION imitating Gothic prepanel work.

EAGLE. Its use as a decorative motive goes back to farthest antiquity, but its revival from Roman and Byzantine designers in the Renaissance was sparing at first. From heraldry it was adapted to painting and carving; conventionalization brought out the familiar decorative uses. The eagle's head, wings, and claws, in conjunction with mythological forms, became rampant in Baroque and Rococo 18th-century work. Empire style, deriving from Napoleon's imperialistic art, employed the eagle widely in carving, bronzes, painting, and fabrics. [72, 574, 805, 1223.]

EAR. In upholstery, the frame of the wing of a wing chair; also, the ends of the top rail crestings in Chippendale chairs.

EARLY AMERICAN. See AMERICA.

EARLY CHRISTIAN. Byzantine art became permeated with Christian symbolism, and remains of this period show wide use of Church emblems, such as the circle, cross, crown, vine, dove, peacock, and biblical figures. They survive in fabrics, mosaics, carvings in stone and wood, painting and metalwork. [186.]

EARPIECE. Scroll across a cabriole leg.

EASTLAKE, CHARLES LOCK, 1836-1906. In an effort to introduce a more conscious method of design into furniture, Eastlake originated a style of furniture compounded of medieval outlines with ornament freely adapted from the Gothic, the Japanese, and the special abilities of the machine. His book *Hints on Household Taste* was published in many editions after 1868 in England and in the United States. With Ruskin he deplores "speedy fashion changes due to machine facility." He holds "that publick taste is corrupt—fashion rules, and few are shocked by sham and pretension" and that "cheap and easy method of workmanship in an endeavor to produce a show of finish with the least possible labor, as well as an unhealthy spirit of competition in regard to price, has continued to cause the value of our ordinary mechanic's work to deteriorate."

This return to pre-Renaissance inspired William Morris and his coterie. It also inspired the very machine-wrights it deplored to go on to design a

535A AFTER EASTLAKE: AMERICAN ROCKING CHAIR c. 1881. Simple framework ornamented only with machined grooves and spindles.

mock simplicity. It encouraged a new vocabulary of ornament derived from the things a machine tool can do. English work in oak and ash, and American design, mostly in cherry, bear incised lines, chip carving, stuck-on bits of molding and turning, falsely architectural excrescences, and pseudoutilitarian hardware. Further crossbreeding came with a craze for things Japanese, producing the mock-Oriental panel decorations, and insertions of tiles decorated with medieval themes. The philosophy found a ready ear in Germany. As a turning point the logic and exposition of Eastlake must not be underappreciated. See also ENGLAND; MODERN FURNITURE; MORRIS, WILLIAM; NINETEENTH CENTURY. [530.]

EASY CHAIR. Any large chair, so padded or upholstered as to be suitable for lounging. The spring and cushion chair is distinctly an invention of the 19th century, although the essential form may be patterned after chairs of the preceding century. The French bergère is probably the prototype of all our easy chairs, although some variation came by way of the English wing chairs and deep armchair of the 18th century. See also UPHOLSTERY.

ÉBÉNISTE (EBONIST). Ebonyworker; French for "cabinetmaker." The craze for ebony in the early 17th century led master craftsmen, then called *huchiers*, to advertise their ability to work in this difficult wood. The name lingered to denote a cabinetmaker of masterful skill.

EBONIZE. The staining of native hardwood to resemble ebony.

EBONY (Diospyros). Tropical wood of general black color, heavy and dense in texture. Of those in current use, the blackest is the Gaboon ebony; the Macassar has stripes of light brownish orange and black-brown.

ECHINUS. Greek egg-and-dart molding.

ECLECTICISM. In design, the practice of using and adapting at will the forms and motives of any previous period. It permits their modification or combination with other styles as freely as the designer's whim dictates, or it may follow rigidly the complete formula of an earlier style. Thus all modern copying or utilization of period styles is eclectic. Periods of eclecticism seem always to follow great periods of constructive designing. The major effort of the 19th century was eclectic, following the great burst of artistic energy of the 18th century. Yet, in retrospect it appears that, to a degree, even eclecticism takes on an original, constructive, and unique aspect when viewed in the light of interpretation and adaptation to current needs and techniques. The various 18th-century revivals were, in their day, eclectic in their use of ancient forms; yet today they appear as well-integrated, distinctive schools. See also NINETEENTH CENTURY.

EDGING. Thin strip of solid wood at the edge of a veneered panel, to protect the veneering.

EGG-AND-DART (EGG-AND-TONGUE) (EGG-AND-ANCHOR). Carved enrichment of an ovolo molding suggesting alternately eggs and darts. An ancient architectural ornament, it is one of the most frequent in carved woodwork of all lands after the early 16th century. [1031.]

EGYPTIAN. Ancient Egypt left a fairly complete record of its daily life in the contents as well as the decoration of its tombs, thanks to the custom of supplying the dead with mundane articles planned to remind the soul of its former associations. From these we may conclude that Egyptian inventiveness supplied the shapes and models for most articles of furniture in ancient times. Subsequent to 1500 B.C. there

appears a rich catalogue of chests and sarcophagi, tables and stands, stools, chairs and folding seats, ingenious in design, sound in workmanship, and with a superior sense of construction.

Folding seats had X-crossed legs with leather seats. Low stools with rush seats survive, as well as low chairs with stiff backs flowing easily into the seat line. The legs are more or less conventionalized animal feet, bull hooves and lion paws supplying motives. Some beds were piles of quilts on frames; others, folding-chair arrangements, but always with a yoke-shaped arrangement as pillow. Tables were commonly simple four-legged structures, well braced. Decoration was

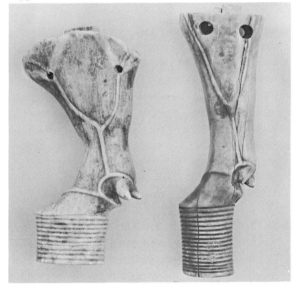

ANCIENT EGYPTIAN FURNITURE: **536** footstool; **537** ivory bull's feet, from couch; **538** folding couch or bed with turned feet. *Metropolitan Museum of Art.*

usually in paint; chairs were often plain white, while chests and sarcophagi were painted in strong colors with bands of geometrical decoration. The motives were largely animal forms; the various lion paws, heads, and other details persisted in all subsequent decoration.

Wood being scarce in Egypt, the character of the wood was often made a feature, and there is evidence of the use of varnishes and natural finishes on sycamore, olive wood, yew, and cedar. Inlaying and veneering were also known, employing for the former pieces of faience, semiprecious stones, ivory, mother-of-pearl, gold, and other metals.

The substance of Egyptian furniture is the basis of most subsequent style. [206, 536, 1071, 1190.]

EGYPTIAN TASTE. A brief attempt was made to naturalize Egyptian forms and decoration around the turn of the 18th century. Napoleon's African campaign in 1798 brought it to France, where it was systematically organized and offered as a style, and the English designers took it over to some degree. As a feature of the Empire style, some details persisted. See also EMPIRE. [793, 988.]

Metropolitan Museum of Art, Bequest of Collis P. Huntington, 1926
539 EGYPTIAN DESIGN: French Empire coin cabinet c. 1810.

ELIZABETHAN. Loosely used, the term denotes the culture of England during the 16th century. The Tudor period is generally limited to the earlier Renais-

sance work, with Gothic elements dominant; the Jacobean includes the period during which the Renaissance spirit was wholly absorbed into English art. At Elizabeth's accession in 1558, the dominant Tudor forms of furniture were based on the perpendicular Gothic architecture; the arts as a whole possessed a homogeneity of spirit and design never after approached. Oak was almost universally used. Outlines were large, straight, and severe, as in the Gothic, with an elaborate use of Italian Renaissance carving. Flemish craftsmen at this time came as refugees and brought French and other versions of the basic Italian Renaissance designs, and with them a host of novelties in the way of fabrics, metal treatment, intarsia, new woods, and uses for furniture, as well as the new decorative details. This process continued until, at Elizabeth's death in 1603, the style had assumed a Continental appearance, but one that was plainly imposed upon older forms. The melon-bulbous leg, the Tudor rose, and decoration by channeling are the most easily identified characteristics. See also ENGLAND. [105, 549, 1201.]

ELLIOTT, JOHN. Philadelphia cabinetmaker known to have made dressing cases and wall mirrors. He died in 1791.

ELM (ulmus). The wood of this family has generally a very light-brown color and a porous, oaklike texture. It appears to have been used for furniture by the Romans, and there are surviving Gothic examples. It appears occasionally in English and a few Continental styles, but principally in provincial work. English chairs of elm, particularly with elm seats, are common survivors of Georgian times. Elms are used extensively today as decorative veneers. The odd figures of the American and English elms, and more particularly the burl of the Carpathian elm, make beautiful veneered surfaces.

EMBLEM. Symbolic and heraldic ornaments passed from their original connotation to a conventionalized, purely decorative, use. Thus, coats of arms, personal insignia and monograms, ciphers and religious symbols are used ornamentally only, with no significance other than the association with the traditional form on which they first appeared.

The use of emblems is particularly characteristic of Elizabethan embroidery.

EMBRASURE. The splay, or reveal, of a window, particularly where deep enough for a piece of furniture, such as a stool.

EMBROIDERY. Decorative needlework; enrichment of fabric by informal design appliquéd or stitched on; one of the oldest arts, it was more or less practiced in every style, both as a trade and as an artistic avocation. See also NEEDLEWORK. [1150.]

EMBROIDERY FRAME. Elaborate, often decorative frame used by dilettantes in the art of embroidery in France, England, and elsewhere, 17th century and after.

EMPIRE. The neoclassic style of architecture and decoration created practically by edict of Napoleon. A committee of artists headed by David in the early years of the 19th century eclectically proposed a complete style based on the imperial forms of ancient Greece, Rome, and Egypt. Architects Percier and Fontaine formulated a full set of designs in 1801. Napoleon's Egyptian campaign force included archaeologists and artists. On their return they added the Egyptian details that so intrigued English Regency designers.

The furniture is rectangular, architecturally massive and excessively sumptuous, rich woods and metal mountings offsetting the rectilinear simplicity. Mahogany, rosewood, and ebony were the rule, with brass or gilt mounts in the forms of swags and festoons, wreaths and laurel branches, torches, mythological figures, and the Napoleonic emblems of the bee, the crown and the letter *N;* later, sphinxes and other Egyptian figures were used. The tripod table and other Pompeiian details are common. Fabrics bore the same ornaments and were executed chiefly in hard textures and strong shades of green, yellow, blue, and red.

The style spread over Europe along with the wave of classical knowledge, and most European and American work is strongly flavored with the Empire essence. It influenced in England men like Sheraton and Thomas Hope; in America, Duncan Phyfe's later work is all in the Empire manner. In Germany it grew into a rusticized version popularly known as Biedermeier. In short, whatever Napoleon's motive in inspiring the step, the fact remains that its spirit suited excellently the rising classicism, and its persistence for more than a generation indicates that it was generally acceptable. [86, 88, 121, 149, 307, 383, 427, 540, 1060, 1270.]

ENAMEL. On wood furniture, a hard glossy finish applied by brushing, then rubbed with pumice stone and oil to a satiny finish. On metal, enamels are baked on.

ENCOIGNURE. Small French corner cabinet. [449.]

Metropolitan Museum of Art, Gift of J. Pierpont Morgan, 1906
540 EMPIRE STYLE, France, 1804-1815. Revolving desk chair, mahogany and ormolu.

EMPIRE

541 FRENCH EMPIRE ORNAMENT, bed foot.
French & Co., Inc.

540A AMERICAN EMPIRE DINING TABLE, New York c. 1830. One of two dropleaf sections with pillar-and-claw pedestal, stenciled decoration.

542 CHILD'S SOFA, New York c. 1825. Scroll arm; mahogany and black horsehair.

543 CENTER TABLE, New York, 1825-1830. Rosewood graining, gilt inlay, stencil and freehand decoration.

EMPIRE

END TABLE. General current term for any small table used in relation to a couch, chair, etc. Small tables of all periods and original purposes are used now as end tables.

ENDIVE. Carved decorative motif, a variation on several acanthus leaves combined. Originally favored in work of the Louis XIV period, it was extensively used by Chippendale.

ENGLAND. The period distinctions of English furniture are somewhat indefinite owing to the variety of labels according to monarchs, designers, typical woods, external influences, etc. Political and economic changes were so rapid after the 16th century that styles are known by their influencing sources as well as by their mature characteristics. More than any other detail, the use of specific woods establishes boundaries of English styles, and a most convenient classification is Macquoid's separation of the ages of Oak, Walnut, Mahogany, and Satinwood.

AGE OF OAK, most typically native, includes all the Gothic development from French sources after the Norman Conquest, through the reigns of the Tudors and the Stuarts. Thus furniture up to 1660 is reasonably consecutive in style; the basic Gothic forms persist, with a growing use of Renaissance details. British sailors and traders, encouraged by Henry VIII and Elizabeth to expand England's sphere of influence,

Philadelphia Museum of Art
545 LIVERY CUPBOARD, English, 15th century.

Philadelphia Museum of Art
544 READING DESK, English Gothic, 14th century. Primitive plank construction.

MAHOGANY, an imported wood, symbolizes the growth of wealth and world power under an imported dynasty, the German Georges of the house of Hanover. The distinctions of the Georgian styles are purely chronological; the real classifications follow the names of the great architects, cabinetmakers, designers, and artists. Their printed works and executed furniture tell us of the Anglicized interpretations of the Dutch Baroque, the French Rococo, the revived classicism of the dilettante archaeologists, the waves of chinoiserie. Chippendale, the Brothers Adam, Hepplewhite, and Sheraton are only a few of the many great talents that made 18th-century furniture synonymous with great design.

AGE OF SATINWOOD is least distinct, chronologically or as a school of furniture style. It represents the flowering of luxury and refinement; exotic, overdelicate, and self-consciously sophisticated, it is more truly the transition from the great age to the debased eclecticism of the 19th century. It foreshadows all the groping of the Regency and Victorian periods.

MEDIEVAL AND GOTHIC

Medieval furniture in England, as elsewhere, was crude and sparse, typical of the dormant state of the arts everywhere.

The Gothic Age established a fairly universal system of furniture, solid and angular in outline, architectural in form and ornament. The development of furniture is marked principally by the passage from the hands of the carpenter to the specialized joiner or cofferer. The former employed solid boards; the latter made framed panels. The coffer and its descendants—ambries, hutches, cupboards [684], and sideboards represented most of the furniture; there were thronelike chairs, forms, joint stools, benches, and trestle tables, and little else. A small amount of beech and elm was used, besides the ubiquitous oak, whose hardness set limits on the style of carving. Gothic structural elements, like arches, tracery, bosses, and deep moldings, were favored carved motives, as were linenfold panels and zigzags. The wood was either painted in colors or left raw. Wrought-iron locks and keys, hinges and straps were conspicuous.

went everywhere, bringing home ideas and riches. Under the less sure hand of the Stuart kings, there were confusion and revolt. James I and Charles I, Cromwell and the Puritan Commonwealth, Charles II and James II are lumped as Jacobean or Stuart or distinguished as Early Jacobean, Cromwellian or Commonwealth, Restoration, Carolean, Late Jacobean. The latter, a transitional period, saw the rise to dominance of foreign forms.

AGE OF WALNUT is one of foreign rulers as well as of foreign furniture styles, but it utilizes a domestic wood. Dutch Baroque came with William and Mary and flowered during Queen Anne's reign.

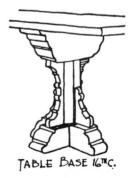

TUDOR GOTHIC (1520)

TABLE BASE 16TH C.

546 CHEST, 16th century. Panel construction, Renaissance detail. *Charles of London*

548 COURT CUPBOARD, dated 1659. *Stair & Company, Inc.*

TUDOR-ELIZABETHAN

The reign of the Tudors, 1485-1603, covers the last phase of the Gothic style and the beginning of the Renaissance [549]. In the reign of Henry VIII the secular power displaced that of the Church, and domestic furniture began a robust development. Italian influences came with Italian architects; but only in details of ornamentation did furniture styles deviate from the established Gothic. Romayne work, scrolls and dolphins were added to the Tudor roses, palmetted bands and zigzags of the carvers' vocabulary. Intricate carving encouraged some use of walnut, more easily worked. Under Elizabeth this Renaissance-Gothic combination attained its height, distinct from any Continental styles. Massive and large-scaled, the structural principles are simple and effective; joints are at right angles, well braced. The huge bulbous-melon turning appears on all upright members; stretchers are square and low. Paneled chairs, draw-top tables, court cupboards, colossal beds with heavy wooden canopies are prodigally ornamented with grotesques, caryatids, foliated scrolls, strapwork, gadrooning, inlaying, and other Italian exuberances. Inigo Jones brought Italian architecture; Italian workmen followed. Religious freedom and commercial advantages attracted French, Flemish, German, and Dutch craftsmen, but their output appears strangely homogeneous.

INTRODUCTION OF FOREIGN DETAIL.

EARLY JACOBEAN

Under James I and Charles I, 1603-1649, the Renaissance continued to submerge the Gothic styles. The straightforward structure and simple outlines persist, but furniture grows smaller, lighter, less ornamented. Flatter carving used the Renaissance motives, including Ionic capitals, weak acanthus leaves, the guilloche and intertwined circles, palmettes, etc. The melon-bulb turning is conspicuously lighter. The gateleg table appeared, and upholstery improved some chairs. The Italian X-chair, footstools, highly carved mirror frames, and turned chairs were common.

547 TABLE, mid-17th century. *Stair & Company, Inc.*

549 BED, Late Elizabethan.   *Metropolitan Museum of Art, Gift of Irwin Untermyer, 1953*

551

Charles of London
Anderson Galleries

552

551 ENGLISH c. 1550. Wall cupboard with seat and arms attached. **552** ENGLISH, Cromwellian c. 1660. Lid, drawers, and doors. Oak, mother-of-pearl inlay; Italian influence. **553** *Left.* WAINSCOT CHAIR, Cromwellian. **554** *Right.* JOINT STOOL, Jacobean c. 1625.

553 – 554

Anderson Galleries

550 SETTLE c. 1680. Rope seat frame with loose cushion.   *Arthur S. Vernay, Inc.*

Charles of London

555 Early-17th-century ENGLISH OAK TABLE with fine melon bulb turning with acanthus carving, gadrooning, and Ionic caps.

Charles of London

557 *Above.* ENGLISH OAK GATELEG c. 1620.

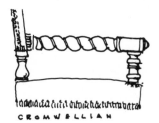

CROMWELLIAN

558 TRESTLE-FOOT GATELEG c. 1660.   *Stair & Company, Inc.*

Charles of London

556 LATE JACOBEAN CABINET. Strong influence of France and Italy appears in the strong geometric panel shapes and the arched perspective.

CROMWELLIAN OR COMMONWEALTH

The Civil War, 1642-1660, a Puritan revolt, substituted austere undecorated furniture for the ornate luxuries favored by the Cavaliers. Simplified turnings followed spool or sausage profiles. Ball- or bun-turned feet came from the Dutch. Carving, inlays, moldings were simplified. Padding appears on the backs as well as on the seats of chairs, and leather decorated in the Spanish manner is used.

560

559 STATE CHAIR with royal cipher of James II. Restoration style c. 1685-1689. **560 SPIRAL-TURNED WALNUT CHAIR,** English or Flemish. Period of Charles II. **561 CHEST-ON-STAND** c. 1685. Walnut base with Spanish foot. **562 WILLIAM AND MARY SCROLL-LEG TABLE.** Walnut burl c. 1690.

559   *Metropolitan Museum of Art, Kennedy Fund, 1918*

561

RESTORATION

Charles II returned in 1660 and ruled until 1685. From his refuge in Flanders he returned with Continental elegances and ideas of luxury, and a train of French, Flemish, and Italian craftsmen who preferred to work in walnut. The court of Louis XIV shed some of its brilliance on the revived English court, and the rising Baroque lushness appeared. Restoration lines are everywhere lines of movement, instead of the static squareness of Early Jacobean work.

Distinctive are spiral turnings, double-curved legs, scrolled feet, large free curves, the Flemish scroll, deep carving with the oft-repeated crown motive, caning and upholstering with fine silks, velvets, brocades, embroideries, stamped leather. Veneering is a new feature, displaying large surfaces of selected grain with inlaid floral patterns—marquetry. Oystering —veneering with cross sections of small branches—was a unique development. Lacquer and painted decoration after Indian and Chinese examples, known since Elizabeth, became a rage: Oriental themes and details were colorfully executed in inlay, paint, and carving. Gesso, silvered or gilded in the Italian manner, also provided brilliant, showy surfaces. Even solid-silver furniture was made for the court.

The demand for luxury created new species of furniture. Rest beds or daybeds, bureaus or desks, sofas, drawer-chests, wing chairs, mirrors, small tables and stands, and great draped beds were accepted by the upper classes as required by the French standard of

562

splendid living. The huge bed, hung with fabrics of absurd costliness and grandeur, reached its zenith during this period. Grinling Gibbons's style of carving set the precedent for most decorative treatment during the ensuing half century.

LATE JACOBEAN

Late Jacobean, often used to limit this period, is named for James II. His three-year reign ended with the Bloodless Revolution of 1688. The entire period, more properly called "Carolean," after Charles II, is typically transitional; oak gave way to walnut, the innate structural simplicity to excesses of Baroque technique, native directness to foreign brilliance.

565

Anderson Galleries

WILLIAM AND MARY

The full-blown Baroque style was brought from Holland in 1688. Continuing the tradition of importation, the French architect Marot brought the rich style of Louis XIV; Christopher Wren worked in a chaste Italian manner; Dutch and English traders continued their Oriental importing; religious tolerance attracted weavers, painters, carvers, joiners. New types and processes produced a revolution in furnishing, and the swing away from excessive grandeur to a simpler domesticity changed the scale and style. Smaller, more intimate rooms had lighter chairs, tables, chests. Chairs were comfortably padded and covered with needlework; legs were mostly turned and braced with serpentine stretchers. The Dutch club foot and the scroll leg inspired the rudimentary cabriole leg; but trumpet, bell, cup, and bun turnings are more typical.

Surface treatment became vital in this epoch, partly due to the need of protecting the delicate veneers, partly to the love of fine finish. High polishes emphasized the carefully matched veneers. Lacquer and japanning still rose in popularity. Seaweed marquetry suggests the minute intricacies of French Boulle work. Walnut is predominant, but many other woods appear as veneers and for contrast in inlays.

563

Anderson Galleries

564

Metropolitan Museum of Art, Bequest of Annie C. Kane, 1926

563 CLOCK, Charles II, London, 1680. **564** MARQUETRY CABINET, late 17th century.
565 MARQUETRY CHEST-ON-CHEST. Early bracket base.

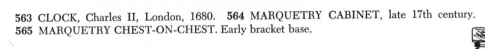

Metropolitan Museum of Art, Rogers Fund, 1910

566 WALNUT AND INLAY.

END OF THE AGE OF WALNUT SHOWS
TRANSITION TO DOMESTIC SCALE.
MASTERY OF CABRIOLE FORM
FORESHADOWS GEORGIAN.

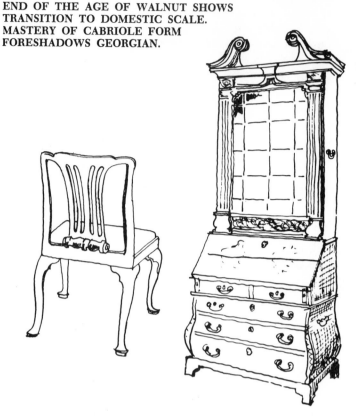

570 SECRETARY, 1705-1710. Walnut, glazing of later date.
Arthur S. Vernay, Inc.

QUEEN ANNE

The reign of Anne, 1702-1714, carries on the Dutch inspiration, developing the elements of comfort, grace, elegance. There is little positive differentiation in the work of the years 1690-1720, but the tendency is toward a more English interpretation of the flowing Baroque outlines. Sleek and sophisticated, there is generally a unity of curved lines in Queen Anne furniture, as well as a restraint of ornament and a better technical understanding of design. The cabriole leg is the outstanding detail, and its skillful association with other curves, as of seat outlines and back members of chairs, produces superb, distinctive designs. Improved technique made stretchers unnecessary after 1710, and pierced back splats became more decorative. Marquetry was subordinated to fine walnut surfaces. Carved motives were the scallop shell, broken and C-curves, and acanthus leaves. New habits introduced new furniture; tea drinking called for hosts of small tables. A craze for collecting china produced the china cabinet. Secretaries, bookcases, fire screens, mirrors, tallboys, love seats, etc., were moderate in size, beautifully proportioned, and ornamented with restraint and charm.

Metropolitan Museum of Art
568 SMALL CHEST c. 1710. Type now called "bachelor's chest."

Arthur S. Vernay, Inc.
567 CHEST-ON-STAND, walnut and burr elm. Unusual foot typical of wide experimentation with cabriole form.

569 WING CHAIR, 1710-1714. Carved walnut, cabriole legs with stretchers.

Arthur S. Vernay, Inc.

GEORGIAN

The furniture produced in the earlier part of George I's reign shows an orderly progression of the Queen Anne style, but two rising factors could not long be withstood: first, the coming of mahogany, and, second, the trend toward magnificence bred by the new prosperity. Until about 1725 walnut was undisputed. More ornate features began to elaborate suave lines. Cabriole legs ended in animal details, such as ball-and-claw or hoof feet. Lion masks, foliated scrolls, complex rock-and-shell ornaments, satyr and other mythological forms were symptoms of the Rococo offshoot of the Baroque style.

The architecture of the great houses after 1725 was classic Italian in the Baroque manner, and the architects did not hesitate to design furniture in the same manner. Thus the classification of "architects' furniture"—pompous, florid, magnificent, denying the simple elegance of the earlier work. Full-bodied architectural pediments, columns, and statuary distinguish the work of Kent, Langley, Vanbrugh, Ware. Gilding was favored, while lacquerwork declined. Bracket and pedestal bases and applied architectural details are typical.

Mahogany had been in some use before this time, but removal of import taxes in 1733 let it compete with walnut. As it excelled walnut in strength, ease of carving, and resistance to decay, its popularity virtually drove walnut out of use.

Most significant about Early Georgian furniture is its completely English quality. The foreign elements, flowing into England for more than a century, had become completely fused into a distinct national style. By 1730, the furniture was English, more so than the Dutch and German rulers. Style and nomenclature no longer followed the monarchs.

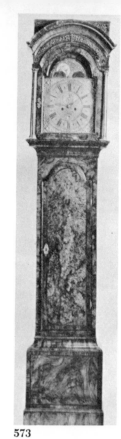

571   *Arthur S. Vernay, Inc.*

573

572

Metropolitan Museum of Art, Gift of Louis J. Boury, 1937

REACTION AGAINST BAROQUE TOWARD RESTRAINT AND GOOD PROPORTION, REFINEMENT OF SCALE AND DETAIL; GRADUAL SUPPLANTING OF WALNUT BY MAHOGANY.

571 GEORGE I ARMCHAIR c. 1725. Walnut with burl veneers. **572 CHAIR** c. 1730. Label of "Grendey." Chinoiserie lacquer. Late date for such stretcher and undeveloped cabriole. **573 WALNUT CLOCK** c. 1730. By William Lambert. **574 CARVED PINE CONSOLE** c. 1730. Naturalistic carving of eagle and dolphins recalls Baroque.

574   *Stair and Company, Inc.*

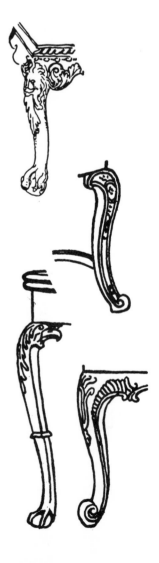

575 MIRROR c. 1715. *Frank Partridge, Inc.*

577 MAHOGANY DESK c. 1745. Revived Palladian influence through architects like William Kent is suggested in composition and detail; carving recalls Grinling Gibbons. Tastefully restrained composition foreshadows quality of developing 18th-century style.

Ginsburg and Levy

576 CABINET, George II. Cream chinoiserie lacquer on gilded stand. Interior gold-powdered scarlet lacquer. *French & Co., Inc.*

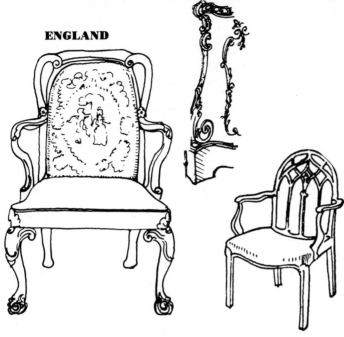

CHIPPENDALE

The name of Thomas Chippendale has become a convenient tag for the entire style of the Middle Georgian period. The reason for this widespread influence lies in his publication in 1754 of *The Gentleman and Cabinet-Maker's Director*. Far from being the first book of this type, it had prototypes in works by the Langleys, Swan, Lock, Jones, Copeland, Johnson, the Halfpennys, etc.; but the *Director* alone was confined to furniture. It illustrated practically every type known, showing the average Early Georgian basis with variations after the more fleeting whims: French, Rococo, Gothic, Chinese. The book was so enthusiastically received everywhere that its patterns became the current style of English furniture.

Of furniture in the style of the *Director*, Chippendale himself produced a minimum. Some of the designs are technically poor, while Chippendale's known work is invariably of superb craftsmanship as well as design. Furthermore, much of his work appears to have been done in collaboration with Robert Adam, whose classicism made the *Director* designs appear old-fashioned.

Chippendale's genius is most evident in the manner in which he amalgamates the various details of Rococo, Gothic, Chinese, and other styles without sacrificing the unity of the design. With all the intricacy of rock-and-shell, fretwork or ribbons, there is always a strong outline and a dominating wood-structural sense that permits great vitality even to renditions or copies by lesser men. Consequently, there are vigorous schools of Chippendale in America (see PHILADELPHIA CHIPPENDALE); Scotland, where most literal copies were made; and Ireland, where the style was so liberally modified as to be recognizable as a distinct manner. (See IRISH CHIPPENDALE.)

The Rococo taste came from France as the style of Louis XV, was greatly restrained in English work, but attained special splendor in gilt mirrors and commodes. The eclecticism of the period also led to an abortive Gothic revival. Interest in chinoiserie and Oriental themes came in periodic waves. All these details, surprisingly welded together, found their way into mahogany.

THE BROTHERS ADAM are notable for their preoccupation with the refined classicism of Pompeii, to the exclusion of the Baroque-Rococo influence that had prevailed. They stopped at no detail as unworthy of their designing, so that furniture and all other interior fittings came under their sway. Classic symmetry was a revolutionary substitute for the naturalism of the older style; this, more than any other characteristic, typifies the influence of the "antique." Scale became fine, sometimes painfully, unstructurally, so. The square line framed everything. Ornaments comprised swags and ribbons, fluting and paterae, rams' heads, sphinxes, griffins, chimeras, Greek key and honeysuckle and Vitruvian scrolls. Painting was used for whole surfaces as well as for ornaments. Marble and scagliola, metal mounts and gilding, all contributed to the effect of rich elegance and refinement.

SATINWOOD appears about 1760, and is coincidental with the refining influence inaugurated by the Adams.

HEPPLEWHITE is credited with modifying the classic influences into furniture of great charm and elegance. Cold angularity was softened into subtle curves. Chairs are his best designs, but there are excellent chests and commodes, sideboards, desks with cylinder tops, tall secretaries, sofas and settees, etc.

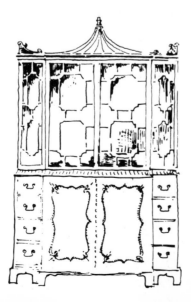

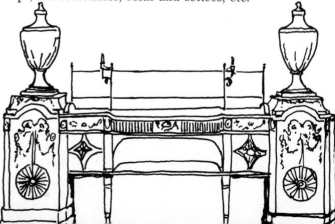

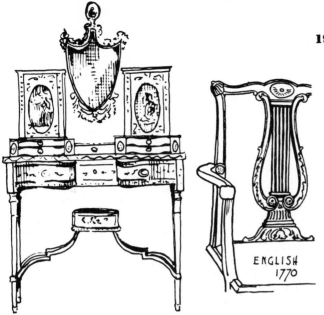

ENGLISH
1770

HEPPLEWHITE

The Rococo influence shows in Hepplewhite's earlier work, but his major work is in straight lines. Tapered legs end in spade feet. Chairbacks were in five shapes: oval, wheel, heart, shield, camel, always filled with pierced splats in delicate designs, sometimes lightly carved. Typical motifs are the three-feathered crest of the Prince of Wales, wheat, ribbons, fine swags, paterae, etc. Hepplewhite employed decorative painting extensively, and sponsored the use of satinwood and fine inlaying.

In 1788, two years after Hepplewhite's death, his widow published his book *The Cabinet Maker and Upholsterer's Guide*, which had much the same effect on his reputation as the *Director* had had on Chippendale's—that is, the whole style is sometimes ascribed to him.

SHEARER collaborated with Hepplewhite and is credited with the familiar sideboard design. His drawings appear in *Designs for Household Furniture* (1788).

SHERATON is known as a designer and publisher of several books on furniture more than as a working cabinetmaker. His book *The Cabinet Maker and Upholsterer's Drawing Book* (1791-1793) purports to show the "present taste in furniture"—probably indicating that many of the designs were not his own. However, the designs shown are so good and so well thought out as to the details of construction that, like Chippendale forty years before, Sheraton served as master to the whole cabinetmaking industry, and his drawings epitomize the contemporary style.

The earlier designs follow generally the same classic antique forms as the Louis XVI style. Rectangular forms are nevertheless graceful; segmental curves are preferred to Hepplewhite's serpentines; many flat areas afford surfaces for inlay and, later, porcelain plaques. Sheraton liked complicated mechanical arrangements—folding tables and disappearing drawers and secret compartments, all ingeniously devised and workably delineated. He covered the entire field of furniture then known, and in tremendous variety.

The French Revolution and the chaotic sequence of styles that followed were too much for Sheraton, as for everyone else. After some brilliant work on Directoire models, the Early Empire style confused him, and his designs appear weak, overornamental, debased. He died in 1806.

It must be remembered that Chippendale, Hepplewhite, and Sheraton, outstanding though they were, held no monopoly sufficient to name the period for them. They were the great lights of a vigorous style, but there were lesser lights and there were cabinetmakers with the craft and grace to execute the designs offered. The production of books on furniture was a thriving industry; and part of every gentleman's education was in architecture, the classics, and design. Among the contributors must be listed Chambers, Manwaring, Ince and Mayhew, Lock and Copeland, and innumerable others.

The tremendous furniture output of the mahogany period can be largely lumped into two types: the Baroque-Rococo, through 1755, and the Classic Revival, after that time. The former, known by fuller proportions, solidity, robust ornamentation, is exemplified in Chippendale's earlier work. The classic work is piously symmetrical, fine-scaled, graceful to a fault, with a tendency toward the finicky. After that, the Age of Stainwood lays the ground for the decline. In the quest for lightness, structure is lost; fine scale becomes mere thinness, novelty leads to the bizarre and eccentric. This is the trend of early-19th-century furniture, the post-Sheraton period as laid down by Sheraton.

RENT TABLE Ca. 1765

"RIBBAND" BACK

578 BREAKFRONT BOOKCASE with secretary drawer c. 1760. Free use of varied ornamental detail well composed.   *Stair & Company, Inc.*

579 CHINESE.   *Arthur S. Vernay, Inc.*   **580**   *Arthur S. Vernay, Inc.*   **581 GOTHIC.**

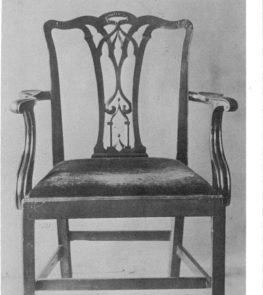

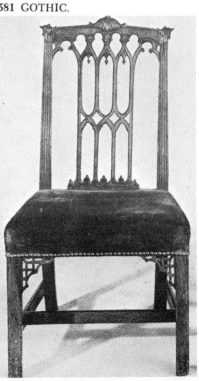

THE CHIPPENDALE STYLE

COVERS A LARGE FIELD OF FURNITURE DESIGNS INSPIRED BY THE PUBLICATION IN 1754 OF *THE GENTLEMAN AND CABINET-MAKER'S DIRECTOR.* VERY LITTLE ACTUAL WORK IS ATTRIBUTABLE TO CHIPPENDALE HIMSELF, BUT HIS PRINTED SUMMARY OF CURRENT STYLE BECAME THE MOST INFLUENTIAL BOOK ON FURNITURE PUBLISHED IN ENGLISH.

Needham's Antiques, Inc.

582 CARVED, GILDED ROCOCO MIRROR c. 1765.

583 CARD TABLE, 1760-1765.   *Metropolitan Museum of Art, Rogers Fund, 1924*

584 CHAIR "IN THE FRENCH TASTE."   *Needham's Antiques, Inc.*

585 FRETWORK URN TABLE.

586 SOFA c. 1765.   *Arthur S. Vernay, Inc.*

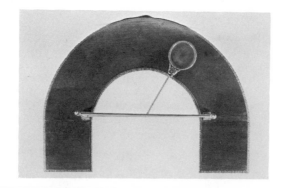

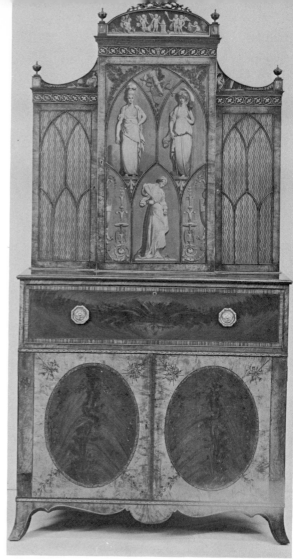

Arthur S. Vernay, Inc.

587 ADAM DESIGN WINE TABLE (plan view above shows drop leaves).

Anderson Galleries

588 SECRETARY BOOKCASE c. 1785. Mahogany and satinwood with typical painted panels. From the collection of Lord Leverhulme.

589 ADAM DESIGN CARVED WOOD SOFA c. 1795.

Symons Galleries, Inc.

SHOWED HEIGHT OF CLASSICISM IN ADAM AND SHERATON IN-
FLUENCES, INCREASINGLY FINE-SCALED ORNAMENT, SATIN-
WOOD, AND DECORATED PAINT SURFACES.

590-591   *Arthur S. Vernay, Inc.*

590-591 DRUM TABLE, HEPPLEWHITE CHAIR with
Prince of Wales feather carving. 592 DRESSING TABLE c.
1795 by Seddon, Sons and Shackleton. 593 HEPPLEWHITE
CABINET c. 1780. 594 SHERATON ARMCHAIR, 1780-
1790.

CLASSIC
TORCHÈRE

Metropolitan Museum of Art, Rogers Fund, 1919   592

ADAM
PEDESTAL

594   *Arthur S. Vernay, Inc.*

Symons Galleries, Inc.   593

ADAM
SIDEBOARD   ADAM ARMCHAIR

595 MIRROR c. 1810, gilded carving. *Symons Galleries, Inc.*

596 SHERATON COMMODE, 1780-1790. Satinwood, tulip-wood banding.

Arthur S. Vernay, Inc.

597 CHINA CABINET c. 1810. Rosewood with metal inlays and fittings.

Symons Galleries, Inc.

598 PAINTED SYCAMORE DAYBED c. 1800.

Metropolitan Museum of Art, Fletcher Fund, 1929

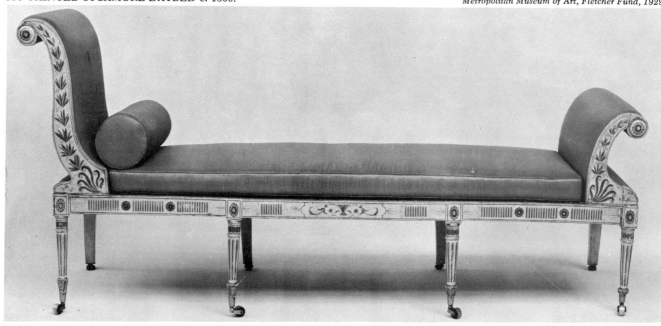

English Furniture at the End of the 18th Century

FAVORED SIMPLEST SURFACES AND GEOMETRIC LINES, DELICATE PROPORTION AND REFINED DETAIL IN PAINT AND INLAY, AND SELECT WOOD GRAINS.

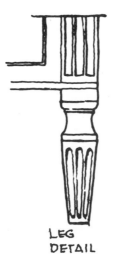

LEG DETAIL

Arthur S. Vernay, Inc.
599 SHERATON CHAIR c. 1790.

Metropolitan Museum of Art,
Gift of Alexander Smith Cochran, 1911
600 INLAID SATINWOOD COMMODE, 1780-1790.

601 MIRROR, gilded.

602 DRESSING TABLE, harewood with painted decorations.

SPADE FOOT

603 CHEST c. 1780. Hepplewhite style, yellow lacquer with Chinese decoration.

604 DESK WITH OVAL PEDESTALS; sycamore, painted decorations in classical style of Pergolesi.

Wood and Hogan

605 DRESSING TABLE c. 1840.

606 DRUM TABLE, 1825-1840.   *Symons Galleries, Inc.*

608 SIDEBOARD c. 1830. Heavier Sheraton
detail in inlay and reeding.

English Pre-Victorian

DURING THE REGENCY PERIOD A CERTAIN STOLIDITY DEVELOPED FROM THE LATE SHERATON, AS TYPICAL OF ONE LEVEL AS THE OVERSTYLIZED CLASSICISM USUALLY CALLED REGENCY WAS OF THE COURT LEVEL.

St. James Gallery

607 MAHOGANY FALL-FRONT BUREAU c. 1810.
French Directoire style, but detail and
workmanship are unmistakably English.

609 REGENCY BOOKCASE c. 1810. Marble
top, brass moldings on rosewood.

Symons Galleries, Inc.

ENGLISH REGENCY

The name is applied roughly to the period 1800-1837, although these dates do not exactly cover the period during which George, Prince of Wales, acted as Regent. The declining influence of Robert Adam gave way to an intensely literal archaeological spirit. Roman types were reproduced wherever possible after the French Directoire and Empire models, or from the ancient sources. For such articles as ancient Rome provided no precedent, an assortment of Roman ornaments was combined or adapted. Bookcases like temple façades, couches after Roman beds, sideboards as bits of architecture were all so literally architectural that both scale and comfort were often lost, the artist's sense of rightness being sacrificed to the archaeologist's enthusiasm. The Adams' typical compo ornaments and painting were discarded for metal inlays and applications; the ornamental features were directly Roman and Egyptian, bronzed or gilded, comparatively sparse, and accepting large surfaces of unembellished wood.

Thomas Hope and Sir John Soane were the foremost exponents of this English version of the French Empire style, but the taste was general enough to leave us drawings and work by Sheraton, Thomas Chippendale, John Nash, George Smith, and others, many illustrated in *Ackermann's Repository of the Arts.* The earlier phases of the style are solid and scholarly in an extension of the great 18th-century classicism. Its orderly development collided with the expansive pressures of the Industrial Revolution. Burgeoning wealth created vast new markets, and in striving for originality and variety, designers and furniture makers verged on the grotesque.

Queen Victoria gave her name to a style covering two-thirds of a century, incorporating new techniques and materials into a hodgepodge of eclecticism, reform and counterreform. (See also NINETEENTH CENTURY; VICTORIAN.)

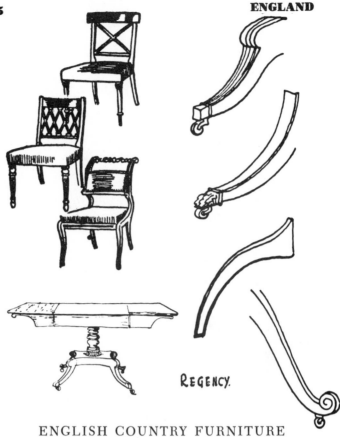

REGENCY.

ENGLISH COUNTRY FURNITURE

Foreign influences usually came in through the court and the aristocracy in the capital, and slowly seeped down through the country aristocracy to the middle classes (where such existed) or the artisans and tradespeople. In England this saturation process was slow. The lower classes were wedded to the simple forms, and the provincial gentry were conservative. Thus, oak furniture prevailed throughout the Walnut Age, and many characteristics of Good Queen Bess's time lived on in furniture of the following century. Stronger individuality and deficiencies in technique gave novelty to the styles when they did come. The dates of much unascribable furniture are therefore in doubt. Sideboards of essentially country type

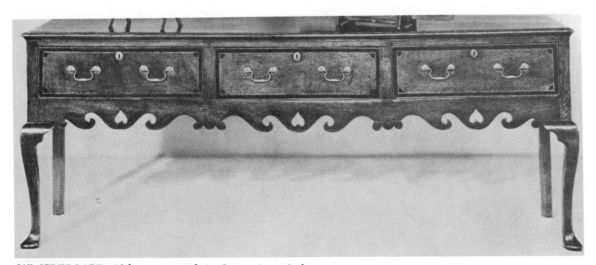

615 SIDEBOARD, 18th century, oak in Queen Anne Style.

**ENGLISH
COUNTRY
FURNITURE**

614 TRESTLE-FOOT GATELEG c. 1680.

Stair and Company

Needham's Antiques, Inc.
610 SIMPLE WINDSOR.

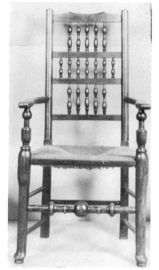

Stair and Company, Inc.
611 RUSH SEAT. Turner's work.

Arthur S. Vernay, Inc.
612 COUNTRY CHIPPENDALE.

use oak for details of walnut style; retaining some Jacobean details, some Queen Anne, they may date from the late 18th century.

The Windsor chair is a unique country development. Chairs, stools, and tables with turned members, and many other articles of utility furniture reveal an innate respect for wood and pride of craftsmanship. [314, 315, 1347.]

ENGRAVING. Method of cutting designs into metal, glass, etc. In some marquetry, fine lines are engraved into the veneers, then filled with a composition to make them contrast with the background.

ENTABLATURE. The horizontal section borne by a column. Each order of architecture has its distinctive entablature made up of architrave, frieze, and cornice. See also ORDERS.

613 WINDSOR, elm.   *Needham's Antiques, Inc.*

ENTASIS. Slight swelling of a column at the middle designed to overcome the optical illusion of hollowness that appears in a perfectly straight column. See also ORDERS.

ESCALLOP SHELL. Cockleshell. See also SHELL MOTIF.

Museum of Art, Rhode Island School of Design, Providence

616 ESCRITOIRE, English, 1850-1860. Papier-mâché.

ESCRITOIRE (SCRUTOIRE, SECRETARY). Writing desk with drawers, pigeonholes, etc. [495, 616.]

ESCUTCHEON. Armorial term for a shield-shaped surface bearing coat-of-arms, monogram, etc. In furniture, fitting over a keyhole or the back plate of a handle. They are usually of metal, but are sometimes ivory, bone, inlaid veneers, etc. See also CARTOUCHE; HARDWARE.

ESPAGNOLETTE. Female busts used as terminal ornaments on posts of cabinets, etc., usually arranged on the upper curves of volutes. Frequent in styles of Louis XIV, the Régence, and Louis XV.

ÉTAGÈRE. Whatnot; a series of shelves supported by columns, used chiefly for the display of curios. Commonest in the 19th century, although graceful examples in exotic woods survive from the time of Louis XVI. [617, 618, 1341.]

EVOLUTE. Recurrent wave scroll used to decorate friezes and bands.

617 ÉTAGÈRE, English, Mid-Victorian.

ESPAGNOLETTE

618 FRENCH ÉTAGÈRE c. 1790. Style of Louis XVI. Acajou, brass gallery.

EVOLUTE (WAVE) SCROLL

FABRICS. See TEXTILES.

FAÇADE. Front, using the word in the architectural sense. The faces of chests, etc., were often treated to resemble architectural façades, particularly in the classic revivals. [151, 175.]

FACING. An economical, technically incorrect method of veneering by covering a thick common wood with a thin layer of better or more decorative wood on one face only.

FAKES AND FAKING. The fine art of counterfeiting antiques flowered with the recent craze for them. The problem would be a simple one if there were some criteria of the genuineness of antiques, but unfortunately the trade is permeated with practices varying from the faintly unethical to the completely fraudulent. The technique of faking has a partly legitimate parentage in the art of restoration. New parts are used to replace old or missing ones in old pieces and are then treated to present the same superficial aspect as the old parts. This is legitimate enough, but the seller must state that parts are replaced or restored. A good craftsman who knows the methods of restoration could take an entirely new piece of furniture and make it look antique. Honor alone can deter him from this fraud and compel him to start, at least, with a truly old original piece.

Some of the tricks are admirable in their ingenuity: fine birdshot makes wormholes; a heavy chain wears off edges; acids and rusty nails stain wood; and burying a board in a barnyard for three months ages it a century. See also ANTIQUES; COPY; REPRODUCTION; RESTORATION.

FALDSTOOL. Portable folding seat, like a camp stool. In religious use, a litany desk. [216.]

FALL FRONT. Drop lid or drop front, as in a cabinet-desk or piano. Sometimes "slant front." [74, 496.]

FALL-LEAF TABLE. Drop leaf or flap table. [87.]

FAN INLAY
FEDERAL
AMERICAN

FAN. Radiating design suggesting a fan, used in chairbacks (18th-century English), a fan-shaped filling, upright or reversed. Windsor chairs with flaring spindles and curved top rails are called "fanbacks." The fan motif is used in inlaid and painted decoration on 18th-century furniture.

FANLIGHT. Elliptical or half-round window over a window or over a door, with radiating design of muntins or leading.

FANCY CHAIRS. Early-19th-century American chairs designed or decorated in imitation of imported models. These often have a charming and revealing style, such as the Sheraton-inspired work of Hitchcock. [78, 324 *et seq.*]

FANCY FURNITURE. Tables, chairs, etc., usually small, intended more for ornamental purposes than for utility.

FARTHINGALE CHAIR. English chair, period of Elizabeth and James I. It was without arms in order to permit the then fashionable wide dresses, called "farthingales," to spread in all directions.

FASCES. Roman decorative motif depicting a bundle of rods with a projecting ax. Recurs in most classical revivals, such as Louis XIV and the Empire.

FASCIA. A broad flat molding; a facing band.

FAUN. Mythological demigod, half man, half goat, used instead of a caryatid. Italian and French Renaissance; Adam.

FAUTEUIL. French upholstered armchair. The sides are open, while the sides of the bergère are upholstered solidly.

FAUX-SATINE (False Satinwood). Cypress crotch, which yields very beautiful veneers similar in color and texture to satinwood crotch.

FAVAS. Honeycomb-like detail characteristic of Louis XVI decoration.

FEATHER BANDING. Herringbone inlay.

FEATHER EDGE. Edge of a board thinned off, as in paneling.

FAN DESIGN·ADAM COMMODE

"FANCY" CHAIR
AMERICAN 19TH CENT

FEATHERED. Certain grains, particularly of mahogany and satinwood, are referred to as feathered when they are cut to show a plumelike figure.

FEATHERS. Feathers, plumes, and bird wings are used as ornamental details in Egyptian work, in the period of Louis XIV, Hepplewhite, and in subsequent styles.

FEDERAL. American period, coincidental with the early years of the Republic, 1780-1830. Beginning marked by the Revolution or end of the Colonial period; it declined by the deterioration in taste after the early stages of the Empire influence. The style is completely classical, traces of antique Pompeiian and Greco-Roman design coming through Adam, Hepplewhite, Sheraton, and Regency influences from England; Louis XIV, Directoire, and Empire influences from France.

The Federal period is the period of Duncan Phyfe. His earliest work echoes the English masters; after 1800, stronger French qualities bring his work to its highest distinction. The Directoire-classic influence so evident in late Sheraton and English Regency is also the basis of Phyfe's best style. Samuel McIntire excelled in Adam interpretations. The Directoire influence was followed by the heavier Empire. By 1830, the decline had set in; furniture was heavy and coarse.

Federal furniture is predominantly mahogany. Some curly maple was used to imitate the satinwood of European models. Cherry and other fruitwoods are common in less splendid furniture; rosewood was used in more costly work after 1820. Maple and pine were stained to imitate rosewood, notably in the chairs of Lambert Hitchcock. Veneering is general. Brass feet and casters, brass ring handles and, to a lesser extent, brass applied ornaments were used. Of the latter, the commonest form was the eagle; the national bird is almost symbolically Federal. China and glass knobs were later used as drawer pulls.

Feet and legs were mostly turned, reeding being more typical than fluting. Lions' paws were carved on feet, lion heads on handles; lyres, swags, festoons, delicate acanthus leaves suggest the Directoire. The Empire style favored cornucopias, pineapples, spiral carved turnings, with leaves, and mostly heavy scrolls employed as brackets, tables, and mirrors, supports, bed ends, etc.

The Federal Era was marked by great interest in architecture and archaeology; leading citizens like Thomas Jefferson brought this enthusiasm to a high pitch. Interiors and furniture reflect in pure outlines and refined detail the classic stateliness of Palladio and Vignola and their European followers. See also AMERICA; PHYFE, DUNCAN; LANNUIER. [619, 828, 869, 1134, 1212.]

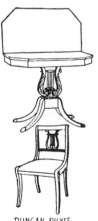

DUNCAN PHYFE

FEDERAL Ca 1815

Weil

619 CHAIR, Sheraton influence.

WASH-STAND

620 FEDERAL DESK, Hepplewhite style, 1780-1800. Tambour doors, fold-over top. Mahogany with satinwood inlay.

Metropolitan Museum of Art, Gift of Mrs. Russell Sage, 1909

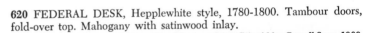

FERRULE. Metal ring or cup, turned or square, fitting the foot of a leg for strength and ornament. Sometimes with caster [1134] in 18th- and 19th-century work. See also SHOE.

FESTOON. Scalloplike series of loops, such as a rope, chain of flowers, drapery, etc., painted or carved for decoration; swag. [1030, 1226.]

FIBER. In furniture, specifically, an African fiber is sometimes used in cheap furniture as a filling for upholstery in place of hair.

FIDDLE BRACE BACK. Windsor chair with two spindles radiating from a projection back of the seat up to the top bar. [318, 321.]

FIDDLEBACK. Chairback whose splat resembles a violin. Queen Anne. [572.]

FIDDLEBACK (Veneer). Parallel curly grain in wood such as maple, mahogany, walnut, koa, and others, like the finely marked sycamore selected for violin backs. See also WOOD.

FIELD BED. Canopy bed of smaller proportions. Planned in the 17th century as one to be carried about, the name came to signify the less monumental types with curved canopy and comparatively low turned posts.

FIELDED PANEL. Panel formed by molding, grooving, or beveling around a plain surface. Also a panel made up of smaller panels.

FIGURE. In wood, certain characteristic markings other than the customary straight grain. These are spoken of as crotches, burls, butts, curls, mottles, feathers, waves, crossfire, etc. See also WOODS.

FIGURE DECORATION. Human, animal, and mythological figures are used in most styles of decoration, more or less conventionalized. They are adapted to the embellishment of structural parts, such as brackets, columns, legs and arms of tables and chairs. They are also used as motifs in every form of flat decoration. See also ORNAMENT.

FILIGREE. Wire work in delicate ornamental patterns.

FILLET. Small band, or fascia, used for separating moldings; also, a small cleat or ledge for supporting loose shelves.

AMERICAN FEDERAL FINIALS.

FINIAL. Decorative terminal, placed vertically to accentuate a point or the ending of a structural feature, such as a post, pediment, or intersection.

FINISH. Generally refers to the process of polishing or preserving the wood in furniture. It originates in two needs; first, the desire to embellish and decorate; second, the need of protection of the perishable material from the ravages of use and time.

The decorative impulse seems the older. The ancient Egyptians, Chinese, Mesopotamians, and Romans used color and design on most of their furniture. The Chinese perfected their lacquer at a very early date. This is an opaque shellac process with many rubbed coats yielding a surface of great depth and durability. The Egyptians used pigment and polychromy more as we know it, and their methods, together with gold and bronze leafing, were handed down through the Roman and Byzantine artists to the Renaissance decorators.

Less elaborate work in the Early and Middle Ages appears to have been untreated; apparently common usage suggested polishing with oil or wax, which method continued in use until the end of the 17th century. Woods were exposed to the light until they darkened somewhat; then were rubbed with oil and beeswax.

Varnishing had been known to the Egyptians, but disappeared until the early 18th century. Martin, a French carriage painter, made a transparent varnish about 1740. This *vernis Martin* so brought out the beauty of the wood that more exotic woods were sought in order to display the beauty of the treatment. The English finishers relied on their oil and wax process and on shellac, which, rubbed smooth, produces a satiny finish, and very little English furniture before the end of the 18th century was given the "French polish," or high gloss, produced by rubbing and polishing gums.

It seems probable that varnish as we know it did not appear until American finishers dissolved resins in hot oils, about 1848. In cheaper work these varnishes were applied without rubbing, producing a cheap, sticky-looking effect.

Finishing has enjoyed much study in recent years. Synthetic lacquers (having nothing in common with Chinese lacquer) developed out of nitrocellulose compounds. They make a tight skin, or film, and yield beautiful finishes. The object in most furniture finishes today is to emphasize the beauty of the wood and to protect the surface with the minimum of gloss, the greatest transparency, and the most resistance to wood's enemies: moisture, dirt, abrasion.

FIR. Family of coniferous trees. American varieties most used for furniture and construction grow on the West Coast in tremendous trees yielding long, wide boards. The wood is very soft, highly resinous, and not susceptible to good finish; its use in furniture is therefore limited to interior parts.

FIRE SCREEN. Metal spark guard. Also, a panel on a pole adjustable to any height to ward off the direct heat of the fire. See also SCREEN.

FISHTAIL. Carving on the top rail of a banister-back chair.

FITMENTS. Articles made up and fitted to the walls of a room, such as cabinets, bookcases, paneling, fireplaces, and built-in work in general (British usage).

FITTINGS. Metal mounts, handles, etc., applied to the completed piece of furniture. See also HARDWARE.

FLAG (FLAGG). Rushes used for weaving seats of chairs. [324.]

FLAMBEAU. Flaming torch used as decoration.

FLAMBOYANT. Brilliant, sometimes overdecorated. Specifically, the Late Gothic of northern Europe, which tended to excessive decoration. See also GOTHIC. [170, 720.]

FLAME CARVING. Finial of a vase, spirally or naturalistically carved to represent a flame; from the Italian Renaissance. [738.]

FLAP; FLAP TABLE. English term for drop leaf.

FLEMISH. See NETHERLANDS.

FLEMISH CABINET · ITALIANATE DETAILS Ca. 1600

FLEMISH SCROLL. Baroque double scroll on chair legs, etc. The lower curve is a C-scroll separated from the upper, a reversed C-scroll, by a right angle.

FLIP-TOP TABLE. Double-top dining or card table that unfolds like a book, supported either by pivoting about to the opposite axis, by a swing leg, or by a runner. [452.]

FLITCH. Part of a log that is sawed into veneers; the bundle of consecutive sheets of veneers when cut.

FLOWER BOXES. Ornamental boxes for the growing and display of plants. During the reign of Charles II, a craze for horticulture came to England from Holland. This prompted the design of handsome boxes in which the bulbs and roots were grown indoors, and for two centuries fine examples were produced in veneer wood and japanned decoration. See also PLANT STAND; PLANTER.

FLEMISH FOOT ENGLAND C 1690

FLOWER BOX ITALIAN IRON

FLUSH BEAD. Bead molding sunk into the surface.

FLUTES; FLUTING. Hollows or channels cut perpendicularly in columns. In furniture, flutings are applied to pilasters, legs, friezes, aprons, etc., particularly after the 16th century. Good flutes are close together and deep, with a sharply scooped curve for the ending. The ridge between the flutes is a fillet.

FLY RAIL. Swinging bracket that supports a flap or drop leaf.

FOIL. Point at the intersection of two arcs. Gothic decorative detail was used in the trefoil, quatrefoil, cinquefoil, etc.

FOLDING FURNITURE was made from earliest times, folding chairs and couches being found in Egyptian tombs. Their mechanical aspects always excite more enthusiasm in the mechanic than in the artist, as few folding pieces present a very attractive appearance. Sheraton's special ingenuity led him into very complex designs, but generally speaking the mechanical demands preclude the possibility of a coherent substantial design. [213, 538, 994, 1074, 1242.]

FOLIATED. Leaf ornaments.

FOLIO STANDS. Folio-size books being more common prior to the 19th century than since, provision was made for their storage in deep cases. The top surface was generally tilted, and adjustable for the accommodation of folios.

FOLD OVER. Desk leaf that doubles over to a table surface. Found in French table desks, Sheraton desks, and American secretaries.

FOOTRAIL. Front stretcher of a chair.

FOOTSTOOL. Low footrest related to a chair. [621, 901, 1094.]

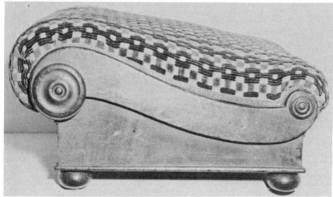

Sleepy Hollow Restorations

621 FOOTSTOOL, mahogany frame in the form of a "Grecian scroll" with applied rosette turnings, c. 1835-1845.

FOOT WARMER. Box-shaped footstool with holes for radiating heat from a hot brick placed within. Sometimes decoratively carved in Early American work.

FOOTBOARD. Panel in the lower end of a bed, or the entire end.

FORM. Old English term for bench or seat, usually long and backless.

FOUR-POSTER; FOUR-POST BED. American term for beds with the corner posts elongated. Probably the field bed or low canopy bed descended to the four-poster simply by omitting the canopy. [39, 109.]

FRAME. Border or case for pictures, mirrors, etc.; also, the wood skeleton of an upholstered chair [1302]. Also, in case joinery, the use of framing parts as a skeleton in place of merely joining the panels of a carcass together. [1.]

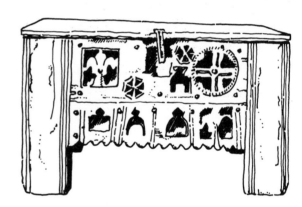

FRENCH GOTHIC CHEST c. 1400

FRANCE. GOTHIC, approximately 1100-1500. Up to 1400, French furniture was indistinct from the whole Gothic style of northern Europe. This was essentially ecclesiastical. Secular art and architecture were in the minority, and domestic work the smaller part of that. Gothic art had the quality of uniformity: architecture, woodworking, the metal crafts, etc., were homogeneous, designed directly from the same impulse, using the same ornaments and motives; a local, nonimported product, scarcely susceptible to outside influence. Social conditions were unsettled; people of high estate lived a seminomadic life, while the submerged classes were too poor to afford or require furniture.

The nomadic, unsettled life established the chest or coffer as the preeminent article of furniture. A portable catchall for bedding, clothing, valuables, it also served as a bench, a serving table, a bed for retainers, and other extemporaneous uses. At first mere planks with heavy iron reinforcements, its weight was the measure of strength. About the 14th century, some genius invented the framed-in panel, a stout frame with thin filler panels that lightened and strengthened the whole structure. There were armoires, cabinets or cupboards; stools and forms, rude tables, chiefly demountable trestles and elementary seat structures. Oak predominated. Carving developed with the style, utilizing architectural details, conventionalized flora, grotesques. Painting was undoubtedly resorted to for decoration; polychromy was used for picking out moldings and ornaments and representational painting in panels.

CREDENCE
C. 1500

With the rise of a semblance of political organization in the 14th century, there arose in France a few individuals capable of dominating or subduing their neighbors and rivals. They acquired wealth and satellites. To their rude courts they imported from Italy and Spain artists, materials, methods, and motives and, at a later date, rulers. Thus a fairly well-defined France was ruled between 1461 and 1515 by Louis XI, Charles VIII, and Louis XII. Their arts and architecture were persistently Gothic, but with decorative details of Italian flavor.

The chest, now more sedentary, became larger to serve as buffet or sideboard, and acquired a permanent base. With sides raised, it became the bench and then the sofa; fabrics and cushions were piled upon it. Permanent tables were still unknown, except minor specialized forms such as the "lectern" for reading, the *pupitre* for writing, the *demoiselle*, a kind of dressing table, and the *basset*, a very small square or round stand, like a tall stool. Beds were merely rough frames, upon which were hung the many draperies; or *lit clos*,

huge boxes with wooden panels. Seatings are described as of three types: the *faudesteuil*, the *banc*, and the *chaire*. The *faudesteuil* (English faldstool) was an X-type conceivably deriving from the Roman curule chair, and seems to have had implications of royalty. The most important *banc* was the ponderous *archebanc*, a coffer set either immovably before the fire or as an integral part of the bed, backed onto the side to serve as clothes closet and bed steps. Lesser *bancs* were the *bancelle*, the *escabeau*, the *selle*, and the simple *forme* or *fourme*. The *chaire*, never quite the same as the English chair, was quite immovable, and mercilessly uncomfortable.

The cabinet appeared as an extension of the wainscoting. The various cupboards, armoires, etc., were fundamentally the same in their ancestry, and evolved by regional and personal distinctions into the entire family of closet forms. It is just as reasonable to ascribe their origin to the coffer equipped with doors in front in place of a top lid.

Besides oak, other native woods were either slightly used or did not survive so well; these may have been beech, chestnut, maple, pine, or elm. Walnut came into extensive use in the 15th century. Pieces with ebony and ivory inlays are known after this date, but may have been imported. Iron hinges, locks, and straps were essential and highly decorative features of the designs.

Gothic architecture about the year 1500 was still vital, evidenced by such structures as the Hôtel de Cluny in Paris, the Palais de Justice at Rouen, the châteaus of Amboise, Blois, and many others. Yet in all occurs a suggestion of classic Italian decoration. Woodwork followed closely with the adoption of antique vases and candelabra, acanthus and rinceau motifs.

THE EARLY RENAISSANCE: FRANÇOIS I, 1515-1547

During these years, the Renaissance rolled into France in great waves of Italian influence that were assimilated and then merged into a coherent style. There were incidental influences: Spanish marquetry (derived from the Moors); German and Flemish details transmitted through craftsmen brought to the court from the North. Walnut waxed and rubbed to a deep finish became the dominant wood; polychromy grew rarer. Surface carving covered everything, and high-relief carving of plastic character was carried to the point of distorting the outlines. Ebony was so prized that a cabinetmaker became—and still is—an *ébéniste*—a worker in ebony. Hardware disappeared as part of the design. The homely Gothic vegetable ornament yielded to the olive, the laurel, and the

French Renaissance

GOTHIC FURNITURE RELICS ARE MOSTLY ECCLESIASTICAL, AND HARD TO FIX GEOGRAPHICALLY OR BY DATE.

622 FOLDING-TOP TABLE dated 1506, oak and linden. Front panel pivots to support opened top. Developed from trestle type that could be taken apart.

623 MARRIAGE CHEST, Late Gothic. Painted paneled sides; style of carved tracery suggests late 15th century.

624 WALNUT CHAIR with box seat, simple linenfold panels. Developed from wall paneling.

625 CHOIR STALL, 16th century. Renaissance carving in back contrasts with Gothic details, typical of Early Renaissance Italian influence.

622   *Metropolitan Museum of Art, Gift of George Blumenthal, 1941*

624   *Metropolitan Museum of Art, The Cloisters Collection, 1947*

625   *Philadelphia Museum of Art, A. J. Wyatt, Staff Photographer*

623   *Wadsworth Atheneum, Hartford, Conn.*

626 BENCH, North Italian style.

Metropolitan Museum of Art, Gift of J. Pierpont Morgan, 1916

627 DRAW-TOP TABLE, 1610-1643. Italian style.

628 CABINET, style of Henri IV.   *Don Ruseau*
Provincial character.

630 WALNUT CHAIR with
medallion c. 1600.

Symons Galleries, Inc.

629 CABINET, early 17th century. Architectural details of clear
Italian inspiration.

631 BURGUNDIAN TABLE, walnut, late 16th century.

634 "CONFESSIONAL" ARMCHAIR, late 17th century. Experimentation with scroll members approaching the cabriole.

632 CABINET dated 1580, Burgundy. Monumental style of Hugues Sambin. *Duveen Brothers, Inc.*

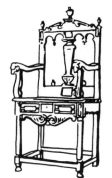

633 DIAMOND PANELS typically Burgundian; Provincial, early 17th century.

BED POST.
FRENCH
RENAISSANCE.

acanthus, although the latter became the endive, never to disappear.

The use of the architectural orders as decoration on furniture was formulated in a work dated at Lyons, 1572, by Hugues Sambin, carver of Dijon. Sambin's plates were the model for a great school of *huchiers*. This guild brought cabinets to their highest development in France. These were architectural compositions in bulk, but with irregular, jagged outlines and Baroque architectural embellishment. Pilasters were commonly used as decoration, often with circular or lozenge panels. The diamond shape, elaborated into stars and other geometric forms, remained a favorite ornament for nearly a century, and persisted in the provinces after that.

The catalogue of ornaments of this period is most extensive. Grotesque figures growing out of almost equally grotesque foliage spread over everything: swans and dolphins, sphinxes, chimeras, griffins, masks and mascarons, caryatids and Atlantes—all were carved in high relief.

The TABLE is conspicuously new during the period of François I. From a disappearing utilitarian device it became an architectural entity. The bases, vigorously carved after Italian models, had greater license in ornament and scale. Smaller tables appeared. The bed assumed a more recognizable form in the structure of four posts that carried the various draperies and curtains. The sheer carpentry of the bed became, in the reign of François I, a monumental affair of pillars and canopy. The wood posts were extravagantly carved.

Chairs were scaled down from the monumental, and were even designed to yield some comfort to women. The exaggerated costume of the time suggested the *caqueteuse*, a light armless chair similar to the farthingale chair of England. About 1580, straw-seated chairs were in use. The flat squab cushions, or *carreaux*, indicate the trend toward comfort.

THE HIGH RENAISSANCE

The style of François I prevailed with variations through the reigns of Henri II, Catherine de Médicis and François II, Charles IX, Henri III, and Henri IV of Navarre. Fierce religious wars upset the logical sequence of furniture evolution and accelerated changes by the in-and-out movement of courtiers, craftsmen, and architects. It was a violent period. The Gothic root withered and died—at least in the capitals. In the provinces it persisted because of the rise of a powerful middle class. Wealth and security seeped down through the classes. Merchants, artisans, and peasants enriched their houses with furniture inspired by that of the local nobles. In adapting these luxuries to their needs, they omitted much of the ornamentation, substituted available woods and fabrics, scaled the gigantic pieces down to their rooms, and tempered the designs to their skill. The result is the school of French Provincial Furniture, known in France as *Mobilier rustique*, as distinguished from *Meubles de luxe*.

The height of the Renaissance in France may be judged from the work executed in Paris between 1550 and 1610. The engravings of Jacques du Cerceau reveal the supreme development of the cabinet. The *armoire à deux corps*, or double-bodied cupboard, had the upper section narrower than the lower; pilasters, paneled and decorated with flat carving, framed the doors, which were often paneled geometrically, as with stars and diamonds in bold relief. Broken pediments crowned many of these structures. Cartouches and flat strapwork carving prevailed over the purer Italian decoration. Table bases were involved compositions of columns, balusters, caryatids, and scrolls. Chairs were architectural in scale, except the unimportant types, which remained stiff and uncomfortable. This phase is sometimes labeled the style of Henri IV, but it cannot be precisely distinguished from the work executed under Louis XIII. [175, 1210.]

LOUIS XIII, 1610-1643

Gaudily splendid, monumental, overpowering, the furniture of this epoch reflected a rich parvenu imperialism. The names of the period are of the great in their fields: Mazarin, Molière, Corneille, Rubens, Descartes, Pascal. A period of great power, it brought the High Renaissance to a vivid climax. Walnut and ebony were the principal woods. Panels, columns, and pilasters of semiprecious stones or molded stucco panels were introduced into cabinets. Marquetry came from the Low Countries. Tortoiseshell and gilt bronze contributed to the lavish air. Carving was in the Flemish style, rich and turgid. Turning was used not only for legs of all types of furniture but also for applied ornament. Turnings with complex profiles were dis-

tinctive of the style, but not so much so as the elaborate geometric panels and deep moldings. This vigorous paneling, likely of Flemish origin, is probably the outstanding clue to Louis XIII furniture.

Cabinets were the pièce de résistance. They covered the whole range from little coffers covered with embroidered velvet to colossal structures carried on twelve ornate supports. They were now no longer necessarily vertical; the buffet form as we know it appeared in Guyenne and Gascony with drawers below. The *bureau* was new, evidently adapted from the cabinet by the addition of a fall front, although the name derives from the cloth used to cover earlier writing tables. Tables with expanding tops for dining were another novelty of the period of Louis XIII. These either were hinged flaps or telescoping types; the bases were commonly turned legs with elaborate detail, although the classic vase or slab shapes were frequently used. The H-stretcher is typical. There was a great variety of small tables, some oval, round, or octagonal, but chiefly oblong. Beds were still great masses of fabric covering the rough wooden structure.

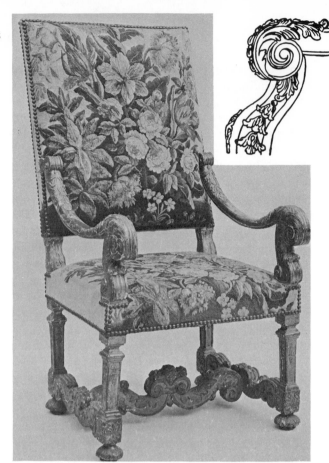

Metropolitan Museum of Art, Fletcher Fund, 1929

639 The regal style of Louis XIV. ARMCHAIR carved and gilded.

640 CABINET, mid-17th-century, beginning of reign of Louis XIV.   *Symons Galleries, Inc.*

Chairs are generally low, possibly due to the current headdress and ruffs. The word *fauteuils* appears in inventories, but uncertainty exists as to whether it indicates the type so called after the period of Louis XIV. The most important change in seatings occurs under Louis XIII in the permanent nailing-down to seats of fixed upholstery. Leather was commonly used for upholstery, and silver or gilt nail-heads were decoratively applied, either close together or in the daisy pattern.

LOUIS XIV—1643-1715—BAROQUE

Louis XIV came to the throne of a self-consciously powerful France, and with deliberation proceeded to focus it into the center of the world. The Gobelin tapestry factory was transformed into the "Manufacture Royale des Meubles de la Couronne." Under Le Brun's direction Jean and Daniel Marot, Bérain, Le Pautre, Leclère, Andrau, engraved designs for furniture. The outstanding cabinetmakers of this period were Boulle, Oppenord, Cucci, Caffieri, Peter Golle. It is significant that these are not French names but Italian, Flemish, Dutch. Yet the product was French, clearly welded into a positive style, for all its foreign roots.

The style of Louis XIV was distinctly Baroque, the robustly exaggerated manner emanating from the Jesuit architecture of Italy. It was sumptuous, large in scale, masculine for all its lavish decoration, and completely symmetrical. The straight line predominated; curves were restrained within severe outlines, lending formal dignity. Panels were simple rectangles, occasionally hollowed at the corners or with semicircular tops, or inset circles and ovals. They were always defined with strong moldings of classic quality. Carving was rich and plentiful, employing animal forms of nature and mythology to express the current love of allegory: masks, satyrs, lions' paws and heads, sphinxes, griffins, dolphins. There were acanthus in endless variety, water lilies, oak, laurel, olive leaves; weapons, musical instruments, agricultural implements, ribbons, festoons, swags, knots. Architectural details were sparingly used for small furniture prior to 1680.

Woods were rich and varied. The simple oak and walnut and even ebony lacked magnificence; elaborate marquetry panels formed large surfaces. Almond, holly, box, pear, and other woods were toned by fire; but this did not suffice, and Boulle perfected marquetry of tortoiseshell, brass, horn, pewter, tin, ivory and bone and mother-of-pearl in intricate detail. Bronze appliqués were imposed upon the whole. Painting was liberally resorted to, strong colors such as red and green being favored. Gilded and silvered furniture was substituted where real gold and silver were prohibitive—although an incredible amount of metal was used for small furniture prior to 1680. The gilding was exceptionally fine, and further distinguished massive armchairs and tables. The "Chinese taste" became a rage, first with the collection of porcelains and finally in the effort to duplicate the lustrous depth of Oriental lacquer. The Brothers Martin perfected the process of varnishing known as *vernis Martin*, of great brilliancy and solidity.

635 CONSOLE TABLE in natural oak. Square baluster legs.

Changed manners affected the forms and variety of furniture. The coffer had completely disappeared, and the monumental cabinet of Louis XIII declined. Outside Paris, cupboards, while developing in the general form, were ornamented in the old style of Louis XIII. In fact, the entire ornamental system retained much from the earlier 17th century. In Normandy a narrow, graceful form for the storage of bonnets is known as *bonnetière* [142]. "Bookcase cupboards" had doors fitted with iron wire grilles. The most important piece of receptacle furniture after the period of Louis XIV is the commode, stemming either from the table with drawers or the coffer on legs, fitted with drawers. Boulle's name is attached to some famous commodes, irrational and pretentious [159]. Others exhibit the curved leg and doe's foot destined to become the cabriole leg.

Beds achieved new heights, literally and figuratively. The woodwork was still a skeleton for manifold draperies consisting of as many as thirty-three distinct parts. Some arrangements of suspended testers were known as "duchess beds" and "angel beds." The canopy of the first hung completely from the ceiling, while the tester of the angel bed was shorter than the

636 CLOCK by Boulle.

638 BOULLE CABINET.

637 GILT PEDESTAL.

641 CARVED OAK OVER-MIRROR PANEL. Combination of straight and curved lines in simple architectural outline is typical of Regency work.

642 ARMCHAIR after design by Berain. Late stretcher from Beauvais tapestry cover.

644 CLOCK, mid-18th century.

French Régence

THE TRANSITION AFTER LOUIS XIV TO A SOFTER STYLE MARKED BY THE ASCENDANCY OF THE CURVED LINE.

643 STOOL, of sinuous plan, vigorous carving in walnut.

645 DESK, mahogany and ormolu. Strong early cabriole leg.

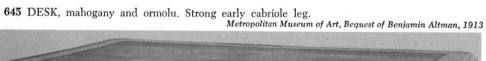

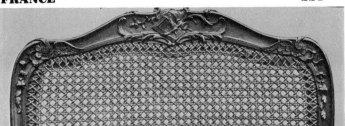

Metropolitan Museum of Art, Rogers Fund, 1927

646 CARVED DETAIL of fruitwood chair top rail.

647 CHEST with coromandel lacquer.

648 CORNER CHAIR
Metropolitan Museum of Art, Gift of J. Pierpont Morgan, 1906

650 CONSOLE BRACKET,
transitional
Louis XVI—Regency.

649 RÉGENCE CONSOLE. Oak.

French & Co., Inc.

bed, and had side curtains looped to the wall. In these types, the actual bed frame or stead was a detached unit handsomely treated in its own right. The rest bed, or chaise longue, was a logical product of this age of luxury.

Of tables, the newest form under Louis XIV is the console type. Decorative tables having become immovable owing to the great weight of the stone tops, elaborate bases were set permanently against the wall, with the hidden side left undecorated. The architectural console became common as a base. Free-standing tables with the double console were developed. Table legs were also turned or flattened balusters. Important types such as these were gilded, but natural or painted woods were used for much smaller tables that were suitable for holding trays, coffee, candelabra, or writing stands; there were toilet tables and night tables and specialized game tables and desks of various types.

SEATS. The etiquette of seating was in this period the philosophy of royalty. Thus, in order of importance ranged the armchair, chairs with backs, joint stools, folding stools, hassocks with gold gimp, hassocks with silk edging. The Louis XIV throne chair was majestic indeed; high, wide, and handsome, it stood upon a dais with several steps. It was solid silver, draped with crimson velvet. The back was eight feet high, draped with full gold embroidery carried by caryatids fifteen feet high. This was the model for important armchairs. They always had stretchers, first H-shaped, and later the serpentine X. Legs were scrolled or flat or turned balusters; the arms were well molded and swung into the back with great curves. The "confessional" was the first of the bergère type, or fully upholstered easy chair. The armless chairs follow the *caqueteuses* of Louis XIII. The sofa was the most important seating invention of the period. The first was a rest bed or canapé, almost bed in shape and upholstery; the word "sofa" appears about 1680, and the later sofas were less fully upholstered. Caning for chairs grew in popularity, and straw-seated turned chairs, called *chaises à la capucine*, were used in the palaces as well as in peasant homes.

Louis XIV died in 1715, but long before this a modification of his style set in. The transitional period was marked politically by the regency of Philippe d'Orléans from 1715 to 1723, when the young Louis XV became king. The term Régence loosely describes the transition from the high style of Louis XIV to the feminine style of Louis XV. The massive square grandeur of Louis XIV relaxed into softer outlines and freer ornament. Curves at first only modified the rectangular forms in corners and ornamental details; later, structural members, such as legs and stretchers, were shaped into flowing lines.

The craze for chinoiserie was responsible for much of the ornamental character of the Régence and Louis XV styles. Louis XIV's explorations and commercial exploitation of the Far East brought to Europe Chinese porcelains, jade, and decorations depicting formalized landscapes and figures. The technique somehow suggested the use of natural forms in decorations; and rocks, shells, flowers, and birds became the basis of a manner dubbed "rock and shell" —*rocaille et coquille;* years later, this was unsympathetically contracted into Rococo, by which name we characterize furniture and manners emanating from this age, having a florid, gaily absurd manner.

The cabriole leg—*pied de biche*, or doe's foot—was no novelty, but in the Régence it became the characteristic shape. It was so curved as to make the vertical line flow evenly into the horizontal of the apron. The typical curve was that of the crossbow.

Ornament was less classical, discarding mythology for nature, though ribbons, foliage, shells, and scrolls were usually symmetrically arranged. Chairbacks have pierced carved splats. In general, the wider range of ornament had delicate movement austerely restrained within clear architectural outlines. The lighter touch also applied to materials; ebony and walnut were too somber, and yielded to fine veneers of polished rosewood and lighter colors.

Robert de Cotte, Berain, Marot, Mansart, Boulle, and others carried over the grand tradition; younger men then in their early phases created novelties destined to be the elements of the Louis XV style. But the style of the Régence was epitomized in the work of Charles Cressent. His supreme creations were commodes, whose cabinetwork was most important as a base for superbly chased bronze appliqués.

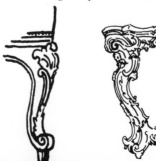

THE FULLY DEVELOPED STYLE OF LOUIS XV AVOIDED THE STRAIGHT LINE IN ANY PLANE.

652 MARQUETRY CYLINDER TOP DESK.

Dalva Brothers, Inc.

651 FAUTEUIL, tapestry cover.
Dalva Brothers, Inc.

653 COMMODE in kingwood and tulipwood. Manner of Delorme. Ormolu mounts by Charles Cressent.

Duveen Brothers, Inc.

LOUIS XV—ROCOCO

The ultimate in decorative furniture is, to many critics, that which was produced in France between 1700 and 1760. Louis Quinze furniture avoided like a plague the appearance of symmetry and the right angle. Every device was employed to alleviate the rectangle. In plan or elevation no piece of furniture was permitted straight lines . . . only flowing lines; everything was rounded so that the eye might follow any line without perceiving the junction of planes. Ornaments were drawn from shells, flowers, musical instruments, pastoral objects like shepherd's crooks and baskets, all naturally and unconventionally rendered. Chinese themes were capriciously misinterpreted. Architecture alone was rejected as a source of ornament.

Marquetry and inlaying assumed primary importance. For large veneer surfaces, rosewood, satinwood, amaranth, and tulipwood were used, while marquetry was made up of most of the exotic varieties known today. Mahogany rose to great popularity, and the native fruitwoods, notably cherry and plum, were used in Paris as well as in the provinces.

Painted furniture grew in demand through the middle years of the reign, the brightest reds, greens, yellows, and black being emphasized with fillets painted in gold and contrasting colors. Lacquering processes were studied, although much woodwork was actually sent to the Orient to be decorated. The delays incidental to this procedure encouraged the development of varnishes whose depth rivaled that of the Oriental lacquers. The Brothers Martin with their *vernis Martin* were phenomenally successful. Gilding, only slightly less popular than during the Louis XIV period, covered console tables and mirrors, chairs, and small tables.

Metal appliqués were universal. The costliest pieces were chiefly decorated by this means. But in more modest furniture the bronzes were more functional, being handles, lock escutcheons, keys, feet, or fillets to protect weak veneers. That both Meissonier and the Caffieris were metalworkers before they made furniture is evidence of the importance of this decoration to the style.

Marble of many colors made tops for commodes and tables: onyx and alabaster were used for small pieces. Imitations of stone were variously successful. Small China plaques were let into tabletops and inlaid in mahogany panels. Mirrors also were set into panels.

The types of furniture follow closely those described previously as originating during the Régence. The commode type was expanded into many forms, among them slant-front desk types. Tables for every purpose shared a common feature—the cabriole leg. Expand-ing dining tables "of the English kind" came from England about 1770; other types were developed earlier. Small tables, or *ambulantes*, had great variety. Console tables were architectural fixtures, the most typical having legs that came together to a point at the base. Special tables were designed for every game. Dressing tables of wide variety, writing tables *(bureaux)*, worktables, etc., made a long list of table shapes.

Comfortable chairs, chaise longues, and sofas were dimensioned to the human frame and shaped for luxurious ease. Chairbacks and seats were low, modified to current costumes and habits. The bergère was made with solid sides and loose down cushions. Armless chairs, designed for voluminous skirts, were as popular as they had been a century earlier. Cane chairs were important, and often had loose cushions of lemon or red morocco. Straw or rush chairs appeared in great variety and imagination.

Chaise longues were significant at this luxurious time. Ladies received *en déshabille* in their boudoirs, and the furniture designed to accommodate this pose varied between a small bed and a large chair. Turkish inspiration provided types of "sophas," or full-length beds, with backs on three sides and a large "ottoman."

Beds developed along more modern concepts, since specialized bedrooms were smaller and warmer. This permitted the diminution of the completely enclosed bed. Though the canopy and draperies were retained, they were minor or decorative, and were generally supported on four posts. The *duchesse* bed had a flat canopy as long as the bed, with the counterpane falling to the floor at the foot. There were straight side draperies. The "angel bed" had equal headboard and footboard, while the half-length canopy hung from the ceiling and had two looped-back draperies at the head [113]. The "Polish bed" had a headboard and footboard, but instead of the high tester a curving dome was carried on four iron rods, with four curtains looped up at the corners [111].

Of the cabinetmakers of the period, Jean François Oeben was supreme, particularly for his marquetry. Philippe Caffieri, Meissonier, Oppenord, Oudry, and many others developed superb techniques to meet the demands of a style essentially unstructural.

LOUIS XVI, 1774-1793—THE CLASSIC REVIVAL

The inevitable revolt from the curved line came long before Louis XVI. But here again the old king outlived the taste he fostered. Some time after 1760, the curve-weary pointedly demanded a return to simple forms and straight lines. The answer came from Italy in an intellectual movement not unlike the early Renaissance—the imitation of antiquity. [117, 141, 375.]

Excavations in Greek and Roman ruins had been in progress for many years, but the unearthing of Pompeii and Herculaneum set off a new spark. Ancient architectural forms became the basis of furniture design even as they had been in the Renaissance. Because the architectural spirit demanded recognition of supports, legs were truthfully expressed as sheer vertical members, forming right angles with the aprons, etc. The vertical was emphasized by fluting and grooving; architecture suggested bases and capitals in the form of moldings and feet. Curves, where they were used, were cut-off segments of ellipses or circles; legs were straightened out entirely. Panels were important in their flatness and absence of decoration, being set off by exquisitely studied moldings. Ornament was classic, mathematically symmetrical, and recalled all the forms of Louis XIV: laurel and acanthus, egg-and-dart, oak leaves and Greek palm leaves, fretwork, rinceaux, ribbons, etc. Fluting was partially filled in (cannellated), the filling ending in small vase turnings or torch effects. Bound arrows, lyres, swans, urns, wreaths, festoons, fanciful animals, etc., were adapted from Greco-Roman sources. Brass

Metropolitan Museum of Art, Gift of J. Pierpont Morgan, 1906
655 DESK CHAIR in green morocco.

THE CLASSIC REVIVAL OF LOUIS XVI, 1760-1790, BROUGHT STRAIGHT LINES AND SIMPLE SILHOUETTES, ORNAMENT AFTER THE ANTIQUE, ALL DECREASING IN ELABORATENESS AS THE REVOLUTION APPROACHED.

654 PAINTED ARMCHAIR by Brizard, 1780-1790.

657 *Center.* CONSOLE, carved oak, marble top.
Metropolitan Museum of Art, Gift of J. Pierpont Morgan, 1906

656 WALNUT ARMCHAIR, 1780-1790.

Metropolitan Museum of Art, Gift of George Blumenthal, 1941

Metropolitan Museum of Art, Gift of Ann Payne Blumenthal, 1943

658 COMMODE, c. 1773, by Riesener. Marquetry, floral decorations. Ormolu moldings and ornamentation by Duplessis.

galleries were applied to tables, commodes, and bookcases: delicate brass or gilt moldings framed drawers. Ornament varied from the earlier style in its delicate scale, its tactful proportion, and the complete denial of the sinuous line.

Mahogany was the preeminent wood. Rosewood, tulipwood, and others were combined in geometric marquetry, arranged as diamond and lozenge patterns. Ebony returned to favor. Black-and-gold lacquer was popular, and much painted furniture of grayish-white, gray-green, and similar soft tones was used. Sèvres China plaques were inset into desks, cabinets, etc.

Jean François Riesener was the great master of the era. Oeben's pupil, he later married his widow. David Roentgen, known only as David; Georges Jacob, and his son, called Jacob-Desmalter after the Revolution; Étienne Avril, Martin Carlin, Leleu, Saunier, Schwerdfeger, Lalonde, Aubert, and innumerable others created masterful designs. A few, such as Montigny, Levasseur, and Séverin, copied or adapted the style of Louis XIV and the technique of Boulle. Others, like Beneman and Weisweiler, worked so closely to the antique architectural ideal that they actually created the later Empire style.

The character and function of the individual pieces scarcely varied from the lines established under Louis Quinze. Commodes, chairs and sofas, desks and tables merely assumed straight lines. A few new shapes appear in chairs by Aubert, excessively classical; such were the curule chairs and seats and sofas with roll-backs, Roman tripods for tables, and a glazed commode, called the "vitrine," for the display of curios. Beds were smaller, following the styles set earlier, with the angel bed the dominant type. Fabrics were of small-patterned silks, (small-patterned) tapestries, and the whole range of Louis XV materials. The vogue for printing cotton and linen created the *toiles de Jouy.*

DIRECTOIRE, 1795-1799; CONSULATE, 1799-1804

The period of the Revolution, 1789-1795, was chaos. A somewhat authoritative government, the Directory, assumed control in 1795. Directoire was essentially simpler Louis XVI adorned with the symbolism of the Revolution—the Phrygian caps, arrows, pikes, triangles, wreaths, clasped hands, the fasces and lictor of Rome, etc. There were "Patriotic Beds." It is improbable that any considerable quantity of furniture was produced during this troubled era, short at best, so that it is difficult to construe a full style out of the few scattered remains. Simplicity, grace, directness, charm; straight lines with restrained classic double curves; the swan, lyre, stars, in addition to the antique and Revolutionary symbols, were the index of decorative motives. Woods were more often native fruitwood, walnut, oak, than mahogany, now that foreign trade was difficult. For the most part the old cabinetmakers continued in their work: Riesener, David, Jacob, Beneman. Two young unknown designers, Percier and Fontaine, worked under Jacob, and in their hands lay the evolution of the developing style.

659 MEDAL CABINET with stone inlays.
By Weisweiler.

660 SECRETARY, 1784, by Riesener, with cipher of Marie
Antoinette. Ebony, gold, and ormolu, black marble top.

661 DESK, satinwood and mahogany, with ormolu
ornaments and moldings. Stamped "Muller."

The Directoire Style

A BRIEF PERIOD OF TRANSITION FROM LOUIS XVI TO SIMPLIFIED DETAIL, DISCARDING REGAL CHARACTERISTICS.

664 PAINTED ARMCHAIR. *Don Ruseau*

662

667 LATE LOUIS XVI SECRETARY (acajou). Late style of Riesener.

668 ALCOVE BED, end of 18th century. Turned, fluted carved posts on one side only.

Don Ruseau

665 DROP-FRONT SECRETARY, Mahogany with Revolutionary symbols in brass inlay.

662-663 CARVED GILT MIRRORS, late 18th century.

666 MARQUISE, painted.

EMPIRE, 1804-1815

The classic Revolution became Imperial under Napoleon in 1804. His absolutism reached into the arts, and the wavering Directoire style was galvanized by edict into a solid formulated manner. Percier and Fontaine's first work, issued in 1801, expressed a system of archaeological copying and adaptation in the grand manner.

The Empire differs from the Louis XVI in the degree to which it absorbs classic forms whole and undigested. It took the few vestiges of ancient furniture literally, and tried to stretch them over the whole field of furniture without modification. The discriminating scale of Louis Seize was lost completely; architectural forms were taken whole rather than as motives for decoration. Absolute symmetry, cubic rectangular or geometric shapes, and heavy solid proportions characterized all pieces. Large surfaces were flat and plain, free of moldings or paneling, to emphasize the highly polished wood grain. The ornamentation consisted almost exclusively of bronze or flat gilt appliqués (the invention of Gouthière in the preceding era) molded into stiffly formalized relief, and tacked on. These motives included military symbols such as the sword and shield, arrows and wreaths and winged figures, torches, and the whole catalogue of ancient symbolism, all coldly archaeological and precise. Napoleon invented a few of his own symbols: the bee and the letter *N*. Cornucopias, palm leaves and laurels

First Empire
in France, 1804-1815

Metropolitan Museum of Art, Rogers Fund, 1920

670 CHEVAL GLASS (Psyche), mahogany; ormolu candelabra and mountings.

669 CHEST OF DRAWERS, mahogany and ormolu, marble top.

Don Ruseau

Metropolitan Museum of Art

671 CONSOLE with sphinx-head capitals.

were stiffened and added to the list; in fact, nothing available to the Greco-Roman researchers was overlooked. Carving was entirely avoided except for the arms and posts of chairs and table legs where they could be transformed into lions or griffins or caryatids.

Mahogany was the overwhelming favorite. The rich deep-red color was favored, along with rosewood and ebony, and other woods were stained in imitation. Knot elm, thuja, and similarly burled veneers were equally rich. Marble, being classic, was therefore acceptable. Fabrics were always deep and rich in color, primary reds, greens, and yellows, deep browns; all were in hard textures, with large imperial patterns or diaper patterns with the usual stars, etc.

Tables were invariably round, generally on a pedestal or tripod base. Tops were often thick marble or porphyry slabs. All cabinet furniture was designed as miniature architecture. Desks varied from table types with superimposed banks of drawers in temple-façade form to the large cabinet type, almost flat with fall front. The drop-front type evolved under Louis XVI as *bonheur du jour* was popular. Beds of the "angel" type were first favored, but the typical Empire bed was the boat style, with richly scrolled ends of the same height.

Chairs and sofas were stiff and clumsy and supremely uncomfortable. The shapes were forced copies of the Greek and Roman ceremonial seats, unwillingly rendered in wood instead of in the original stone and bronze. The chaise longue developed a rather new type—the Recamier type and the *méridienne*. With the eclipse of Napoleon, the impetus and the style disappeared together. See also EMPIRE. [123.]

673 "BONHEUR DU JOUR," mahogany secretary with flat gilt bronze ornaments.

672 NAPOLEONIC MONOGRAM in Beauvais tapestry.
Metropolitan Museum of Art, Gift of Mrs. S. E. Minton, 1899

674 EMPIRE BED with mirrored ends.   *French & Co., Inc.*

PROVINCIAL FRENCH

The foregoing classification of French styles is essentially Parisian. The great body of people in the provinces was only partly aware of or interested in these developments. The local styles were of course constantly modified by the new influences, but the degree of acceptance was always subject to local conditions. These included degrees of wealth, climate, available materials and skill, and local custom and prejudices. As a whole, the provincial furniture is honestly designed for family life, as distinct from the *meubles de luxe* of the capital, and in its restrained scale, constructional quality, and charm forms a distinct body of styles.

The bourgeoisie and peasantry of the 17th century acquired wealth but continued to live simply. Their furniture comprised only the essentials: a closed bed, a few straw-bottomed stools, a cupboard or hutch. The few additional pieces of the 17th century were receptacles: wardrobes, cabinets, various forms of buffets. In Flanders the Gothic forms persisted. The wealthier provinces, like Burgundy and Gascony, adopted the style of Louis XIII enthusiastically and have clung to it ever since. The long reign of Louis XIV witnessed in the provinces little more than a development of Louis XIII, but the style of Louis XV struck so responsive a chord that the 18th century became known as *le siècle de Louis Quinze*. In many sections they continued to make furniture in this mode until the end of the nineteenth century. Louis XVI was only partially accepted, the classic details being imposed upon the curved Louis XV forms. The Empire style simply passed the provinces by.

The buffet and cupboard forms are the most important provincial types. They evolved out of sheer utility and had characteristic shapes and names in different regions. The armoire also developed in variety according to local usage. Beds were more or less closed in, according to the climate; those in Provence were open at an early date, while the mountainous sections of the Vosges, Auvergne, and Savoie retain the *lit clos,* a room within a room. Straw-seated chairs were treated with innate distinction everywhere; some distinctly minor forms are interesting. The *panetière,* or breadbox, is universal, as are wall shelves and knife boxes.

Local types of decoration often survived even when the design books from Paris suggested new ideas. Normandy long exhibited traces of her Viking ancestry. Alsace showed Germanic or Swiss traces in painting; the metalworkers of Provence and Limousin developed handsome steel mounts as hinges and handles. The available woods made for variations; oak

675 "CHAUFFEUSE," walnut.
676 DRESSER-BUFFET from Gascony; diamond-point panels of Louis XIII style may indicate date c. 1650.

Anderson Galleries

Above. EARLY-17th-CENTURY INSPIRATION.

677 REGENCE-STYLE MIRROR.   678 COMMODE. Carved into the solid walnut are details of early Louis XV style, freely interpreted.

PROVINCIAL FRENCH CUPBOARD TOP

FRANCE

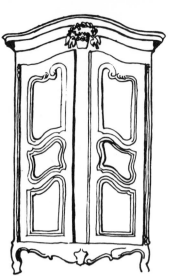

681 KNEADING TROUGH, Arles. Naturalistic carving fitted into mixed outlines of Louis XV and Henri IV turnings.

679 SETTEE with straw seat and loose cushions; details of early style.

682 SMALL MIRROR of Louis XVI inspiration. Gilt on white.

680 WALNUT CHEST dated 1780. Signed "Ohneberg EB 1773." (Bordeaux?). Mixed details of Louis XV and Louis XVI styles in functional design.

684 CREDENCE SIDEBOARD, Arles, Rococo inspiration with earlier and local details in carving and hardware.

Putting Antiques

685 Rustic type of DOE'S FOOT LEG, suggested by cabriole. Similar adaptations are seen in 19th-century American work.

in Normandy with brass fittings; walnut and the fruit-woods trimmed with polished steel in Lorraine; walnut in Savoie; even the imported tropical woods in the Saintonge region; all tend to differentiate not only the technique of carving but also the whole style of the piece. [91, 92, 226, 371, 492.]

FRENCH FURNITURE AFTER THE EMPIRE

The nineteenth century was in France as elsewhere a period of esthetic indetermination. Styles floundered from outright copying or eclecticism to misbegotten attempts at conscious organization. After Napoleon there was a tepid Restoration, no more successful in art than in politics. An abortive Gothic revival, a heterogeneous Louis-Philippe manner, and various resurgences of the classic spirit followed, and finally a burst of Renaissance revivalism—the SECOND EMPIRE, 1852-1870. France accepted leadership in the arts at this time, and the École des Beaux-Arts was its spokesman. Classicism was eroded by a current of Oriental faddishness that elevated the upholsterer above the cabinetmaker. No substantial change in viewpoint came until the very end of the century when the Art Nouveau attained a vogue and a mild success in accessory arts. But its furniture, as illogical but not so charming as Louis Quinze, was less appreciated, and faded out before 1910. See also ART NOUVEAU; NINETEENTH CENTURY; UPHOLSTERY.

MODERN FRANCE

France's liberal approach to design has been a spur to advanced thought the world over. After World War I, work in the decorative arts was summarized in an International Exposition of Decorative Art in 1925. Many divergent currents of thought appeared here—the constructivists and functionalists of Germany and Holland, the romantics of France and Italy trailing Art Nouveau and Directoire grace [501]. For once, the French with their Art Moderne took no clear stand. It fell largely to Germany émigrés to lay the foundations of the International Style. See also MODERN FURNITURE.

683 SMALL TABLE, RÉGENCE SPIRIT, much simplified in the copying—probably end of the 18th century.

Anderson Galleries

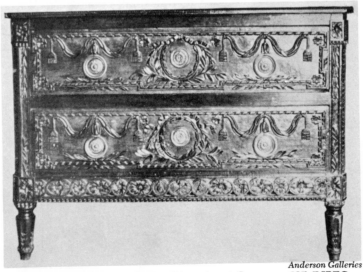

Anderson Galleries

686 FRUITWOOD CHAIR, Directoire influence. 687 DIRECTOIRE COMMODE from Provence. Revolutionary symbols carved into the solid walnut. 688 LOUIS XVI ORNAMENTAL DETAIL applied to country-style armchair.

Don Ruseau

FRANCIS (François) I. King of France 1515-1547. Builder of châteaus of Blois, Chambord, and Fontainebleau. In them the Renaissance had its first great French expression. It was really a mingling of flamboyant Gothic and Italian Renaissance ornament, more Italian than French. Walnut was favored in the South, oak in the North. Cabinets, tables, and chairs were rich, and profusely carved and inlaid.

FRENCH BED. Roll-end bedstead without posts.

FRENCH FOOT. Scrolled or spiraled foot, ornamented as with a dolphin. Also, a slightly outswept foot as used by Hepplewhite. [50, 72.]

FRENCH POLISH. Process of finishing wood with a high gloss by applying successive films of shellac in spirits. See also VERNIS MARTIN.

FRET (FRETWORK, FRETTING, or LATTICE-WORK). Interlaced ornamental work, either perforated or cut in low relief on a solid ground, usually in geometric patterns; also the tracery of glazed doors and windows. A Chinese importation, it was sparingly used on the Continent but taken up avidly by the Georgian masters. Particularly characteristic of Chippendale's Chinese manner, it was also adapted to his Gothic designs. [108, 409, 579, 1052.]

Flat fretwork, as painted and inlaid, comes down from the Greek and is also a feature of Arabian and Moorish design.

FRIESIAN; FRIESLAND. Scratch carving in simple geometric designs, such as the wheel. In Pennsylvania Dutch work it is found as decoration on rude pine Bible boxes, spoon racks, etc.

FRIESLAND CUPBOARDS. Important cabinets with rich carved cornices in the Baroque style, made in Friesland (Netherlands) in the 17th century. Prototype of KAS. [798.]

FRIEZE. Central part of the entablature, between the architrave and cornice. A flat member, it is usually the surface most decoratively treated with formal ornament, inscriptions, painted or inlaid detail. See also ORDERS.

FRINGE. Ornamental edging used in upholstering furniture; made of twisted threads, yarns, tassels, etc., of silk or other materials, often with metal. See also UPHOLSTERY.

FRISE (FRIEZE). Heavy woolen or linen and cotton upholstery cloth with uncut nap.

FRUIT MOTIF. Motif in Italian and Tudor carving; also used in Grinling Gibbons's work.

FRUITWOOD. The woods of the various fruit trees have always been used for small furniture, especially in provincial work. These woods are usually hard and durable, and polish well. Pear, apple, and cherry are the most used woods of this class.

FUNCTIONAL. In general use as applied to furniture, serviceable, utilitarian, designed primarily for use rather than for decoration. Specifically, in modern design the school that eschews the decorative nature of furniture in order to emphasize its special utility. It is the outgrowth of Louis Sullivan's edict that "form follows function." Only those factors that directly concern function may be accepted as elements of the design. Analyzed closely, it will appear that pure functional design tends to restrict the outward expression of functional forms within the narrowest bounds, resulting in abject poverty of aesthetic interest. On the other hand, the scope of total room composition is emphasized.

Owing to the conflict between functional and decorative approaches, pseudofunctionalism in furniture is rampant. Fake structural forms and construction methods lack both straightforward functional design and the intrinsic beauty of traditional forms. See also INTERNATIONAL STYLE; MODERN FURNITURE.

FURNITURE. American usage limits the word to movable articles, equivalent to the French *meuble* or German *möbel*. In England the term is more inclusive, embracing every type of equipment, whether portable or built in. Thus "chimney furniture" includes the accessory furnishings of the fireplace: fenders, andirons, tools, etc. The room paneling and built-in fittings are also furniture.

DECORATIVE FURNITURE includes all types of more or less utilitarian pieces to which is applied some effort at beautification. In former times every article of use was treated ornamentally except the crudest utilitarian objects. Modern practice has discarded much of this decoration, and even furniture has been exempted from the erstwhile need of elaboration; the decorative aspect of rooms is conceived to be a matter of composition of abstract elements rather than an association of many objects of individual ornamental claims. Most furniture today is designed in terms of modern utility, but with the decorative aspects of former periods. This cannot be correctly called "period furniture," since it modifies proportions, woods, finishes, structural methods, purpose, or other features that in a true period copy should follow the example of the original.

GABLE. Triangular-peaked, like a roof. The shape occurs in European cupboards of the Romanesque Era [457] and in Gothic coffers. Decoratively, it appears as Renaissance pediments, and persists through the 19th century. [804, 1056.]

GABOON. *(a)* Ebony of the blackest variety, which comes from the Gabon region of Africa. *(b)* A light, inferior mahogany from the Gabon region, known in Europe merely by this name.

GADROON. Ornament carved on edges either of flat areas or of turnings resembling short convex or concave flutes or ruffles. It is common in Elizabethan work, Italian Renaissance work and all styles influenced by Italy. A characteristic decoration of bulbous supports in Elizabethan carving. Chippendale used it extensively for borders and top edges. [226, 810, 1035.]

GALLERY. Small railing of metal or wood, or a raised rim, around the tops of tables, cabinets, buffets, etc. Various works had pierced brass galleries. Chippendale style shows pierced wooden fretwork galleries. [153, 1256.]

GALLOON (GALON). Narrow tape used as gimp in the finishing of upholstery.

GAME TABLE. One of the earliest specialized types of tables developed for games, such as dice, cards, chess or draughts, backgammon etc. Sixteenth-century examples have needlework tops in patterns required for the various games; the ultimate development occurred in 18th-century England. See also CARD TABLE. [158, 1277.]

GARGOYLE. Grotesque figure originally used in architecture as decorative rainspout. Best known in Gothic examples, it was adapted for purely ornamental purposes in some medieval and Renaissance woodwork.

GARLAND. Floral decoration, freely arranged.

GATELEG TABLE. The whole classification of tables in which one or more drop leaves are supported by a leg or gate that swings away from a central fixed structure. According to Nutting, the gateleg must have a stretcher; if the stretcher is lacking, the type is known as "swing leg." Gatelegs were made with as many as twelve legs, and appeared in every style dur-

GADROONING

JACOBEAN GATELEG

ing the 17th century. In the nineteenth century the gateleg table retreated to provincial use, its place being taken by swing-leg types in the more advanced style centers. [13, 558, 622.]

GEOMETRIC PATTERN. Abstract design based on simple mechanical lines, such as squares, triangles, circles, etc.

GEORGIAN. In England within the period of George I, George II, George III—1714-1795. The first three Georges ruled an England of swelling importance, though their personal influence was not great. The interchange of ideas with the rest of the world, the wealth and growing leisure and fine living promoted the adoption of modes and manners from abroad, as well as the products of the ingenuity of native designers and craftsmen. The rising importance of individual designers made their personal styles the fashion, so that, unlike the period of Louis XIV, we think of a given period as that of Chippendale, Hepplewhite, Sheraton, or the Adam brothers. Naturally, much of their material overlapped, was interchanged with or borrowed from the same sources, so that we are at a loss to find an adequate name for the whole period. For that reason they are often lumped as Georgian.

Early Georgian usually begins with the passing of Queen Anne, 1714, and includes the style up to the ascendancy of Chippendale, about 1745. The style is a heavier, richer Queen Anne, substantial, and not excessively Rococo. There are much gilding and lavish upholstery. Chairs and tables have brass casters. Decorative details include the scallop shell on cabriole legs, eagles' heads on chair arms, satyrs' heads, lions' and ball-and-claw feet; cabinets were of solid architectural proportions. Mahogany was used, but some walnut work was still done.

Later Georgian styles are better known by the names of designers such as Chippendale, Hepplewhite, Sheraton, etc. See also ENGLAND.

GERMANY. The Teutonic peoples derived their first ideas of furniture from Rome, there being evidence of turned members of chairs and tools drawn from Roman models. Scandinavian elements of rich open-work carving, dragons and intertwined floral decorations occur on earlier medieval coffers. Chests on high legs, with sloping lids like a gable roof, display both Celtic and Byzantine ornamentation. Other chests are embellished with many iron bands. Construction and decoration are crude and elementary Romanesque.

GERMAN ROMANESQUE

The Gothic architectural influence reached domestic furniture early in the 15th century, but the Romanesque tradition remains in peasant work for several centuries. Chests decorated with mingled Romanesque and Gothic motives occur in low Saxony, in Holstein, in the Hartz Mountains, and elsewhere sufficiently to indicate that the type was general in the Netherlands, northern France, Scandinavia, England, and Alpine lands.

The later Gothic stage saw the evolution of chests with doors, variations known as credences, dressoirs, etc., in the lower Rhine district, parallel to the various cupboards of Flanders, France, and England. Linenfold decoration was universal. The post-and-panel method of construction was the great contribution of this age to cabinetwork, and from it developed all the drawer and cabinet forms.

There is a distinct line of demarcation between North German and South German types, due both to the nature of the accessible woods and the exposure to outside influence. North German work employs oak and follows the intricate ornament of the Scandinavian countries. South German work is in fir and pine, and exhibits North Italian influences coming both from the Alpine countries and from Flanders.

689 BENCH with reversible back, 15th century German. Gothic vine carving.

690 BAVARIA(?), dated 1693. Armoire with painted decoration of Gothic design.

Liebhold Wallach

691 SOUTH GERMAN, dated 1772. Medieval form persists —with inlaid decoration suggesting Rococo.

Liebhold Wallach

693 ROUND TABLE from Lübeck, early 18th century. Turnings are native characteristics; the whole form has a rich Baroque quality.

Metropolitan Museum of Art

692 SOUTH GERMAN (Augsburg), 16th century.

694 SACRISTAN CHEST, Salzburg, mid-18th century. Double-bodied buffet type of fine Baroque outline. Walnut, inlaid.

In South German work occurs a wide range of coffers and cupboards in all stages of evolution, with the carved ornament freely Gothic of the flamboyant school. Green and red paint emphasized the planes. Box settles, turned chairs of a type common in England two centuries later, and trestle tables are of well-developed type. A distinct form of bedstead has square posts and side pieces and a short wooden canopy at the head. See also GOTHIC. [93, 102, 178, 221, 343, 346, 457, 466, 484.]

THE RENAISSANCE

The free cities of southern Germany had a flourishing trade with northern Italy, and the first signs of the Renaissance appeared there. Woodcuts of furniture by Peter Flötner of Nuremberg appeared about 1542, showing Italian Renaissance details, and there are cupboards extant, probably of his workmanship, which show a mature appreciation of the Lombard forms. Classic ornament and intarsia are employed. Flötner's austere style was the prevalent type for a generation, but after 1580 the richer plastic decoration, with a larger vocabulary of ornaments, becomes the rule. Pilasters taper toward the base; heavily projecting consoles, lion motifs, scrollwork, and cartouches appear, and the trend toward the exuberant richness of the Baroque has begun. Examples of about 1600 from Ulm, Frankfort-am-Main, and Augsburg are parallel in the elaborate Late Renaissance tradition to the work of Flanders and northern France. Veneered panels of walnut and ash and intarsia enrich the fir and pine surfaces. Augsburg had a specialized cabinet industry, and the earliest Baroque forms appeared there about 1620. Elaborate joinery, such as mitering, broken corners, undulating moldings, all superseded carving. Chairs were four-legged board types, folding chairs and, later, armchairs with square legs. Turned

695 ARMOIRE, Austria or Bavaria, end of 18th century. Classic influence of Louis XVI style. Provincial version, fine carving in pine, probably originally painted.

696 BEDSTEAD, Louis XVI influence.

Both photographs, Liebhold Wallach

baluster legs displaced the latter in the Late Renaissance. This style clung to much of the South German work until after the mid-17th century.

In North Germany oak furniture continued to be made in the Gothic structural tradition through 1550. Cologne and Münster were centers of cabinetmaking and carving, and there the Early Renaissance first appears in the work of John Kupfer and Aldegraver. In Luneberg and Schleswig-Holstein restrained Italian ornament was merged with the Gothic. Schleswig-Holstein early produced the more exuberantly carved cupboards with metal ornament and scrollwork, while other regions followed with the imposition of Late Renaissance ornament upon Late Gothic shapes. The corner cupboard appeared about this time in Dithmarschen.

The bed with carved posts and canopy frame appeared in North Germany about the middle of the 16th century. Chairs for state uses were inlaid with ivory and silver. Lesser ones were elaborately carved and turned. Cabinets were of wide variety and were decorated with elaborate carving, architectural features, and intarsia panels. In these particulars, the High Renaissance remained the source of much German cabinetwork until the later 18th century.

BAROQUE

The substitution of bold-scale moldings, surfaces, and shapes for excessive applied plastic ornament differentiates the Early Baroque of Holland from the Late Renaissance styles of Germany. This took place about 1660, but the austere Dutch curves were speedily enriched in Nuremberg, Augsburg, Frankfort, and other centers of German skill. Frankfort cupboards were richly curved, lush in outline and modeling as a whole. To the north, Hamburg walnut cupboards of 1680 were severely, vigorously architectural, with heavy cornices and high raised panels. Pointed ovals, base with drawers and large bun feet, with richly carved enclosed leaf, flower, and fruit ornaments characterize these excellent ornate structures.

Spiral-turned legs are universal in earlier Baroque tables and chairs, but about 1690 the cabriole leg was widely accepted, indicating the penetration of the forms evolved at the court of Louis XIV. The Augsburg cabinetmakers followed the French lead with both ebony and Boulle tortoiseshell. The court of Frederick I was furnished with pure Louis XIV forms; from this time on, all the palaces borrowed directly from Paris, while the lesser workers lagged with the older styles.

This is particularly true of the Régence. This transitional style was readily taken up in the royal castles of Germany, and inspired lower-caste furniture for many years. Few new forms appear in important work; it is henceforward essentially French, with a variable time lag. Burgher furniture along Régence lines forms a fairly national style in South Germany; inlays after Boulle, and intarsia in ribbon patterns are characteristic. Bombé commodes and high chairbacks with smooth wooden splats are common.

ROCOCO

The Rococo style of Louis XV permeated German cabinetmaking through the period 1730-1790. Spreading from Belgium and Lorraine, spheres of French influence, the lavish naturalism of the French court styles was brought into Bavaria by the architects François de Cuvilles and Georg Knobelsdorff; the decorative sculptors Johann Hoppenhaupt and Johann August Nahl (1710-1781) luxuriated in magnificent carved decorations for backgrounds and furniture alike. Consoles, mirror frames, commodes, chairs deluxe and canapés were embellished with birds, fruit, and flowers, garden tools and musical instruments, carved, gilded, and painted in the French manner. North German palaces vied with those of Munich. Frederick's New Palace in Potsdam, like the Solitud near Stuttgart; others in Munich, Wilhelmthal, and the

GERMAN ROCOCO
COMMODE

Electors' castles on the Rhine and the Main being masterpieces of the style. It is noted, however, that most of the *meubles de luxe*—the bronze mounted commodes and writing tables, etc.—were actually made in Paris.

The German Rococo on its own initiative indulged in more unrestrained fantasy than its prototype. The bombé-shaped and loaded cornices are less airy, more solidly brilliant, and possibly excessive in the best work of Würzburg and Mainz. Chairs bear a strong resemblance to the simpler Dutch and English types, although the German cabriole shape is distinctive. Bright paint colors carved furniture of Bavaria and Austria.

Metropolitan Museum of Art, Bequest of John L. Cadwalader, 1914
697 TYPICALLY LATE BAROQUE CHAIR, 1725-1750, with Rococo elements.

698 GERMAN ROCOCO. Writing table of Frederick the Great. Chinoiserie decoration.

Dalva Brothers, Inc.

699 SMALL PEDESTAL SECRETAIRE; early 18th century.
Pictorial inlays of ivory, mother-of-pearl, enamels. Bronzedoré
mountings.

BIEDERMEIER

After 1830, the style settled down recognizably to
express easy comfort on a lightly classical foundation.
Light native woods, light birch, cherry, pear, apple,
maple, and ash were displayed to advantage, without
other ornament, in commodes and chests, tables, large
secretary-desks and cabinets. Curved chairs and sofas
were upholstered with horsehair, calico, and rep, and
bore infinite variety of graceful ornament based on
swans and griffins, cornucopias and domestic flowers
and fruits. Gothic bits were added to the ornamental
repertoire about 1840. But there was no solid Gothic
revival. This style is so dominantly middle class, so
comfortably gauche that it took its name from the
comic-paper character Papa Biedermeier, who expressed his simple political views in *Fliegende Blatter*.

The growing comfort and wealth of the mid-century
period undermined this simplicity and brought various
neo-Rococo and merely lavish picturesque effects. The
weakening of the genuine feeling for style is evidenced by the acceleration of the changes in style;
and by the end of the century pure eclecticism permitted Renaissance, Turkish, and Far Eastern neo-
Empire and neo-everything styles to come and go with
individual whims.

GERMAN CLASSICISM

The classic influence arrived after 1770 through
both French and English channels. The German cabinetmakers made writing tables and commodes, chairs
and cupboards in the familiar proportions and some
of the austerity of the Parisian manner. The classic
straight lines were more floridly ornamented. David
Roentgen surpassed many of his French contemporaries with his cylinder desks, commodes, writing
tables, etc., using light mahogany, superb marquetry
and ormolu mounts. As in France, the classic continued in essence to be an urban style, the provinces
retaining the exuberant curves of the Rococo, but
about 1800 the influence of Hepplewhite and Sheraton had penetrated these strongholds. The middle-
class furniture of Napoleonic Germany has an
appreciable style of its own, its later phases being
known as Biedermeier [138]. The early years of the
century produced a group of designs of light graceful
furniture, classic in form but devoid of excessive ornament, executed in light mahogany, pear, ash, cherry,
and poplar. The smooth veneered surfaces of the Empire style are common, but the proportions are better
and they have a livable human quality. Painted furniture was also popular.

700 CYLINDER DESK of mahogany and bronze, by David
Roentgen. End of 18th century. Clock and candlesticks of
the period.

701-702 ARMCHAIR AND TABLE, Munich, c. 1820.

703 SIDE TABLE c. 1810.

704 BIEDERMEIER SOFA c. 1820.
Gothic tracery detail.

705 HIGH CABINET with desk drawer. Mahogany, Munich, c. 1820.

706 BIEDERMEIER STYLE c. 1826.
Cylinder front.

707 GERMAN CHAIR, 18th century. Motives familiar in Scandinavian and Celtic work. Elements of the Windsor chair appear here also.

appreciation of the revolutionary ideas of William Morris led to the growth of the *Jugendstil*. This "Youth Style" as a German "Art Nouveau" produced little directly, but established a system of thought and art training more comprehensive, unified, and progressive than in other countries. After World War I, the movement toward functional form found its prophets in Germany, where the Bauhaus examined the reasons for design under the direction of Walter Gropius and Mies van der Rohe. Other powerful personalities, like Peter Behrens and Eric Mendelsohn, moved dynamically toward other objectives. The ferment was largely dispersed by the Hitler regime. The United States was the principal gainer. After 1945, Germany did not at once resume its role in design leadership. See also MODERN FURNITURE; NINETEENTH CENTURY.

GERMAN FOLK STYLES

As elsewhere in Europe, the fashionable styles in northern lands reflected only the tastes and symbols of the aristocratic class. Some of these styles filtered down through the lesser nobility, through the rich burghers, the merchants and the moneyed, and in the process the styles accommodated themselves to indigenous skills and tastes. There was always, however, a firm level of native or peasant taste that exhibits more of local skill. Woodcarving is a local art where wood is abundant and appreciated. From the Alps and the Black Forest to the birch woods of Sweden, carvers were skillful before outside influences were known. German craftsmen produced unique furniture in provincial regions from earliest times right up through the Industrial Revolution. [195.]

Not only wood but ceramics, iron, brass, glass, and everything available went into utilitarian objects of fine native design. The ceramic stove is a singularly successful product of these regions. [708.]

MODERN

The essential philosophy of the modern International Style grew largely in Germany, where an early

708 AUSTRIAN STOVE, 1589. Tile.

GESSO. Plastic preparation used for raised decoration. In Italy it was extensively employed on furniture in the Middle Ages and afterward. It was never very extensively used elsewhere, although, gilded, it was popular for a time under Charles II in England. [266, 755, 1078.]

GIBBONS, GRINLING, 1648-1721. English carver and designer. John Evelyn brought him to the notice of Christopher Wren, who employed him as a carver on St. Paul's and on Windsor Castle. His work and influence are the basis of English carving after that time. Most typical of his work are the garlands and festoons, birds and animals and other typically Baroque details exquisitely executed in rich high relief. The carving was usually done in pine, limewood, or similar close-textured woods, later nailed to the paneling and gilded on mantels, paneling, ceilings, overdoors, and important furniture. He combined superb draftsmanship, a remarkable sense of composition, and inspired craftsmanship. See also CARVING.

GIBBS, JAMES, 1682-1754. English architect, follower of Palladio. Like many of his contemporaries, he designed the furnishings as well as the structure. His *Book of Architecture* (1728) was one of many on the subject.

GILDING. Decorating with gold, either by application of gold leaf or powder in a liquid vehicle, producing a sumptuous effect.

GILLINGHAM, JAMES. Philadelphia cabinetmaker, born in 1736; he produced simple furniture of fine quality.

GILLOW, FIRM OF. English cabinetmakers, first known about 1728, who constructed much furniture during the 18th and 19th centuries.

GIMP (GUIMPE). Narrow flat tape, more or less ornamental, used as a trimming or finish on upholstery and drapery.

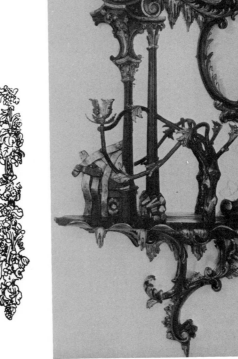

Symons Galleries, Inc.

709 GIRANDOLE, English Rococo, c. 1760, Chippendale design. Black and gold.

GIRANDOLE; GIRONDOLE. Wall bracket or chandelier, often with a mirror back. Later in the 18th century the mirror was made circular and convex— and was used alone. (Sometimes called bull's-eye mirror.) [72, 709, 866.]

GLAZED DOORS. Doors fitted with glass, often with a lattice pattern of woodwork, or tracery.

GLAZING. In painting, glazing is the application over the finish paint of a thin wash coat that is then wiped off, thereby modifying or subduing the base color. It produces a mixed, soft tone. Glazing is definitely not polish, or the application of a gloss, as on chintz.

GLOBE STAND. Wood or metal stand of pedestal, tripod, or other shape designed to hold terrestrial or celestial globes. Like other objects of scientific interest, they were given serious artistic treatment in the 18th century.

ENGLISH GLOBE STANDS LATE 18TH CENT.

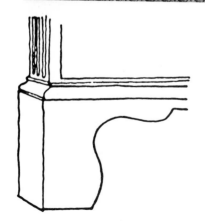

710 PHILADELPHIA CHIPPENDALE
CHEST by Gostelowe, 1775-1780. Serpentine front, original Adam brasses.

711 LABEL OF
JONATHAN GOSTELOWE.

Both photographs Pennsylvania Museum of Art, Philadelphia

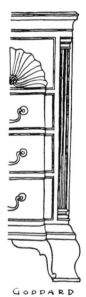

GODDARD

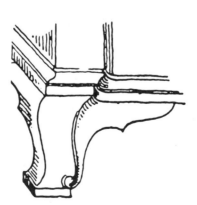

GLUE. Adhesive material of various kinds, used in veneering, joinery, etc. Good gluing provides the tightest joint of wood known. A proper glue joint will break less readily than the wood it holds together, but this implies good glue, good joining, and accurate fitting. Much study is now being given to adhesives for wood, with the object of producing waterproof joints, by a simpler process than the customary hot-glue method.

GOBELIN. French family of dyers, established in the 15th century, began to make tapestries in 1529. In 1662 their factory was purchased by the government and transformed into an upholstery manufactory under the direction of the painter Le Brun. This actually marks the beginning of the period of Louis XIV. During the 18th century they made chiefly tapestries, and in 1826 they added the manufacture of carpets. The industry is still conducted by the state.

GODDARD, JOHN. Latter half of the 18th century. An American cabinetmaker, he worked in Newport, R.I., with his son-in-law John Townsend. Produced distinct form of block-front desks, cabinets, secretaries, chests, etc., with shell carving. Bracket feet, usually ogee in shape and finely carved or in clustered shapes are also typical. See also RHODE ISLAND SCHOOL; TOWNSEND, JOHN. [1295.]

GONÇALO ALVES. Dense hardwood from Brazil. Color is light tan with red-brown stripes, with some curl.

GONDOLA (GONDOLE). Chair or sofa whose back curves downward continuously to form the arms, so called because of its supposed resemblance to an 18th-century gondola.

GOOSENECK. Double curved arch of the pediment of highboys and the like; also called swan-neck or broken arch.

GOOSENECK PEDIMENT

GOSTELOWE, JONATHAN, 1744-1795. Philadelphia cabinetmaker; produced distinguished mahogany furniture of Chippendale Baroque influence. A man of property and education, he made furniture of the finest type for a rich clientele. Nutting rates his identified work ahead of that of Savery. [710.]

GOTHIC. To the Romans, Gothic symbolized the barbarians of the North. To the Renaissance artists the name implied the unclassical, rudely homemade efforts of the Dark Ages, where men had lost the classic touch. Yet today the Gothic is regarded as having the primary greatness of a complete, spontaneous art system. The reason lies in our recognition of the underlying impulse; the deep need of people to construct, beautifully, the things they require out of the materials at hand. The only stable power of the time being the Church, the chief artistic expression was ecclesiastical. The cathedral was the triumph of Gothic art. Secular and domestic expressions lagged far behind. Gothic domestic furniture is therefore almost an anomaly.

ENGLISH PLANK CHEST ON FEET

Gothic architecture grew from the Romanesque, the style of Christian Europe between 800 and 1200. Vestiges of ancient Rome, particularly the round arch, were crossed with Byzantine showiness and the ancient semibarbaric themes of the Teutonic peoples, debased architectural forms with naturalistic and geometric ornament. The Gothic structural system developed in stone the notion of the skeleton framework. The great pointed arches, the pillars and buttresses are decorated with moldings and details of unique and logical type. These details were carried through into the detached wood furniture. Altars, screens, and other ritual furniture were magnificent, and in complete harmony with the architecture.

Secular Gothic art stemmed from the castles of the feudal barons. Such governing powers as they were able to seize and to hold were largely personal matters. The state of almost continuous warfare kept them moving about; their furnishings and their material wealth went with them from castle to castle. With mobility as the basis, chests and coffers were the principal articles of furniture; these carried clothing, bedding, valuables; they could be used as beds and seats for the retainers. Later, chests were mounted on feet or stands, but it was not until the 15th century that there appears a consistent type of furniture fore-

712 CHEST, Alpine manner, c. 1500.

Metropolitan Museum of Art, Fletcher Fund, 1930
713 NORTH ITALIAN GOTHIC CHAIR, 1450-1500, from Church of San Orso, Val d'Aosta, Piedmont.

714 CHEST, South German. Panel construction, scratch carving, nonecclesiastical quality.

shadowing the various cupboards, chests, and cabinets. These were invariably of oak. Earlier types were plank boxes, heavily bound with iron straps and locks, often with gabled tops. Later, flat-top chests had sides ornamented with carved representations of architectural forms. Finally the logic of the stone skeleton of buildings was applied to furniture; a sturdy framework held panels of thinner wood, which in itself created an ornamental type. The panels were further ornamented with linenfold, tracery, or painted designs. See also CHEST.

Chairs were almost a royal prerogative. Under nomadic conditions, folding chairs were carried only for the lord and his lady; when court was set up, a thronelike structure of canopy and dais was literally the court. Below sat the lesser ones, importance diminishing as distance grew. Seats with hinged or pivoted back rails developed from the practice of sitting on chests, the back adjustable to serve from either side.

Beds were chiefly textile; curtains and canopy and bedding were easily transportable. The framework of exposed wood appeared after security warranted such permanent structures. Beds retained their enclosure character until rooms became small enough to afford privacy and warmth. See also BED.

Tables for dining, like the refectory types, were unknown in secular use. For dining, boards were set on trestles: hence, "set the table." From the monastery came the desk idea, originally a portable box set on a collapsible frame. The box grew flatter, forming a worktable with a lift lid covering writing materials.

All this furniture, usually of unpolished oak, borrowed its decorative character from Church art. Carving in oak makes for large-scale, not too fine detail. Familiar floral forms, vines and leaves, with grotesque animal and human representations were often humorously rendered. Simple structural embellishments, such as grooves, moldings, and paneling, were typical; in later Gothic work these were scaled down to represent

715 TABLE, Alpine, c. 1500.

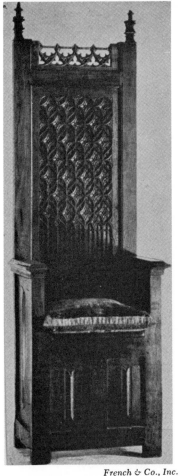

CABINET CRESTING

FRIEZE

CORNICE COVE

Metropolitan Museum of Art, Rogers Fund, 1905
716 OAK CHEST, France, late 15th century.

French & Co., Inc.
717 FRENCH CHOIR STALL, c. 1500.

Gothic Furniture

719 CREDENCE CUPBOARD, France.

718 COFFER-SEAT, Oak. Combines paneling with chest. 15th-century panel types.

720 WALNUT CHEST, France, early 16th century.
Metropolitan Museum of Art, Gift of George Blumenthal, 1941

721 SMALL BENCH, Late Gothic, pierced tracery.

722 PRIMITIVE GERMAN CHAIR, plank construction.

723 CREDENCE-BUFFET CABINET.
Late-style Gothic carving.

architectural arches, tracery, façades. Cusped arches, trefoil, quatrefoil, etc.; ogee curves and deep, full moldings were essential in the style everywhere. Painting later became general.

The Gothic as a style had extremes of type according to locale. In Italy there never was a true Gothic; Italian Gothic was merely the imposition of a few northern motives on a persistent classic taste, diluted with Eastern (Byzantine and Saracenic) forms and motives. Spain was Moorish through the early Gothic stages; even in her 15th-century Gothic a strong quality of Oriental light and shade is evident. France was scarcely a political entity. The style centered in the Île-de-France types, and spread with local variations from North and South. The Teutonic and Scandinavian lands worked in individual styles. The rise of secular nationalism came with the Renaissance, when Church influence in politics and in art waned. [126, 148, 169, 173, 225, 232, 343 *et seq.*, 544, 753, 1017, 1144.]

LATE GOTHIC COFFER

GOTHIC REVIVALS. England had a brief interest in the Gothic after 1740; and ornamental forms, fondly imagined to be in the "Gothic taste," were incorporated into furniture by Chippendale and others. Cusped arches, ogee curves, and similar rudiments were accepted as Gothic: there was no further effort or understanding of the whole concept of Gothic structure. [423, 533.]

Early in the 19th century another revival gained more momentum. Architecture profited chiefly; the Gothic became the accepted style for churches and, somewhat less, for schools. In furniture in America, England, and France it remained only a source of a few ornamental motives [137]. Somewhat later, Eastlake and William Morris and his school fostered an abortive attempt to reintroduce Gothic handicraft methods to combat the machine development. [532, 880.]

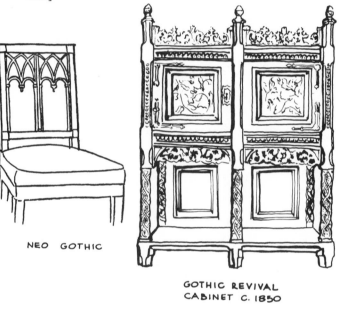

NEO GOTHIC

GOTHIC REVIVAL
CABINET C. 1850

GOUGE CARVING. Rudimentary form of decorative carving found in cruder styles such as the Gothic in Spain and England. Usually simple chisel marks in rhythmic repetition. [724, 1200.]

724 GOUGE CARVING, American box, early 17th century, suggestion of Gothic work.
Wadsworth Atheneum, Hartford, Conn., The Nutting Collection

GOUTHIÈRE, PIERRE-JOSEPH, 1740-1806. French bronze worker (*ciseleur*), famous for unsurpassed metal mounts for cabinets.

GRAIN. Wood fibers tend to assume characteristic arrangements in different species. When boards are cut, the cross sections of the fibers reveal these arrangements in patterns, which the cabinetmaker employs in the design much as the pattern or texture of fabric is used in draping and tailoring. See also WOOD.

GRAINING. Process of painting to resemble the color and figure of wood.

GRANDFATHER'S CLOCK. Tall clock case. [419.]

GRANDMOTHER'S CLOCK. Floor clock of smaller dimension than grandfather's clock.

GRECO-ROMAN. Refined decoration style of late classical antiquity, roughly 200 B.C.-A.D. 200. Appeared in 18th century through the excavations of Herculaneum and Pompeii, and formed the basis of the 18th-century classical revivals. In itself a free mixture of style in Egypt, Greece, and Rome, it was liberally misunderstood and misnamed.

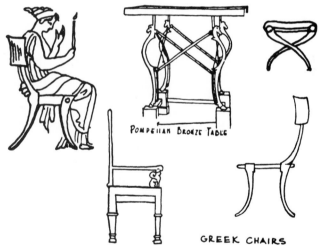

POMPEIIAN BRONZE TABLE

GREEK CHAIRS

GREEK, ANCIENT. The Golden Age of Greece, 1200-300 B.C., has left scant remains of furniture, but vase pictures and sculpture show many well-developed types of beds and couches, chairs and tables [205]. In literature we find references to "chests of cedar . . . gilt and inlaid with ivory." Chairs were gracious in outline, with sweeping curves on legs and backs. The form often suggests bronze rather than wood. Couches were elongated thrones, suggesting Egyptian origin, like much other Grecian furniture. Tables were low and portable, even as they occur in

Asia Minor today, and bronze animal legs and feet are found. Chests or coffers are found in an architectural-roofed shape, decoratively painted.

Turning, inlaying, carving, painting, encrusting with precious stones, gilding, etc., were widely practiced, and construction methods were good. The native olive and cedar, yew, box, and ebony seem to have been employed, and upholstery with silken cushions was known before 300 B.C.

GREEK FRET. Greek key pattern; repeated square hook-shaped forms as a band decoration.

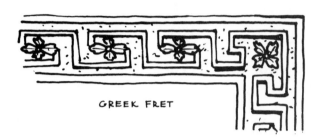

GREEK FRET

GRIFFIN (GRYPHON). Mythological beast, half eagle, half lion. Grotesque, occurring in much Late Italian Renaissance, French Renaissance through Louis XIV, and the work of Adam and Sheraton, and again in the Empire style. [89.]

GRILLE. Metal or wood latticework used in bookcase doors, cabinets. They were of brass or gilt wire in a variety of woven patterns and often had fabric curtains behind them. [152, 1158.]

GRISAILLE. Painting in various gray tints, representing solid bodies in relief. Fashionable in furniture decoration of the late 18th century. [588.]

GROS POINT. French coarse stitch embroidery used for upholstering chairs, etc.

GROTESQUES. Fantastic figures or part figures as decoration.

GUERIDON. Small French table for candles and small articles. [202.]

GUILLOCHE. Continuous running or band ornament of interlacing circles, found in every style after the Assyrian. [463.]

GUIMPE. Gimp.

GUINEA HOLES. Scooped out corners in 18th-century English card tables as receptacles for coins. [1267.]

GUMWOOD. Three species of gumwood are used in furniture: sweet, tupelo, and black gum. Sweet or red gum has a pinkish hue, especially in the sapwood. Tupelo has a tan-gray color, while black gum is the lightest, and has the most decided figure. All gums are susceptible to warping unless they are very carefully kiln-dried. They are commonly used for structural parts in less expensive cabinetwork, as they are strong and stain easily to resemble mahogany or walnut.

GROTESQUE

GRIFFIN (FRENCH)

PROVINCIAL FRENCH

DIRECTOIRE GUERIDON

GUERIDON LOUIS XIV

GUILLOCHES

H-STRETCHER. Typical stretcher construction, as in some Windsor and Chippendale chairs. A stretcher from front to back leg on each side is connected through the middle by a third member.

HADLEY CHEST. Early American chest, first found in Hadley, Mass. Typical tulip carving over front rails as well as the three panels. Often with a drawer. [354.]

HAIG, THOMAS. Partner of Chippendale.

HAIRCLOTH. Fabric woven of horsehair, colored or small-figured, typical of mid-19th-century upholstery. A mixture of horsehair and linen was used by the 18th-century English upholsterers.

HALF COLUMN. Engaged column against a flat surface or rounded pilaster.

HALF-HEADED BED. Short posted bedstead without canopy.

HALF-TURNING (SPLIT SPINDLE). Turned members sawn in half, lengthwise, usually applied to a flat surface as ornament, particularly in English and American Jacobean, Italian and German Renaissance. Also used as spindles in chairs (Jacobean) with the smooth side to the sitter's back. [11, 137, 242, 725, 873.]

Wadsworth Atheneum, Hartford, Conn.
725 HALF TURNINGS (split spindles) as decoration on American oak chest dated 1694.

HALFPENNY, W. AND J. 18th-century English architects and designers.

HALL CHAIRS. Formal, ornamental chairs, originally named by Manwaring.

HALL CLOCK. Grandfather's, or any tall, clock case.

HALL TREE. Stand or framework, wood or metal, for coats and hats, etc. [1299.]

HALVING-IN. Method of joinery. See also CONSTRUCTION.

HANDLE. Knobs or pulls on drawers and doors. The types and materials have varied in all periods to such an extent that handles constitute a sure index to the period of a piece of furniture. Wood, metal, glass, ivory, etc., have been adapted and designed in characteristic forms; the better the designs, the more harmoniously related was the hardware to the case, as to size, spacing, shape, material. See also HARDWARE.

HANGING. Bed and window curtains and portable wall coverings are hangings. Medieval construction provided no finish for interior walls, so that men of wealth carried with them to their various transient abodes hangings that provided grace and comfort to the harsh castle interiors. Bed curtains and window curtains were variations of these same draperies, as these were still architectural features. The latter were almost always plain fabrics, such as fustian, but the wall hangings early took on highly decorative character. The conventionalized patterns of medieval weaves became tapestries, which in turn became in the hands of the French weavers, representations of paintings, including the representation of a gilt frame.

Leather hangings of Spanish or Saracenic origin, with typical stamped embellishment and coloring, were popular on the Continent during the 16th and 17th centuries.

Papers, pasted to the wall displaced textile hangings very largely in the 18th century.

HANGING SHELVES; BOOKSHELVES; PLATE SHELVES. Oldest surviving examples of these types are found to be of crude type, particularly in England and France. The latter are exclusively Provincial and are of mid-18th-century character. English oak shelves of Early Jacobean date are carved abundantly, with double-arch shapes. 18th-century shelves developed with the craze for china collecting: Chippendale's school produced jigsawed variations on Chinese themes with Gothic accents. Hepplewhite's book illustrates simple types, some with turned uprights. Many of these types have survived, made of mahogany or satinwood with inlay and painted decoration. Amer-

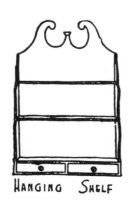

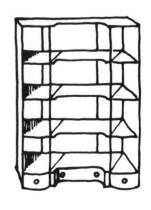

HANGING SHELF

726 YEW WOOD c. 1765.

Symons Galleries, Inc.

728 ROCOCO MANNER,
late 18th century.

727 MAHOGANY c. 1770.   *Needham's Antiques, Inc.*

ENGLISH
HANGING SHELVES,
LATE 18th CENTURY.

ican hanging shelves after 1750 are of similar style, usually plainer. The country types of pine are rarely decorated, but show inventiveness in decorative outlines. [450, 726, 1332.]

HARDWARE. Fittings of metal were originally intended to strengthen the heavy board construction of chests, etc., and early became decorative features as well. Earliest Gothic chests have beautifully wrought iron straps and corners, hinges and locks, hasps and keys. As stronger joinery became the rule the metal fittings were allowed to lapse into decorative desuetude. Renaissance furniture relegated hardware to an inferior place; brass and bronze replaced iron, and mounts virtually disappeared. Functional details such as hinges and locks were subdued, largely through technical improvements. Gothic hinges had exposed leaves that were fashioned into such decorative shapes as the dolphin, cock's head, loop, and H-hinges. These designs persisted, especially in ironwork and in rural districts, but sophisticated Renaissance work used butt hinges, concealed like the countersunk locks, etc. This left only keys and key plates and handles as decorative members; these were fine in scale and delicately wrought, often chased. Handles or pulls were either knobs or drop handles. Pear, tear, and ball shapes were common drops, while bails were gracefully formed and fitted with ornate escutcheons or back plates. Later Baroque and Early Georgian work employed

silver extensively. [15, 359.]

The Rococo style revived interest in metalwork. Bronze appliqués were a mainstay of the ornamentalist, and much of the effect of Rococo furniture derives from the contrast of exquisitely chased bronze and gilt metal against the background of fine veneer. Handles, key plates, etc., were particularly fine. Chippendale's handles were ornate Baroque-Rococo compositions, and form an essential contrast with the mahogany.

The classic revivals brought new hardware designs, severe in outline and fine in scale. Ring handles were general in Regency and all Empire styles, and decorative metal appliqués of classical themes were universal. Mirrors were metal ornamented, and galleries and beadings of brass were common.

Late-18th-century handles began to utilize glass, ivory, and porcelain. These remained throughout the 19th century. The turn of the century featured copper and leather, and modern styles added chromium, aluminum, and the plastic materials.

HAREWOOD. Greenish-gray wood, actually sycamore or, in America, curly maple, stained or dyed to a thin gray tone. Originating in England in the 18th century, it was used chiefly for inlays and decorative veneering. Widely favored in early modern work in France, England, and America, in spite of its tendency to lose the dye and to assume a greenish cast.

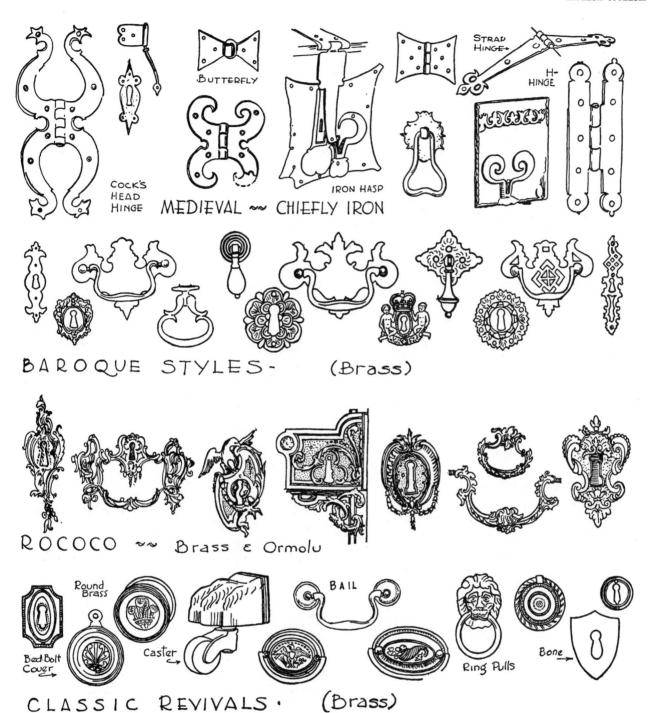

COCK'S HEAD HINGE

BUTTERFLY

IRON HASP

STRAP HINGE

H-HINGE

MEDIEVAL ~~ CHIEFLY IRON

BAROQUE STYLES - (Brass)

ROCOCO ~~ Brass & Ormolu

CLASSIC REVIVALS · (Brass)

Bed-Bolt Cover

Round Brass

Caster

BAIL

Ring Pulls

Bone

CHINESE BRASSES

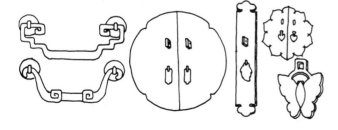

SABOT   KNEE   LOUIS XVI

Israel Sack, Inc.

731 HARLEQUIN TABLE. Pigeonholes and writing bed rise when top leaf is unfolded. American Hepplewhite c. 1790.

HARLEQUIN TABLE. Table invented by Sheraton in which the center part rises automatically when the leaves are raised, revealing fittings and compartments for toilet articles or writing materials. Recently adapted to bar and cellarette uses. [731, 1386.]

HARVARD CHAIR. Three-cornered chair with all turned members; Early American (17th-century) version of a Gothic type found throughout the Continent in Late Gothic and Early Renaissance stages. [732.]

HASP. Hinged part of a hinge lock, used decoratively in Gothic and Spanish cabinets.

HASSOCK. Thickly stuffed upholstered footstool showing no wood.

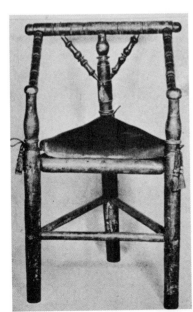

732 "HARVARD" CHAIR, English Cromwellian. *French & Co., Inc.*

HATRACK. Nineteenth-century hall furniture, ranging from wall rack with hooks or pegs to freestanding structure with box bench, mirror, etc. See also COSTUMER; UMBRELLA STAND. [1299.]

HEADBOARD. The entire head section of a bed; or the boards within the head framework.

HEART AND CROWN. Baluster-back chair whose cresting has cutouts of these shapes.

HEART-BACK. Shield-back chair, Hepplewhite type.

HENRY II; HENRY III. Medici kings of France whose Italian preferences imposed Italian forms upon the French Renaissance-Gothic of Francis I. Their style was completely Baroque Italian, but more highly carved and decorated, featuring interlaced strapwork, delicate reliefs, cartouches, etc. See also FRANCE.

HENRY VIII. The first English monarch to look away from England's insularity, Henry VIII literally imported the Renaissance into England. The lessening of Church influence affected the design of furniture, and the influx of Italian motives enriched the heavy, severe furniture of earlier days. For the most part shapes remained Gothic, but unquestionably Italian ornamentation appeared. See also ENGLAND. [106.]

HEPPLEWHITE
WINDOW SEAT

HEPPLEWHITE, GEORGE. Died 1786. It is known that he worked for the firm of Gillow and that he began to make furniture in London about 1760. He collaborated with the Adam brothers much as did Chippendale, and produced furniture in a more rational, simple version of their taste. Some of his work modifies the earlier French styles; his later output develops the classic outlines. Two years after his death his widow, Alice, published *The Cabinet Maker and Upholsterer's Guide* "from drawings by A. Hepplewhite and Co., Cabinet Makers." As only ten of the drawings are signed "Hepplewhite," it is assumed that this work illustrates the prevailing fashions interpreted by many contributors. See also ENGLAND. [43, 46, 453, 593, 733, 734.]

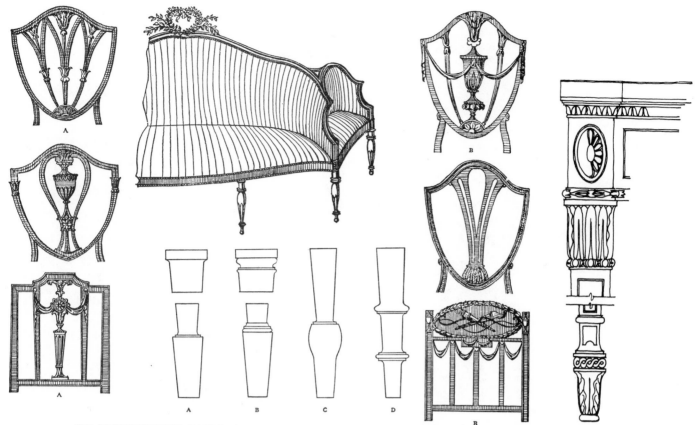

733 HEPPLEWHITE DESIGNS FOR CHAIRBACKS, "CONFIDANTE," TURNED AND SQUARE FEET. From the 1794 *The Cabinet Maker and Upholsterer's Guide.*

Israel Sack, Inc.

734 HEPPLEWHITE MAHOGANY CARD TABLE, Massachusetts, c. 1812.

HERALDIC EMBLEM

HERALDIC FORMS. Early furniture being a noble prerogative, it often carried the arms or other heraldic marks of the noble owner. Thus, reproductions of such furniture, mainly of the Middle Ages, Tudor English, Renaissance, Italian, German, French, and Spanish, are emblazoned with symbols which in themselves are no more decorative or significant than a monogram.

HERCULANEUM. The excavation of the Roman city of this name after 1719 revived interest in the decorative arts of the Romans. This persisted throughout the 18th century, particularly as the inspiration of the classic styles of Louis XVI and the Adams.

The name specifically was applied by Sheraton to a type of upholstered chair in the antique style.

HERRERA, JUAN DE. Spanish architect, reign of Philip II—1556-1598; his name applied to the style of the period, noted for austere, harsh design. A reaction to the brilliant plateresque style preceding it, it was followed by the even more exuberant Baroque called churrigueresque. See also SPAIN.

HERRINGBONE. Inlay banding in which the alternately slanting grain produces a chevron or herringbone effect. Louis XIV and Queen Anne particularly. [1030.]

735 HIGHBOY, English, c. 1690. William and Mary, recalls contemporary styles in France, including suggestion of Boulle design in seaweed marquetry.

H-HINGE. One with exposed, long flat leaves that when opened resemble the letter *H*. See also HARD-WARE. [443, 1035.]

HICKORY. Strong, tough, elastic American wood, good for bent parts, or parts where thinness and strength are required, as in Windsor chairs. Oak color and texture; it is too hard to work easily.

HIGHBOY. Tall chest of drawers, usually in two sections, the upper chest being carried on a tablelike structure or lowboy with long legs. The form is essentially English, the earlier chests on turned stands appearing in the early 17th century. Transported to the American colonies, it developed with William and Mary and Queen Anne influences into the unique and characteristic highboy of Colonial America of the 18th century. See also CHEST; TALLBOY. [26, 735.]

Henry Ford Museum, Dearborn, Mich.

737 NEW ENGLAND QUEEN ANNE, 1720-1730. Burl walnut.

Henry Ford Museum, Dearborn, Mich.

736 William and Mary manner in AMERICAN HIGHBOY of burl walnut. Early 18th century.

738 NEW YORK HIGHBOY c. 1800 (linen press), attributed to Michael Allison.

Anderson Galleries

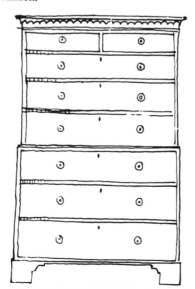

739 CONNECTICUT CHIPPENDALE CHEST-ON-CHEST c. 1760. Cherry.

Israel Sack, Inc.

Anderson Galleries

740 ENGLISH TALLBOY c. 1760. Secretary drawer.

Metropolitan Museum of Art, Rogers Fund, 1913

742 FRENCH EMPIRE SECRETARY of highboy type, amboyna wood with ormolu mounts.

741 SWEDISH, mid-18th century.
Influence of English forms.

Henry Ford Museum, Dearborn, Mich.

Metropolitan Museum of Art, Rogers Fund, 1921

743 HIGH CHAIR, Ohio, 1840-1850. Made by Shakers.
744 CHILD'S CHAIR, English, c. 1650.

HIGH CHAIR. This special long-legged seat for young children has been given affectionate attention to design since earliest chair history. [743, 744.]

HIGH RELIEF. Deep surface carving. See also CARVING.

HINGE. Simple mechanism that permits doors, lids, etc., to swing on a pivot center. Decorative forms are characteristic of the various styles. See also HARDWARE.

HIP. Same as knee, in speaking of the part of a chair or table leg of cabriole shape. More exactly, the horizontally elongated part of a cabriole leg above the line of the seat rail as found on English chairs from 1700 to 1760. [262.]

HISPANO-MORESQUE. Spanish style with Moorish influence. See also SPAIN.

HITCHCOCK. The Hitchcock chair is an American type, 1820-1850, named after Lambert Hitchcock of Connecticut. The typical form derives from a Sheraton

HITCHCOCK

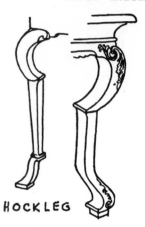

HOCKLEG

"fancy" chair, and has a typical "pillow back," or oval-turned top rail, straight-turned front legs, a rush or caned seat enclosed in thin wood strips. Most often these were painted to simulate rosewood, with a unique powdered-gold stencil of fruit and flowers. See also CHAIR. [78, 325.]

HOCK LEG. Cabriole leg with a curve and angle under the knee.

HOGARTH CHAIR. English chair, early 18th century, of the decorated Queen Anne style. Has hoop back and pierced splat, with a heavy-kneed straight cabriole leg.

HOLLAND, HENRY. English architect, 1746-1806, fostered the use of Greco-Roman details.

HOLLY (Ilex). Hard grayish-white wood, among the whitest of all woods, with small flecked grain. Used primarily for inlays, it has been favored in modern work for larger surfaces.

HONEYSUCKLE. Basis of conventional ornament; the anthemion of Greek origin, it was revived with other classicism in the Renaissance in every form of decoration. See also ORNAMENT.

HOOD (HOODED TOP). Shaped top, usually curved, on a highboy, clock case, etc. See also BONNET TOP.

HOOF FOOT. Hoof-shaped base of a leg, representing principally the goat hoof on a cabriole leg. See also CABRIOLE. [1222.]

HOOP BACK. Chairback whose uprights and top rail form a continuous curve. Bow back in Windsor chairs.

HONEYSUCKLE ORNAMENT

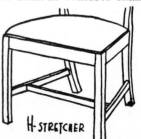

H-STRETCHER

HOPE, THOMAS, 1769-1831. English writer, architectural dilettante, who was influenced by the Empire designs of Percier and Fontaine. His book *Household Furniture and Interior Decoration* (1807) formulated an archaeological classicism for furniture that was not well received but nevertheless epitomizes the classical massiveness of the period. See also ENGLAND; NINETEENTH CENTURY. [312, 745.]

HOPE CHEST. Dower chest; traditional form of furniture for storage of trousseaus. See also CHEST.

HORSE. Primitive trestle or stand to support table-top or board.

HORSEHAIR. See HAIRCLOTH. [1138.]

HORSESHOE ARCH. Arch whose curvature is more than half-circle. Occurs in Moorish decoration.

745 THOMAS HOPE, drawings from *Household Furniture . . .* (1807).

HORSESHOE BACK. In Windsor chairs, outward sweep at the base of the bow of the back.

HORSESHOE TABLE. English wine table, 18th century. See also HUNT TABLE; WINE TABLE.

HOUSING. In joinery, grooving of one piece of wood into another.

HUCHIER (French). Cabinetmaker, chiefly one who makes fine cabinets by the panel method of construction.

HUNT TABLE. Semicircular table with an open middle fitted with pivoted device for bringing bottles to any point of the radius; sometimes with drop leaves

or other expansion. English, late 18th, 19th centuries. See also WINE TABLE. [587, 1239.]

HUNTING CHAIR. Sheraton design with a slide in front upon which to rest the feet.

HUSK. Drop ornament, such as the cornflower or catkins of shrubs, arranged in diminishing series. From classical times down.

HUTCH. From the French *huche*. A chest or cabinet with doors, usually on legs. An early form descending from the Gothic and disappearing after the 17th century. Its principal interest is as progenitor of the chest—court-cupboard sideboard. The type was common in France and Italy and particularly in Early Jacobean England, whence it came to America.

IMBRICATION. Decoration resembling fish scales, adapted from the antique Roman in the Italian Renaissance.

IN THE WHITE. Any cabinetwork or woodwork in the raw state, before the wood is finished.

INCE AND MAYHEW. English firm of cabinetmakers and upholsterers published *The Universal System of Household Furniture* (1762) illustrating their designs. Many of them were based on Chippendale's work, and much of the actual furniture is in a lesser Chippendale manner.

INCISED LACQUER. Decoration carved into lacquer that has been built up in layers of sufficient thickness.

INCISED ORNAMENT. Deeply cut engraved or carved work, the entire being cut *into* the surface rather than raised from it. [1144.]

INDIAN GOODS. All Oriental objects imported into Europe from the latter 16th century to the middle 18th century were called Indian goods.

INITIAL. Initials, monograms, etc., were favorite decorative devices from ancient times. Conventionalized letters of monarchs' names, up to Napoleon, were frequent in State furniture. Personal furniture, such as dower chests, toilet cases, writing boxes, etc., were often monogrammed.

INLAY. Designs formed in wood through the contrast of grains, colors, and textures of wood, metal, ivory, tortoiseshell, mother-of-pearl, etc., inserted *flush* into the wood. The process is one of the oldest of the arts, the Egyptians surpassing many later peoples in their skill. Ancient records indicate that this was the most prized of the woodworkers' arts. In the Renaissance the earlier work appears to have been inlaid into the solid wood; only later reappears the ancient method of assembling the small pieces comprising the whole design in veneers, and laying and gluing them to the background wood. [159, 174, 699, 791.]

INTAGLIO. Carved design cut into the surface; differs from cameo cut on which the design is raised from the surface. [32.]

746-747 INTARSIA PANELS in Louis XVI cabinets.
Dalva Brothers, Inc.

IMBRICATION

IONIC

INITIALS

INTARSIA. Form of wood inlay, especially of other materials, such as ivory and metal, derived from Oriental ivory inlays. It first appeared in European work in Siena, in the 13th century. [360, 746, 791.]

INTERNATIONAL STYLE. Modern functional manner, so called from its freedom from nationalistic traditions of decoration and its development along similar lines in many countries. Inspired purely by material and purpose, which today vary only slightly in different lands, furniture tends to assume a similar appearance everywhere. See also FUNCTIONAL; MODERN FURNITURE.

INTERRUPTED ARCH. Arched pediment, the center or top part of which is cut away. [1041.]

INTERRUPTED PEDIMENT. See BROKEN PEDIMENT.

INVERTED CUP. Turning profile of cup shape typical of Jacobean and later work. See also TURNING.

IONIC. Greek and Roman order of architecture, distinguished by double voluted capital. See also ORDERS. [1208.]

IRISH. Early in the 18th century a cabinetmaking industry developed in Ireland to the extent that con-

siderable furniture was exported to Britain and the colonies. The style was identical with contemporary English work, and there appear to be "no decisive criteria . . . for discriminating what is Irish and what is English" (Hinckley). Superficially, certain heavy aprons and exaggerated carving in masks seem distinctive. Much of this work, dating 1730-1750, is called Irish Chippendale.

IRISH CHIPPENDALE. Type of mahogany furniture probably made in Ireland by local craftsmen in the mid-18th century after designs in Chippendale's published works. It is solid, rather heavy in form, and ornamented with disconnected flat carving. Lion masks and paw feet are characteristic. [748.]

IRON: Iron figures in furniture in both cast and wrought form. Earliest wood construction relied on iron reinforcement more than on joinery, as in the hinges and straps of Romanesque and Gothic work [341, 544]. Spanish design made extensive use of such elaborate wrought-iron features as stretchers [1205] and beds, as well as applied ornaments. Iron casting produced important furniture components in the 19th century, finally reaching a considerable repertory of furniture designs clearly conceived in terms of that material. Outdoor furniture of Victorian vintage is most familiar. Cheapness and ease of mass produc-

748 IRISH CHIPPENDALE, 1730-1750, mahogany side table. *Metropolitan Museum of Art, Bequest of John L. Cadwalader, 1914*

751 IRON BED, 19th century. Tubing bars, cast ornaments, and spring-steel strapping. Crystal Palace, 1851.

SPANISH WROUGHT IRON

749-750 CAST-IRON STOVES, New York State, 1843-1845.

Henry Ford Museum, Dearborn, Mich.

752 FLORENTINE WROUGHT-IRON TORCHÈRE, 16th century.
Anderson Galleries

tion was second only to the attraction of its plasticity and durability. Utilitarian articles, like stoves, sewing-machine stands, table bases, small receptacles, and ornaments, are a considerable legacy of Victorian design. [749.]

ITALIANATE; IN THE ITALIAN MANNER. In design, refers to Renaissance details as imposed upon regional styles in northern Europe and England in the late 16th century and after. [164, 462, 551.]

ITALY. If we divide man's history into the ancient era, the Middle Ages, and modern times, we must look to Italy for the source of the arts of the modern world. Geography made Italy the heir of the Roman Empire; it also gave it the seat of the Church, and dominance of trade operations through the Middle Ages. The feudal system and its Gothic church art never flourished in the lively trading cities of Italy, Venice, Genoa, Rome, Milan, Florence. [133, 176, 191, 198, 211, 217, 253.]

Exploration and commerce engendered a spirit of free inquiry, and the Renaissance was born. Established dogma, pat, static ideology quivered before the heretic questionings of mathematicians, geographers, artists, poets, and philosophers. These rediscovered the works of the ancient Greeks and Romans and fostered the cult of Humanism, the glory of individual man. This was the *Renaissance*, a rebirth, a new conception of the exploring mind. At first the Church opposed it as revived paganism; then turned toward it gradually. The material blessings were accepted most readily. The classic pagan arts were less difficult to Christianize than the philosophy. Italian church art, never truly Gothic, vied with secular art to reproduce and interpret the glories of Greece and the grandeur of Rome.

The chronology of Italian furniture is therefore based on the unfolding of the Renaissance. For convenience the following distinctions of period may be observed.

1. PRE-RENAISSANCE period, 1100-1400. Insincere, misunderstood Gothic on a base of classic Romanesque, Byzantine, and Saracenic art.
2. QUATTROCENTO, 1400-1500. The Early Renaissance, a style of classical purity, simplicity.
3. CINQUECENTO, 1500-1600. The High Renaissance. The first half was the great period of the Renaissance.
4. BAROQUE, 1560-1700. The Counter Reformation in art, a Jesuit movement.
5. SETTOCENTO ROCOCO, 1700-1750. Secular prettification of the Baroque.
6. FOREIGN INFLUENCE, 1750-1900. All the eclectic revivals; the impulses originating chiefly in France and England and including the classic styles of Louis XVI, Hepplewhite, Adam, etc.; Directoire, Empire, mid-19th-century, etc., in freely modified versions.

PRE-RENAISSANCE

Italian furniture of the Middle Ages, unlike the homogeneous Gothic style, shows the classic-Romanesque basis, enriched with Byzantine and Saracenic motives. Crusaders, sailors, merchants, and explorers brought influences from the Near and Far East and Africa. Wealth and power were largely in the hands of the rich merchant families; their palaces displayed a cosmopolitan, secular style; but only a minimum of furniture was needed. [341, 713, 753.]

The chest (Italian *cassone*), as elsewhere, was all-important, but continued to be made of planks and

heavy boards long after the superior framed-panel construction was the rule in France. In the Piedmont and other localities touched by the Alpine styles appear evidences of Gothic details, such as pointed arches, etc., but their Gothicism is superficial. Venice has pierced tracery carving, with Persian overtones. Flat surfaces were painted with landscapes or textile patterns, sometimes raised with gesso and sometimes inlaid with mosaic and marble (Cosmatesque work) or with ivory or bone in fine geometrical patterns (certosina) in Moorish style.

The Italian climate discouraged the enclosed bed, in place of which Oriental fabrics and rugs were used, probably with light four-post frames. [119.]

QUATTROCENTO

Renewed interest in ancient art endowed all furniture of the Early Renaissance with an architectonic outline. Chests and cupboards, heretofore box forms, had bases, pilasters, and cornices, scaled down from architecture; the architectural profile is a distinguishing Renaissance feature. Their bases were pedestals, solid to the floor, rather than feet. The chest type was modified into new shapes for specialized purposes. The *cassapanca* was a *cassone* with back and sides to form a settee; cushions were added for comfort. The "credenza" was a low sideboard with doors and drawers. [430, 475.]

Chairs were principally straight rectangular structures *(sedia)* large and dignified and uncomfortable, with flat arms at right angles to the backpost; the seats were padded at an early date. The X-chair shows many variations; from the Moorish folding chair came the Savonarola chair [214] interlacing curved slats with carved wooden back and arms [215], often with certosina ornament. The Dante chair had four curved legs continuing into arms, with a fabric or leather seat and back. *Sgabelli* were wooden side chairs; some had three legs doweled into the seat, with a flat board back; others had bases of two carved slabs. [217.]

Tables derived largely from the long trestle type, with turned baluster legs or shaped slabs, but four-leg types with box stretchers appeared early. There are many incidental table forms. [1198, 1204.]

Austerely restrained surfaces in the early phase became highly decorated as the period waxed. Ornament was purely classic in character, with pilasters and scrolled volutes, fine moldings enriched with egg-and-dart, dentils, etc.; panels, with foliated scrolls, were delicately carved. Gilding and polychromy in strong colors, landscapes, and conventional painting decorated flat areas and moldings.

753 ITALIAN
GOTHIC ARMCHAIR, 14th century.

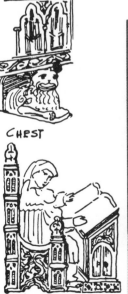

CHEST

ITALIAN GOTHIC

DURING THE 15th CENTURY THE MEMORY OF ANCIENT ROME INSPIRED THE
ARTS OF THE RENAISSANCE AT THE SAME TIME THAT THE GOTHIC OF
THE NORTH REACHED ITS ZENITH. NEVER TRULY UNDERSTOOD OR DEVEL-
OPED, GOTHIC IN ITALY FADED OUT AS CLASSIC ARCHITECTURE ROSE TO
UNIVERSAL DOMINANCE IN THE 15th AND 16th CENTURIES.

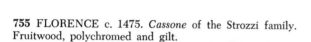

754 "STIPO"—walnut writing
cabinet, 16th century.
Anderson Galleries

755 FLORENCE c. 1475. *Cassone* of the Strozzi family.
Fruitwood, polychromed and gilt.

Metropolitan Museum of Art, Kennedy Fund, 1913

756 TUSCAN CARVED
WALNUT PRIE-DIEU,
16th century.

757 SACRISTY CABINET, painted on walnut,
late 15th century.   *Metropolitan Museum of Art, Rogers Fund, 1945*

760 CASSONE, 16th century. Walnut, gilt carving.

Frick Collection

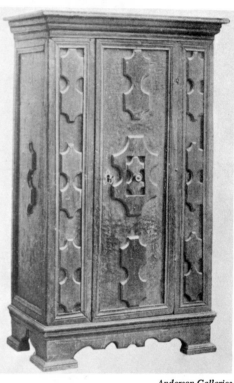

Anderson Galleries
761 FLORENTINE
IRON TORCHÈRE.

Metropolitan Museum of Art, Bequest of Benjamin Altman, 1913
759 DANTE—folding chair—Venice, after 1550.
Carved walnut, red velvet cushions.

Anderson Galleries
758 UMBRIAN CABINET, 16th century.

762 REFECTORY TABLE, Bologna, 16th century.

French & Co., Inc.

763 CARVED WALNUT CABINET, end of 15th century.
Di Salvo

764 MIRROR, carved polychromed wood. Venice.
Anderson Galleries

765 PANELED WALNUT CABINET. Tuscany, early 17th century.
Anderson Galleries

766 TABLE in two semicircular parts, walnut.
French & Co., Inc.

767 VENETIAN BAROQUE ARMCHAIR, walnut; 17th century.
Anderson Galleries

768 SILVERED WOOD TORCHÈRE, 17th century.

769 FLORENCE, 16th century.
Metropolitan Museum of Art

770 VENETIAN TORCHÈRE, silvered wood; 17th century.

771 BED, carved walnut and wrought iron; 17th century.

773 BAROQUE CABINET c. 1700.   *Anderson Galleries*

772 OCTAGONAL CENTER TABLE, walnut, Tuscany, 16th century.

Anderson Galleries

BY 1700, ITALY HAD CEASED TO EXPORT THE
BAROQUE RENAISSANCE, WHICH BEGAN TO FLOW
BACK IN THE FRENCH FORMS OF RÉGENCE AND
ROCOCO.

All photographs, Olivotti

774 ARMCHAIR of French Régence inspiration; Venice
c. 1700.

775 SECRETARY-CABINET.
Fanciful shape in dramatic veneers.

BAROQUE SHAPES SHOW TECHNICAL VIRTUOS-
ITY, TASTE FOR EXTRAVAGANT OUTLINE.

776 BOMBÉ CHEST.

777 ITALIAN ROCOCO DESK, walnut veneers.

FRENCH ROCOCO IDEAS WERE ENTHUSI-
ASTICALLY TAKEN UP IN 18th-CENTURY
ITALIAN FURNITURE.

779 SOFA, Louis XV influence.

Lavezzo

Olivotti

778 PAINTED SEDAN CHAIR c. 1775.

780 CHAIR in Louis XV manner.
Olivotti

781 CABINET, mid-18th century.
Rococo, distinctly Italian.

French & Co., Inc.

782 POLYCHROME BEDSTEAD,
Baroque, early 18th century.
Olivotti

THE CLASSIC REVIVAL IN ITALY FOLLOWED
THE MANNER OF LOUIS XVI AND ENGLISH
INTERPRETATIONS BUT MAINTAINED A DIS-
TINCTLY ITALIAN IDIOM.

272

Metropolitan Museum of Art, Gift of George Blumenthal, 1941
783 ARMCHAIR, classic Italianized Louis XVI;
painted and gilded; 1770-1785.

Metropolitan Museum of Art, Rogers Fund, 1923
784 LOMBARDY, 1770-1780. Painted and gilded console and
mirror in the manner of Albertolli.

785 CONSOLE TABLE AND MIRROR c. 1800.
Brunovan, Inc.

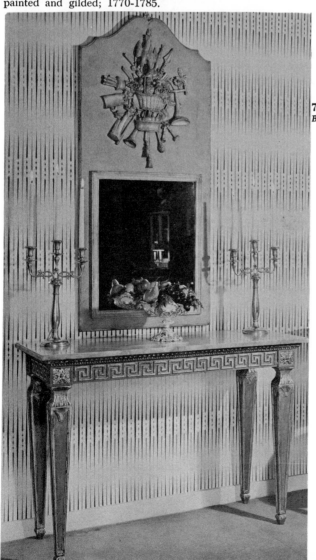

791 INLAID COMMODE, end of 18th century.
French & Co., Inc

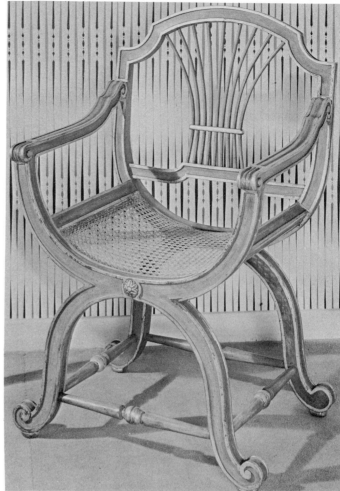

788 NEOCLASSIC CHAIR c. 1835. *Brunovan, Inc.*

792 TRUMEAU, Directoire simplification.

793 CHEST. *Don Ruseau*

Italian Neoclassic, 1800-1835

789 TRUMEAU. *Brunovan, Inc.*
790 EMPIRE COMMODE, Egyptian detail.

786 BEDSTEAD, late 18th century. *French & Co., Inc.*

787 LYRE TABLE.

A few general characteristics run through almost all Italian furniture of the 15th and 16th centuries.

1. The wood is universally walnut, oiled or waxed to a deep, rich tone.

2. Ornament is sparing, but increases progressively from the simplest early style to a highly decorative character later. Paint and gesso, even inlay, are less common in later work, while carving becomes the principal resource for decoration.

3. Proportion is architecturally large and stately, proper to large rooms; even chairs were larger than in modern usage, so that most Renaissance furniture is overlarge and uncomfortable by current standards.

Italian furniture is distinguishable by local styles. Tuscany, centering in Florence, led in the Early Renaissance. Her style was refined and nobly restrained. Siena is noted for painted and gilt furniture, while in Lombardy the certosina inlay was favored. Venice produced inlays in varicolored woods (intarsia), and later turned to highly decorative painted work of capricious form. Genoa and Liguria are known for distinctive four-door cupboards. Rome developed the rich style of carving that came to dominate all Cinquecento furniture.

CINQUECENTO

High Renaissance furniture developed consistently out of the early style, adding, embellishing, expanding types and decoration. Dignified formal richness is achieved by bold carving, free and brilliant, utilizing the whole vocabulary of classical decoration. The acanthus leaf has infinite variety; likewise guilloche, rinceaux, flutings, animal forms, gargoyles, caryatids, scrolls and volutes, imbrications, gadrooning, paterae, molded panels, pilasters, and architectural cornices, intarsia, etc. Newer are cartouches, strapwork, turned rosettes, broken pediments. Paint appears less frequently; gesso is rare; carving in positive relief is abundant.

The large, formally bare room of the Quattrocento became richer, fuller, more sparkling; though in similar scale, chairs were made more comfortable by cushions, tables were used in greater variety, beds were built as four-post frames, chests had animal feet, sideboards appeared in divers shapes, and the whole catalogue of furniture grew. Carving was universally rich but judicious. The period was indeed one of the golden ages of furniture.

BAROQUE

The Baroque style consists chiefly of an exaggerated, emphasized fullness of size, scale, and proportion. It is not necessarily overrich in ornament,

although lavish carving is typical. So is unorthodox treatment of accepted Renaissance features, such as ornate broken pediments, tremendous scrolls, profuse sculpture, deep moldings, theatrical effects of light and shade. Twisted turnings, broken and reversed curves, inlays and appliqués of brilliant materials— marble, ivory, gilt, bronze—all contribute to the rich effect, but the classic architectural silhouette vanishes.

The style is a logical outgrowth of the High and Late Renaissance. Its exaggerations are characteristically the aftermath of a good mature style in its decadence. (The period 1560-1800 is often called in Italy "Decadenza.") The great architects Vignola, Palladio, and Michelangelo witnessed and promoted the transition; among their successors Bernini most crystallized the change. The architects' part in the evolution of the Baroque was stimulated by the Counter Reformation, the movement fostered by the Jesuits to win back the Catholics wavering toward the Protestant movement. The means was partially this showy, theatrical dramatization of the power and wealth of the Church. Paradoxically, the effect on furniture was most pronounced in the secular product, and most sustained in the northern lands from which the Reformation flowed.

The distinctive features of Baroque furniture are apparent after 1580, and as such set a fashion for state apartments and *meubles de luxe* in France and England and the Germanic countries. Its splendor rendered it incapable of being scaled down or simplified; it furthermore was usually a group design, so that the individual pieces are often either downright ugly or meaningless or unbalanced by themselves. A design was studied, not as a unit of furniture, but as a composition of wall and ceiling, with architectural features and chairs, mirrors and candelabra and consoles all one indissoluble picture. The detached furniture elements are therefore apt to be illogical, even absurd.

The earlier Baroque, 1560-1650, is a purely Italian outgrowth of the Late Renaissance; the later phases show French, Flemish, Spanish, Dutch, and English traits. Italian Baroque foreshadows the style of Louis XIV, and later echoes it. Wall furniture flourished in this formal atmosphere; tall cabinets, console tables, and wall seats superseded the *cassone*. The dominating cabinet, a great architectural structure, came from France. Sculptured bases, with cherubim, mermaids, lions, eagles, and Negroes in composition with scrolls, shells, and leaves were gilded and polychromed. The middle sections had small panels veneered or molded or carved within restrained outlines; the top features again burst forth in a glory of pediments, involved in profile and loaded with carved ornament.

Table bases in the same style carried tops of marble,

pietra dura, scagliola, or painted imitations. Chairs with flowing outlines, excessively carved and gilded, were upholstered with large-patterned velvets, silks, and stamped leathers; nailheads were arranged in decorative patterns. Mirrors were larger, particularly as to frames, which were most intricately carved.

Beds of the earlier styles were still four-posters, light and graceful. As the style wore on, the panels were made larger to permit more painting area for landscapes and robust floral compositions.

SETTECENTO ROCOCO

Italy's declining commerce reduced wealth, and the declining quality of craftsmanship and materials in this period is significant. The best craftsmen found profitable occupation in France, Germany, and England. The movement was not one way; to Italy flowed the technique and ideas of the expanding nations. The later Baroque, and more particularly the Rococo, are cosmopolitan, Italianized. By 1675, the general scale of furniture was smaller, prettier; gracefulness supplanted grandeur. Still lavishly decorated, the motives favor foliage and ribbons, rocks and shells, Chinese forms, all increasingly naturalistic. Asymmetry and the curved line were the rule. Capricious gaiety is the tradition of the early 18th century. Régence and Louis XV influences from France, William and Mary and Queen Anne from England were exaggerated, distorted, often badly designed and unsuitably adapted. The effect was theatrical, romantic, superficial, and charming.

Venice alone retained some of her prestige and wealth, and therefore led in the production of furniture; consequently, most Italian Rococo work is described as Venetian. Painting over inferior wood and joinery achieved effects cheaply; using not only formal motives but landscapes and marble—and even wood—imitation. Bombé commodes and fancifully wavering outlines in chairs and mirrors, sofas and beds are recognized as vulgarized Louis XV.

THE CLASSIC REVIVAL

The Classical Revival came well after the excavations in Pompeii and Herculaneum had stirred the revolt toward ancient simplicity in France and England. Almost at the end of the 18th century, Italian classicism was able to borrow from the mature Louis XVI, Adam, and Hepplewhite styles. Rejecting the cold formalism, it achieved symmetry and brilliance with paint, marquetry, marble, and gilding. Louis Seize was interpreted in designs by Piranesi, Pergolesi, Albertolli. Milanese commodes inlaid with light wood are typical.

ITALIAN DIRECTOIRE. Northern Italy was essentially French, but untroubled by Revolution as the 18th century ended. The Directoire style lent itself to prettification, and was so accepted. Greco-Roman details from Pompeii and Herculaneum were revived in their native province. Swans, lyres, scrolls, and fine detail were liberally naturalized, more exuberantly than in French furniture. Carving, gilding, painting, inlaying, and veneering reached new heights of technical virtuosity. Much of the Directoire outlived the succeeding Empire style. [329, 379, 447, 514.]

EMPIRE. The Empire style substituted the heavier Roman, Greek, and Egyptian forms for Greco-Roman airiness. This style, engendered by imperial command, had less national distinction than any prior to it; the general description of its traits applies as well to the Italian as to the French. More walnut was used, and less ormolu. The Imperial manner lingered long after Napoleon's fall; it was, in fact, the accepted formal style for much of the 19th century. In less important work Italy followed the swiftly successive eclecticisms of France and England during the 19th century.

IVORY. Elephant tusks, and less properly the tusks of some other animals, have been used for decorative and small utilitarian articles since prehistoric times. Egyptian sculptures in ivory are among the finest remains of their art, and Early Christian, Mohammedan, and Far Eastern and Gothic ivories also reveal the skill lavished on this material.

Its use in furniture is ancient, but size limits it to decorative features. Inlays, mounts, ornamental plaques, small caskets, etc., were used by the Egyptians, Romans, and Byzantines, among others. In the 18th century its use for ornamental details was revived, and again it appears in details of some modern work, notably the designs of the more elegant French school. [215, 501, 930.]

JACOB, GEORGES, 1735-1814. Cabinetmaker of the Louis XVI period. Father of Georges and François-Honoré, recorded as Jacob-Frères, also known as Jacob-Desmalter, who refurnished the royal residences for Napoleon after designs by Percier and Fontaine. See also FRANCE. [190, 287, 292, 438.]

JACOBEAN, from the Latin Jacobus (James). General term for English styles up to 1688. Early Jacobean comprises reigns of James I, 1603-1625; Charles I, 1625-1649; and the Commonwealth, 1649-1660. Late Jacobean covers the Restoration period, including Charles II, 1660-1685, and James II, 1685-1688. The period represents the growth of foreign influence and the passing of the oak styles. Furniture becomes lighter and more adaptable, with ornament changing from Early Renaissance types to Baroque. See also ENGLAND. [454, 551.]

18ᵗ CENT JAPANESE

JAPANESE STAND · 1637

JAPAN. Japanese domestic usage requires but little furniture. Chests and cupboards are invariably built in, with sliding panels as doors. For sleeping, mats are unrolled on the floor, and seating is similarly on mats. Tables are rare, being extremely low and portable. Such furniture as appears is usually lacquered and highly polished. Japanese lacquer is flecked with gold and decorated with fine-scaled flower, animal, and landscape motives.

JAPANESE INFLUENCE. In Western furniture it appeared after 1870 as part of the fad for Orientalia. With little precedent in actual utility, the influence

Ginsburg & Levy

794 JACOBEAN INFLUENCE, Massachusetts, c. 1680. Chest with typical paneling.

795 JAPANESE CHEST.

796 JAPANESE TABLE FOR GAMES.

took the form of irrelevantly applied details on East-lake and Arts and Crafts bodies. Incised black lacquer panels and bamboo turnings are most easily identified. The bamboo forms flourished for several decades, from 1880 to 1910 in minor furniture; it was naïve and sometimes charming in an unsubstantial way. Since 1945 the Western world has become interested in the applicable aspects of Japanese culture, and there is now much borrowing of general ideas if not of actual details. The sparse Japanese interior is reflected in some modern American work, as in the clean, direct taste of utilitarian objects. [335.]

JAPANNING. The art of coating surfaces of wood, metal, etc., with various varnishes, dried in heated chambers. The process dates from remote antiquity in the East, but reached Europe only about 1600. In France it attained remarkable excellence under Louis XIV, who installed in the Gobelin factory Lemoyne and other artists to imitate the Oriental styles, which they called *laquage*. The Dutch traders developed a considerable commerce in lacquered work, even carrying European furniture to China to be decorated. They also tried both taking Dutch "joyners" to China and bringing Chinese artists to Holland. The latter move seems to have been more successful. The extensive traffic between the Dutch and the English, as well as that between the courts of Charles II and Louis XIV, created a vogue for "Japanned work" in England, and the years of Charles II's reign and later produced quantities of cabinets, mirrors, screens, etc. The earlier work in both France and England was in high relief, which gave way to flatter decoration of flowers and foliage in Georgian times. It was also called "bantam work," and was incised as well as flat. The technique declined toward the last part of the 18th century, such work as was designed by Robert Adam for this medium being inferior to the Queen Anne and earlier Georgian work. See also LACQUER. [14, 1038.]

JARDINIÉRE. Ornamented box or jar or stand, intended to hold flowers.

JEWEL BOX. Early coffers were specially made for storage and transportation of jewels [342]. Cabinets 'n more permanent households became objects of furniture virtuosity in the High Renaissance. [178, 180, 629.]

JEWELING. Surface carving to simulate jewels.

JIGSAW. Saw for cutting interior work, such as pierced work, fretwork, latticework, etc. Originally operated by a treadle, it was one of the first machines

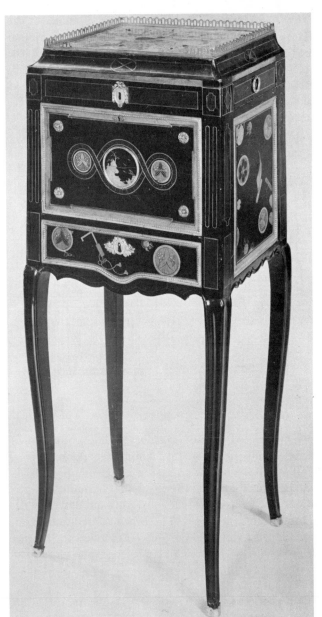

797 BLACK JAPANNED CABINET, French, *French & Co., Inc.* 1767, by Levasseur.

to which power was applied. As a consequence, jig-sawed detail is typical of the earlier machine age of the 19th century. Inevitably it ran away with its designers, and an easy characterization of the period 1830-1890 is by this lacy wood ornament. Not only furniture but façades of houses were draped with better or worse decoration of this type.

JOINERY. The technique or mechanics of furniture and woodwork. Joinery is to the interior designer what masonry is to the architect. It is the oldest term for the craft, and literally means the joining together of pieces of wood. See also CONSTRUCTION.

JOINT STOOL. Jacobean stool with turned legs, originally with mortise-and-tenon joints. [797, 1177, 1245.]

JONES, INIGO, 1573-1652. Leading architect of the Early English Renaissance. Apprenticed to a joiner and sent to Italy to study, he was imbued with the spirit of classical architecture as exemplified by Palladio. On his return to England, he inspired the use of these forms, under the patronage of Charles I. He designed furniture in the current Baroque Italian style.

JOINT STOOL

STYLE OF INIGO JONES

JOUY. Printed fabrics, usually on fine cotton, produced at Jouy near Paris by Philippe Oberkampf, from 1760 to 1815. The patterns were most commonly realistic designs on classic themes, with charming compositions of all classical ornaments, fruit and flowers with plaques and landscapes. These prints are extensively reproduced today, and also serve as models for fabrics printed with subjects of timely interest. See also OBERKAMPF.

JUGENDSTIL (Youth Style). Decorative style in Germany roughly contemporary with L'Art Nouveau in France about 1895-1912. Rebellious and self-conscious, it failed to materialize as a substantial or mature style in furniture. See also NINETEENTH CENTURY.

KAS. Dutch cabinet or sideboard; appears in the Dutch-American colonies of New York and the Delaware Valley; sometimes carved walnut, also pine, cherry, or maple; paneled and painted with rather primitive ornaments of vases and flowers. See also ARMOIRE. [172, 798.]

KAUFFMANN, ANGELICA, 1741-1807. Swiss painter and decorative artist. Came to London in 1766, where she executed murals and ceilings, many designed by Robert Adam. Her classical compositions appear as decoration on much painted furniture of the last third of the century, whether inspired by her

Metropolitan Museum of Art, Rogers Fund, 1908
798 DUTCH CABINET (Friesland), 17th century. Carvings in architectural panels suggest origins similar to Grinling Gibbons's work.

799 NEW YORK DUTCH KAS of pine and oak planking, early 18th century. The shape and motives of the painting indicate ancestry in Dutch prototypes.
Metropolitan Museum of Art, Gift of Miss Sarah Elizabeth Jones, 1923

work or actually painted by her being uncertain. Her husband was Antonio Zucchi, likewise a painter of murals and decorations under the auspices of the Brothers Adam. Their influence on the work of Hepplewhite, Sheraton, and others is unmistakable.

KENT, WILLIAM, 1684-1748. English architect and furniture designer of the Golden Age. Probably the first English architect to make a practice of designing the movable as well as fixed furniture of his rooms. His work is insistently architectural, employing columns, entablature, and pediments on cabinets and bookcases; his side tables and desks and most smaller pieces become heavy and massive as a result of this ornamentation.

KERF. A saw cut. Sometimes on curved work a series of saw cuts against the grain, not quite through the board, permitting the bending of the wood into curved shapes.

KETTLE BASE, FRONT. Bombé-shaped case, with swelling or bulging front and/or sides. Of Baroque inspiration in the early-18th-century Continental work, it occurs in fine American Late Colonial. [36, 365.]

KEY and KEY PLATES. Decorative keys and back plates were features of Gothic cabinets; in Spanish and Italian work in iron; in brass and gilt in French cabinetwork. See also HARDWARE.

KEY PATTERN (Greek fret). Ancient Greek band ornament of interlacing lines at right angles. Carved on Mid-Georgian and inlaid or painted on English Regency furniture. See also ORNAMENT.

KIDNEY TABLE, BENCH, DESK, etc. Oval shaped with concave front, applied to dressing tables or writing tables, etc. Appears in 18th-century furniture of France and England. Especially favored by Sheraton. [503, 800.]

Symons Galleries, Inc.
800 KIDNEY DESK with arcaded gallery, early-19th-century English.

KILN DRIED. Lumber dried by artificial means in warm chambers. The heat is regulated to prevent the too sudden loss of moisture to avoid checking, warping, and other defects. Besides speed, kiln drying is superior to air drying because the remaining moisture content can be precisely controlled.

KINGWOOD. Conspicuously marked dark reddish-brown wood similar to rosewood, used for inlays and veneers in flatwork, periods of Louis XV, Queen Anne, Late Georgian.

KLISMOS. Ancient Greek chair, prototype for Classic Revival. See EMPIRE. [305.]

KNEADING TABLE. Utilitarian furniture of the provinces of Europe, now used as tables and side tables. Provincial French ones are particularly decorative. [1248.]

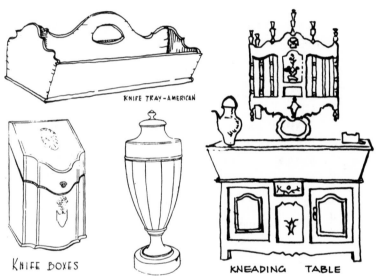

KNIFE TRAY-AMERICAN

KNIFE BOXES

KNEADING TABLE

KNEE. The upper, convex curve or bulge of a cabriole leg, sometimes called "hip."

KNEEHOLE. Desks, chests, or bureaus are sometimes built with an opening in the center, between the two banks of drawers; so called because they make room for the sitter's knees. Sometimes this space is filled partway from the back with a door compartment [35, 491, 577, 1380.]

KNIFE BOX—KNIFE CASE. Box cases for table silver, usually in pairs, stood on buffets or side tables in 18th-century English dining rooms. They first appear at the end of the 17th century, made of walnut with sloping lids and curved fronts. The later ones of mahogany were often inlaid and mounted with silver. In the late 18th century a vase form appears, often of satinwood. [1070, 1113.]

KNOB. Handle of wood, metal, glass, etc., usually turned always with a single stem, distinctive to the various styles. Elaborately chased metal gilt knobs feature Louis XVI furniture. Small wooden and ivory ones were used in fine 18th-century English work, and large glass and china knobs were used on 19th-century work in the United States. See also HARDWARE.

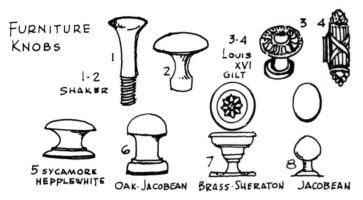

FURNITURE KNOBS

1-2 SHAKER

3-4 LOUIS XVI GILT

5 SYCAMORE HEPPLEWHITE

OAK-JACOBEAN

BRASS-SHERATON

JACOBEAN

KNOB TURNING. Turning of knobs in series, used on some 17th-century work.

KNOCKED DOWN. Constructed in sections to be easily assembled after shipping.

KNOLE. House in Kent, England, repository of quantity of Tudor and Stuart furniture, including earliest upholstered work. Specifically, sofa having cushioned headrests hinged to the arms and held by ratchets; original, circa 1610.

KNOP. Bunch of leaves or flowers. Also the old spelling for knobs, occurring as a swelling or vase shape on a turned shaft.

KNOTTY PINE. In good old work the knotty parts of pine were scrupulously avoided, only the clear wood being used except where painted. The removal of paint revealing these in renovated paneling and furniture, it is mistakenly assumed that the knots were purposefully chosen. Wide advertising has created a vogue for knotty pine, but it does not follow that this is historically correct or good.

KNUCKLE. Carving on the outside end of chairs, principally of Chippendale and Windsors.

KNUCKLE JOINT. Joint, as at separable leaves of a drop-leaf table, resembling a finger joint.

KOA. Dense, dark-brown hardwood from the Philippines, having pronounced stripes and cross stripes like curly maple.

LABELS are one of the most reliable proofs of antiquity. The practice of burning in or carving names or initials, dates, etc., began with the *ébénistes* of 17th-century France. Paper labels are common in 18th-century English work, and the practice carried to America. The best-preserved labels are in almost secret places in the interiors of cabinets, etc. [1300.]

LABURNUM. Hardwood, moderately durable, yellowish in color with brown streaks. It takes a high polish. In ancient Rome it was known as Corsican ebony. It appears on veneered surfaces in the furniture of the Louis XV period and in English post-Restoration furniture. In the latter the branches or saplings were cut transversely and matched to produce the concentric markings known as "oyster shell." See also OYSTER PIECES.

LACEWOOD. Australian oak having fine regularly spaced flakes yielding a lacelike appearance; light mahogany color.

LACQUER. Oriental lacquer is a high dense finish acquired by tedious padding up and rubbing down of many coats of spirit shellac. This has nothing in common with modern lacquer, which is a compound of cellulose derivatives. These dry so rapidly that they must be sprayed by compressed air. Such lacquers now possess many qualities not found in varnish or shellac finishes, such as resistance to heat, moisture, and acids. It can be rubbed to a clear satiny finish that emphasizes the beauty of the wood; it is also made opaque, like paint, and tinted to any shade. In speed, ease of handling, and resistance to wear it is more economical and more efficacious than older materials such as varnish and shellac. See also FINISH. [407, 1330.]

LADDER BACK. Chairback with horizontal slats or rails resembling a ladder. Common types in Pilgrim furniture and in the simpler Chippendale work. [247.]

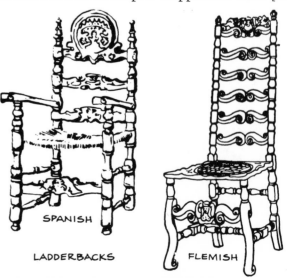

SPANISH

LADDERBACKS

FLEMISH

LADIES' DESKS. Lighter and smaller desks on legs, developed in France and England after 1690.

LAMBREQUIN. Drapery around the top of a bed.

LAMINATE. The binding up of layers; in wood panels three, five, or more layers are laid alternately across the grains for strength and durability. See also PLYWOOD; VENEER.

LAMINATE MATERIALS in modern work are chiefly synthetic sheet surfacings such as Formica, etc., designed primarily to provide more durable or cheaper finished surfaces by bonding to a plywood panel.

LAMPADAIRE. Pedestal in the classic manner, designed to hold a lamp or candles; French Empire.

LANCET. English pointed Gothic arch.

LANDSCAPE PANEL. Wood panel with the grain running horizontally.

LANGLEY, BATTY AND THOMAS. English architects, early 18th century. Their published early designs were after the grandiose French manner. Batty Langley was one of the leaders of the earliest Gothic revival.

LANNUIER, CHARLES-HONORÉ. Cabinetmaker, born 1779, arrived in New York 1803. Working in a skillful Directoire manner, he had wealthy patrons in the entire Hudson Valley and down to Maryland. His style encompassed Empire as his popularity grew. His label on many fine pieces has come to light, and he is regarded as the peer of Phyfe. He died in 1819. See also FEDERAL. [210, 1268, 1275, 1346.]

LANTERN CLOCK. Shelf clock suggesting the shape of a lantern; late-17th-century English, often in brass. Also called "birdcage clock." See also CLOCK.

LATHE. Machine for shaping turned parts by the application of cutting edges against the revolving wood. See also TURNING.

Albany Institute of History and Art

801 Bed labeled Charles-Honoré Lannuier c. 1817. Mahogany, satinwood, gilt bronze.

Ginsburg and Levy

802 LANNUIER WORKTABLE, New York, 1815. Maple with gilt bronze.

803 MARBLE-TOP SIDE TABLE c. 1810. *Ginsburg and Levy*

Israel Sack, Inc.

804A LABEL OF CHARLES-HONORÉ LANNUIER.

804 WARDROBE signed "H. Lannuier, New York." Select crotch-mahogany veneers. *New-York Historical Society, New York City*

LATTICE. Carved crisscross pattern in cutout work, found in chairbacks, highboy pediments, etc. Metal is sometimes used for lattice chairbacks.

LAUREL. Hardwood of deep brown color. Best known for furniture is East Indian laurel, having a pronounced wavy grain.

LAURELING. Decorative banding of laurel leaves, usually on a half-round molding.

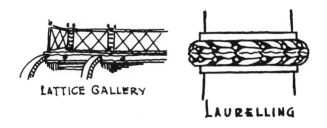

LATTICE GALLERY

LAURELLING

LAVABO. Washstand. [1338.]

LAZY SUSAN. Revolving tray for condiments, American. See also DUMBWAITER.

LE BRUN, CHARLES, 1619-1690. French architect, painter, designer; first director of the State Gobelin factory. A great organizer as well as a great artist, his personality is the dominant force in the vigorous style of Louis XIV. He brought together French, Flemish, and Italian artists and coordinated their work and styles. His mastery is reflected in the magnificent royal works of the age.

LEAF. *(A)* Conventionalized or naturalistic leaves are among the earliest and most continuously used decorative forms. The acanthus leaf is the basic floral decoration; it lends itself to infinite shapes and variations. The laurel leaf, water leaf, and other shapes occur constantly in decoration.

(B) Drop leaf is the hinged part of a table, desk, etc.

(C) Loose leaf is inserted into the opening of an extension table to provide additional surface.

LEAF SCROLL FOOT. Base of a leg with foliated design.

LEATHER. The tanned skins of animals. Furniture uses chiefly those of cattle, calves, sheep, goats, and pigs. These are treated in many ways for strength, permanence, and decorative interest. Dyeing and surface coating yield an unlimited palette, and a great variety of textures are a product of manufacture as well as of nature. The heavier skins of cattle—steers, cows, etc.—which are too thick for upholstering, are split into several thicknesses. The topmost, or buff, extremely thin, is reserved for choicest small articles. The following layer, or top grain, is the choicest for upholstery, accepting the flaws and irregularities, the vestiges of bruises and scratches on the living animal, as part of the beauty of the material. The succeeding layers, having no such natural surface, are treated with imitations of top grain or of the characteristic surfaces of other hides, such as pig, ostrich, walrus, or snake, or with pebbling, glosses, etc. Such mechanical treatment is superficially more perfect, or more regular, than the natural hide. In such leathers the fiber is looser and therefore weaker. Skins, sometimes not tanned and with the hair not removed, were used in the most ancient periods, before weaving was known; and afterward for its strength and availability. There seems never to have been a time that it was not used for seats, but it comes into special favor in styles of the masculine character. All the earlier Renaissance types, particularly the Spanish and English, especially favored leather upholstery. Special processes of embossing, tooling, painting, and gilding leather were disseminated by Spanish craftsmen in the 16th and 17th centuries. Everywhere, chests, coffers, chairs, screens, etc., were covered with leather and studded with nailheads arranged in decorative patterns. Table tops and desk tops have been covered with leather since Renaissance times, as have been decorative features and accessories, such as handles. Oxhide and calf were supplemented in the Late Louis XIV work by Morocco, a fine goat leather that was also favored by Chippendale and subsequent designers, but cattle leather has always maintained its preeminence by reason of its strength and size. Today the many methods of surfacing leather for texture and color make it more desirable than ever. [213, 250, 254, 479, 1150, 1277.]

LEATHERETTE. Artificial leather made of cellulose-coated cloth embossed with familiar leather textures.

LECTERN. Reading desk of wood, metal, or stone. [805, 983.]

LECTUS. Roman beds or couches. The *lectus lucubratorius* and *lectus cubicularius* were respectively fitted with and without incidental conveniences as reading desks, receptacles for things at hand, etc. The *lectus triclinarius* was a lower couch, used when dining.

LEG. In the various styles, legs of furniture are among the most distinctive features as guides in determining

time and place of origin. A few general types have
their individual styles and imitations, such as the
cabriole, turned, tapered, fluted, concave, animal, etc.
See also style headings such as CHIPPENDALE; TUDOR.

LEPAUTRE, JEAN, 1617-1682. French designer,
School of Louis XIV; published *Livre de Miroirs,
Tables de Guéridons,* and other works on furniture,
which influenced design in Flanders and England.

LEPPEL BORTIE. Pennsylvania Dutch spoon rack
of wood. [82, 1110.]

LIBRARY STEPS. Various devices for providing
access to the higher shelves in libraries. They appear
frequently in England, and during the last half of the
18th century in many forms, chiefly combined with
benches, chairs, tables, etc. The ladder part unfolds,
sometimes providing a handrail. [807.]

LIBRARY TABLE. Large table with drawers usually
in pedestal form. English name for any flat-top desk,
usually known in America as pedestal or kneehole
desk, often provided with space for books. See also
KNEEHOLE; WRITING DESK.

809 LIBRARY STEPS in table, English
Regency, 1830-1840. *Symons Galleries, Inc.*

808 ENGLISH REGENCY CHAIR
unfolds into steps. Oak, c. 1810.
Symons Galleries, Inc.

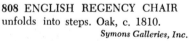

LIGNUM VITAE. West Indian wood, the heaviest known. It was used for veneering in the Late Stuart period.

LIME-WHITENED. Sixteenth-century painted furniture was first bleached with a solution of lime. The removal of the painted surface at later dates exposed this whitened surface, which is sometimes referred to as "pickled finish."

LIMEWOOD. Light-colored, close-grained wood that cuts as well across as with the grain, rendering it excellent for carving. Favored by Grinling Gibbons.

LINEN PRESS. Two boards closed together by pressure of a large wooden screw. Linen placed between the boards and pressed down while damp came out smooth. Linen presses appear in Dutch interior pictures of the 17th century, and some survive from the period of Charles I. Some 18th-century types were made part of the chest of drawers planned to hold linens. See also PRESS. [386, 810.]

Metropolitan Museum of Art
810 LINEN OR CARD PRESS, Italian, 16th century.

LINENFOLD. Gothic ornamental panel treatment representing the folds of linen, probably originally after the folded napkin on the chalice in the Catholic ritual. It appears to be exclusively a North European motif, abundant in Gothic 14th-, 15th-, and 16th-century remains from Gothic France, the Netherlands, and the Teutonic countries. In England it survived another century along with the persistent Gothic quality of the Tudor, Elizabethan, and Jacobean styles.

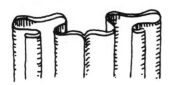

LINEN FOLD

LINEN-FOLD PANEL

LIVERY CUPBOARD

It is invariably executed in oak, in panels of seats, armoires, cupboards, chests, etc. It appears that a special molding plane with profiled knife was used for tooling out the long ridges. [169, 173, 345, 465, 624, 970, 1072.]

LION MOTIF. One of the most ancient decorative symbols, probably typifying the royal nature of the furniture of early peoples. In Egypt, lion paws and heads, alone, were terminal decorations, rather naturalistic. In Gothic representation they appear more as grotesques or in heraldic shapes, the symbolism of lion couchant and rampant being represented in the carving and painting of furniture. Renaissance work employs the lion sporadically, although the paw and head were almost uninterruptedly used. The Empire style revived its use to a great extent, probably as much for symbolic as for historical or decorative interest. Brass castings of heads and paws appear frequently; handles of the lion-and-ring form are typical.

LIP MOLDING. Small convex molding around drawers, originally intended as a dust stop in Queen Anne and Early Chippendale casework.

LISTEL. Same as "fillet," a flat, plain molding.

LIT CLOS. French "closed bed"; paneled enclosure of wood around a bed, sometimes free standing, sometimes in a corner. Chiefly provincial French, 17th-19th centuries.

LIVERY CUPBOARD. Early English food cupboard. Livery is probably a contraction of "delivery." Food was stored here and distributed to the household and to the poor. Ventilation was a necessity, often provided by grilles of wooden spindles, or tracery. See also AMBRY; CUPBOARD; ENGLAND.

LOBE. Section or profile in rounded form.

LOBING. Gadrooning.

LOCK, MATTHIAS. English carver and furniture designer. In collaboration with Copeland, published several books on ornament between 1752 and 1769. Early work a flamboyant Rococo character, later almost exact copies of the Adam style.

LONG CLOCK. Grandfather's, hall, or tall clock.

LOO TABLE. Oval table designed for the old game of loo. English 18th century.

LOOP-BACK. Oval chairback; also Windsor bow back, without arms.

LOOP HINGE. Early type of hinge consisting of two intersecting loops.

LOOSE SEAT. Same as slip seat; separate wood frame, upholstered and let into the framing of the chair seat.

LOPER. Sliding arms that support the fall or drop front or lid of a desk. Also the sliding runners of an extending table. [442, 498.]

LOTUS. Ancient flower ornament. The principal Egyptian floral motive, it appears in more or less ornamental uses in all ancient work, and may have been the basis for many later flower decorations.

LOUIS-PHILIPPE. King of France, 1830-1848, era of transition from declining Empire style to exuberance of mid-19th-century Industrial Revolution experimentation. Economic rise of bourgeoisie plus romanticism fostered by growing interest in Orient opened the field for uninhibited novelties. Generally, decorative taste reverted to Rococo and Renaissance, aggravated by the freedom in duplication and complication offered by early machine processes. See also NINETEENTH CENTURY.

LOUIS QUATORZE. Louis XIV, King of France, 1643-1715. Greatest period of French achievement; furniture style is marked by Baroque magnificence. Masculine character declined after 1680; proportions reduced, lines softened. Latter part was the Régence. See also FRANCE.

LOUIS QUINZE. Period of Louis XV, King of France, 1715-1774, marked by culmination of feminine Rococo style; dainty scale, free naturalistic ornament, rounded surfaces and flowing lines. See also FRANCE.

French & Co., Inc.
811 LOUIS XV WRITING TABLE, parquetry.

Frick Collection
812 LOUIS XVI WRITING TABLE, octagonal legs.

LOUIS SEIZE. Period of Louis XVI, King of France, 1774-1792, marked by revival of ancient classicism; severe rectangular lines, architectural ornament. See also FRANCE.

LOUNGE. Type of couch in late-19th-century work, often with one end high as a pillow.

813 LOVE SEAT, Italian Directoire, c. 1810.   *Brunovan, Inc.*

815 ENGLISH LOWBOY, William and Mary oystered veneers.

French & Co., Inc.

814 LOVE SEAT, Irish(?), Late Georgian with satyr and lion masks.

LOVE CHEST. 18th-century Pennsylvania Dutch chest, with the initials of the bride and groom.

LOVE SEAT. Double chair or small sofa. Queen Anne and later. Also, "courting chair." See also SETTEE. [813, 1310.]

LOW RELIEF. Carving or built-up work, not highly raised from or sunk into the ground. See also CARVING.

LOWBOY. English low chest or table with drawers. Beginning in Jacobean times by raising a chest on a stand, it continues through English and American work of the 18th century in various forms as dressing tables, side tables, etc. [23, 815.]

LOZENGE. Diamond-shaped. Panels, overlays, inserts, etc., of this shape occur in Renaissance work of all descriptions. [216, 463.]

Wadsworth Atheneum, Hartford, Conn.

816 AMERICAN LOWBOY, William and Mary, c. 1700. Walnut.

817 LOWBOY, Massachusetts c. 1700. Slate top.   *Ginsburg and Levy*

Israel Sack, Inc.

818 LOWBOY, Philadelphia c. 1750. Queen Anne, stocking drake feet. Walnut.

Albany Institute of History and Art

819 LOWBOY, Albany, New York, third quarter 18th century. Probably base of a high chest.

Henry Ford Museum, Dearborn, Mich.

820 LOWBOY, Philadelphia Chippendale, walnut c. 1750. Beginning of the lavish style.

Ginsburg and L.

821 LOWBOY, Philadelphia c. 1760. Mahogany. The rich manner of Savery.

LUNETTE. Semicircular space. In furniture, a half-moon shape filled with carving, inlay, or painting. In Gothic oak furinture, lunettes were carved, while in English Late Georgian work they were often inlaid or painted with fan-shaped designs.

LYRE MOTIVE. A naturalistic representation of the lyre figures in Greek decoration that was adapted by the Renaissance artists. It appears sporadically in all design, and was featured strongly in a free form in Louis XIV and Louis XV decoration. In the style of Louis XVI it occurs in symmetrical form, and in comparative forms in England. Sheraton employed it conspicuously, as did the entire school of the Empire and Empire influence in England and America. Duncan Phyfe designed table supports, chairbacks, mirror standards, etc., with this motif, delicately executed, with brass wires representing the strings. It is also found in Biedermeier work in Germany and in Italian furniture of the early 19th century. [76, 296, 822, 1264.]

Albany Institute of History and Art

822 LYRE DETAIL, CARD TABLE c. 1815. Attributed to Duncan Phyfe.

MACASSAR. Dutch East India port from which is shipped the striped ebony called Macassar.

MADRONE. Brown-red burl of sound, regular texture and figure, from the Pacific coast.

MAGAZINE STAND. Portable racks for magazines developed in Victorian England in a type called Canterbury; there were endless variations as magazines proliferated. [185, 823.]

MAGNOLIA. American tulip tree: wood is light straw color with slight figure. Suitable for exposed parts of furniture and face veneers.

MAHOGANY. Reddish-brown wood of medium hardness, great strength, and among the most beautiful for texture, ease of polishing, variety of grain and figure. Today mahogany includes several botanical species, chiefly the *Swietenia* of the West Indies, South and Central America, and the *Khaya* of Africa. The American mahoganies were the first known. The Spanish explorers were quick to appreciate its splendid properties, and its early importation and use in cabinetwork is attested by the 16th-century date of some fine Spanish Renaissance remains. Other countries were

slower to use it. Queen Elizabeth is said to have been interested in some mahogany brought by Sir Walter Raleigh, but no headway was made in England against the domestic oak and walnut until the 18th century. In 1721, the heavy tariff against mahogany was modified, and it rapidly supplanted other wood in fine work, retaining its ascendancy for many years. The Cuban and San Domingan varieties were preferred; these had a hard firm texture that nevertheless carved well. Its original light color changed gradually to a deep rich lustrous tone, and the various figures, such as crotch, rope mottle, fiddleback, etc., stimulated the designers' imaginations. Later, Mexican and South American mahoganies came into the market, each with special characteristics. The African varieties were accepted as true mahogany in the later 19th century. They are lighter in weight and softer in texture, with rarer appearance of the beautiful eccentric figures, but they have distinct features, such as fine stripings and cross-fire markings that recommend them. Philippine trees such as the tanguile and lauan are not recognized as true mahogany, although referred to as "Philippine mahogany."

Mahogany is the essential ingredient of the great 18th-century school, which Macquoid calls the Age of Mahogany. Not alone England, but France, Spain, and Italy have used the wood more or less continuously since that time. The Empire period featured it extensively; the Federal period in American work is essentially a mahogany style.

823 ENGLISH MAGAZINE RACK, early 19th century.

Israel Sack, Inc.

Each style developed a special treatment of mahogany that is significant. Georgian England had a light red-brown tone, the result of polishing with beeswax, slightly red-tinted. Empire mahogany was rich red, highly polished. Until very late years a popular misconception in America held mahogany to be a blackish-red wood, the result of universal dark staining and overvarnishing in American furniture practice. [90, 386, 508, 1264, 1354.]

MAIDOU. East Indian wood prized for decorative veneers, both in the long grain and the fine, with even burls resembling amboyna.

MANWARING, ROBERT. English designer and furniture maker, published *The Cabinet and Chair Maker's Real Friend and Companion* in 1765. Heavy and highly ornamented chairs, resembling those of Chippendale, are shown. Few surviving pieces with his mark are known.

MAPLE. The *Acer* family is the distinctly American wood. While known in Europe in a few varieties, its preeminence in the Western Hemisphere is due to its prevalence, its fine structural properties, and its decorative interest. The early colonists were quick to recognize and use maple, and we have the example of much Early American maple furniture as a guide to its use. There are hard and soft maples, with varied figures and textures, such as curly, bird's-eye, wavy, blister, and quilted figures, usable in the solid lumber or as veneers. It varies from very hard to medium, with a high ratio of strength and resistance to shock and splitting; it works well and can be polished very smooth.

The texture of maple is very hard and smooth, the fibers and pores being exceptionally small. It is almost white in color in the harder varieties, the softer maples being light tan or yellow-brown. Recent furniture practice has been to stain or glaze maple to a red-brown shade that purports to be the color of Early American antiques; this is neither accurate nor beautiful and it is to be hoped that commercial producers will soon abandon it and utilize the true light beauty of the wood.

MARBLE. Remains of marble furniture from Egypt, Greece, and Rome are not uncommon, whether resulting from a considerable use or its ability to survive being conjectural. Ceremonial chairs, or "thronos," from classic Greek times are known, and inspired the "curule" chair of the classic revivals. The type was copied by the Romans in elaborately sculptured chairs of state. Remaining Roman table bases indicate that these likewise were handsomely adorned and combined with bronze, used as supports for marble tops.

Metropolitan Museum of Art
824 OFFERING TABLE, ancient Egyptian marble.

The Romans undoubtedly used the highly colored Italian marbles as well as the classic white, while Byzantine remains show a preference for these colors. The Italian Renaissance revived the use of marble, neglected by the Gothic designers, and the process of inlaying marbles into wood or stone surfaces was either revived or rediscovered. Baroque Italian and, to a greater degree, French work of the 16th and 17th centuries favored marbles, and in the magnificent furniture of Louis XIV and XV it appears most frequently as tops of buffets, commodes, tables, and side tables. The Italian precedent did not reach England to any considerable degree until the 18th century; after 1720, however, the vogue for marble grew. At first only white marble was imported, and it became customary to stain this to imitate the costlier varieties. About 1738, colored marbles native to England were employed in furniture, and the search abroad was for still more exotically hued stone. After 1750, porphyry, lapis lazuli, alabaster, and other semi-precious stones were used as tops. With the diminishing scale of furniture toward the end of the century, the use of marble tops waned; the decline was also hastened by the new skill in coloring and veining of *scagliola*—a composition. The Adams used these imitations extensively.

Italy, with a declining aristocracy, carried marble effects so far that whole rooms and their furniture were painted to simulate highly figured marble.

The Empire style revived the classic use of marble. It survived the style and was probably most characteristically used in the furniture of the 19th century throughout Europe and America. The styles of Louis-Philippe, Victoria, and the marble-topped era in the United States favored the dull tone of gray-and-white marble. Dressers, washstands, tables, and commodes were generously covered with the stone, the habit persisting almost to the end of the century. [88, 1071, 1224, 1231, 1284.]

MARBLEIZING; MARBLING. Wood painted to simulate marble was probably used in all times, but we have actual examples surviving from the 17th century in Italy, France, and England, and later throughout Europe. Painted columns, commodes, and tables were often combined with real marble.

MAROT, DANIEL. Architect and designer of furniture, born in Paris about 1660, died in Holland about 1720. Studied under Lepautre and Boulle; went to Holland to escape religious persecution; under patronage of the Prince of Orange he designed important public and residential work. As architect to William III of England he issued many designs, but to what extent they were executed is not known. Much detail of Hampton Court Palace bears his characteristic form, whether it was his actual design or not. Marot's style is the quintessence of the Baroque style of Louis XIV. His designs for Boulle typify his ability to compose extravagant detail into an architectural whole. His fireplaces and wall treatments also incorporate the richest assortment of motives into sound compositions. In lesser hands the effects are garish, but Marot's designs, employing all manner of rinceaux and festoons, animal and geometric forms, with every color and texture, are firmly held together. His talent inspired Dutch, French, and English artists for almost a century; Chippendale, Kent, and most other designers of the age appear to have profited by his work in no small measure.

MARQUETRY. Inlay of contrasting wood into a background of veneer. See also INLAY; PARQUETRY. [82, 369, 482.]

MARQUISE CHAIR (French). Wide bergère armchair, completely upholstered. [666, 827.]

MARRIAGE CHEST, COFFER. See DOWER CHEST. [755.]

MARTHA WASHINGTON. (1) Chair. Simple lined high-back narrow chair with open wood arms. Hepplewhite or Sheraton feeling in American work, late 18th and early 19th century. [70, 828.]

(2) Sewing cabinet. Small worktable with wood receptacle or cabinet for materials, American, 1780-1850.

825-826 MARQUETRY DESK AND COMMODE, late Louis XV style. The geometric design is parquetry.
Dalva Brothers, Inc.

827 MARQUISE CHAIR, English, c. 1730.   *Arthur S. Vernay, Inc.*

828 MARTHA WASHINGTON ARMCHAIR, Massachusetts, c. 1800. Sheraton style.

MASK. Decorative motive of great antiquity, representing a human or animal face, distorted, conventionalized, or naturalistic. Found in practically all European styles. [1179.]

MATTRESS. Thick pad or cushion, filled with feathers, down, spring, hair, wool, cotton, etc., and placed upon the springs of a bed. The loose cushion of an upholstered chair (squab or *carreau*) is sometimes called mattress in old writing.

MAYHEW, THOMAS. English Georgian designer. See also INCE AND MAYHEW.

McINTIRE, SAMUEL, 1757-1811. Woodcarver of Salem, Mass. Distinctive style and superb craftsmanship distinguish his mantelpieces, overdoors, and other carvings for furniture and architectural embellishment. [54, 1260.]

MEANDER PATTERN. Same as GREEK FRET. See also ORNAMENT.

MECHANICAL FURNITURE. Beginning with Gothic benches fitted with reversible backs, some approaches to design have always favored devices that give an object more than a single or fixed use. Sheraton brought to a peak many such devices and mechanisms, but he had a great body of Continental ingenuity to draw on. German cabinetmakers in particular had delighted in complex mechanisms directed at compactness, security, secrecy, or simple gadgetry. In 19th-century work new processes and materials met new demands with a torrent of inventions, as demonstrated in the records of the United States Patent Office. Inspired variously by health fads, transportation methods, space realignments dictated by new industries and economies, new mechanical operations, new machine potentials, or the amusement of simple novelties, metal spring seats and mattresses, adjustable chairs and beds, furniture that folded or opened or that disappeared or became something else was regarded with respect. Some achieved real usefulness and even esthetic interest. Swivel chairs, sofa beds, expanding tables, lighting adjuncts are contemporarily acceptable. Fitted receptacles like television cabinets and refrigerated bars are, like musical instruments, variably successful in furniture terms. On the other hand, furniture designed for specific technical use, including transportation seating, office furniture and equipment, mechanical objects such as barber and

829 SEWING TABLE, Salem, Massachusetts, 1800-1810, by Nathaniel Appleton; carving attributed to SAMUEL McINTYRE.

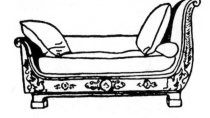

MÉRIDIENNE. Short sofa unique to the French Empire period. It had one arm higher than the other.

METAL FURNITURE. The ancients left remains of much furniture in bronze and iron, though its greater durability rather than favor may account for the excess of metal relics over wood. Egypt, Assyria, Greece, and Rome used bronze in a magnificent way, and among the best evidences of their styles and craftsmanship are table bases, chairs, torchères, etc. In India, China, and Japan, likewise, brass, bronze, and iron articles of great antiquity are found, and yield a clue to the artistic power of dead ages.

Ironworkers in the Middle Ages attained superb skill, and in this medium executed almost every article of furniture then known. In addition, wood pieces were both ornamented and reinforced with a prodigious amount of wrought-iron straps and bands, hinges, locks, and handles.

830 WROUGHT-IRON TABLE BASE, Florentine 16th century. 831 CAST-IRON BED, Spanish, shown at the Crystal Palace, 1851.   *Anderson Galleries*

Brooklyn Museum
829A PATENT OSCILLATING ROCKING CHAIR, 1869.

dentist chairs, are highly successful in their directness of design and suitability of materials and appearance. [521.]

MEDALLION. Circular, oval, square, or octagonal plaque painted or carved with decorative figures, ornament, etc. French Renaissance and Italian work used medallions of stone set into the wood; the Adams brothers used cameolike medallions of pottery or painted wood. See also ROMAYNE WORK. [625, 659.]

MEDIEVAL. See GOTHIC.

MEISSONIER, JUSTE AURÈLE, 1693-1750. French designer; developed Rococo style to greatest extravagance. Introduced Italian features, such as broken shell-shape curves. Published *Le Livre d'Ornements*.

MELON BULB. Thick bulbous turning, typical of Elizabethan and Jacobean furniture. Thicker, more ornate types are early; later forms were smaller and not carved. Found less typically in Continental styles. [1201.]

MENUISIER. French word for cabinetmaker or joiner.

832 CAST-IRON GARDEN CHAIR, American Victorian, 19th century.

833 METAL MOUNTS ON KNIFE BOX c. 1770, by Lewis Fueter, New York, silversmith.

In the earliest phases of the Renaissance in the Mediterranean countries, the skill of the medieval ironworkers survived, and in Spain and Italy there are iron chairs, bedframes, torchères, table structures, etc., of superb design and technique. Wholly metal furniture declined during the later Renaissance, but the use of metal details as accessory to wood increased to the point where in the late 18th century it represented the principal means of ornamentation. Modern times and machine processes have rendered us essentially metal-minded, and the quest for a metal furniture technique is as old as the movement to create furniture in current moods. The metal bed, both brass and iron, of the late 19th century is the example par excellence of the trend and its success. It seems entirely logical and proper to make such structural frameworks of metal. Chairs of tubular steel answer supremely the contemporary cry for forms readily adapted to cheap machine production. Their shapes are peculiarly expressive of the material and the process. They are exceedingly comfortable, easy to handle and to keep in good condition. Many other articles of furniture may also be made wholly or in part of this strong light material, but ingenuity of design and public demand are still far behind the technical possibilities.

Sheet-metal work is likewise in a tentative state. Excellent utilitarian cabinets, chests of drawers, bookcases, etc., are possible technically, but timid taste and the exigencies of commercial production have retarded the development of other than office furniture.

METAL MOUNT. See HARDWARE; ORMOLU. [833.]

MEUBLES. French for movable furniture.

MEUBLES DE LUXE. The luxurious furniture that set the standards of most great styles. The extremely decorative furniture in the great rooms of Continental palaces was really built more for show than for use; its large scale, profuse ornamentation, and extreme cost render it unsuitable as inspiration for the design of average modern furniture.

MIDDLE AGES. See GOTHIC.

MIRROR. Looking glasses of polished metal were known in ancient times, but the mirror of silvered glass appears in the Early Renaissance. It was costly and available in small sizes, so that the important frame both exaggerated its size and emphasized its value. In Italy the typical form was a rich architectural profile, of simple shape; in the North the frame was elaborately outlined and richly carved. Jacobean mirrors, the earliest English types, were small, and heavily framed in the Italian manner. Some were framed in smaller bits of mirror leaded together. The carved wooden frame predominated with the advent of the Grinling Gibbons type of carving. The Louis XIV style inspired large mirrors with firm architectural outlines, richly carved and gilded or silvered. Under Louis XV these assumed irregular shapes in lighter frames. English mirrors of the Chippendale School were in the Rococo manner, with a constant tendency toward greater size; these were often pieced together in intricate frames. The classic types, like the characteristic Adam mirrors, were very large and of simple shape, outlined in thin gilt frames of Pompeiian inspiration. Trumeaus, of this time, were mirrors set into the paneling of rooms, as overmantels, etc. Smaller mirrors were in general use for dressing; these were frequently mounted on stands. In America the elaborate Rococo mirrors were simulated in jigsawed outline. The later classic revivals produced mirrors of strong architectural feeling. See also CHEVAL GLASS; TRUMEAU.

835 ENGLISH, 17th century Jacobean. Small pieces of glass leaded together.

837 ITALY, late 17th century.

836 ITALY, 16th century.

EARLY MIRRORS HAD SMALL GLASS IN LARGE ORNATE FRAMES.

834 ITALY, late 15th century.

838, 839, 840 THREE AMERICAN COURTING MIRRORS, 1780-1800.

Metropolitan Museum of Art

841 GERMAN, 17th century. Carved wood, gilded.

BAROQUE MIRRORS WERE LARGE AND ORNAMENTALLY COMPLEX.

843 RÉGENCE.   *French & Co., Inc.*

842 RÉGENCE c. 1700.   *Don Ruseau*

844 RÉGENCE, Louis XV.   **845** ENGLISH, Mid-Georgian, pre-Chippendale.   **846** QUEEN ANNE, 1700-1720.   **847** ENGLISH OR AMERICAN c. 1740?

848 ENGLISH, Early Georgian. *Needham's Antiques, Inc.*

849 PRE-CHIPPENDALE c. 1745. Early Rococo influence. *Symons Galleries, Inc.*

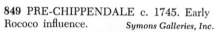

850 AMERICAN, 1740-1760. *Israel Sack, Inc.*

851 ENGLISH ROCOCO, symmetrical, c. 1770.
French & Co., Inc.

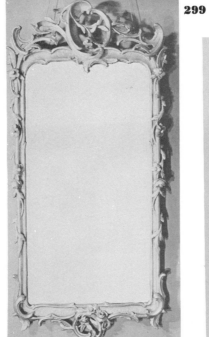

Symons Galleries, Inc.
855 ENGLISH, late 18th century.

854 ENGLISH c. 1785.
Symons Galleries, Inc.

Symons Galleries, Inc.
853 BALANCED ROCOCO, English c. 1760.

ENGLISH ROCOCO MIRRORS.

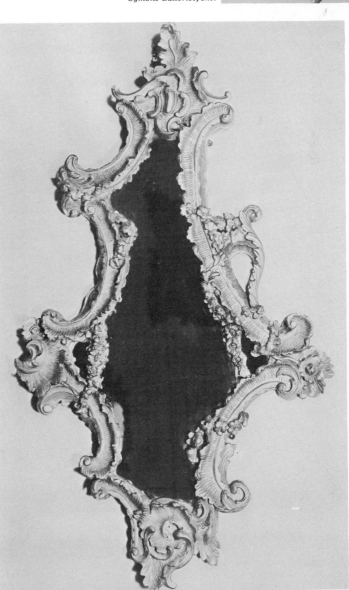

852 ENGLISH ROCOCO, asymmetry less accomplished than the French equivalent.
Symons Galleries, Inc.

French & Co., Inc.

856 LOUIS XVI, painted and gilded.

Don Ruseau

857 TRUMEAU, style of Louis XVI. Painted and gilded.

Di Salvo

858 NORTH ITALIAN c. 1780. Style of Louis XVI.

859 TRUMEAU, painted russet on gold ground.

Metropolitan Museum of Art, Gift of J. Pierpont Morgan, 1906

860 TRUMEAU, painted and gilded.

Di Salvo

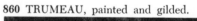

Needham's Antiques, Inc.

862 ENGLISH, Adam inspiration.

Brunovan, Inc.

861 VENETIAN, Louis XVI derivation.

864 ADAM, late 18th century.   *Symons Galleries, Inc.*

863 ITALIAN DIRECTOIRE.   *Olivieri*

865-866 TWO GEORGIAN
CONVEX MIRRORS
c. 1800.

Symons Galleries, Inc.

868 LOUIS XVI design framed in engraved glass
and ormolu.

Symons Galleries, Inc.

French & Co., Inc.

867 VENETIAN BAROQUE, mid-18th century.
All glass framing, cut, etched, and colored.

Ginsburg and Levy

869 AMERICAN c. 1810. Shows view of New York from Weehawken.

ITALIAN EMPIRE CHEVAL MIRROR

Needham's Antiques, Inc.

870 ENGLISH c. 1780. Late Adam design.

871 NEW ENGLAND HEPPLEWHITE c. 1800. Mahogany, inlaid.   *Israel Sack, Inc.*

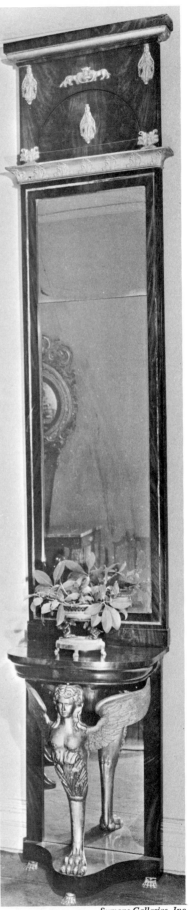

Symons Galleries, Inc.

872 FRENCH EMPIRE c. 1810. Console or pier glass. Mahogany, gilt mounts.

MIRROR

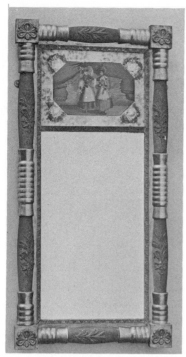

873 AMERICAN c. 1830. Gilt
half-turnings on black wood.

874 LACQUERED WOOD DRESSING MIRROR made
in China c. 1790 for the English trade.

877 NEW YORK c. 1815, made for the Livingston
family. Now in Museum of the City of New York.

875 VICTORIAN SHAVING
STAND.

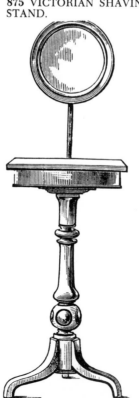

876 ENGLISH VICTORIAN.

MISSION. Spanish missions in southwestern North America (California, Mexico, etc.) were built by missionaries and Indians of native materials in a crude, substantial style. The furniture was heavy and square. In the early 1900's the Arts and Crafts Movement, reaching America from England, appropriated the heavy, homemade air of the missions, using heavy square oak, with crudely obvious mortise-and-tenon jointing (usually faked) and finished with a smoky or fumed dark stain. Upholstery was of leather, for ornament appliqués of hand-hammered copper, large nailheads, or simple cutout patterns were popular. The style lacked charm or subtlety; its clumsy weight and decorative poverty quickly condemned it and by 1913 it was extinct. [927.]

MISSION

MITER (MITRE). Joint in a molding where it changes direction, usually at 90 degrees.

MIXING TABLE. Side or serving table arranged with compartments for bottles, etc., and a flat work space for mixing drinks. See also WINE TABLE. [1241.]

MODERN FURNITURE. Viewed in terms of design, modern furniture may be considered as the product of development following World War I. Its roots, however, go back into the early phases of the Industrial Revolution. Continuing processes of invention, retrogression and adaptation have been led by an expanding style-conscious economy. During the whole century following the application to tools of power—water, steam, internal-combustion engine, and electricity—furniture making remained essentially a handicraft. With few exceptions, changes were confined to organization of production methods as opposed to technological advances in the product itself. Also remaining from past ages was the vocabulary of historic furniture design. [878 *et seq.*]

Mass production buried the artisan-designer. The designer became a detached anonymity, more salesman than artist, sternly governed by the production director, the mechanic. Often the designer and the production man were the same person. The factory idea, not new by 1830, hastened the growth of the industry, paced in turn by a mushrooming market. Population growth and new opulence followed the opening of new lands, but even in old countries the Industrial Revolution created new furniture buyers.

Most of these new customers wanted only furniture designs that had become fixed in their minds as status symbols, handed down from the courts and the nobility to the lesser strata, and particularly to the enriched bourgeoisie. The bulk of design, therefore, was commercial adaptation of the great old themes. The fashion cycle was accelerated by the frantic eclecticism of the designer-decorators, who were hard put to keep ahead of the latest overpopularized researches and revivals. In the metropolitan fashion centers, such designers, aided by skilled craftsmen-artisans, kept the wheel of style turning. Their innovations, inventions, and researches inspired the commercial factories that flooded the market with each new wave.

Even the reform movements were smothered by acceptance and mechanization. Resurgences of classicism and Rococo and Renaissance, reform movements like those initiated by Henry Cole, William Morris, and the Pre-Raphaelites, Eastlake and the cottage style, *Secession, Jugendstil*, Mission, and Art Nouveau [94] were eagerly seized upon and hybridized. Salesmen exploited the "story"; machinists worked out compromises; popular interest rose and fell. The market became so big that most movements made only a slight dent here and there. Significant innovations were usually of very small personal proportions, barely noticed at the time. Now recognized as turning points are the few clear cases of design coming to terms with the limitations and potentials, when recognized, of the machine.

The London Crystal Palace Exhibition of 1851 summarized the tendencies of the new potential: mostly bombast, novelty, excess in line, and overloaded ornament; loss of functional expression and scale. There was much substitution of materials, showing the effort to use machine products to solve problems of cost or structural weakness in handicraft. Welding metal into tubes and joining them by the same process appears in a French chair by Gandillot in 1844. Although painted and shaped to imitate a wooden chair, its slender members and joints reveal its true material. By 1840 in Vienna, Michael Thonet had rendered a Regency chair design in curved veneer strips. At the Crystal Palace he showed the same idea in steam-bent wood rods. The full strength of the continuous grain made joints so located and constructed as to reinforce rather than weaken the structure. Millions of chairs—cheap, light, strong, and

878   *Metropolitan Museum of Art, Edward C. Moore, Jr., Gift Fund, 1926*

878 L'ART NOUVEAU TABLE c. 1899, designed by Edward Colonna. **878A, B, C, D** SIDE CHAIR (1912), DESK CHAIR (1905), BRONZE UMBRELLA STAND (1902), DESK (1903), designed by Hector Guimard. **878E** SIDE CHAIR c. 1899.

878A, B

Collection, Museum of Modern Art, New York, Gifts of Mme. Hector Guimard

878 C

878E

878 D

handsome—were produced through this technique.

Another technique dating from mid-19th century that was to have far-reaching effects was the notion of laminating thin layers of wood plaidwise, the cross grains balancing strengths and stresses—plywood. The first general notice of extensive application was in chairbacks designed by Belter. Glued layers of rosewood and walnut, pierced and shaped, gave effects of openwork carving in curved planes, but with a cross-grain strength impossible in solid wood. New machines made veneer cutting cheap, and thin woods were extensively used in industrial packing, etc. Glued together in cross grains, early veneer panels were only as good as their adhesives. The idea of large surfaces with fancy-faced veneers spread rapidly, however. About 1900, bird's-eye maple [928], circassian walnut, crotch mahogany, and other exotic cuts of wood distinguished much commercial furniture.

The upholsterer's work changed significantly in mid-19th century. Development of springs permitted soft, bulky shapes. The Oriental craze was expressed in cushiony overstuffed effects merging with excessive drapery and permitting a show of rich fabrics and trimmings. Originating in France after 1830 are the divan, the *confortable*, the *confidante*, the *pouf*, the *borne*, the ottoman, etc. See also UPHOLSTERY.

While Great Britain spawned the philosophical views of design, America was preoccupied with mechanical aspects. An enormous catalogue of "Patent Furniture" appeared in the half century up to 1900. Unheard-of combinations of furniture functions occupied one species of designer. Others developed such specialized furniture as barber chairs and dentist chairs, while whole schools attacked the techniques of sitting and lying, working and resting. Unconcerned with visual effect, these products were essentially machines to which were added applied decorations of no relevance whatever.

Thus the 19th-century concept of furniture lost itself in mechanical practicality on one hand, in visionary esthetics on the other, while the bulk of the enormous production met neither the mechanical nor the esthetic problems directly. Where real advances did take place, their true significance was obscured for decades. Architects and painters figured largely in the philosophical discussions, as they had in ages past; and, as in the past, they proved that furniture design is best done by furniture designers. This is not to underestimate the vital impulse of the parent art and allied arts and crafts. Robert Adam, as the greatest of architect-designers, probably occupies that niche through his dependence on Thomas Chippendale. Palladio, Berain, Marot, Percier and Fontaine, Inigo Jones, Gibbs, Kent, Thomas Hope, Brunel, Baillie, and Mackintosh, H. H. Richardson, Stanford White, Frank Lloyd Wright—all the greatest architectural innovators and spokesmen—achieved something less than their greatest forcefulness in the design of actual furniture.

Conversely, the trade schools and shop organizations tended toward excellence of technique and conservatism in design. The British Art Workers Guild (1883), the Deutsche Werkbund Movement, and similar anticommercial organizations emphasized the craft approach and an educated base for designers. In America, Gustave Stickley promoted the Craftsman School from a simple rationale like that of the English Arts and Crafts. These were popular movements with a businesslike view of market objectives, not precious

theorizing. If the effects in furniture were transitory, the impact on interior decoration was positive in sweeping away the cluttered effects of 19th-century rooms and encouraging a sense of scale and quiet orderliness in room design.

These influences did not stem the antiquarian impulses that had come to dominate furniture thinking by 1910. After the Eastlake influence of the 1880's, England and America reverted to the great classics— Rome and the Renaissance. On the Continent the Biedermeier influence had never lapsed, and the reign of Napoleon III revived interest in Empire. An awakened Palladianism restored attention to the 18th century in England, while its counterpart in the United States launched the preoccupation with Americana, still current. The search for antiques—and their commercial reproduction and inspiration—began in the 1890's. Architecture, and furniture and its literature in this vein were—and are—the most favored expression. Early reproductions showed a curious lack of observation or a cavalier willingness to adapt. "Colonial" designs of the 1890's were wide of the mark in detail, materials, and finish. Up to World War I there were essays in Empire (then called post-Colonial), and mixtures of colonial Queen Anne, Adam, Hepplewhite, and Chippendale that were almost uniformly negative. After 1920, the old designs came to be more authentically reproduced, thanks to the educational influence of magazines, museums, and well-publicized collections, and especially to the new merchandising

878F SIDE CHAIR, 1900, by Charles Rennie Mackintosh. **878G** OFFICE CHAIR, 1904, by Frank Lloyd Wright. **878H** TUBULAR STEEL, 1927, by Mies van der Rohe.
Collection Museum of Modern Art, New York,

878F   *Gift of Glasgow School of Art*   378G   *Gift of Edgar Kaufman, Jr.*   878H   *Knoll Associates, Inc.*

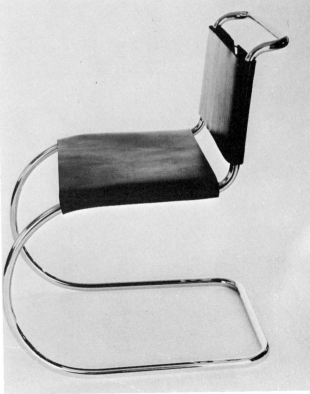

techniques of the large stores. Similar commercial production explored Italian Renaissance (a bow to the classic Italianism of the 1893 Chicago Fair); the Rococo Louis Quinze after the Paris fashions of the *haut monde* and the Beaux Arts School; the English Oak Era, spurred weakly by a similar movement in England, the aftermath of the Pre-Raphaelite quest for sanctity in handicraft Gothic.

There was as well a separatist movement, the Art Nouveau. Its protest against academic art was more articulate than its realization in furniture, but its thrust was different and aimed in the direction of new thinking. Henri van de Velde showed his Art Nouveau in Paris in 1895. Characteristic are the whiplash curve, free renderings of fruits and flowers, and fine workmanship in good materials. The style tended to be oversweet, and it cloyed swiftly. (See also ART NOUVEAU.) Van de Velde opened a school—the Bauhaus—at Weimar in 1902 under the patronage of the Duke of Weimar. Most of its significance rests in its pupils. Groups like De Stijl, abstract theorists in all the arts, grew out of such origins. Another school at Darmstadt had Peter Behrens, Hans Christiansen, and Ludwig Habich working under Joseph Olbrich. The various forces coalesced in the first decade of the 1900's into the Deutsche Werkbund, aimed at consolidating the active forces in art education and production. For the most part their design was simple and unaffected, sound in construction theory and practice. Architects like Jacobus Oud, Walter Gropius, Rietveld, Eric Mendelsohn, Mies van der Rohe, and Le Corbusier came from this background. After the war the new Bauhaus at Dessau encouraged reexamination of the basics of

Knoll Associates, Inc.

878J BARCELONA CHAIR, 1929, by Mies van der Rohe.

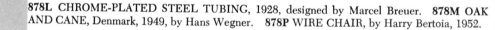

878L CHROME-PLATED STEEL TUBING, 1928, designed by Marcel Breuer.   **878M OAK AND CANE,** Denmark, 1949, by Hans Wegner.   **878P WIRE CHAIR,** by Harry Bertoia, 1952.

Frederick Lunning

Knoll Associates, Inc.

Thonet

furniture design. The International Style became international largely through Hitler's dispersal of the brains and talent of this institution.

In Vienna the Secession was organized in 1896 by Josef Hoffmann, Roller, Klimt, Moser, Olbrich, and others. It pioneered in the application of the English Arts and Crafts. In 1903 the Wiener Werkstätte appeared. Architects, many pupils of Otto Wagner, formulated a coherent style, and by the time of World War I, their thought dominated house design and decoration in Europe.

Design in the Scandinavian world enjoyed the intelligent direction of artists' associations, which have been a consistent force in the clarification of design ideas. Passing gently from the prevailing classicism of the 19th and early 20th centuries, Scandinavian design followed a mannerly rationalization. Coordination of industry and commercial output with design education has produced a complete repertory of gracious furniture, soundly constructed and economically able to compete in export with the most advanced furniture manufactories. Among outstanding designers may be listed Hans Wegner [334], Finn Juhl [1334] and Arne Jacobson in Denmark, Alvar Aalto in Finland, Karl Malmsten [333] in Sweden.

English furniture design followed a conservative course after William Morris. His general precepts of honest workmanship and direct design were widely accepted [880]. The Arts and Crafts Exhibition So-

878N Designed by Charles Eames   *Herman Miller*

878O Designed by Jens Risom

878Q, 878R PEDESTAL TABLE, CHAIR, AND OTTOMAN designed by Eero Saarinen, 1948.   *Knoll Associates, Inc.*

878K BENTWOOD by Thonet. Vienna, 1870.
Museum of Modern Art, New York

ciety, founded in 1888, set a quiet standard for a certain level, maintained by architect-designers like Charles Rennie Mackintosh, furniture designers like Ambrose Heal, Gordon Russell, Ernest Gimson.

The 1925 Paris Exposition of Decorative Art brought together many of the divergent currents of both prewar and postwar European design. Most of the exhibits were of a plush, romantic style, descended in part from Art Nouveau, with some reminiscence of Directoire and Empire, much influenced by advanced painting from Cubism through Abstractionism and Dadaism. In the elegant vein was exquisite cabinet-work in rare woods, metals, ivory, and glass by Ruhl-mann, Dufrene, Leleu. There was much of bizarre rebelliousness, strident color and pattern—the shapes of jazz. There was also a strain of constructivism, of both true and false functionalism, as expressed by students and observers of the new Bauhaus and the functionalists in Germany, the Netherlands, and Scandinavia.

The Bauhaus influence grew steadily in Europe during the late 1920's. Le Corbusier's Pavillon de l'Esprit Nouveau (Paris, 1925) showed plated tubing for everything but chairs, which were historic Thonet bentwood. Marcel Breuer went on with Mies van der Rohe's tubing designs, producing the cantilevered chair about 1928.

The impact of the Paris Exhibition on the United States was earth-shaking. The country was hungry for just such motivation. A new artistic-intellectual class of Europophiles had sprung up from its war contacts. A booming economy and the burgeoning craft of merchandising created and exploited a new art hunger. The Americans came to the Exhibition empty-handed; they went home carrying everything they saw. Until 1930, there was a riot of novelty and invention in the world of design and decoration. It was the Jazz Age, and cacophony was the theme. Indiscriminately, the new was accepted as the good. Sincere European designers arrived and developed personal mannerisms—men like Paul Frankl, Joseph Urban, Wolfgang Hoffmann. Their mannerisms and interpretations created a wave of copying of all the diverse European schools—Wiener Werkstätte, the English rationalists, Cubism, the Bauhaus, Swedish neoclassicism, Orientalism. Odd shapes, like the sky-scraper bookcase, and bizarre color and glorified amateurism in line and craftsmanship flourished side by side with an overrefined lush French manner.

A decade of economic stringency abolished much of this rebellious falseness, and substituted a reasonable functionalism whose early gaucherie was subtly influenced by sentiment from both Scandinavian and Italian sources. Sensitivity to architectural thinking was a strong influence, and the 1940's saw the rise

of an architecturally oriented school of furniture designers and manufacturers. George Nelson's engineering esthetic, Charles Eames's molding techniques, Jens Risom's Scandinavian wood logic, Harry Bertoia's light metal framings, among many others, supplement the furniture efforts of architects like Eero Saarinen and Marcel Breuer.

These influences have by no means found universal application in the United States. A strong traditionalist sentiment still operates, and on every level there is a great industry founded on historic styles. The unceasing quest for novelty by a growing affluent class has created a debased vocabulary called "contemporary," justifying stylistic liberties with historic themes. This has filtered down to lower commercial levels, encouraging mass-production industries to ignore the refinements of good reproduction. Fine design in well-made medium-price furniture is more abundant than ever before, but by no means universal.

MODILLION. Projecting brackets, usually enriched with carving, at regular intervals under the cornice in the Roman Corinthian, Composite, and Ionic orders.

MOHAIR. Upholstery fabric, originally made from the hair of the Angora goat. The Moors introduced it into Spain, whence it spread to England and northern Europe. It is mentioned in English inventories of the 17th century, but these appear to have been woven partly, if not entirely, of silk.

MOLDING (MOULDING). A shaped profile applied to a continuous member to emphasize the difference in planes or to provide decorative bands of light and shade. Any break in a continuous flat surface may be considered a molding if it is designed to catch light and shade as an accent or embellishment. Certain general types of moldings have been in use since the earliest architectural decoration. These are broadly classified as (1) flat or angular, (2) single curved, (3) compound curves. All types are variously embellished. The flat or angular types include (1) the band, face, or facia, continuous flat members, raised or sunken into and parallel with the main surface; (2) the fillet, listel, or regula, a narrow band, usually projecting; (3) the chamber or bevel, an inclined band; (4) the splay, a large bevel.

The simple curved moldings are (1) the cavetto, a concave molding of a quarter circle, though the section may be flatter or more elliptical; (2) ovolo, the reverse of the cavetto, a convex quarter circle or flattened shape; (3) the flute, a semicircular groove that may be flatter; (4) the torus, a convex bulging shape of approximately a half circle; (5) the astragal, a small

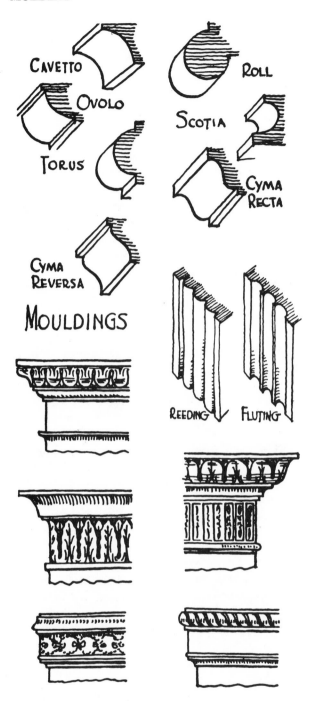

MOULDINGS

the ovolo, wreath form for the torus, bead-and-reel for the astragal; anthemion and acanthus for the cyma recta, water leaf for cyma reversa.

The Gothic moldings were deep hollows, generally roll moldings with fillets. The ornaments were less often continuously than spasmodically applied, or at the terminals of the shape.

MONEY DISHES. Scooped-out saucerlike spaces in card tables for holding money or counters. Also called "guinea holes." See also CARD TABLE.

MONEY MOTIVE. Decoration of flat overlapping desks, like scaling.

MONK'S BENCH. Early Gothic form possibly originally with refectory tables, often with carved aprons or stretchers. Also a type of BOX SETTLE or SETTLE (q.v.) with top hinged to form back. [879.]

879 MONK'S BENCH, Canadian, pine.   *Montreal Museum of Fine Arts*

torus or bead; (6) the scotia, a hollow molding of more than the quarter circle of the cavetto; (7) the roll molding, about three quarters of a circle. The compound moldings are (1) the cyma recta, (2) the cymatium, and (3) the cyma reversa, or ogee, all serpentine or double moldings; and (4) the beak mold, with the upper part concave and the lower convex.

Historically, certain ornaments have been used for specific profiles, the styles varying chiefly in technique. For example, the egg-and-dart is classical for

MORESQUE. Moorish; the style of decoration left in Spain by the Moors, in which high color, abstract geometric patterns of fine detail, and gilding are features. See also SPAIN. [350, 930.]

MOROCCO. Goat leather, used in fine upholstering in Louis XIV, Chippendale, and other styles.

MORRIS, WILLIAM, 1834-1896. English artist, architect, poet; formed in 1862 firm of Morris, Marshall, Faulkner & Company for practice of decorative arts. Chiefly motivated by a free interpretation of the medieval, Morris was a leader of a group of liberals in art and politics who tried to stem the tide of machine development by fostering handicraft de-

Metropolitan Museum of Art. Rogers Fund, 1926
880 CABINET by William Morris, door panels by Burne-Jones.

signing in simple naturalistic forms, producing textiles both printed and woven, wallpapers, carpets, furniture, stained glass, metalwork, book printing and binding, etc., embracing the whole field of design. This thought was the springboard for the development of subsequent European and American design philosophy, which after many divergent movements culminated in the Modern movement. See also NINETEENTH CENTURY. [880.]

MORRIS CHAIR. Large easy chair of the late 19th century with adjustable back, loose cushions forming the seat and back rest within a wooden frame. Said to have been invented by William Morris.

MORTISE. Hole or slot in wood, into which the tenon or tongue fits; one of the most important joints in woodworking. [622.]

MORTLAKE. English tapestry mills established near London by James I in 1619, discontinued during the reign of Charles I.

MOSAIC. Decorative inlays of small pieces of wood,

glass, stone, etc., conventional or pictorial in effect; Roman and subsequent.

MOSS. Vegetable growth from the South, used as upholstery stuffing in cheap furniture.

MOSS EDGING. Heavy pile cording used as a decorative edging in upholstery; first appeared in Italy, France, and England late in the 17th century.

MOTHER-OF-PEARL. Hard inner layer of shells. Its brilliant color after cutting and polishing has suggested its use for inlays since the 16th century. First applied in the East, it was adopted by the French, Dutch, and English in the 17th century. In England it often replaced tortoiseshell in Boulle work. Early-19th-century work in England and America abounds in mother-of-pearl inlays.

MOTIF (MOTIVE). Distinctive feature or element of design or ornament; theme.

MOTTLED. Spotted, speckled, or blotchy figures in veneers.

MOUNTS. Metal fittings or ornaments applied on furniture; most important in the style of Louis XV, when bronze appliqués were responsible for most decorative effects. Some mounts are utilitarian, such as handle and key plates, hinge ornaments, corner and angle protection, for inscriptions, etc.

MUDEJAR. Mixed Moorish-Christian style of Spain, 1250-1500, marking the transition from Mohammedan to Christian art by partial assimilation of Gothic and Renaissance forms. Some Moorish traits still persist. See also SPAIN. [1145.]

MUFFIN STAND. Small tier stand for plates, used in tea service in England and America.

MULE CHEST. Evolutionary type of coffer or chest with one or more drawers beneath the lid section.

MULLION. Vertical bar dividing the panes of a traceried window. In furniture, the tracery in glazed doors of bookcases, etc.

MUNTIN (MUNTING). Inside vertical members of a door or window frame, such as the divisions between the glass or wood panels of a door.

MUSHROOM TURNING. Shallow cup turning, either in a leg section or as a finial.

MUSIC DESK; MUSIC STAND. Table with inclined top for holding music in front of the player. Decoratively treated in 17th-, 18th- and 19th-century English and Continental work. [884.]

MUSICAL INSTRUMENTS. The less portable instruments, such as pianos, organs, etc., have been treated as furniture because they could not be stored away. From the Renaissance to the present we have examples of elaborate casework designed for these instruments, and in late years the phonograph, the radio, and television have been added. The tendency is to simplify the cases for the instruments to the minimum, avoiding the architectural or decorative cabinet idea. In the past, however, some notable forms, such as the spinet shape, have developed around instruments. [881, 966.]

MYRTLE. Light tannish-yellow wood with fine burl markings, excellent for fine inlays and veneered work; from the Pacific Coast.

881 EUROPEAN WORKBOX PIANO. 882 CLAVECIN, Paris, 1802. 883 WHATNOT OR MUSIC STAND, English c. 1800.

882

Symons Galleries, Inc.

883

881 *Metropolitan Museum of Art, Crosby Brown Collection of Musical Instruments, 1889*

Metropolitan Museum of Art, Crosby Brown Collection
of Musical Instruments, 1889

884 MUSIC STAND, Italian, 19th century.

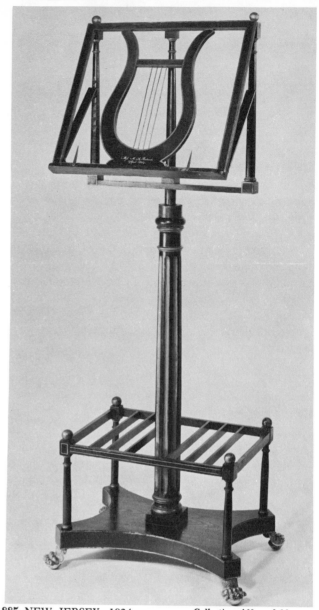

885 NEW JERSEY, 1824. Collection of Newark Museum

"N." Napoleon's monogram, used as a decorative motive in French Empire style. Occurs in bronze mounts, and is embroidered or woven on chairbacks.

NAILS (upholstery). Nails with ornamental heads are used for finishing in upholstery work. In some

888 NAIL-STUDDED LEATHER-COVERED CRADLE, American, 18th century.

Israel Sack, Inc.

886-887 VICTORIAN ENGLISH MUSIC STANDS.

styles they are arranged to make patterns, such as the daisy pattern in the French period of Henry II, and on screens, coffers, etc. Large nailheads are characteristic of Portuguese and some Spanish work. [162, 213, 254, 342, 1151.]

NECKING. Narrow molding or collar around the upper part of a column or post.

NEEDLEPOINT. Upholstery covering of woolen threads embroidered upon canvas.

NEEDLEWORK. Hand embroidery. The art is as old as weaving. Many techniques create different textures; these include embroidery, tapestry work, patchwork, appliqué, etc.

NEOCLASSIC. Revivals of interest in the ancient manner, such as the Renaissance, Adam, and Empire styles. See also CLASSIC. [138, 790.]

NEO-GOTHIC. Revivals of Gothic detailing, principally after 1830 in England and America; to a lesser extent in Continental work in furniture. [330, 410, 533.]

NEO-GREEK (Greek Revival). Classic Greek influence in early 19th century, particularly American work of Late Empire style, 1815-1845.

NEST OF DRAWERS. Quantity of small drawers or boxes contained in a case; a diminutive chest of drawers, chiefly English, 18th and 19th centuries.

NEST OF TABLES (Nested Tables). Set of several tables, graduated in size so as to fit one over another.

NETHERLANDS. The Low Countries, now Holland and Belgium, shared the homogeneity of Gothic art. Flanders as an entity produced only slight variations from the typical oak styles. In the 16th century it was under Spanish rule, and was thereby exposed earlier than other northern lands to the Mediterranean Renaissance. Italian influences likewise came up via France. Thus Elizabethan England and South Germany, through propinquity, felt the repercussions of the Italian Cinquecento, and imposed upon their current Gothic forms the lush Italian plastic and inlaid ornamentation.

Antwerp, Brussels, and Liège had important furniture makers early in the 1500's. Vredemann de Vries's book, about 1600, shows compositions with architectural pilasters, scrollwork, grotesques, and robust applied ornaments in beds and cupboards, credences and tables and chairs.

Metropolitan Museum of Art

889 NETHERLANDS, 17th-century writing cabinet, Hispano-Moresque influence in ivory inlays in rosewood and ebony.

890 DUTCH, 17th-century cabinet. Renaissance details are prototypes of succeeding English and American work.

NETHERLANDS
BAROQUE
CABINET
18TH CENTURY

Flemish Late Renaissance cupboards are distinctive. Square panels are boldly molded and carved; table and chair legs are recognized by the use of blocks interrupting the turned parts. The method of upholstering betrays Spanish origin, and is reflected in English Jacobean work.

The Baroque came into northern Europe through Flanders. The house of the painter Rubens, built after his return from Italy in 1613, shows bold scale and a rich architectonic conception. Furniture is in the same spirit. Four-door cupboards of oak, paneled with ebony, are square and firm, the cornices adorned with cartouches and leaves. Chairs become broader to accommodate the spreading costumes. Dutch Early Baroque, according to the paintings of the old masters, is simpler, quite devoid of plastic ornament, but full scaled and restrainedly embellished with deep moldings. Walnut became important after 1660, and inlays or exotic veneered panels enriched the surfaces. Twisted turnings are universal; oval bulb legs and bun feet are equally popular. The great "Friesland" cupboards are unique. Portuguese influences are present in chairs with embossed leather. The Dutch traders brought bits of styles from everywhere, but the Oriental touches are most interesting. Chinese porcelains, collected avidly, demanded cupboards for their display. Chinese lacquer was imported and imitated endlessly. But nothing exceeds in importance the development of the cabriole leg, partially inspired during this period by the Chinese. From India the Dutch borrowed the arcaded chairback. Dutch imports and exports of the latter 17th century are the real basis of English Baroque furniture of the Age of Walnut.

Dutch power waned early in the 18th century, and Flanders was virtually a French province after 1700. Henceforward the French style of Louis XV dominates Dutch and Flemish furniture. [13, 160, 172, 249, 251, 487, 1195, 1211, 1298.]

NEWPORT SCHOOL. Mid-18th-century Rhode Island group of cabinetmakers, including John Goddard, the Townsends, Job, John (father and son), and Christopher, and descendants. Concave shell and block forms in chests, secretaries, and clock cases, are among the best work of the period. [1382.]

NIGHTSTAND; NIGHT TABLE. Bedside table.

NINETEENTH CENTURY. The Industrial Revolution is the story of furniture in the nineteenth century. The factory and the machine were not alone new; design concepts had new meanings, and there was a whole new class of furniture owners. Actually, the factory was an 18th-century idea. The pattern of the Royal Manufactory in France was repeated in England in private furniture manufacturing enterprises employing as many as 400 workmen, favoring specialization within each trade. Then came the highly specialized tools and finally the application of power to the tools. All this made production of parts so cheap and rapid that the mass market had to follow. This vast output was no longer conceived in terms of a particular person or taste. [134, 323.]

This speedy mass production allowed no time for considering either the special capacities of the machine as a design factor or the changing symbolism of furniture for its public. The enormous reservoir of furniture ideas that had accumulated over the previous centuries was tapped for every impulse and motif. At one time or another in the 19th century, they were all embraced—or at least those bits that lent themselves to simulation by the machines and technicians of the time. The key to design in this era is the excess of ornament: easily produced adornment for its own sake, unrelated to the corpus of the furniture object.

Academic classicism had a deep appeal for northern European scholars, courts, and designers. The new archaeology, beginning with the German Winckelmann's work in Pompeii and Herculaneum, reinforced by the explorations of Englishmen after the Brothers Adam, took strong root in Scandinavia, Germany, and Austria. It was actually more correct, less derivatively inspired than the Louis Seize in France, and it flowed more naturally into the Empire. What Giedion calls the "ruling taste" created in France the Empire, a synthetic style developed by Percier and Fontaine at Napoleon's order (1801). In its sweeping haste it reduced the bulks of furniture to their simplest shapes, and added distinction by appliqués of historically correct ornaments. Because the simple forms and the applied ornaments, whether metal, carved wood, or stencils, were easy and satisfying for every talent, we see aspects of this style persisting throughout the century, from Madrid to St. Petersburg, from Stockholm to Chicago.

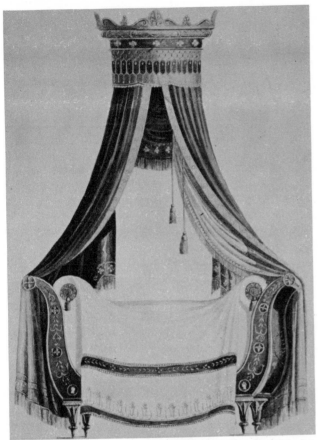

from Ackerman's Repository of the Arts,
Cooper Union Museum, New York City

891 REGENCY BED c. 1828.

892 REST BED, German, 1827.

893 BIEDERMEIER, 1800.

In its earliest phase in France, the Empire represents a retrogressive phase of the style of Louis XVI. Led by Jacob Desmalter (who signed himself simply "Jacob" as a revolutionary gesture), and based on the work of the German border *ébéniste-entrepreneurs* Riesener and Roentgen, the Empire was universally popularized. Berlin and Vienna were the outposts of classicism at the turn of the century, and there it became Biedermeier—reduced from the palace styles of Karl Schinkel in Berlin and Franz von Klenze in Munich to a comfortable middle-class adequacy. Thus, most Swedish, Danish, and German work of the period 1800-1830 is more classical, cooler and better composed than the prototypes in France and England. In Italy, on the other hand, a freer taste showed up in centers like Milan and Venice. Highly individualized and fanciful, some of the best work of the genre is ascribed to Giuseppe Soli and Gioconda Albertolli [784]. The style was so assimilated as to remain the basic idiom to the present day.

At the source in France, however, the Empire theme swirled indecisively in the crosscurrents of politics and taste and class struggle through the period of the Bourbon Restoration. By the time of the 1830 July Revolution, the aristocratic tradition had been substantially washed out. Louis-Philippe's decade saw a vulgarization of curved lines, an unrestrained and sometimes incoherent ornamentation, and, most significantly, the acceptance of eclectic free choice as a basis of design. Delacroix and other painters enamored of the Oriental theme set off a quest for the picturesque. In furniture, it appears as spineless upholstery, a predominance of fabric over frame, soft cushiony bulks distinguished only by rich covering and exuberant tailoring. The debasement of furniture design by the upholsterer is the most significant revealing expression of the mid-19th century. The artisan-designer lost out to the machine. The ease of producing applied ornament—machined wood, molded, stamped, embossed, electroplated, printed—obscured furniture mass and outline beneath the flood of trimmings.

The frantic search for ornament revived interest in the Rococo, which had never really disappeared in the provinces [975]. The neo-Rococo never caught the finesse of the 18th century. Its curves were less restrained, failing of continuity and coarsened in carved detail. This style was not without effect in Germany and Austria, often with a special naïve charm, sometimes more or less incongruously wedded to the Biedermeier.

The English middle class, not immediately affected by upheavals in Continental politics and manners, came to dominate style in furniture during the first half of the century, as they acquired wealth in the

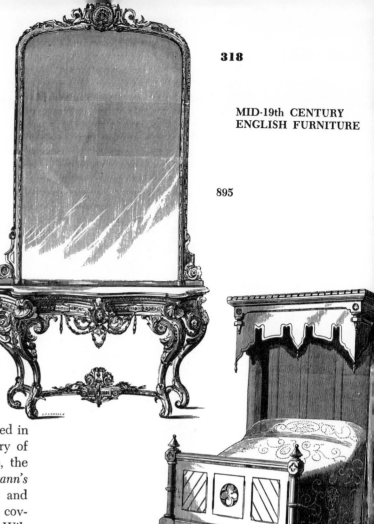

894

895

900

most expansive economy of its time. Sheraton died in 1806, leaving in his publications a total summary of the achievements of Chippendale, Hepplewhite, the Adams, and the 18th-century schools. *Ackermann's Repository of Art* (1808) adds Thomas Hope and George Smith to the style now labeled Regency, covering the decline of George III, George IV, and William IV up to the accession of Victoria in 1837. Regency furniture includes a wide range of classical motives—Greek, Roman, Egyptian, and assorted hybrids. Designers' names disappeared, and architects concerned themselves very little with furniture, so the field was open for the manufacturer-designer of commercial production, aimed at an unspecified, faceless clientele. Palace furniture and exhibition designs give a picture of overelaborate, strained designs that are not representative of the mass of everyday furniture.

894 BED c. 1870, Renaissance detail. **895** CONSOLE, Louis XIV inspiration. **896** REGENCY c. 1835. **897** LATE SHERATON, 1840 (?). **898** LOUIS XIV c. 1860 (?). **899** SCOTTISH BARONIAL c. 1880 (?). **900** BED, Neo-Gothic.

899

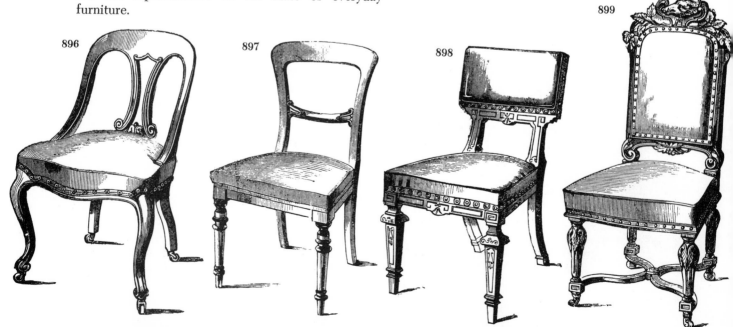

896   897   898

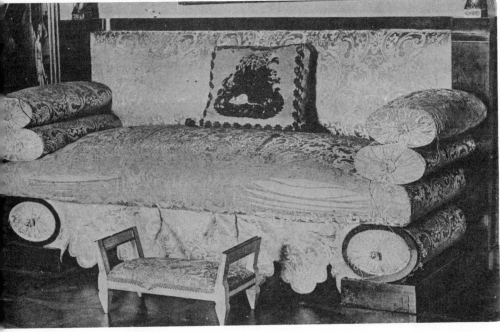

901 BIEDERMEIER, upholstery tour-de-force with Egyptian flavor. German c. 1850.

902 DETROIT c. 1865. Infinite variety in detail of parts, derived from Windsor, Empire, and current English models. Millions of such chairs were made from 1840 to 1900.
Henry Ford Museum, Dearborn, Mich.

The only architects who showed any interest in furniture were proclaiming the heathenness of classicism and advocating a return to the Gothic. Augustus Pugin carried on the medievalism of his father in his work on the interiors of the Houses of Parliament. The Gothic Revival owes much to this impetus. But there were conflicting arguments for such diverse styles as the Elizabethan and the Jacobean, the Early French Renaissance of François I, then the grandeurs of Louis XIV, and finally Orientalism. After 1835, the decline in taste accelerated, reaching its climax in the Crystal Palace Exhibition of 1851.

Probably the best result of this agglomeration of overblown craftsmanship was to make clear to a few the dishonesty of design (1) based entirely on pseudo-archaeology, and (2) using the machine to imitate handwork. Three men—Henry Cole, Owen Jones, Richard Redgrave—spurred a reform movement aimed at understanding the directness of the machine process. Ruskin turned about from this point and reverted to the Gothic of the hand and the simplest tools. His circle, the Pre-Raphaelites, took in Eastlake and finally Morris, but this stream was an intellectual movement that probably did not even run parallel to the mainstream of popular Victorian design. [532.]

AMERICAN CHAIRS, 1840-1880. *Left to right:* 903 BALLOON BACK, Louis XV derivation, 1850-1870. 904 LATE EMPIRE, 1840-1860, fruit and flower carving, haircloth, slip seat. 905 PLANT STAND, marble top, 1850-1870. 906 RENAISSANCE ECHOES, round cane seat, 1860-1875. 907 EASTLAKE INFLUENCE, 1870-1880, machined lines and carving.
Henry Ford Museum, Dearborn, Mich.

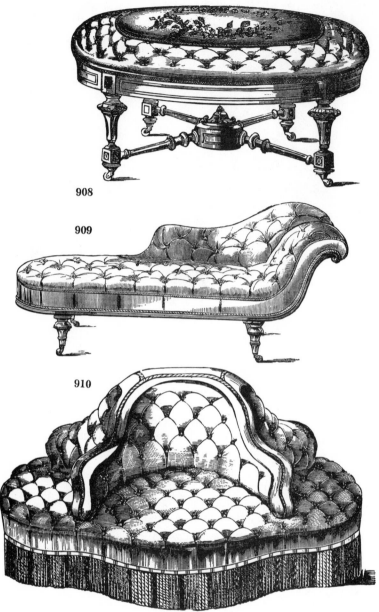

908

909

910

908 BENCH OR POUF for use in center of room. 909 CHAISE LONGUE. 910 BORNE OR ISLAND SEAT, no wood exposed. 911 Sofa with mixed Renaissance-French detail.

ENGLISH UPHOLSTERY WORK, 1850-1880.
From catalogue of Hampton and Sons, Furniture Collection of Grand Rapids Public Library

911

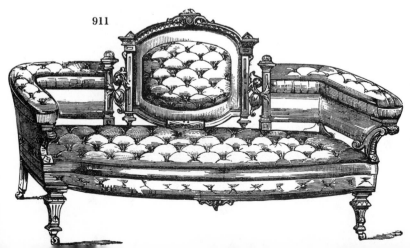

The Crystal Palace Exhibition did call attention to a widespread interest in technological experimentation with methods and techniques as well as with machines. New materials and new uses for materials were examined. Metals were handled in new contexts, turning their known virtues to unfamiliar uses. Papier-mâché was at its height and was shown here with inlays of mother-of-pearl, in the Islamic style. Michael Thonet's bentwood technique was germinating about this time in Vienna, his designs growing perfectly logically from his process. His basic chairs appeared before 1860; the technique may be considered one of the outstanding furniture achievements of the century.

The great bulk of work of the century after 1840 was anonymous in design and commercial in production. For several decades it remained conservatively Renaissance [1120], stressing comfort, not overly decorated (contrary to general opinion). After 1860, Louis XIV yielded to Rococo, as in France. In the provinces much of the Georgian of the prior half century persisted as current style. Quite possibly much of what is sold today as authentic antique may date from this era of eclectic, painstaking copying of Tudor and Queen Anne and Chippendale.

The reform influence was felt throughout the field after 1880; but instead of turning toward better design, it sought variety. This bred stylism: probably the superficially Oriental was strongest. As in France, the neo-Renaissance gave way to suggestions from the East, Near and Far, Turkish rooms, Persian and Indian themes. Just as Italy and Spain in the Renaissance had been influenced by Islam, as the Portuguese and Dutch in the 17th century brought home reminiscences of India, and as the England of Queen Anne and the early Georges reveled in chinoiserie, Europe now exploited a mistaken idea of Oriental culture, including the Japanese. Harmless and impermanent in Europe, its worst effect was to encourage Oriental craftsmen to make "bazaar" rubbish.

It was France that inspired most of the changes in fashion as the political pendulum swung from Republic to Empire to Republic. Napoleon III and Eugénie presided over a great revival of elegance, this time with the upholsterer overriding the carver. A species of Louis Quinze curvature with puffy upholstering was the hallmark. There was tremendous expansion of the furniture vocabulary, as well as an overemphasis on the furniture object in relation to the main composition of the room.

In America, an explosively expanding economy and geography absorbed the French influence avidly, although the Gothic Revival (roughly 1820-1850) took more from English Pugin than from Viollet-le-Duc [423]. Prior to that, the Federal style had merged naturally into the Empire. After 1800, the classic of Greece and Rome suited the philosophy and esthetic of the new Republic. Duncan Phyfe could not have been alone in making the transition from Sheraton to Thomas Hope; New England and the southern seaboard saw the same evolution. French imports included not only fashion plates and furniture but also designer-craftsmen like Honoré Lannuier. The Greek Revival was the mainstream in architecture through 1850, and furniture followed closely. Neo-Gothic began to edge in after about 1830. Reacting to the formal symmetry of the Greek was the so-called "picturesque." It aimed to be quaint, small-scaled, and personal. The prevalent wood construction took easily to lacy cutout detail, to board-and-batten walls. In furniture, only a few details lent themselves to transfer to the accepted comfortable outlines.

Most significant here are the advent of power and the machine. The designer-craftsmen stayed in the eastern cities. Boston, New York, and Philadelphia set the standards because they had the designers. Still, hundreds of new towns, settlements nearer the source of the woods, found that they could supply some of their furniture needs at home. They had wood and power and a market right there. The design mattered little; they copied—in their fashion—what they saw and liked from the few pieces they had brought with them, and they found they could do things with their lathes and saws and primitive shapers that were different, which is in itself a virtue in the American ethos. Individuality was the keynote, coupled with

a fine business sense. Among hundreds of such enterprises in New England after 1815, we single out Lambert Hitchcock in northern Connecticut for the mass production of his famous "fancy" chair, the "poor man's Sheraton." Parts for these chairs went to Charleston by the thousands for assembly and local sale. The idea was too good for enterprising Yankees to leave as a monopoly to Hitchcock: Carl Drepperd is authority for the estimate of over 8,000 American chairmakers in 1830—for 12,700,000 people.

The product of this far-flung industry varied by whim. Much was derived from the Regency-Directoire shape familiarized by Phyfe and made machinable by innumerable adapters clear to the Mississippi Valley. Their style ranged freely, and so did the scope of their production. Cabinets and case goods and beds came from everywhere in New England, central New York and Pennsylvania, up the Great Lakes and down the rivers. By 1870 some of these had become important industries serving the seaboard cities. Grand Rapids, Rockford, Jamestown, the factories in central Pennsylvania, West Virginia, and North Carolina—all have their roots in such beginnings.

What they sought for design inspiration is a vague story. There were a few itinerant designers who visited the plants long enough to leave a parcel of sketches. How well they wrought is conjectural because the product of the era generally indicates a ruthless adaptation to the vicissitudes of the mechanical production process. The Late Empire, Louis Quinze Victorian, Eastlake and the neo-Renaissance,

912 BELTER CHAIR c. 1865. Back carved in laminated rosewood.   *Wadsworth Atheneum, Hartford, Conn.*

912A, 912B DRESSER AND BED c. 1860, by Belter. Laminated rosewood.   *Brooklyn Museum*

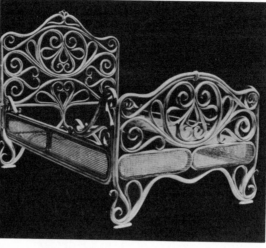

913 *Left.* VIENNA c. 1850. Thonet's first work simulated Late Regency design. **914** *Center.* BED c. 1890 (?). Exuberant manipulation of the bending technique in beech and cane. **915** *Right.* Thonet's basic chair after 1860, the forecast of functional directness.

Photographs, University of California (Los Angeles) Art Department

Mission and Colonial revivals were freely adapted—and accepted—with a generally specious critique. Techniques outran design. Molding took the shapes that the machine found natural, and carvings made separately and stuck on were just as effective if made of composition. Turning and shaping developed virtuosity. Sheer bulk of wood made for grandeur, and multiplication of themes for richness. The development of plywood permitted larger surfaces that lent themselves to adornment with figured veneers.

If the status of the designer was ambiguous, that of the inventor or the technician never was questioned. The latter improved machines and found things for them to do. Early in the power era, lathes began to turn out miles of simple turnings, like the "spool," which found its way into the spool bed about 1850. Routing and simple carving imitated plastic ornament. Veneer cutting was simplified and cheapened. Lamination may have originated with Belter, whose highly modeled chairbacks were carved into crossbanded layers of rosewood. Laminated panels were made by former "box-and-shook" mills in New England, although it was several decades before adequate adhesives made plywood trustworthy.

The inventor had his field day in the 19th century. Thousands of patents were granted for mechanical furniture whose uselessness was second only to complexity of manufacture or operation. A favorite subject was the bed that retreated into a piano, a bookcase, a library table, or another bed, sometimes accompanied by dressing tables or a few incidental accessories. There were trick chairs, desks, dressers, and therapeutic devices. Few worked and few went past the patent papers, but the enthusiasm recorded for them in print gave them a life of their own.

916 GRAND RAPIDS c. 1880, by Berkey and Gay. American interpretation called Eastlake style. This assimilates about everything the reformers decried. Richly ornamented with inlay and painting, it typifies the lavish, superior craftsmanship of the time. **916A** MAHOGANY TABLE with inlaid top. American c. 1881. **917** GRAND RAPIDS, c. 1898. The mass-production low-price end of the scale resorted to bulk and machine virtuosity.

916A
Brooklyn Museum

916

917

Both photographs, Furniture Collection of Grand Rapids Public Library

Photographs, Grand Rapids Furniture Museum

919

918

920

921

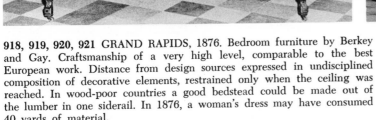

918, 919, 920, 921 GRAND RAPIDS, 1876. Bedroom furniture by Berkey and Gay. Craftsmanship of a very high level, comparable to the best European work. Distance from design sources expressed in undisciplined composition of decorative elements, restrained only when the ceiling was reached. In wood-poor countries a good bedstead could be made out of the lumber in one siderail. In 1876, a woman's dress may have consumed 40 yards of material.

922 ALSACE c. 1890. Jacobean theme in decoration of a cabinet. Stepped top for display of *objets d'art*.

921A DESK, 1878, American.

Brooklyn Museum

The large cities did not give up the premium market. There remained in many of the larger centers an important cabinetmaking industry that closely followed European fashions and maintained a high level of craftsmanship. Most of this work reproduced the classic French, English, and Italian antiques, more or less faithfully. Most museum exhibits of American Victoriana show this phase rather than the commercial product of the time.

923 GERMANY. Early 20th century buffet showing influence of decorative reform movement. **924** GRAND RAPIDS, 1887. Bedroom furniture "designed in the manner of Richardson." **925** ENGLISH, cottage style. Board construction recalls Eastlake Gothic. **926** MICHIGAN, 1892. Desk-bookcase of "golden oak"—a functional idea, with unrelated decorative elements inexpertly composed.

Furniture Collection of Grand Rapids Public Library
924

924B

925

924A RENAISSANCE INFLUENCE, c. 1881, American. OAK HALL TABLE, **924B** MAHOGANY ARMCHAIR.
Brooklyn Museum

924A

926

Original design in America had little success. Closest to a domestic idiom was the Mission style, arising after 1895 from two sources: (1) the crudely direct work of the Spanish missions to the Indians in the Southwest; (2) the English cottage or Arts and Crafts Movement. Dissimilar as these two may appear to be, their reduction to basics coincided superficially with the functional gropings of the Chicago School of architecture. The furniture efforts lacked the appeal and stamina of the architectural philosophy that presently blossomed in the work of Sullivan, Wright, and other forerunners of the 20th century. The Mission withered before the onset of World War I. So had an abortive neo-Colonial about 1900, the Art Nouveau, and a cottage Louis Quinze bird's-eye maple, various adaptations of Jacobean and Adam and Italian Renaissance. The tenures of such styles were brief and overlapping. After the war there were recurrent revivals of all these, along with a Spanish craze generated by a Florida land boom. The Early American theme in its simpler versions rose to dominance, side by side with well-studied schools of 17th- and 18th-century English and Provincial French.

928

contained some of the features of *L'Art Nouveau* and others that were borrowed from the English Arts and Crafts and also from ancient Egyptian forms of art. The French school has already failed in the efforts to establish a permanent style, and the indications are that the efforts of the German and Austrian Secessionists will prove equally futile, because in both cases the workers have merely attempted to do something different; to evolve a new thing by combining the features of the old. In other words, they began at the top instead of beginning at the bottom and allowing the style to develop naturally

A LARGE WRITING DESK FOR THE LIBRARY OR WORKROOM

928-929 BED AND DRESSER SUITE, 1899. Bird's-eye maple veneered on large panels and shapes. Moldings and carvings accommodated to machines' abilities leave only weak reminiscence of Louis XV motivation.

from the sure foundation of real utility. The leaders succeeded in making things that, whatever their relative merits, were a new departure; but this once made, it stood as a completed achievement that might be imitated, but could hardly be developed, as it lacked the beginnings of healthy growth.

But during the same period in this country things were on a different basis. Out of the chaos of ideals and standards which had naturally resulted from the rapid growth of the young nation, a vigorous and coherent national spirit was being developed, and amid the general turmoil and restlessness attendant upon swift progress and expansion, it became apparent that we were evolving a type of people distinct from

A TYPICAL CRAFTSMAN LOUNGING CHAIR.

A LARGE OAKEN SETTLE UPHOLSTERED WITH CRAFTSMAN SOFT LEATHER. THE PILLOWS ARE COVERED WITH THE STILL SOFTER AND MORE FLEXIBLE SHEEPSKIN.

927 CRAFTSMAN FURNITURE, 1898. Utility to the point of crudeness. Mission's lack of grace doomed it to a brief doctrinaire appreciation; nevertheless it attained wide distribution.
Page from The Craftsman *magazine*

NONESUCH; NONSUCH (English). Chest showing in inlay a representation of the castle of Nonesuch built by Henry VIII. The typical picture, however, appears in chests of the time from Germany and Scandinavia.

NORMAN. Style of the French conquerors of England after 1066; a rugged, bold, large-scaled manner basically Romanesque, employing the sparing ornament and hard outlines of medieval fortress architecture.

NORMANDY. Furniture of the province of Normandy, in France, has a simple, refined rustic character somewhat reminiscent of the product of Colonial New England. See also FRANCE; PROVINCIAL.

NOTCHING. Simple form of decoration found in primitive woodwork.

NULLING. Quadrant-shaped (in section) carved ornament, similar to gadrooning.

NURSERY. Furniture specially designed for infants and small children, including bassinets and cribs, bath tables, high chairs, diminutive chairs and tables, toy chests and wagons, etc.

OAK. Coarse-textured, hard, durable wood valuable for woodworking. It occurs everywhere in the temperate zones, in a wide range of varieties. The northern part of Europe was originally covered with oak, so that practically all Gothic work is in this wood. Its displacement by walnut and other woods in Germany and Europe north of central France occurred in the 17th century. It is the typical wood of all the Gothic styles, of the Tudor and Jacobean styles in England, and the Early Renaissance in Flanders and Germany.

OBERKAMPF, CHRISTOPHE PHILIPPE, 1738-1815. French textile manufacturer, creator of the *toiles de jouy*.

OCCASIONAL TABLE. Small table for incidental use, as coffee and tea tables, end tables, book tables, lamp tables, and other less definite uses.

OEBEN, JEAN-FRANÇOIS (died 1765). French *ébéniste*, an outstanding designer of Louis XV Rococo style. Made celebrated "Bureau du Roi," completed by his pupil Riesener.

OGEE. Classical molding having a cyma or double curve; also, two S-shaped curves, the convex curves meeting at a point or fillet, as used in the sides of an arch. Ogee-headed panels are found in Georgian casework, and in the tracery of bookcase and cabinet doors. See also MOLDING. [40.]

OGEE BRACKET FOOT. Cabinet foot with cyma reversa profile, found in American and some English work, late 18th century. See also GODDARD. [1045.]

OGIVE; OGIVAL. Pointed arch, distinctly Gothic.

OLIVE WOOD. Hard, close-grained wood, greenish-yellow in color, with irregular dark markings. It takes a high polish. It has been used by the Mediterranean peoples since time immemorial, as indicated by Egyptian, Greek, and Roman remains and documents. It is found as inlays and veneers in furniture of the French Renaissance, and of England after Late Stuart times. English Regency and Continental Empire styles favored the burl figures. Ash burl is often substituted for the olive.

ONION FOOT. Oval-shaped cabinet foot.

ONLAY. Overlay; decorative appliqué, as of veneers. [918.]

OPPENORD, GILLES-MARIE, 1672-1742. French cabinetmaker and designer, Louis XV style.

ORDERS. The orders of architecture are the standardized ornamental types of columns, with their associated bases, capitals, pedestals, entablatures, etc. They are based on the Greek and Roman remains,

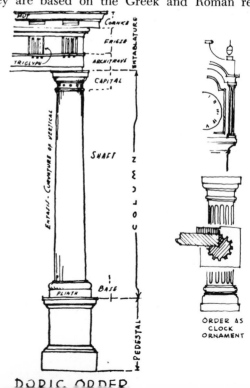

DORIC ORDER

having been originally classified by Vitruvius during the reign of Julius Caesar. He defined three Greek orders, the Doric, Ionic, and Corinthian, and five Roman orders, the Tuscan, Doric, Ionic, Corinthian, and Composite, reducing the proportions and profiles of each surface, molding, and ornament to exact rules. Later Roman and Byzantine work deviated increasingly from these standards until they were completely lost, to be rediscovered and revitalized in the Renaissance.

The significance of the orders in furniture design lies in the application of architectural forms by Renaissance designers. Case furniture of all types was profiled with base and cornice moldings, and increasingly the column form was used as applied and, later, free-standing ornament. Vertical members like table legs were made into miniature columns. The whole structural significance of the orders was lost in their universal use as applied ornament. This idea of trying to make a piece of furniture resemble a scale model of a building reappears in every revival of classicism. In contrast is the homogeneity of the design whose ornamentation is an essential part of the whole structural method, exemplified in Gothic and French Rococo furniture.

ORIENTAL. The Near East has produced relatively little major furniture. Furnishings in the Islamic lands depend mainly on carpets and fabrics; the small tables, low seats, and small cabinets look portable and have jewel-like decoration of inland ivory and pearl or of representational painting [174]. Mosque furniture is more commonly found, and includes reading desks and Koran stands with fine ritual decoration of flat delicate carving and inlay. Farther east, India and adjacent lands show little furniture in the European sense until the 18th century. Wood and ivory turning were old accomplishments, and Indian themes of grillwork of turned members entered the European vernacular through trade with the Portuguese and Dutch.

Where Chinese influence and taste enters, we meet a very ancient knowledge of furniture. Drawings and clay models remaining from earliest history show everyday use of tables and chairs and cabinets, but remains of actual furniture in China cannot be dated before the 14th century. (See CHINA.) In the Japanese royal treasure stores, however, there are pieces of Chinese furniture of the 7th and 8th centuries that are not too different from known Chinese work of the Ming and Ching dynasties—1368-1644 and 1644-1912 respectively.

ORIENTALWOOD; ORIENTAL WALNUT. Australian wood of the laurel family; brown with blackish stripes and cross figures and mottles. Polishes well and is generally desirable for furniture. Also called "Queensland walnut."

Metropolitan Museum of Art, Gift of Mrs. Russell Sage, 1911
930 PERSIAN (SHIRAZ) JEWEL BOX, 19th century. Wood inlaid with ivory.

Metropolitan Museum of Art, Gift of Mr. and Mrs. Robert W. de Forest, 1910
930A SCREEN, EGYPTO-ARABIC, 14th to 15th centuries.

931 SYRIAN (DAMASCUS) CHEST, 18th century. Walnut, carved and inlaid with mother-of-pearl.
Metropolitan Museum of Art, Rogers Fund, 1922

932

933

932 CARVED WOOD, Chinese, 18th century.
Charles Gracie and Sons

933 TABLE, Chinese, 19th century. Lacquered wood inlaid
with mother-of-pearl.
Metropolitan Museum of Art, Rogers Fund, 1909

934 THRONE, Chien Lung, 1736-1795. Carved lacquer.
Victoria and Albert Museum, Crown Copyright

934

935 SCREEN, carved and lacquered. *Charles Gracie and Sons*

936 KOREAN CHEST, 17th century. Framed burl panels with brass butterfly hinges. Painted screen background. *Charles Gracie and Sons*

ORMOLU. From the French *or moulu;* gilded brass or copper mounts for furniture principally used by the French *ébénistes* of the 18th century, and the followers of their styles. [368, 417, 937.]

ORNAMENT. The term "ornament" applies to every manner of embellishment to make one surface contrast with another, whether consciously applied or intrinsic in the nature of the material or design. Ornament is achieved by means of color, texture, or relief. Certain more or less conventionalized forms used as the basis of ornamental designs are called motifs.

Color ornament may be contrast in surfaces or it may be applied to a surface in the form of designs. These may be painted or inlaid; in textiles, printed, woven, embroidered, etc. Texture of the quality of the surface may be varied by the combination of woods, metals, etc.; in fabrics of monotone color the weave may be interrupted or varied; woods are inlaid with metals or other woods for contrasting texture; metal and glass surfaces are varied to yield contrasts. Relief ornament is accomplished by cutting into or building up the background surface in forms of recognizable design. This implies carving in high and low relief, scratch-and-gouge carving, molding, etc.; also their imitations in composition, stucco, applied relief ornaments, etc.

Motifs are produced spontaneously or borrowed and modified by peoples at various times. The manner of treating ornamental motifs is always characteristic of a people or their style, and serves as an index to the style. Certain motifs have been used since dim antiquity, yet the individual variations are an unfailing guide to the time and place. Motives are classed as abstract or naturalistic. Abstract forms grow from

937 ORMOLU, French Empire. *French & Co., Inc.*

938 ORMOLU, Louis XVI commode. *Dalva Brothers, Inc.*

simple imaginative use of lines, as circles, triangles, dots, crosses, etc., in rhythmic repetitions. Naturalistic ornament derives from the representation of visual things, chiefly plants and animals. These may be realistic or conventionalized, according to whether they truly pictorialize the object or merely symbolize it in more or less recognizable simplification.

The simplest structural form may be considered ornamental, if it is adapted in the slightest way to uses other than pure structure. Thus an arch is ornamental if any other than the true stone structural principle is employed. A column treated with bases, capital, fluting, etc., is *ornamented*, but the use of the column itself in furniture is *ornamental*. All architectural forms reproduced in furniture may be considered ornament. The use on furniture of ornaments planned for the embellishment of buildings is similarly architectural, but the scaling-down process has developed a distinct sequence of ornamental forms. Certain styles, such as the Renaissance and other classic revivals that look backward to ancient times, employ these architectural forms; others, like the Gothic and phases of the Rococo, derive their ornamental character from the deft manipulation of lines, planes, color, and organic details.

Ancient Egypt conventionalized its flora and fauna in paint and sculpture. Animal forms, such as bulls' feet and lions' heads and paws, and flowers like the lotus, were used on furniture. Greece and Rome enlarged the list, developing the acanthus leaf, the water leaf, lions, eagles, ox skulls, flowers and fruits in garlands and festoons, mythological or partly real animals and figures as chimeras, grotesques, satyrs, caryatids, etc.; also compounds of lines such as flutings, dentils, scrolls, volutes, etc.; and repeated motives in rhythms like rinceaux, eggs-and-darts, guilloches, undulating vines, etc.; also breaks in planes and surfaces, such as moldings, panels, coffers. Gothic art deviated from these conventionalized classes by working out at first hand a series of naturalistic representations of familiar fruits and flowers, grotesque animals, etc., in combi-nation with moldings; also all-over patterns, diapers, and other rhythmic repeat designs. The Renaissance scrapped the Gothic system and resurrected the ancient patterns, but quickly changed them to their means and fancy, so that Renaissance classicism is usually distinguishable from the antique. The Baroque-Rococo styles carried modification to the extreme of losing sight of the source and creating a wholly distinct category of ornaments. Revival after revival has only used the old as a starting point; the ornament of every period is finally the index to that period.

OTTOMAN. Upholstered seat or bench having neither back nor arms; so named after the Turkish influence in the early 18th century. [908.] During the English Regency period "ottoman" seems to have had a special connotation of a divan. *Ackermann's Repository of the Arts* (1817) shows a form of overstuffed sofa with back and arms.

OUDRY, JEAN-BAPTISTE. 18th-century French designer; as director of Gobelin works after 1736, he influenced Rococo style.

OVAL BACK. Chair shape, best developed by Hepplewhite somewhat after French precedent. [295.]

OVERLAY. Ornamental veneer applied upon the surface rather than inlaid into a veneer surface.

OVERMANTEL (Mirror or Panel). Chimneypiece dominating room design called for an important element over fireplace. Trumeau was one such development, with mirror subordinate to carving and painted areas. Horizontal emphasis appeared in the late 18th century in English and American work.

OVERSTUFFED FURNITURE. Chairs, sofas, etc., in which the wood frame is completely covered by the upholstery, only minor decorative woodwork being exposed. See also UPHOLSTERY.

OVOLO. Convex classical profile, usually the full quarter of a circle. When enriched with the egg-and-dart molding, it is known as "echinus." Both the plain and garnished types occur in much Renaissance detail. See also MOLDING.

OYSTER PIECES; OYSTERING. Veneers cut as cross sections of roots and branches of some trees, such as walnut and laburnum saplings, lignum vitae, olive wood, and some fruitwoods. The irregular concentric rings resemble oyster shells. A favorite device of the English designers from the end of the Jacobean period to the end of the 17th century. [360, 815.]

ORNAMENTS

GOTHIC WOOD

SABOT

SPANISH SHELL BRASS

LOUIS XVI WREATH ORMOLU

BRASS GALLERY

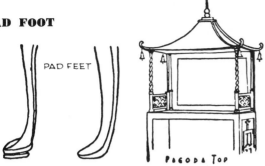

PAD FOOT. Simple flattish end of a cabriole leg, similar to club foot without the disk at the base. [572.]

PADAUK; PADOUK. Vermilion, or Andaman redwood; a heavy brilliant wood from Burma, having the texture and polish of rosewood. Appears to have reached Europe early in the 18th century and to have been used extensively by the French *ébénistes*. In England the solid wood was used for fretwork.

PAGODA. Temple or sacred tower in Burma and China. The Chinese influence popularized their distinctive sweeping roof shape as the crowning motif for cabinets, canopies, etc., in England and France, 18th century. [409.]

PAINTED FURNITURE. Any opaque colored finish on wood, hiding the actual wood grain, whether lacquer, enamel, or simple paint, decorated or plain. The practice of painting furniture is very old. Most Egyptian relics are painted, and much of the furniture of the Far East is finished in lacquer. Medieval furniture was liberally polychromed; in this age appeared the practice of painting common woods in imitation of rarer ones. Naturalistic motives supplemented stenciled conventionalization. Florentine work of the 15th century developed a style of pictorial decoration over gesso [755]. Painted furniture spread from here throughout Italy, and by the 17th century over all Europe, lingering in provincial districts and emerging as distinct styles. Most 17th-century work on important furniture followed Chinese themes, but distinct provincial mannerisms appeared in the Alpine styles in Switzerland, in Alsace, and in Scandinavian lands. Settecento (18th-century) work in Italy in a free Ba-

roque style displays Rococo ornamentation with landscapes, floral panels, arabesques and grotesques, elaborating on the French Rococo manners of Watteau, Pillement, etc., with Chinese themes liberally interspersed. Colors are light and bright. The Louis XVI style brought delicate pastel shades, gray and white. Painted furniture reached its apogee in Italy about the end of the 18th century in the so-called Venetian style. [161, 340, 466, 781, 1043, 1055, 1073, 1163, 1327.]

In provincial work painting substituted for carving. The naturalistic painting in Pennsylvania Dutch work echoes the motives carved in wood in Germany; compare painted Pennsylvania chest 347 with its German prototype 346, or the two Dutch Kas 798 and 799. (See also 22.) Special painting techniques were invented out of necessity as well as from fancy. Such were the gold-powder stencils of Hitchcock, as well as the imitation rosewood widely used in his time [78, 543]. Graining in imitation of wood was practiced on and off after Gothic times, and where brushes were scarce devices

Liebhold Wallach

940 AUSTRIAN, 19th century (?). Headboard painted in Baroque manner. **941** BLANKET CHEST, New York State, c. 1825. Dark green ground with polychrome floral decoration. The small trunk from New Hampshire has a black ground.

939 PENNSYLVANIA, early-19th century dower chest painted brown over red on pine.

New-York Historical Society, New York City

941　　　　　　*Henry Ford Museum, Dearborn, Mich.*

like sponge painting were resorted to. See also GILDING; MARBLEIZING; POLYCHROME.

PALISANDER. French name for rosewood, particularly the straight-grained varieties from India.

PALLADIO, ANDREA, 1518-1580. Italian architect; formulated a free version of the classic orders, which he used in domestic architecture in northern Italy. His published work most strongly influenced architecture in England and America. Several features, such as Palladian windows and columns, perpetuate his name.

PALMATED. In Stuart oak furniture, a running band of half circles containing a crude leaf form, resembling palmettes.

PALMETTE. Conventional representation of the palm leaf. First known in Assyrian and Egyptian work, and adapted in subsequent styles.

PANEL. Board held in place by a framework of rails and stiles that are grooved to receive it. The sunken panel has its surface beneath that of the framework, the edges of the panel not necessarily molded. The flush panel has the same height as the frame, and is usually molded; the raised panel is always molded. Modern plywood boards are spoken of as panels. Paneled effects are sometimes secured by framed moldings or painted frames. [455.]

PANEL-BACK CHAIR. Wainscot chair.

PANETIÈRE. Bread box, especially decoratively treated. French Provincial. [942.]

PAPIER-MÂCHÉ. Molded compound sometimes used as a base for small japanned and lacquered ar-

942 PANETIÈRE, 18th century Provincial French.

Elux C. Putting

943 PAPIER-MÂCHÉ ARTICLES of American workmanship, 1845-1870.

Bruce Buttfield

ticles, late 17th and 18th centuries. In the early 19th century it had a great vogue in Europe and America; tabletops, boxes, trays, etc., of papier-mâché being decorated with Eastern designs. [328, 616, 943.]

PARCEL GILDING. Method of applying gilt to carved or flat surfaces in which only parts of the design are gilded. General after 15th century.

PARCHMENT PANEL. Linenfold paneling.

PARQUETRY. Mosaic of woods laid over a ground in geometric patterns, in which respect it differs from marquetry, which is in more pictorial designs. In earlier work it was inlaid directly into the solid wood, especially in Italian and French work, and in England in Age of Walnut. In Louis XV and equivalent English and Italian work, it reached great virtuosity. [377, 448, 944.]

944 PARQUETRY CYLINDER DESK, Louis XV, tulipwood and rosewood.

French & Co., Inc.

PATERA. Small round or oval carved ornaments. In the latter half of the 18th century, the classic revivals, such as the Adam and Louis XVI styles, brought paterae to the decoration of friezes, chair splats, mirror crestings, and many other things.

PATINA; PATINE. Color and texture of the surface produced by age and wear. In wood furniture the varnish, shellac, or oil has a tendency to deepen, yet retains transparency; edges wear smooth, and sharp outlines are softened. These characteristics may be duplicated to some extent, but a fine patine is a most essential characteristic of good antiques.

PEAR-DROP HANDLE. Small brass pendant drawer pull, typical of late-17th-century English work.

PEAR-DROP ORNAMENT. Frieze decoration in Hepplewhite and Sheraton work. A series of small arches ending in pendant ornaments.

PEARWOOD. Hard, close-grained wood; takes a fine polish. Found chiefly in provincial furniture, especially in France, Austria, and South Germany, 18th and 19th centuries. The color in old pearwood furniture varies from light, warm tannish pink to a medium tobacco brown. The best furniture pearwood comes from the Tyrol. It is also used extensively for inlaying, often stained black to imitate ebony.

PEDESTAL. Stands for vases, candelabra, or lamps, sculpture or other objets d'art appeared as decorative adjunct during the Renaissance. They are found in block form and in simple shaft types, resting on bases of solid or branched form. In some styles they have been adapted to utilitarian purposes as the sideboard pedestals of 18th-century England, fitted with warming chambers, provision for storage of silver, liquor, etc. Banks of drawers carrying flattop desks are called pedestals. [637, 881, 946.]

PEDESTAL DESK. Banks of drawers carrying a flat top, such as a writing or library table. Best development in England after mid-18th century. [604, 945.]

945 PEDESTAL DESK, English c. 1750.   *Arthur S. Vernay, Inc.*

950, 950A VICTORIAN PEDESTALS.

PEDESTALS IN THE METROPOLITAN MUSEUM OF ART

946 GILDED WOOD, period of Louis XVI.
947 BOULLE STYLE, GAINES, ebony and brass. 948 FRENCH GOTHIC, oak, 16th century. 949 ITALIAN, 16th century, sgabello type, walnut. 951 ITALIAN ROCOCO, 1730-1750.

949   *Rogers Fund, 1944*

Gift of J. Pierpont Morgan, 1906

946

Gift of J. Pierpont Morgan, 1916

Rogers Fund, 1948

Gift of Edouard Jonas, 1922

947   951   948

PEDESTAL TABLE. Table, usually round or oval, borne on a single central column or pillar with spreading feet. Pedestals are also used in pairs. Ancient Roman types were made in bronze. The type recurs extensively in late-18th-century English designs, chiefly by Sheraton, after whom Duncan Phyfe modeled some superior designs. [952, 983, 1233, 1386, 1390.]

PEDIMENT. In classical architecture, the triangular top over a portico or gable end. In furniture, a similar feature at the head of cabinets or other tall pieces. The pediment came to furniture with the rest of the architectural repertoire. Italian furniture after the 16th century, French after the 17th, and English furniture at the end of the 17th century employ this feature in the classical triangular and rounded forms, and as Baroque broken pediments. In these the line stops short before the apex, leaving a gap for an ornamental finial. The swan-neck pediment consists of two opposed flat S curves.

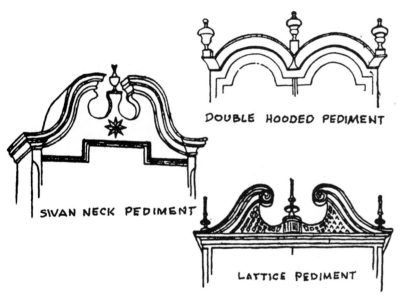

PEG. Wood pin or dowel run through a hole in the corresponding member as a fastener or joint. Peg generally implies an exposed peg; such a joint is not necessarily better than the universal blind peg or dowel. They are used as decorative notes in reproductions of simple sturdy furniture, such as Colonial maple, etc.

PEMBROKE TABLE. Small rectangular drop-leaf table with drawer, the leaves supported by brackets in the frame. Earliest recorded, made by Chippendale for Garrick about 1771. Named after the Earl of Pembroke. [953, 1235.]

PENDANT. Hanging ornament or drop. [737.]

Museum of the City of New York

952 PEDESTAL TABLE, American Empire, c. 1825. Mahogany, marble inset in top.

Israel Sack, Inc.

953 PEMBROKE TABLE, American Chippendale, c. 1765. Pierced cross stretcher. **954 HEPPLEWHITE PEMBROKE TABLE,** inlaid mahogany. Baltimore, c. 1790.

954   *Israel Sack, Inc.*

PENNSYLVANIA DUTCH. Eastern Pennsylvania was largely settled in the 18th century by German and Swiss peasants, with a sprinkling of Swedish and Dutch. Uninfluenced by the English styles of the seaboard, they reproduced the homely straightforward cabinetwork of their homelands, adapting the traditional ancient forms and methods to their slightly changed needs and materials. Using the native pine, maple, walnut, cherry, and other fruit trees, they simplified rather than expanded the ornamental vocabulary of their ancestors. Turning and shaped-outline sawing, such as scallops and zigzags, and scratch-and-gouge carving and simple vigorous molding were employed, but most decorative effects were obtained by painting. Clean colors were used and embellished with naïve, fanciful motives of fruits and flowers, animals, people, names and dates, etc. The usual range of farmhouse chairs and tables, chests, cabinets, beds, etc., occur, but there were in addition some unique types. Bridal chests are outstanding; workboxes, kneading tables, hanging cabinets and boxes for pipes, spoons, spices, etc., are distinctive, and comparatively unknown in settlements of other national origins. The basic imported types were only slightly changed with the passing of generations, and outside influences

955

956

Three photographs, Philadelphia Museum of Art
Photograph by Andrew Wyatt

957

PENNSYLVANIA DUTCH FURNITURE

955 ROCKING HORSE, painted wood, 19th century. 956 CRADLE, pine and walnut, mid-18th century. 957 WALNUT CHEST OF DRAWERS, mid-18th century. 958 PAINTED CHAIR c. 1810. 959 MARRIAGE CHEST, dated 1784. Painted dark red with white panels.

958

Henry Ford Museum, Dearborn, Mich.

959

scarcely touched them for almost 150 years. This quality of slow change, as well as the directness and naïveté of the designs, is typical of all peasant or rural styles.

The name is corrupted from the word *Deutsch,* or German, as these Teutonic people described themselves, rather than from any Holland Dutch association. [15, 42, 161, 320, 347, 450, 955, 1110, 1331.]

PERCIER, CHARLES, 1764-1838. French architect. In collaboration with Pierre Fontaine formulated the Empire style in their books published 1801. See also EMPIRE; FRANCE. [311, 1338.]

PERGOLESI, MICHEL ANGELO. Italian decorative artist. He arrived in England about 1770 and worked for Robert Adam as a painter of ceilings, walls, furniture, etc., in the classic manner. Published a series of *Original Designs,* painting motifs. [604.]

PERIOD FURNITURE. Furniture of a distinctly recognizable style, period in history, school, or time. The special characteristic of historical periods may be woods or finishes; manner of inlaying, painting, carving; distinctive bulks or details, such as legs, posts, frames, hardware, or many of the details that distinguish the style of one place or time from another. The characteristic types of a place may be borrowed by another of the same or another time, producing through its interpretation another style. Thus the Gothic period has distinct character in separated lands; the Gothics of Italy, France, Germany, Flanders, and England are separate and distinct, yet have certain points in common. The Renaissance as a major period is separable into Early, High, and Late, with minor separations in various countries, but it must also be classified by the country that lends its furniture distinctive traits. The Baroque, Rococo, and styles of classicism are large classifications of period furniture, too comprehensive to be descriptive; therefore the further distinction of exact time and place.

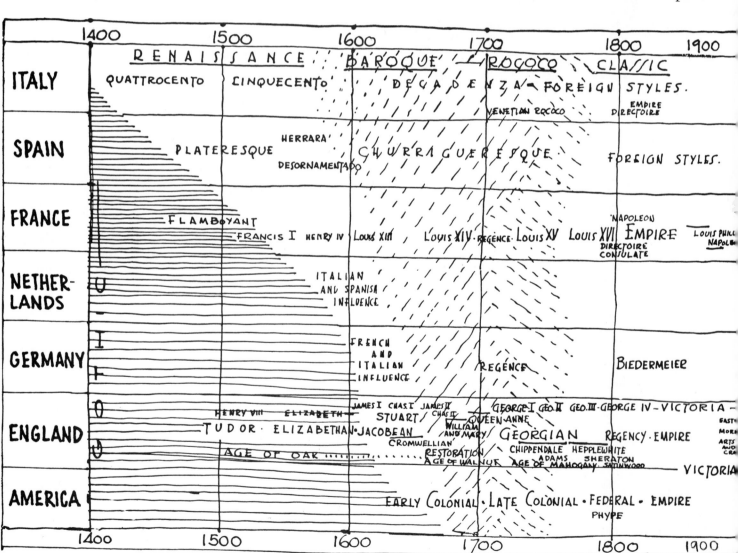

PHILADELPHIA CHIPPENDALE

PIE CRUST TILT TOP

PHILADELPHIA CHIPPENDALE

960 PHILADELPHIA CHIPPENDALE HIGH-BOY, c. 1750. Walnut, broken arch top with flame finials. The American Rococo reached a climax in this school.

Israel Sack, Inc.

PHILADELPHIA CHIPPENDALE. Distinct school of mid-18th century centering in Philadelphia, then a center of Colonial wealth, and following the elaborate style of Chippendale in fine mahogany, with some walnut and maple. Rich carving is characteristic: the outstanding names are Savery, Gostelowe, Randolph, Affleck, Tufft, Colwell, Trotter. Notable are highboys and lowboys and chairs of characteristic Chippendale outline. [37, 278, 414, 738.]

PHILIPPINE MAHOGANY. Family of woods from the Philippines botanically unrelated to American *Swietenia* or African *Khaya*, so-called true mahoganies. Philippine varieties, such as red and white lauan, tanguille, almon, bagtikan, have some characteristics of mahogany, including similarity in texture and grain, color and coloring capacities, versatile pattern possibilities, strength and firmness, resistance to disease and decay; great virtue and adaptability in themselves but not subject to disguise, as the differences are obvious to a moderately informed viewer. A great plywood industry has arisen in the source countries of these woods; and the product is offered under many names, principally for interior finish, boatbuilding, etc. In furniture it suffers unjustly from a denigrating competition with mahogany, and could probably achieve popularity on its own merits.

PHYFE, DUNCAN. Duncan Phyfe's earliest work was done in Albany in the Adam-Hepplewhite style of sound but undistinguished design. Arriving in New York about 1790, he built up an excellent trade with his exquisite workmanship and designs based on the Sheraton-Directoire manner. His productions in the best style cover about 20 years; there is little in any

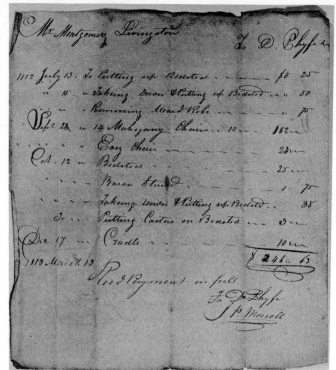

John S. Walton, Inc.
961 DUNCAN PHYFE'S BILL to Mr. Montgomery Livingston, March, 1813.

furniture, American or European, to excel in beauty or technique the grace of these interpretations. After 1820, the Empire styles bore down too heavily even on his mastery, and from that date on there was a steady decline in both artistry and quality. Phyfe died in 1854.

Phyfe's earlier work was almost exclusively in mahogany, meticulously chosen. After 1830 he used much rosewood. The lyre motive commonly associated with Phyfe appears in chairbacks and table bases. Delicately carved lines were favored, with fine reedings or flutings to accentuate lightness. Carving of leaves, plumes, and animal motives were lightly executed after the Pompeiian example. [63, 189, 309, 961, 1091, 1137, 1259.]

PIANO. Housing of musical instruments was an important branch of cabinetmaking from its earliest days. During the Renaissance the development of instruments like the clavichord, the harpsichord, etc., was accompanied by rising extravagance in case design, culminating in Baroque compositions of monumental grandeur. Typical refinement and restraint came with the Classic Revival. Late-18th-century English work is chaste and often superlatively appropriate, as in the spinets of Late Georgian England and Federal America. After 1830 recurred a tendency to Baroque scale and ornamentation that persisted through the 19th century. Mass production and price competition reduced the importance and quality of casework to the contemporary view of the piano as an instrument to be housed in an unadorned functional case. [881, 966.]

962 PHYFE CARD TABLE, from the Rhett family, Charleston, South Carolina.

Ginsburg and Levy

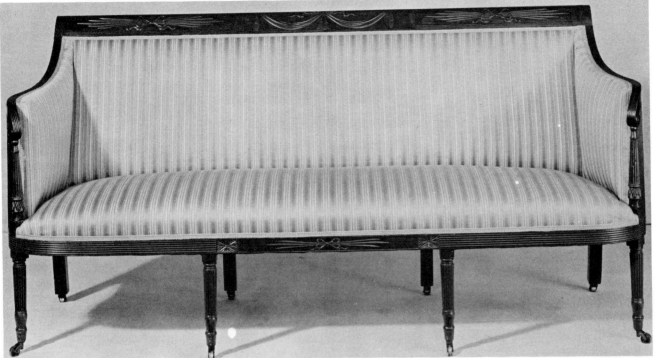

963 SHERATON-STYLE SOFA attributed to Duncan Phyfe, New York, c. 1800.   *Israel Sack, Inc.*

PICKLED FINISHES. Cloudy white patina over light wood, originally produced by the removal with vinegar of the plaster base of painted wood. Old English painted furniture usually had a pine structure (for reasons of economy). The rough surfaces were smoothed out with plaster, which remained when the top paint fell away. The effect is now widely reproduced on many woods. See also LIME-WHITENED.

PICTURE FRAMES. See FRAME; MIRROR.

PIECRUST TABLE. Small table, usually round with edge carved or molded in scalloped outline.

PIED-DE-BICHE. French for "deer's foot"; slight curvature applied to a leg, ending in a cloven foot. Forerunner of the cabriole leg, occurring in Late Louis XIV-Régence work and in contemporary English furniture.

PIER GLASSES AND TABLES. Wall mirror hanging between windows or in a narrow space, usually over a table of console type. See also MIRROR. [872, 895, 967.]

PIERCED CARVING. Openwork carving in Gothic tracery; Baroque and Rococo detailing, as in chairbacks, crestings, aprons; 19th century, as in chairs. [624.]

PIETRA DURA. Hard composition of fragments of marble and other fine stones, usually arranged in designs and highly polished for use as tabletops, etc. Italian Renaissance *et seq.*

PIGEONHOLES. Manifold small compartments in desks and cabinets for papers, etc. [1386.]

PILASTERS. Rectangular or half-round pillar or column placed against a surface.

966 PIANO, American, c. 1830.   *John S. Walton, Inc.*

965 PLANTER, English Sheraton, c. 1790.

PILGRIM. The style of the New England Puritans, 17th century. [6, 137.]

PILLEMENT, JEAN, 1719-1808. French decorative painter known for Chinese compositions.

PILLOWBACK. Top rail of sharp elliptical section, distinctive in Hitchcock chairs.

PINE. The pine chiefly used in furniture is the soft pine, generally the white pine of the northeastern states, the sugar pine of Idaho, and the soft pine of the Pacific Coast. European pines are used locally; Spain, Italy, the Alpine lands, the Scandinavian and North European countries produce distinct varieties. By reason of its availability, its ease of working, and satisfactory performance, pine is among the first woods chosen, especially for provincial or rustic work. This trait is distinctive of pine; it is invariably associated with simple country furniture, with the exception of its use, inspired by economy, as a base for painting or veneering. Of the latter, 18th-century English work is the outstanding example, since the loss of the paint leaves an interesting whitish patina. (See LIME-WHITENED; PICKLED FINISHES.) The knots were allowed to remain where they were, to be painted over; knotty pine was probably never deliberately used for decorative effects prior to the age of reproductions. In Spain the reddish pine of the mountainous sections was used in inferior cabinetwork; the same holds true in Italy. Alpine cabinetmakers traditionally used pine

Olivieri

967 PIER GLASS AND CONSOLE, Italian, end of 18th century.

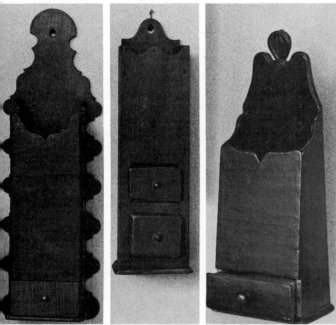

964 PIPE BOXES, New England.

for chests, cabinets, etc. It was either painted entirely or in decorative patterns. The same with local variations is true of all northern Europe, and the style appears in America in the Dutch, Swedish, and German settlements. New England pine was usually left raw, or treated to an oil finish that produced a dark tone, or it was occasionally painted.

Pine carves very easily, for which reason it was extensively used by early Georgian cabinetmakers. In other places carving still was rare, so that finely carved pine is not common. Early-19th-century America developed many processes of painting on pine in imitation of other woods.

PINEAPPLE. Conventionally rendered fruit motif used as finial, particularly early in 19th-century American bedposts. [822, 962.]

PIPE BOXES. Folk-furniture forms serve homely uses. Such are simple receptacles for pipes, tapers, tobacco, etc., as well as a great variety of adjuncts to everyday comfort. As artifacts they are reminders of the development of comfortable middle-class life in Europe and America through the 18th and 19th centuries. [964.]

PLANE WOOD. Maple leafed, or London, plane tree is the English sycamore, a very white, tough, hardwood used in England for painted chairs and structural members subject to strain.

PLANT STAND; PLANTER. Receptacle for potted plants, common in Victorian work and later; often with metal linings and in a wide diversity of shapes. [965.]

PLAQUE. Ornamental medallion of metal, porcelain, or other material, circular or elliptical in shape and inserted into the woodwork of cabinets and other furniture in the 18th century. Sèvres and Wedgwood are the best-known names of makers in France and England. Bronze plaques in the antique manner were used in Empire and Regency work.

PLASTICS. Synthetic materials, products of the laboratory, are molded into shapes or fabricated from sheets, bars, tubes, blocks, powders, etc., in modern furniture because of (1) their ability to resist agencies ordinarily destructive to finished wood, or because of (2) relative ease of manufacture, reducing costs. There are many derivatives of resin, cellulose or protein, such as phenolics, ureas, cellulose, acrylics, polystyrenes and vinyls, which by heat or pressure, or both, are formed into finished products as boxes and containers, into sheets for further fabrication, such as the laminate group (Formica, Micarta, Textolite, etc.), into yarns for weaving (nylon, rayon, Dacron), or solids for molding or cutting and assembling (Lucite, Plexiglas); the vinyls for every surface coating or molding as flooring, wall coverings, etc. They range from foams and fluffs for cushioning—Dacron, polyurethane, etc.—to materials of extreme hardness and durability, whose fatigue point is still unknown. There are finishes for wood and metal. Adhesives, glues, bonding agents for every material and process have virtually eliminated the natural product.

Virtually every material in furniture manufacture is susceptible to modification with some member of the plastic family. Many of the properties are substantially reproduced; some better, some questionable. But beyond question is the superiority of many of these products in durability and the time-cost factor of production. See also LAMINATE MATERIALS; PLYWOOD; SYNTHETIC MATERIALS.

PLATE PAIL. Receptacle for plates, pail shaped, usually of wood with a brass handle. They were necessitated by the long distances between dining rooms and kitchens in the 18th century. They were usually made with lattice sides to permit warming, and with a slot or open side to allow easy access to the plates. [945.]

PLATE WARMER. Sideboard pedestals of George III's time were fitted as plate warmers by lining with tin and fitting with an iron heater. Later they were

made as separate articles of furniture. See also PEDESTAL.

PLATEAU. Platform or stand on low feet used in the center of dining tables to raise the center decorations above the table level. They appeared toward the end of the 18th century, and were variously made of painted wood, papier-mâché, glass, or metal.

PLATEAU MIRROR. Adjustable mirror in a frame attached to a platform or tier of drawers, usually set on a chest for aid in dressing. [44, 386.]

PLATERESQUE. Period 1500-1556 in Spain; reign of Charles V marked by brilliant style, suggesting silversmith's work—*platero*. See also SPAIN.

PLINTH. Block, square or octagonal, used as base of a column; also the base of a chest when solid to the floor.

PLUMWOOD. Yellowish wood with deep brown-red heart, hard and heavy. Old furniture, of country origin, made of this wood is sometimes found.

PLYWOOD. Several thicknesses of plies of wood glued together so that the grain of any one ply is at right angles to the grain of the adjacent ply. Wood is weak across the grain, strong the long way of the grain. Thus the alternation of grains produces the maximum strength of the material all ways. The cross-grain fiber weakness, the tendency to expand and contract from heat and moisture are counterbalanced in the various plies, so that inch for inch of area and thickness plywood has much greater strength than solid wood.

Plywood is made in two ways: (1) *veneer construction,* in which several thicknesses of veneers are glued together, (2) *lumber core,* with a thick central layer of semiporous wood to which are glued thin veneers at right angles, equal in number and thicknesses on both sides. Thus, a 5-ply plywood panel 3/4 inch thick might have a basswood core 1/2 inch thick; on each side is glued a veneer *crossbanding* 1/16 inch thick, at right angles to the core; then a face veneer on each side, about 1/16 inch thick, at right angles to the crossbanding. Odd numbers of thicknesses are the rule.

The advantages of plywood over solid wood are:

1. Its greater strength in every way.
2. Its comparative freedom from warping, checking, swelling, etc.
3. Its use of woods with no structural strength as face veneers for more decorative results.
4. The lower cost when fine face veneers are used, compared to solid lumber in fine woods.
5. The ability to match grains and make many panels of a finely figured wood and to use the grains more freely.
6. Its superiority in curves and shaped work.
7. The possible great size of panels, for economy in handling and fabrication, and for structural rigidity.

Technical advances since World War II have changed plywood to a versatile product with properties subject to scientific controls, extending its usefulness and beauty. Beyond its applications to industry and construction, its scope in furniture making is broader than ever. Cores of wood chips are actually reconstituted wood with dimensional stability and economy of production. Veneers of unlimited range are bonded with special materials and processes. Plywoods are made in the farthest corners of the world, often near the source of the timber.

The basic idea of plywood was perceived by early woodworkers familiar with wood grains and their properties. Sheraton specifies for light fretwork cornices over beds that they be made of three thin layers of wood, the center thickness running crosswise to the two outer ones. Veneering in the 19th century discovered that a face veneer on a thick solid base had to be balanced with a compensating veneer on the inside. (The lack of this produces the convex surfaces with rather charming effect in Biedermeier and similarly naïve work, but the charm is not reproducible.) Belter made special use of the idea to gain strength for his pierced and molded chairbacks. The first United States patent on plywood came in 1865, and in the 1880's special plants for its manufacture were built in Russia.

Later in the 19th century, veneer-cutting processes, molding, and laminating received extensive study, but gluing materials and methods lagged, and plywood endured a period of questionable acceptance. The plastics industry plus electronic methods have brought the science of laminating veneers, plastics, metals, etc., to a leading commercial-furniture raw material.

The molding of plywood into shapes produces receptacle elements like drawers and boxes, chair shells and forms, and structural members like parts of chairs and tables. Strong at bends and angles, these facilitate joining of parts.

POLE SCREEN

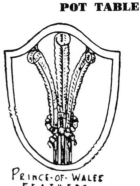

PRINCE-OF-WALES FEATHERS

POLE SCREEN. Small fire or draft screen adjustably mounted upon an upright pole. See also SCREEN.

POLISHES. The process of obtaining a smooth and glossy finish on wood by means of friction and a polishing material is as old as furniture. The early methods were chiefly by applying a film of oil or wax and rubbing it to a satisfactory surface. In the early 1700's the French began to apply successive films of dissolved shellac by means of a pad, producing a hard glossy shine known as French polish. See also FINISH.

POLLARDED WOOD. Pollarding is the removal of the crown or top branches of trees, leaving the main stem intact. This produces a peculiar grain in the wood. In France walnut is pollarded, while in England oak, poplar, willow, and elm are so treated.

POLYCHROME. Multicolored. Polychromy in furniture, or the embellishment by paint, is the most ancient decorative device. Egyptian remains are trimmed with simple bandings, ornamental figures, and representational pictures, all in strong color. The practice undoubtedly was favored in other ancient styles. In medieval furniture the moldings were commonly picked out with color and gold. Medieval Italian practice favored whole surfaces of color, often over raised figures of gesso [755]. Northern European furniture was often wholly painted in red or green; in some rural sections, such as the Alpine lands, a picturesque style of painted decoration still survives. The Renaissance made much of polychromy; in the earliest phases color was sparingly used in furniture, but by the 15th century decorative painting on cabinets, coffers, etc., was the rule. In its later phases, particularly in the Baroque style, paint and gilding were extensively used to emphasize profiles and to embellish whole areas with fantasies in the typically extravagant manner. See also PAINTED FURNITURE.

POMPEII. The buried cities of Italy preserved a complete record of ancient Roman life. The excavations at Pompeii and Herculaneum, begun in 1753, stirred enough interest in the classic arts to terminate the Baroque-Rococo rage and inaugurate the period of the Classic Revival. French and English architects studied the ruins, and from their reconstructions formulated the neoclassic styles known as Louis XVI, Adam, Hepplewhite, Sheraton, etc. See also ADAM; ENGLAND; FRANCE.

POPLAR. Pale yellow, smooth-textured softwood, light in weight and lacking in structural strength. Used chiefly for interior parts in furniture and cores in plywood; slightly, in imitation of better wood. In England in Stuart times used for wall paneling.

PORTUGAL. Early development collateral with Spain, but Portuguese exploration after 15th century inspired a particularized point of view in the well-developed local cabinetmaking craft. Colonies in the Indies sent back techniques of inlaying, wood turning in ebony and ivory, metal mounts, and intricate surface patterns, resulting in a recognizable Indo-Portuguese style. Most distinctive are bedsteads and tables with composition of fine turnings closely grouped in a grill effect, clearly recalling Indian work. Otherwise, Portuguese work used all familiar Spanish devices—leather, wrought iron, flat carving with a Moorish feeling. The South American colonies echoed and sent back similar variations on the same themes. By the 18th century, Portuguese furniture art, like its Spanish corollary, subsided into the general movement of European design. [171, 254, 1147.]

POT TABLE. (Pronounced *poe*.) Commode stand, usually cylindrical, with a door, originally a bedroom accessory and now used decoratively. Often with

POMPEIIAN

968 POT TABLE, American (?), 1835-1845. Mahogany fluted Doric column, marble insert in top.
Munson-Williams-Proctor Institute, Utica, N.Y. (From Fountain Elms)

969 POUDREUSE, Provincial Louis XV style in fruitwood.

Don Ruseau

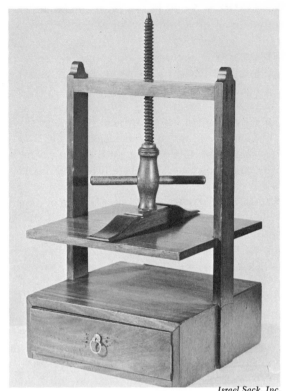

Israel Sack, Inc.

970 PRESS FOR LINENS, American, 18th century.

marble top in a wood ring, and with a semiconcealed door. Originally French, 19th century, hence basically Empire in design. [428, 968, 1337.]

POUF. Large upholstered cushionlike seat, usually round and backless, with legs the only wood showing. Appeared in France about 1845, important through 19th century. [908.]

POWDER TABLE; POUDREUSE. Small dressing table, usually with folding mirror and side leaves exposing compartments for cosmetics, etc. Originating in Louis XV work. Best examples are simple provincial types from French and Italian sources. See also DRESS-ING TABLE. [969.]

PRESS. Box with screw plate for pressing linens, became larger in 18th century for clothes. Finally name became "clothespress"—presently "closet." Decoratively treated in Europe after 17th century. Also, linen press. [5, 810, 970.]

PRIE-DIEU. (1) Chair with high back and very low seat, used for kneeling in prayer. The back has a shelf to carry the book; the seat is cushioned and is hinged to form a receptacle for books. Italian, 14th century and later. (2) Small cabinet with shelf for kneeling, like a low lectern, at prayer. [756, 971.]

PRIMAVERA. White mahogany; light straw-colored wood whose texture and working properties are similar to mahogany from Central America.

PRINCE OF WALES PLUMES. Decorative motive of three ostrich feathers, badge of the heir apparent of England; favored by Hepplewhite as the filler-design of chairbacks.

971 PRIE-DIEU, Canada, late 17th century, pine.

Musée de la Province, Quebec

PROVINCIAL. Styles so labeled refer to work done away from but after the inspiration of the style leaders in the capitals. There is a time lag; and often elements of the style, once accepted, persist long after the original impetus has stopped. Thus the fashions of the courts in Paris spread gradually through the lesser nobility of France and contiguous lands. Ideas were freely adapted to local materials, skills, and preferences. The process creates distinctive manners, sometimes of great taste and charm, often naïve, sometimes merely inept reminiscences. [184, 195, 276, 451, 677.]

Provincial styles flourish and even transcend their inspiration wherever there is a social or economic hinterland with a rising standard of living. Craftsmen isolated from metropolitan sources would nevertheless learn of new forms and incorporate into their work what they could glean of such novelties. At a time when there was no commercial furniture, all new work had to be either imported or produced by local craftsmen. The latter had three sources of ideas: first, the direct example of the import; second, the sketch or verbal description brought in by the client or his own memory; third, books, drawings, or sketches, such as Chippendale's *Director.*

Provincial furniture bloomed most luxuriously in France in the 18th century [91, 92]. The total body of such work is enormous and, as exemplar of good design, of richer inspiration than any other school; this is not to detract from English inspiration of the same era, as suggested by the many publications. The Biedermeier style may be said to be entirely provincial versions of the French Empire. The motivation, formulated and followed for perhaps two decades in Paris, spread over the Western world, and persisted for most of a century. In local versions and revivals the Empire-Biedermeier idea appears in St. Petersburg and Stockholm, in Naples and New York in the

Montreal Museum of Fine Arts
975

975 CUPBOARD, French Canada, late 18th century, suggests Régence detail.

973

973 BANQUETTE of French Empire style, country origin. **974** SPANISH CHAIR, 19th century. After French Provincial model.

974

972 18th–CENTURY TABLE, Canada, in Provincial style of early 17th century. *Montreal Museum of Fine Arts*

Lo Mejor de España

972

1840's, the 1890's, and even the 1930's—always a little different. The special touch of time and place is later recognizable; and so is born a "provincial" style.

Farther than the provinces, colonies acted in the same way to produce like-unlike types of furniture, essentially poor-man's versions of the home product. Improvisations in materials and skills, for special uses as well as for exigencies, relics in Spanish, Dutch, French, Swedish, English, and Portuguese colonies all bespeak their origins as well as their vicissitudes.

In provincial styles are found items, originating in utility, that had no place in higher social levels—such

980 PINE CHEST, Austria or Bavaria, shows traces of Louis XVI influence. Early 19th century.

are the *panetière* of France [942], the cobbler's bench and dry sink of America. See also ENGLAND; FRANCE; SPAIN. [1162.]

PULVINATED FRIEZE. Cornice molding having a convex face. [735.]

PURITAN. Of furniture, the 17th-century New England style. The English Puritans revolted against the worldliness of the court, and substituted simple functional forms, as in the English Cromwellian style.

PURPLEHEART. Dense hardwood from Caribbean

977-978 COUNTRY-MADE TABLE AND CHAIR, Spanish Southwest United States, 19th century, vestiges of cabriole leg and Spanish turnings.

979 PINE CUPBOARD with diamond panels recalling style of Henry IV, Canada.

976 SECRETARY, walnut. Provincial French style of Louis XV.

977-978 *Museum of New Mexico*

QUATTROCENTO

South America. Violet or purplish, it is used for inlay and ornamental purposes. Also called "amaranth," "violetwood."

QUADRANT. Metal device of quarter-circle shape used to support some fall fronts in desks; English and American, late 18th and 19th centuries, generally brass. [495.]

QUARRIES. Small panes of glass, square or lozenge-shaped, used in the doors of bookcases, 18th and 19th centuries.

QUARTERED. Method of cutting the log into four quarters through the center, and then into parallel boards in order to produce a grain having a cross section of the rays.

QUARTET TABLES. Nest of four tables.

QUATREFOIL. Gothic form made from the conventionalized four-leaf clover, the four intersecting curves being enclosed in a circular shape.

Anderson Galleries
982 QUEEN ANNE FALL-FRONT SECRETARY, early ogee foot, pulvinated frieze, walnut veneers.

QUATTROCENTO. Early Italian Renaissance, 1400-1500, characterized by development of classic architectural formality. Dignified, austere furniture, chiefly in walnut. See also ITALY. [981.]

QUEEN ANNE. English ruler, 1702-1714, during whose reign the Netherlands-Baroque strain imported by William of Orange continued to develop, producing chiefly walnut furniture of excellent style. Chiefly identified by the developed cabriole leg, the best types are chairs, china cupboards, secretaries, etc. See also ENGLAND. [18, 32, 182, 265, 418, 478, 486, 565, 1044.]

QUIRK. Narrow groove molding, a sunken fillet or channel.

981 QUEEN ANNE CHAIR, mature cabriole leg.
Needham's Antiques, Inc.

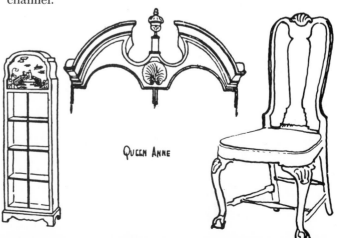
QUEEN ANNE

983 READING STAND, Japan, 1662. Gold lacquer.

Metropolitan Museum of Art, Hewitt Fund, 1910

984 FOLDING LECTERN, Spanish, 15th century, walnut.

Metropolitan Museum of Art, Gift of George Blumenthal, 1941

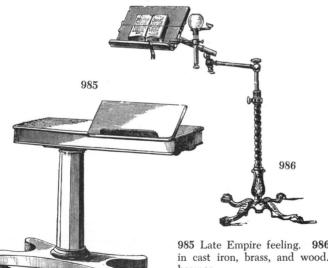

985

986

985 Late Empire feeling. 986 19th CENTURY GADGETRY in cast iron, brass, and wood. Flexibility at the cost of coherence.

RABBET (Rebate). Rectangular slot or groove in joinery. Also, a recess in the meeting stiles of cabinet doors so that one shuts against the other to form a dust-proof joint. See also CONSTRUCTION.

RACK. Stand or frame for various purposes, such as a bookrack, magazine rack, hat rack, music rack. It may be either a piece of furniture in itself or part of another piece. Decorative racks for various purposes are found in many styles, and possess charm and interest for collectors typical of such minor furniture.

LETTER RACKS in England were vertical strips of wood ornamented with fretwork, etc., with hinged leaves to hold letters.

SPOON RACKS were primitive affairs while wooden spoons were in use; after Elizabeth, spoons of soft metal, such as pewter, came into use, but were too soft to be kept in a drawer. The spoon rack therefore grew in importance in lesser homes.

RADIATES. Carved or inlaid rays, as in a shell or fan motif.

RAILS. Horizontal members of framed furniture. In beds, the long sidepieces. In casework, the framing that holds the sides together.

RAKE. The angle of a slanted or splayed member, such as a chairback or table leg, that is not strictly vertical.

RAMP. In chairs of Portuguese, Queen Anne, and corresponding American types, a sudden curve ending in an angle at the end of the post. Characteristic of the type called Hogarth chair.

RAM'S HEAD. Classic decorative carving, borrowed from ancient Greece and Rome and used in all styles employing antique ornament, such as Louis XIV, Adam, etc. Probably originally a symbolic representation on sacrificial altars.

RAM'S HORN. Voluted finial treatment, as in chair arms. [13.]

RANDOLPH, BENJAMIN. Philadelphia cabinetmaker of the period of the Revolution; made chairs in the Chippendale manner as well as the typical Philadelphia highboys.

RANDOM JOINTS. Joints in either veneer or solid board walls or floors, in which there is no attempt at matching either grain or width of boards.

RANGE TABLES. Several identical small tables planned to be used together as one long table.

RAT-CLAW FOOT. Sharp skinny claws grasping a ball, as the decoration of a cabriole foot; English, after 1740; also found in American work.

RAYONNANT. Middle period of the Gothic style, about 1225-1420. Radiating lines form typical ornament.

READING DESK; READING STAND. Small table with top adjustable to hold a book. Found in 18th-century English work chiefly, although similar book-stands, occurring in later Renaissance work on the Continent, evolved from the medieval lectern. Known in the Far East; also in Muslim regions as Koran stand. See also BIBLE BOX; LECTERN. [983.]

REBATE (RABBET). Rectangular groove cut in wood members to permit the insertion of a tongued member, in joining frameworks.

REFECTORY TABLES · ENGLISH · ITALIAN · SPANISH

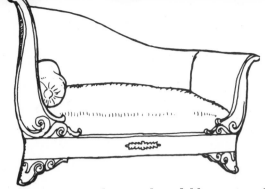

RÉCAMIER. Chaise longue shaped like ancient Roman bed or reclining couch with gracefully curved high end. Directoire and Empire styles, named after Mme. Récamier. See also MERIDIENNE.

RECESS. Niche, alcove, or any depressed or sunken surface.

RECESS CABINET. Tall shallow cabinet designed to be set within a recess or niche; late-18th-century English.

RECESSED STRETCHER. Middle or cross stretcher of chair or table set back from the front legs. See also H-STRETCHER.

REDWOOD. Red-brown wood from Pacific Coast, too soft for most furniture construction. The burls are highly decorative, and are sometimes known as "sequoia."

REEDINGS. Two or more beads set closely in parallel lines, either flush with or raised above the surface they decorate. The reverse of fluting. Late 18th century. [44, 1069.]

REFECTORY TABLE. Long narrow table so called after the refectory or dining room of the monks in ecclesiastical institutions of the Middle Ages. Heavy stretchers are close to the floor. [547, 762, 1200.]

987 ENGLISH REFECTORY TABLE, mid-17th century, oak. Guilloche-carved aprons, turned baluster legs.

Stair & Company, Inc.

989 LATE-17th–CENTURY CARVED OAK ARMOIRE, Early Régence style. Expressed in fine architectural scale, directness of outline, and harmonious composition of ornamental detail.

RÉGENCE. French period covering the end of Louis XIV's reign, until the accession of Louis XV, about 1680-1725. It is marked by the transition from massive straight lines to the gracious, curved, intimate style of Louis XV. [91, 260, 284, 361, 420, 502, 641, 843, 1187.]

REGENCY. English period, roughly 1793-1820, durring part of which George, Prince of Wales, later George IV, acted as Regent. Furniture style is marked by declining classic influence of Pompeiian studies, and increasing use of Roman, Egyptian, and earlier Greek styles. It coincides with the Directoire and Empire styles. See also ENGLAND; HOPE, THOMAS; NINETEENTH CENTURY. [310, 609.]

RELIEF. Raised ornament or sculpture in which the carving is raised or cut above the background. Various styles are characterized by high- or low-relief carving. See also CARVING.

RENAISSANCE (Renascence). Literally a "rebirth" of interest in the culture of ancient Greece and Rome, the Renaissance terminated the medieval Gothic styles. Instead of continuing the Romanesque-Gothic development in the arts, it went directly back to classic sources, and adapted the ancient architectural and decorative themes. The movement began in Italy, attaining its major momentum in the 15th century; it spread to Spain and France in the 16th century largely through Church and political contacts. Flanders, a Spanish colony, imported the Renaissance early in the 16th century. It spread to England in a gradual way over a period of a century, being slowly imposed on the firmly entrenched Gothic art. The same was true in northern Europe; Gothic art yielded slowly to the classic forms in the Germanic countries. By the middle of the 17th century deluxe furniture everywhere was clearly Italian classic; but Gothic traces persisted in lesser furniture for another century.

Early Renaissance Italian furniture was marked by simplicity of outline and detail, a definitely architectural profile with classic moldings and sparing ornament of classic acanthus, rinceau and animal forms. This developed by the enrichment of ornament and outline, and by general elaboration. It was this later phase that first reached other countries, so that the earliest distinctly Renaissance features in France, Flanders, and England are quite elaborate. There never had been a true Gothic feeling in Italy, and the classic themes were therefore purer than in the North, where essentially Gothic shapes and moldings remained, to be modified by more or less Italian details.

Roman orders in the form of colonnettes and pilasters were applied to furniture; these carried the full complement of bases and cornices, pediments, etc., so that cabinets, etc., were scaled-down architectural compositions. Where the Gothic had depended on free renditions of familiar flora, naturalistically applied, Renaissance ornament was highly conventionalized. With greater variety, it was more stylized.

The great change in furniture came in the increased variety of types. Secular life in the Middle Ages had been, for the nobles, a rather nomadic affair; the peasants led poverty-stricken and insecure lives. With the change in political conditions came economic improvement, security, and a substantial middle class. Home life improved; furniture became essential, and developed into many new forms. Practically all types of furniture appeared, at least in rudimentary forms, between 1500 and 1700; older types assumed shapes now recognizable as social conditions and customs approached the standards of modern times. See also individual countries.

RENT TABLE. Eighteenth-century English round or octagonal pedestal table with drawers marked with days of the week or dates. They were used by the landlord as a sort of filing arrangement in collecting rents. [1385.]

REPLICA. Reproduction or copy of a piece of furniture, usually old or of historic period; accurately copied from the original in all details of material, technique, detail, and finish. See also REPRODUCTION.

988 ENGLISH REGENCY ROSEWOOD CABINET. Sphinx heads and brass wire grilles.

Needham's Antiques, Inc.

REPOUSSÉ. Decorative sheet-metal work in which the design is hammered forward from the back.

REPRODUCTION. "Reproductions" in furniture refer to copies of old pieces of historic styles. Good reproductions follow the original in all matters of material, method, and detail throughout; it is a moot point whether the finish and patina with all the marks of wear should be duplicated. An accurate copy if made in the period of the original would be a replica. But if made later it would be a copy or reproduction, and if sold as a genuinely old piece it would be a fake. Commercially made pieces that merely follow the general external form without regard to material or the technique are copies or adaptations, more or less accurate; they are called reproductions only by commercial courtesy.

REST BEDS. All types of chaise longues, daybeds, lounges, and couches planned for repose during the day hours in preference to the formal bed. Appearing in France during the early Louis XIV period, when beds had become excessively large and formal, it was at first merely a cushioned settee or bench. Called couches in England, they took form with one high end; these were caned or rush-covered, with loose cushions thrown over. In Régence France they were more comfortably upholstered. England reflected these types in Restoration and Queen Anne "daybeds," which uniformly were of extended chair form. The Louis XV epoch produced the most luxurious styles, feminine in scale and ornamental character. In the ensuing period the chaise longue developed as a combination of two or three pieces, sometimes two bergères with a footstool between, or a large bergère with lengthened footstool. The daybed form was developed from the simplified bed, and appeared in Italy and France at the end of the 18th century. See also CHAISE LONGUE; DAYBEDS; SOFA. [892, 990.]

Rest Beds

THE GOTHIC *ARCHEBANC - COUCHETTE* WAS THE PRIMITIVE CHEST MADE WITH ENDS, AND LONG ENOUGH TO LIE DOWN ON. THIS SUGGESTED A DELIBERATE FRAMEWORK WITH YIELDING SEAT AND ARRANGEMENT FOR PILLOWS.

990 "ARCHEBANC - COUCHETTE," French, Late Gothic, Renaissance detail.

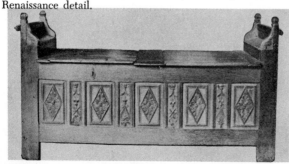

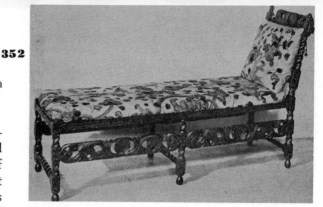

Anderson Galleries
991 ENGLISH DAYBED, Charles II. Carved walnut, crewel embroidery cushions.

Metropolitan Museum of Art, Rogers Fund, 1922
992 REST BED PENNSYLVANIA c. 1725. All turned parts except adjustable back; probably rush seated. Maple, painted red.

Henry Ford Museum, Dearborn,
993 PHILADELPHIA QUEEN ANNE, mid - 18th century. Mahogany, double spoon-shaped splats.

994 NETHERLANDS, 18th century. Folding chair-bed, fla upholstery in marquetry frames.

Cooper Union Museum, New York City

REST BEDS DEVELOPED GRACE AND COMFORT AS
UPHOLSTERY TECHNIQUES ADVANCED IN LUXURY-
LOVING FRANCE OF THE 18TH CENTURY.

Metropolitan Museum of Art, Rogers Fund, 1922

995 FRENCH (PROVENCE) RÉGENCE. Walnut.

996 CHAISE LONGUE, style of Louis XV.

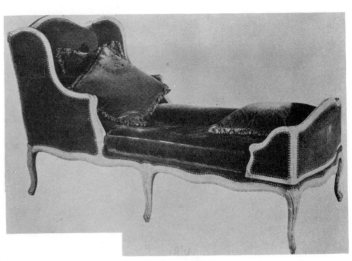

Don Ruseau

997 "LIT DE REPOS," Louis XV. Beechwood.

Metropolitan Museum of Art, Rogers Fund, 1922

998 HEPPLEWHITE RECAMIER c. 1785. Mahogany.

Needham's Antiques, Inc.

999 CHAISE LONGUE, French. Painted frame of
Louis XVI style.

Don Ruseau

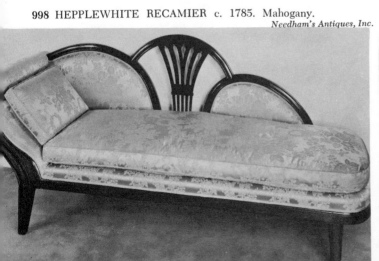

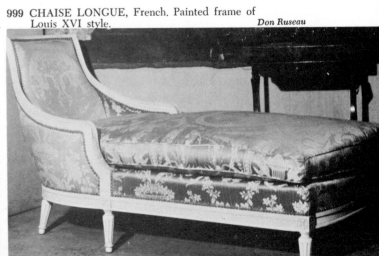

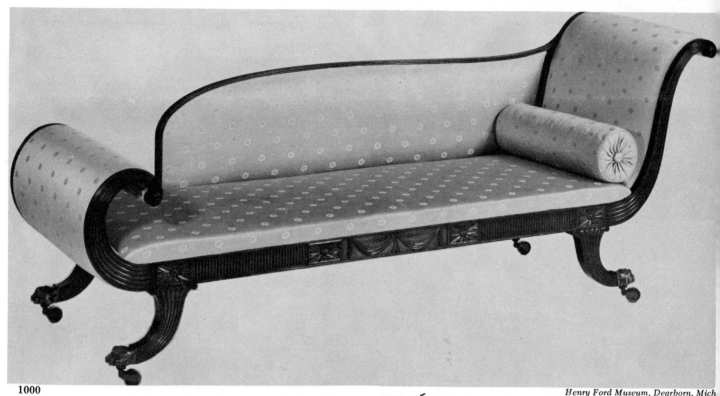

1000

1000 RÉCAMIER c. 1810, possibly by Duncan Phyfe. Vigorous carving accentuates strong structural lines.

1001 MÉRIDIENNE, French
Empire. Mahogany with ormolu.

1002 VICTORIAN ROSEWOOD, c. 1850,
by John Belter. From the Springfield home
of Abraham Lincoln.
Henry Ford Museum, Dearborn, Mich.

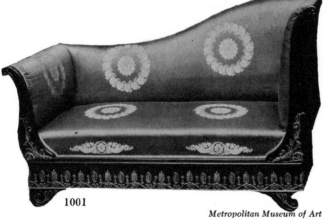

1001

Metropolitan Museum of Art

1002

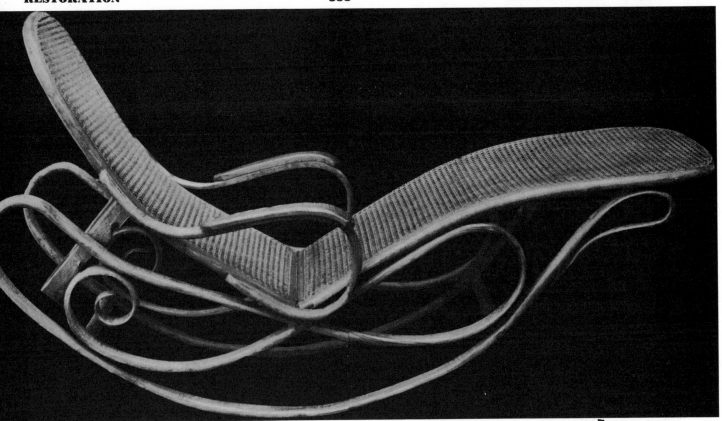

1003 BENTWOOD REST-BED ROCKER, Thonet, Vienna.

Photograph, University of California (Los Angeles) Art Gallery

RESTORATION. Period in English history, succeeding the Puritan Revolution, beginning in 1660 with the restoration of the monarchy of Charles II and ending in 1688 in the Bloodless Revolution. It is the first part of the Age of Walnut. Ornament is highly decorative, gay and frivolous, lighter than the preceding styles but still simple and rectangular in the main, although lesser structural members, such as stretchers, arms, crestings, etc., are given highly curved and scrolled ornament. Strong French influences came with the immigration of craftsmen, and the Flemish forms were brought by the returning nobles. The decorative forms include spiral turnings, molded geometric paneling, floral scrolls, carved crowns, and scroll feet. Grinling Gibbons's rich deep carving is representative. The wealth, security, and social aspirations of the time are reflected in the free use of changed forms in tables, chairs, and cabinets. They are no longer portable, and are more decorative. Daybeds and luxurious upholstery became common. The Baroque influence appears in the Restoration's sweeping curves and generous ornamentation, which caused oak to be replaced by the more easily worked walnut. The period is also referred to as "Carolean," "Late Jacobean," "Charles II." [256.]

RESTORATION, FRENCH BOURBON. After the fall of Napoleon's Empire, the brother of Louis XVI became Louis XVIII, who was in turn replaced in 1820 by another brother, Charles X. Neither personally had time to affect greatly the trends in design, except so far as the venture into Algeria started a romantic movement marked by essays into Orientalism. In 1830, Louis-Philippe ended the succession. [313, 1303.]

RESTORATION CHAIR. A typical English 17th-century form with high caned back, turned legs, and richly carved scroll design on front stretcher and top rail. [256.]

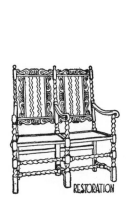

RESTORATION

RESTORATION CHAIR

RESTORATION OF ANTIQUES. Old furniture may ethically be restored to its original condition, which may include the addition of minor or missing parts. The danger in buying "restored" pieces is that the greater or most characteristic original sections have been replaced around a few unimportant relics, as in the use of an old tabletop upon a new base. The distinction becomes a fine one, and is another pitfall in the path of the antique collector.

REVOLVING CHAIRS were in use in Gothic times and reappear widely in the 18th century as part of the quest for comfort. It remained for the mechanical urges of the mid-19th century to promote the idea to common commercial use. Contemporary use in domestic work is freer but still tentative. [201, 878 N.]

RHODE ISLAND SCHOOL. 18th-century American style centering in Newport, R.I., and chiefly in the manner of John Goddard and his son-in-law, John Townsend. The blockfront in chests, secretaries, desks, and dressing tables is practically unique; other features are the Rococo shell, the steep scroll pediments, ogee bracket feet with fine shallow carving. Mahogany predominates, but some maple, walnut, and cherry woods were used. See also GODDARD, JOHN; TOWNSEND, JOHN.

RIBAND; RIBBAND. Ribbon ornament. In some Chippendale chairs the splats simulate elaborately arranged ribbons. Ribbons in bows or knots were important in Louis XVI decoration and were charac-

teristically treated in German Rococo work of the 18th century.

RIBBON. See RIBAND.

RIBBON STRIPE in wood is a straight-banded grain effect, common to mahogany, walnut, and similar woods with a long straight grain and bands of alternate soft and hard textures.

RIESENER, JEAN-HENRI, 1734-1806. French cabinetmaker, period Louis XVI; learned craft under Oeben. Celebrated for his marquetry work. [377, 658, 660, 667, 1004, 1040.]

RIM. Rolled-up or raised edge, as on small 18th-century English and American tables. Dished top.

RINCEAU. Continuous ornament of spiral or wavy form, sometimes called the branching scroll when intertwined with stems and leaves. [190.]

RISING STRETCHER. Serpentine or X-stretchers curving up toward the intersection; found in Louis XIV and allied styles.

ROCAILLE. Earlier term for Rococo.

ROCKING CHAIR. The rocker is a curved slat fastened to the feet of a chair to permit it to be rocked back and forth. It is practically peculiar to America and is fundamentally a rustic or inelegant type, dating chiefly after 1800. Several unique types

1004 COMMODE by Jean-Henri Riesener. Monogram of Marie Antoinette in Sèvres plaque and in *bronze-doré.*
Dalva Brothers, Inc.

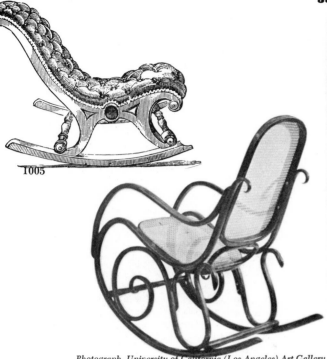

Photograph, University of California (Los Angeles) Art Gallery
1005 ROCKING CHAIR, Mid-Victorian.   **1006** BENTWOOD ROCKER, Thonet, Vienna. Late 19th century.

Philadelphia Museum of Art

ROCOCO

1007 ENGLISH ROCOCO CHAIR, c. 1765. **1008** CLOCK. MEISSEN FIGURES in framework of *bronze-doré*.   **1009** AMERICAN GIRANDOLE, c. 1775, Philadelphia.

Needham's Antiques, Inc.

Dalva Brothers, Inc.

were evolved in New England, such as the Salem rocker, the Boston rocker, etc., having high comb backs and thick scroll seats. These were characteristically painted and decorated in the fruit-and-flower manner popularized on Hitchcock's chairs—a delicate stenciled ornament somewhat in the Biedermeier manner. [77, 83, 136, 157, 1094.]

The Victorians made much of the rocker. Among the "patent" designs are platform rockers, spring rockers, "jolting chairs" with wild claims for therapy as well as for comfort or utility. The Turkish rocker was a huge wire-frame, soft upholstery construction carried on four helical springs on a platform, period from 1890-1915.

ROCOCO. A phase of European art of the 18th century, reactionary to the classical spirit. In France, Louis XIV furniture and decoration had been characterized by a solid, pompous classic grandeur. The succeeding style of the Early Régence years lightened these forms by the introduction of curves, generally symmetrical and exquisitely balanced, and contained within a rectangular framework. These gave way to an extravagantly free naturalism, accepting curved irregular forms as their basis. Rocks (*rocailles*) and shells (*coquilles*) provided the decorative forms in the gardens of Versailles, and were translated into carved and painted ornaments for interior decoration; the name, at first "Rocaille," became "Rococo" many years after the style had waned.

Rococo forms are most characteristically asymmetrical, elaborately ornamented with flora and fauna

SWEDISH ROCOCO

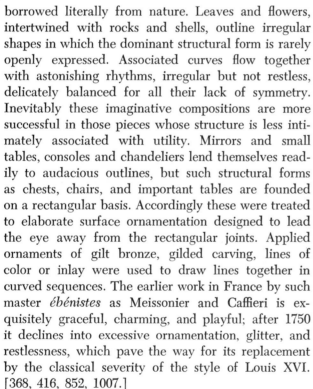

1010 ITALIAN (?) CONSOLE. Unrestrained freedom of scale, choice of animal and plant forms. *French & Co., Inc.*

1011 TUSCAN "CASSAPANCA," late 18th century. *Olivieri*

borrowed literally from nature. Leaves and flowers, intertwined with rocks and shells, outline irregular shapes in which the dominant structural form is rarely openly expressed. Associated curves flow together with astonishing rhythms, irregular but not restless, delicately balanced for all their lack of symmetry. Inevitably these imaginative compositions are more successful in those pieces whose structure is less intimately associated with utility. Mirrors and small tables, consoles and chandeliers lend themselves readily to audacious outlines, but such structural forms as chests, chairs, and important tables are founded on a rectangular basis. Accordingly these were treated to elaborate surface ornamentation designed to lead the eye away from the rectangular joints. Applied ornaments of gilt bronze, gilded carving, lines of color or inlay were used to draw lines together in curved sequences. The earlier work in France by such master *ébénistes* as Meissonier and Caffieri is exquisitely graceful, charming, and playful; after 1750 it declines into excessive ornamentation, glitter, and restlessness, which pave the way for its replacement by the classical severity of the style of Louis XVI. [368, 416, 852, 1007.]

Elsewhere the style persisted variably for an undefinable period. The Germanic countries accepted and adopted it as the basis of most 18th-century work. A glittering Rococo distinguishes the interiors of most palaces and important structures long after the classical features of the Louis XVI style were accepted. In England, Rococo mannerisms were cheerfully absorbed by all designers and imposed upon more local forms in all degrees of ingenuity together with reminiscences of Gothic and Chinese. Notably, most English

Rococo never achieved the balanced asymmetry of the French. The classic revolution inspired by the Brothers Adam swept away much of the gay freakishness, but traces of the Baroque freedom of the Rococo remain in the most esteemed work of Chippendale, Hepplewhite, and their contemporaries. In mid-19th century a return to Rococo offset the excesses of the Empire, but it was rarely again handled with characteristic lightness and ease. In Italy, extreme liberty prevailed, and an excessive naturalism, representative of outdoor life in grottoes, sometimes went beyond the bounds of taste.

ROENTGEN, DAVID, 1743-1807. Known as David. Outstanding French cabinetmaker, period of Louis XVI. Born a German, his principal shop was at Neuwied, but he catered chiefly to the French court.

ROLLTOP. In desks, a tambour or flexible cylindrical hood drawn down as a lid.

ROMAN (ancient). Etrurian bronze remains show an early conventional style similar to the archaic Greek-rigid lines and austere decoration. Later Roman work, indicated by bronze and stone remains and painted and sculptured representations, shows that Rome in her great period borrowed and interpreted all the known styles instead of creating her own. Egypt, Greece, and the East contributed basic forms that were amalgamated and enriched in infinite variety

ANCIENT ROMAN

to serve the luxurious, urbane standard of living. In general, the evolution of the style began with a severe, rigid, limited list of pieces, expanding in size and adding ornamentation and delicacy. The last phase, amply revealed in the buried cities of Pompeii and Herculaneum, show the late Alexandrian-Greek traits, referred to as Greco-Roman.

Chairs appear in four types: *curule*, with square seat and legs in X shape (originally a folding stool, the back was added later); *bisellium*, a double chair or settee, the wood frame of turned members, or carved to represent horses' or mules' heads; *solium*, a thronelike chair with back, for the head of the household; *cathedra*, a chair for the exclusive use of women. Skins or pillows with rich fabrics were used loosely. [208, 209.]

Bed and couch, *lectus*, had the general form of beds known today, with a platform of cushions carried on turned legs, often inlaid, painted, or mounted with metals. A pillow rest at one end served as an armrest as well, for the couch was also used for dining, which was done in a semireclining position.

Chests or cupboards, known as *armaria*, for the storage of arms probably were the origin of the "armoire."

Tables were of all shapes, bronze remains suggesting round tripod types, and rectangular shapes resting on carved slabs or pedestals.

There were in addition a great many styles of tripods, pedestals, stools, etc., of which the forms are conjectural. They employed many means of decoration and finish: carving, inlaying, turning, metal appliqué, painting, engraving, veneering, varnishing, etc. It seems probable that the ancient Romans employed the metals, woods, ivory, and stones known then, much as we now import and utilize such products from the whole world.

ROMANESQUE. European style following the fall of the Roman Empire, roughly 500-1100 C.E. Architecture followed debased Roman style, stiff and barbaric,

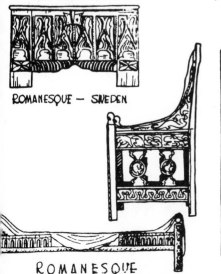

ROMANESQUE — SWEDEN

ROMANESQUE

using coarsely rendered animal and plant forms. Chaotic life encouraged little furniture making. The style is most significant as the parent of the great Gothic style. [231, 457.]

ROMAYNE WORK. Ornamental form of human heads carved upon roundels or medallions, deriving from the Italian and occurring among the earliest Renaissance ideas in English, French, and Flemish Gothic furniture. See also MEDALLION.

ROPE MOLD. 18th-century decorative molding, quarter or half round, spirally channeled to simulate a rope. See also CABLE.

ROSE. The rose motif, highly conventionalized, is an ancient one, and recurs in simple form in most styles. The full rose was adopted as the Tudor badge in England after the 15th century, and frequently appears carved in simple form as a decoration on furniture. In Louis XV and other Rococo work the naturalistic rose is common.

ROSETTE. Rose-shaped patera or disk ornament.

ROSETTES

ROSEWOOD. Several species of tropical woods from India and Brazil are grouped as rosewood, so called from the odor of the newly cut wood rather than from its color. It is heavy, dense, resinous and of a deep redbrown color, richly streaked and capable of being highly polished. It was used in fine European furniture of the 18th century as veneers and ornamental inlays; in the 19th century the solid wood was used extensively for furniture in Europe and America. The French *palissandre* is the Indian variety. The German *Rosenholz* is generally called "tulipwood" in England and America.

ROTTENSTONE. Soft, finely powdered stone used with oil in polishing wood.

ROUNDABOUT CHAIR. Chair with a leg in front, one in back, and two on the sides. The back, rather circular, is carried on three legs. Found in English and Continental and American work of the 18th century. Also called "Roundabout Conversation Chair," mid-Victorian free-standing seat for several persons

1012A ROUNDABOUT CONVERSATION CHAIR, English, c. 1850.

1012 ROUNDABOUT CHAIR, English, c. 1705. Queen Anne-style club foot, walnut.

facing in different directions. [25, 34, 245, 268, 280, 1012, 1012a.]

ROUNDEL. Any ornamental disk or motive enclosed in a circular shape, such as a rosette, medallion, patera, etc.

ROUTING. Decorative engraved lines made by a portable revolving spindle.

ROYCROFT SHOP. Establishment at East Aurora, N.Y., founded in 1895 by Elbert Hubbard on the ideas of William Morris. Produced furniture of Mission-English Arts and Crafts type.

RUDDER. The rudder, butterfly, or flap is a support for the leaf of a drop-leaf table, similar to a ship's rudder in outline.

RULE JOINT. Hinged joint, as between a tabletop and flap, which leaves no open space when the leaf is down.

RUNIC KNOT. Interlaced ornament typical of early northern European work, such as the Celtic, Scandinavian, German Romanesque, etc.

RUNNER. Sometimes the rocker of a rocking chair. Also a guide strip for a drawer, either on the side or on the bottom. [442.]

RUNNING DOG. Continuous ornamental band or wave motive, also called "Vitruvian scroll."

RUSH. Rush stalks were used in medieval times as a covering over stone floors. Later they were plaited into mats. These were sometimes used as beds in the Tudor period.

Rush seats in chairs and stools are known to have been made by the Egyptians. Probably they were always used after this time, but remains are scant. 18th-century chairs with rush bottoms survive everywhere in Europe and America, being also known here as "flag" seats. [324 *et seq.*, 334.]

RUSTIC FURNITURE. (1) Utilitarian objects, usually of such direct functional design as to excite the interest of specializing collectors. Almost always homemade or of amateur manufacture of common materials, they command antiquarian interest and may be used as objects of atmosphere furnishing. Such are: dry sinks, water benches, cobbler's benches, and other artisans' fixtures; barber shelves, schoolhouse desks and benches, printer's type frames, kitchen dressers, and cupboards. (2) Garden furniture of the 18th century was decorated with details resembling the natural growth of trees, as drawn by Chippendale, Halfpenny, and Manwaring. The last named designed chairs utilizing the whole smaller branches, Mid-19th-century furniture, picture frames, etc., made extensive use of this theme. [126, 1243.]

RUSTICATION. Architectural treatment of masonry in which the joints are marked out as grooves. This effect is simulated in furniture of architectural character of the 18th century.

S-SCROLL. Decorative form, carved or applied, in the shape of an S, either continuous or broken. Used as corner and apron ornament in Baroque and Rococo styles.

SABOT. Metal shoe fitting bottom of cabriole leg. [369, 811, 826.]

SACK BACK. Windsor chair with double bow back.

SACRISTY CUPBOARD. Ecclesiastical cabinet or cupboard in which are kept vestments, sacred vessels, etc. [435, 757, 1104.]

SADDLE. Chair seat scooped away to the sides and back from a central ridge, resembling the pommel of a saddle. The best examples occur in Windsor chairs with thick pine seats.

SAFE. Strongbox, usually of metal; in old times of heavy wood with metal straps. Sometimes applied to food cupboards of vermin-resisting construction.

SALEM ROCKER. New England rocking chair after 1800. Has heavy scrolled seat and arms, a lower back than the Boston rocker, light straight spindles, and a heavy top rail with scroll.

SALTIRE. X-form stretcher.

SAMBIN, HUGUES. 16th-century French designer, cabinetmaker, carver, engraver; his engravings show the development of Renaissance forms in Burgundy, where the Italian influence had practically obliterated the Gothic. Much work of the rich Burgundian Italian type is credited to him or his followers. His *Book of Designs* was published in 1572. See also FRANCE. [632.]

SANDALWOOD. Hard yellow-brown wood from southern India, distinguished by its fragrant odor. Used in Oriental (chiefly Indian) woodwork and furniture.

SAPELE. African hardwood resembling mahogany with fine stripe and uniform red-brown color.

SARACENIC. Influence of Mohammedan design, reaching Europe after 700 through Spain, and during the Middle Ages through the Italian trading centers. Motives are fine-scaled, abstract interlacings or geometric forms and some conventionalized floral details. Inlaying with ivory, bone, brass, and stone is typical. Fine fabrics were first brought to Europe from Saracenic sources. See also ITALY; ORIENTAL; SPAIN. [930, 1032.]

SASH BARS. Framework of glass doors in cabinets.

SATINWOOD. Light-honey-colored, hard texture, fine-grained wood susceptible to a high polish. Best varieties from Ceylon and India, but also found in the West Indies. Historically, most favored in later 18th-century English work, its use marks the transition from the Baroque solidity of Chippendale to the lightness of Adam, Hepplewhite, and the later designers. [596, 600.]

SATYR. Mask motif representing the head or whole figure of mythological satyr. It occurs profusely in Greco-Roman work and in all classic revivals.

SAUNIER, CLAUDE CHARLES. French cabinetmaker, Late Louis XV, Early Louis XVI periods.

SAUSAGE TURNING. Continuous turning similar to the spool turning, frequent in 19th-century American furniture; similar to 17th-century rustic turnings in Germany and England.

SAVERY, WILLIAM, 1721-1787. Philadelphia cabinetmaker who worked in a highly ornamented Chippendale style, probably the most elaborate produced in Colonial America. His highboys and lowboys are outstanding examples of American cabinetmaking; some maple and mahogany chairs and serpentine chests of drawers attributed to him are quite simple. It is probable that some of the work loosely identified as Savery's was made by other Philadelphians of the period or later. See also PHILADELPHIA CHIPPENDALE. [32.]

SAVERY LOWBOY

S SCROLL

SAVONAROLA CHAIR. Italian Renaissance X-shaped chair of interlacing curved slats and wooden back, carved or inlaid with certosina work. See also CURULE CHAIR; DANTE CHAIR; ITALY. [215, 759.]

SAWBUCK. Table frame or base having X-shaped supports. The type occurs in Gothic work in northern Europe and in the Early Renaissance in Italy. By this name is generally implied the rustic American type common in New England, although the most decorative examples appear in the Swedish- and German-influenced furniture of the Delaware Valley.

SCAGLIOLA. Hard plaster composition containing bits of marble, granite, alabaster, porphyry, or other stones. It is capable of being highly polished, and therefore is suitable for use as tops of tables, chests, etc. It is likely that the Romans used it, but the process was lost until the early 17th century. After that time Italian workmen carried it over Europe and it is common in English Georgian work. Robert Adam employed scagliola constantly for decorative and utilitarian purposes.

SCALE. Relative size; proportion of a piece to its surroundings and to other pieces.

SCALING; SCALE PATTERN. Imbrication; a surface ornament resembling the scales of a fish. Frequent in 18th-century carving throughout Europe, it occurs often in conjunction with carved shells and acanthus leaves.

SCALLOP. Carved shell ornament after the escallop shell. Typical of Spanish work where it is used alone; also common in the Rococo style as a center of floral ornament. See also SHELL MOTIF.

SCANDINAVIA. Sweden, Norway, and Denmark sustained a unity of artistic expression through the Middle Ages. From the age of the Vikings there survived a system of intricately interlaced ornaments, birds and beasts and vines, vaguely suggesting the Romanesque, the Celtic, and even Far Eastern design. Gothic architecture came in French, English, and Germanic forms, but the ornamental system of the lesser arts was not seriously affected. In the seventeenth century some quality of Renaissance work cropped out in Scandinavia, but it was a tentative exploratory gesture [474, 741]. The southern decorative styles were accepted slowly and modified greatly to adorn the basic native furniture of essentially rural peoples. In the 18th century the nobility imported extensively from Germany and England. The mixed strains were handled with grace and artistic insight. As the style filtered down to the lower classes, the ornamental motives of Louis XV and Rococo England were pleasantly adapted to the honest pine chests

1013 SWEDISH CUPBOARD, c. 1600. Bold carving shows Elizabethan influence. **1014** BOX BED, Swedish, 17th to 18th centuries. Folk-art decorations and construction.

1015 SCANDINAVIAN ARMOIRE, late 17th century. Baroque influence in the North was tamed to vigorous angularity and deep shadows.

and beds and cupboards. Painting and, to a lesser extent, carving, were freely used on flat areas. The aristocrats followed closely the patterns of the Baroque-Rococo-Classic Revival, but an unmistakable local quality is present in most renditions in these manners. The Empire style had longer life than elsewhere, developing under the patronage of the Bernadotte family into a gracious, refined style that lasted into the 20th century.

This style resolved itself into a school of distinguished reminiscent form that held sway, continually simplifying, through the first third of this century. Responding to the impulse of the International Style, Sweden, Norway, Denmark, and Finland alike maintained an orderly progression toward a furniture ideal, stressing wood craftsmanship and finish, restrained experiments with form, comfort, constructibility, and appropriateness to new living conditions and manners. Widely exported, furniture from Scandinavian lands has been a powerful influence generally. [334.]

SCHOOL. Style, era, period, manner; type of a given time, place, or designer.

SCISSORS CHAIR. Folding X-type of chair, known in Egyptian, Roman, Byzantine, and Italian Renaissance work. In medieval times it was actually a folding chair, but the type became solid as furniture ceased to follow its owner about in his rovings. See also CURULE CHAIR; DANTE CHAIR; FALDSTOOL; SAVONAROLA CHAIR; X-CHAIR.

SCOOP SEAT. Dipped or dropped seat, one in which the front rail is slightly concave to fit the body. [48, 410.]

SCOTIA. Hollow or concave molding, approximately quarter round. See also MOLDING.

SCRATCH CARVING. Crude form of carving usually done with a V-chisel. [714, 1016, 1169.]

SCREEN. Screens as furniture are ornamental frames or panels for protection from observation, draft, or the heat of a fire. The framework has variously been cov-

1016 SCRATCH CARVING in New England box, dated 1677.
Wadsworth Atheneum, Hartford, Conn.

Metropolitan Museum of Art, Gift of J. Pierpont Morgan, 1916
1017 FRENCH GOTHIC SCREEN, oak; early 15th century.

ered with leather, paper, textiles, etc., and may be made in only one panel or of several leaves or panels hinged together. Small one-panel screens have been decoratively treated to serve as fire screens; these usually stand on a pair of feet and are called "cheval screens." The type known as "pole screen" has a smaller panel, fixed to an upright pole upon which it may be raised or lowered. These frequently had tripod or pedestal bases.

The earliest known screens occur in China in the 2nd century B.C. Some of these were made with mica or glass panels to permit a sheltered enjoyment of the view; others were carved and inlaid with jade and metals. Screens from this time on were painted with landscapes, texts, memorable events, or simple scenes of everyday activity; others were covered with embroidered silks, using natural forms and inscriptions. These were often made of many panels, some having as many as 40. The Japanese screens more characteristically are of 6 panels, with the landscape pattern spread entirely across the whole, instead of each panel being framed and decorated independently, as were the Chinese.

In Europe the screen developed from sheer necessity in the drafty halls and to protect against the tremendous fires of the Middle Ages. Records indicate that Edward II had screens, but of what material we are not aware. Henry VIII's inventory lists "scrynes of purple Taphata frynged with purple silke, standing uppon feete of tymbre guilte silvered and painted." Among the possessions of Charles I sold after his execution were "china skreens"; the rage of Oriental screens spread until they were common throughout England. Leather-covered screens came from the Continent and were likewise highly decorated with pastoral scenes, Chinese pictures and characters, birds and flowers, or formal diaper patterns typical of the Spanish and Flemish leatherwork. Wood, leather, textile, and Oriental screens appear on the Continent after the Middle Ages. In France the period of the Régence produced handsomely paneled and carved wood screens. With the feminine character of the style of Louis XV, screens were often curved at the top and covered entirely with tapestry, embroidery, or other textiles matching the hangings and chair coverings; some were painted canvas with the fashionable pastoral scenes; some with Coromandel lacquer and many with "India paper" with small flower and figure patterns. Mirrors were often set into the upper part. Under Louis XVI the classic rectangular shapes returned, with fabric panels set within carved and gilded frames. Later, during the Directory, large panels of painted papers were used in the Japanese manner but employing timely pictorial motives. Shelves were sometimes added to screens, either fire or tall screens, as aids in reading or writing. [1017.]

Symons Galleries, Inc.

1018 *Center, left.* English, 18th century. Painted leather.

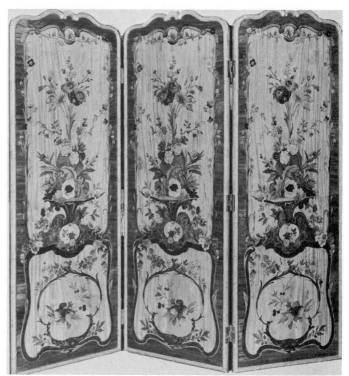

Symons Galleries, Inc.

1019 *Center, right.* French, Louis XV. Marquetry and parquetry panels.

1020 JAPANESE PAINTED PAPER SCREEN, Tokugawa period, 1603-1867. The pattern is continuous over six panels.

William Rockhill Nelson Gallery, Atkins Museum (Nelson Fund); Kansas City, Mo.

1021 *Lo Mejor de España*

1022   *C. R. Gracie & Sons*

1021 SPANISH, wood panels after old door designs. **1022-1023** JAPANESE SHOJI PANELS made into folding screens.

1023

1024 CHINESE LACQUER, incised and colored.
Symons Galleries, Inc.

1025 MASSACHUSETTS c. 1790. Hepplewhite. Folding candle shelf.

1026 NEW YORK, late 18th century. Printed cotton facing; mahogany frame, small drawers.

1027 FOLDING WINGS, adjustable height, English c. 1810.

1028 FRENCH ROCOCO, 1725-1735. Silk brocade panel.

1029 SCREEN made for Marie Antoinette, 1788, by Jean-Baptiste Claude Sené.

1026 *Metropolitan Museum of Art, Rogers Fund, 1941*

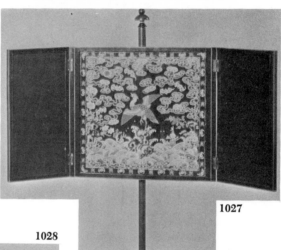

1025 *Israel Sack, Inc.*

1028

1027

1029   *Metropolitan Museum of Art, Gift of Ann Payne Blumenthal, 1941*

Symons Galleries, Inc.

Metropolitan Museum of Art, Gift of Louis J. Baury, 1935

Ginsburg and Levy

1030 SCROLL-TOP DETAIL of American secretary, late 18th century. Exceptional variety of ornamented moldings and carved detail.

SCRIBANNE. Secretary-commode made by the Dutch and Flemish and imported into France, middle 18th century.

SCRIBING. Method of fitting together surfaces whose profiles are not identical straight lines.

SCRIPTOIRE; SCRITOIRE; SCRUTOIRE. See ESCRITOIRE; SECRETAIRE.

SCROLL. Ornament of spiral or convolute form.

SCROLL ARM. Chair terminating at the hand in a scroll. Very simple in Early Renaissance work [214, 254), later Baroque treatment exaggerated the curvature and carving [257.] Some Windsors show sensitive detailing.

SCROLL FOOT. Curved foot not fully articulated with the block above, as in a cabriole leg. [184, 1137.]

SCROLL LEG. Seventeenth-century Baroque work in France shows attempts to embellish legs other than by turning and carving; curves ending in scrolls at either end [258, 260, 562, 1282] were intermediate steps in the development of the cabriole leg.

SCROLL TOP. Broken pediment formed by two S or cyma curves; also swan-neck. [36, 1030.]

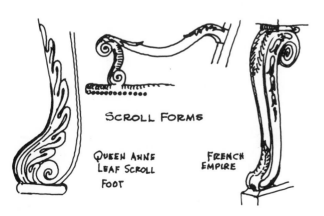

SCROLL FORMS

QUEEN ANNE
LEAF SCROLL
FOOT

FRENCH
EMPIRE

SCRUTOIRE. Enclosed desk for writing. See also SECRETAIRE; SECRETARY.

SEAT. The whole class of seat furniture comprising chairs, stools, sofas and settees, chaise longues, etc. Specifically, it refers to the horizontal surface of a chair or similar piece of furniture.

SEAWEED MARQUETRY. Delicate interlacing designs in inlay suggesting marine plant life. Originating in Italy, the type was best developed in England, late in the 17th century. [735.]

SECESSION. Style in design originating in Vienna about 1896. Precursor of the later "Modern" Austrian style, it followed no accepted types, modifying the French Art Nouveau and other reactions to traditional style. More than most of its contemporaries, the Secession style was generally applicable and had elements of grace, directness, and an easy charm now identifiable in the Wiener Werkstätte creations. Joseph Hoffman, Moser, etc., were early exponents; the influence came to America through designers like Joseph Urban, Paul Frankl, and others. See also MODERN FURNITURE; NINETEENTH CENTURY.

SECOND EMPIRE. France, under Napoleon III, 1852-1870, a period of artistic ferment and opulence, marked in furniture by an overrich mixture of Rococo and Renaissance detail. See also FRANCE; NINETEENTH CENTURY.

SECRET DRAWER. Small, hidden compartments in old chests, bureaus, desks, and the like, for private or valuable papers. Rarely very secret, but the old cabinetmakers delighted in providing these difficult-of-access places. [487, 1031, 1056.]

1031 SECRET DRAWERS in peak of secretary. Viennese. See 1056.

French & Co., Inc.

SECRETAIRE; SECRETARY. Closed desk, usually with drawers below and bookcase above. In Europe sometimes called "bureau." [138, 159, 1032.]

THE SECRETARY IDEA BEGAN WITH THE FALL-FRONT DESK BOX OR PORTABLE FITTED CHEST SET UPON A TABLE, A CHEST, OR A FRAME TO HOLD FIRMLY THE WORKING SURFACE AT A COMFORTABLE HEIGHT. AS THE BASE UNIT SOLIDIFIED AND BECAME THE COMPARATIVELY IMMOVABLE DESK, SUPERSTRUCTURES FOR BOOKS AND DOCUMENTS WERE ADDED UNTIL THE END RESULT, A VERTICAL WALL COMPOSITION OCCUPYING LITTLE FLOOR SPACE, BECAME ONE OF THE MOST DECORATIVE ELEMENTS OF THE FURNITURE REPERTOIRE.

1032 Spanish *vargueño*, 16th century. Portable chest-desk of Moorish inlay surface upon a stand of Renaissance design.

1033 FRENCH, style of Louis XIII. Storage units and desk box imposed on traditional "bureau."

1034 ENGLISH "SCRUTOIRE," 1690-1700, walnut.

1033

1032   *Hispanic Society of America*

1034

Metropolitan Museum of Art, Gift of Mrs. Elihu Chauncey, 1930

1035 Italian, late 16th century. Walnut writing cabinet with the arms of the Strozzi family. (The fall front is missing.) Typical animal feet, gadrooned base.

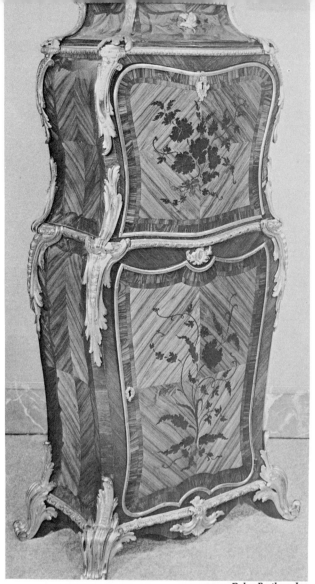

1036 LOUIS XV PEDESTAL SECRETARY. **1037** ENG-LISH c. 1710, Queen Anne. Green lacquer, gold Chinese decoration. Mirror-faced doors. **1038** LOUIS XV TRANSITIONAL. Drop-front secretary, black lacquer, chinoiserie. **1039** LOUIS XIV. *Secretaire à abattant* by Boulle.

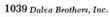

18th—Century Cabinet Desks—France and England

1040 FALL-FRONT DESK, dated 1790, by Jean-Henri Riesener. Marquetry with ormolu mounts.

THE TALL SECRETARY ("BUREAU" IN ENGLAND)
DEVELOPED BY THE ADDITION OF A CABINET SEC-
TION OVER THE SLANT-FRONT DESK.

1042

Metropolitan Museum of Art, Rogers Fund, 1911

1043 *Metropolitan Museum of Art, Fletcher Fund, 1925*

Metropolitan Museum of Art, Bequest of Annie C. Kane, 1926
1041 THE BAROQUE MANNER, English c. 1700. Black
lacquer.

1042 *Upper.* ENGLISH, Queen Anne, walnut fall front.

1043 *Lower.* VENETIAN, 18th century. Applied engravings.

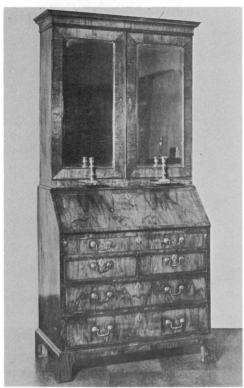

Needham's Antiques, Inc.

1044 ENGLISH c. 1720. Walnut.

Philadelphia Museum of Art, A. J. Wyatt, Staff Photographer

1046 PHILADELPHIA CHIPPENDALE, second half of 18th century.

1045 ENGLISH c. 1755. Mahogany.   *Needham's Antiques, Inc.*

1047 MASSACHUSETTS, 1760-1775. Blockfront, fine scrolled hood.   *Israel Sack, Inc.*

1049   *Ginsburg and Levy*

1048 BLOCKFRONT SECRETARY, New England.
Height of the Colonial period.   *Ginsburg and Levy*

Metropolitan Museum of Art
1050 Blockfront extends over lid.

INTERIORS WERE PARTICULARLY WELL DESIGNED IN THE STATELY
SECRETARIES OF THE THIRD QUARTER OF THE 18TH CENTURY.

1051 KETTLE BASE, broken pediment,
carved ogee feet, doors ogee paneled.
Metropolitan Museum of Art

1055 ITALIAN, painted chinoiserie, 18th century.

Olivieri

1053 AMERICAN c. 1800. Sheraton style.   *Ginsburg and Levy*

1054 LOUIS XV PROVINCIAL STYLE.

Don Ruseau

Israel Sack, Inc.

1052 AMERICAN c. 1765. Fretted pediment.

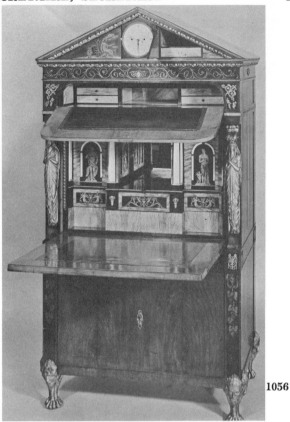

French & Co., Inc.

1057 *Symons Galleries, Inc.*

1056 VIENNESE, late 18th century. Complex mechanisms, secret drawers behind clock.

1057 ENGLISH c. 1805. Sheraton, mahogany inlaid chest-desk with breakfront bookcase.

1058 MASSACHUSETTS c. 1780. Hepplewhite style. Tambour center, serpentine tambour below.

1059 MASSACHUSETTS, Sheraton c. 1800. Secretary bookcase.

1059 *Philadelphia Museum of Art*

1058   *Israel Sack, Inc.*

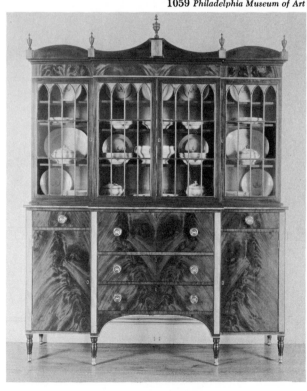

Philadelphia Museum of Art, A. J. Wyatt, Staff Photographer
1061 PHILADELPHIA, 1825-1827, by Quervelle.

Dalva Brothers, Inc.
1060 FRENCH, made for Lucien Bonaparte. Decorated on four sides to be free standing.

1062 GERMAN EMPIRE, Biedermeier.

1063 PHILADELPHIA, 1818-1820. Attributed to Michael Bouvier.

Atheneum of Philadelphia

SECRETARY DRAWER. Addition to a bookcase, chest, table, cabinet, etc., of a drawer with conveniences for writing, usually with a fall front to make a level bed. [165, 495, 504, 1380.]

SECTIONAL FURNITURE. Furniture made in units that complement each other, but present a finished appearance if used separately. Bookcases, desks, chests, cabinets, sofas, etc., are arranged to form large units when placed together. Chiefly modern commercial work.

SEDAN CHAIR. Enclosed portable chair borne on two long poles carried by two men. They appeared in Italy after the Middle Ages, and their use spread with the growth of luxury during the 16th, 17th, and 18th centuries. They were often elaborately decorated and luxuriously upholstered. [778, 1153.]

SEDDON, THOMAS and GEORGE. English cabinetmakers, late 18th and early 19th centuries; supplied furniture for Windsor Castle. [1386.]

SEGMENTAL ARCH. Arch made of less than half of a circle, the curve ending sharply.

SEGMENTAL CORNERS. Panel corners broken by curved lines, typical of Régence work.

SEGMENTAL PEDIMENT. Unbroken curved pediment, the arc of a circle.

SELLA. Ancient Roman name for most seat forms; also occurs in Early French Renaissance usage.

SEMAINIER (French). Tall narrow chest or chiffonier with six or seven drawers, planned for supply of personal linen for each day of the week. [389.]

SERPENTINE. Waving or undulating surface. A serpentine front, as in a commode, has the center convex or protruding, while the ends are concave. [40, 53, 366, 390, 710.] Reversed serpentine fronts have a more complex curve. Serpentine stretchers are X-type with curves. [476, 816.]

SERRATED. Zigzag or sawtooth ornament of Gothic origin; a form of notched dentil.

SERVER; SERVING TABLE. Side tables in dining rooms; generally higher than an ordinary table, and fitted with drawers for silver. [1064.]

Charles of London

1064 ENGLISH TUDOR c. 1600. Originally each of such shelves was called a "desk." Shelves were added or subtracted to form more complex cabinets or simple serving boards or sideboards.

1065 LOUIS XVI, by Riesener. *Frick Collection*

SERPENTINE FRONT

SERPENTINE STRETCHER

1066 ENGLISH, Sheraton.

1069 MASSACHUSETTS c. 1800. Sheraton serpentine front with candle slides.

1067 LOUIS XVI "COMMODE DESSERTE."

1068 NEW YORK EMPIRE, 1830-1835. Stenciled decorations on mahogany, marble columns. Columnar ends rotate to reveal shelves.

1070 HEPPLEWHITE c. 1790. Wine bin at right, slide trays at left.

1071 SERVER—English Regency in "Egyptian taste." Shelves fold in.

SETTECENTO (Italian). Eighteenth century, the 1700's.

SETTEE. Light open seat about twice the width of a chair, with low arms and back, sometimes upholstered. [77, 1072 *et seq.*]

SETTLE. All wood settee with solid wood ends, and occasionally a wooden hood; Tudor times and later, in England, generally of oak; in America of pine, rarely of maple, sometimes walnut in Pennsylvania. Usually built solid to the floor, and sometimes with a hinged seat over a box [1346]. See also BENCH; CHAIR TABLE. [550.]

SÈVRES. Porcelain objects from the manufactory at Sèvres, France, established 1756 and taken over by the government of Louis XV in 1759. Made plaques, medallions, etc., which were used as decoration inserts on furniture, as desk fronts and table tops, particularly favored in the highly decorative styles. [202, 1004.]

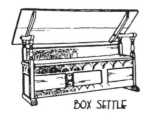

BOX SETTLE

Settles

GOTHIC BENCHES SERVED AS BENCHES AND BEDS FROM THEIR BEGINNINGS. BY THE 15TH CENTURY ARMS OR BACKS WERE ADDED FOR COMFORT.

Metropolitan Museum of Art, Bequest of George Blumenthal, 1941
1072 FRENCH 15th century, linenfold paneling.

1073 ITALIAN BAROQUE PAINTED CHEST with removable back. Shows decline of portability and increasing decorative interest. Probably 17th century.

Olivieri

1074 AMERICAN, 17th century. Chest use abandoned, this seat opens out to form a bed.

Wadsworth Atheneum, Hartford, Conn.

1075 ENGLISH TUDOR STYLE, early 16th century. Linen-fold paneling. This type appears to derive from the detachment of wainscot.

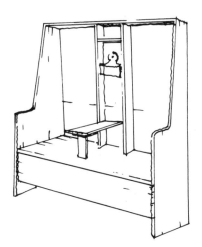

1076 NEW ENGLAND, early 18th century. Pine bench with wings and hood.

1077 TUSCAN, carved walnut, 1600-1630. Hinged seat derived from *cassone*.

ENGLISH

382

1078 ENGLISH, 1720-1730. Early Georgian double chair gilded and decorated, gesso.

Metropolitan Museum of Art, Fletcher Fund, 1924

EARLY
GEORGIAN

1079 NEW YORK, Sheraton c. 1800. Painted black with colored decoration.
*Metropolitan Museum of Art, Gift of
Henrietta McCready Bagg and Ida McCready Wilson,
1936, in memory of their mother, Ann Carter McCready*

1080 VENETIAN, late 18th century, Louis XVI inspiration. Carved wood, polychromed.
*Metropolitan Museum of Art,
Bequest of Annie C. Kane, 1926*

**FULLY UPHOLSTERED SETTEES
APPEARED IN THE 17TH CENTURY.**

1081 ENGLISH c. 1610.
Early Stuart settee at Knole.

1082 EARLY GEORGIAN c. 1725.   *French & Co., Inc.*

1083 Venetian, late 17th century.

1085 *Bottom, right.* MASSACHUSETTS c.
1800. Sheraton style.   *Israel Sack, Inc.*

1084 Bentwood, late 19th century.   *Thonet*

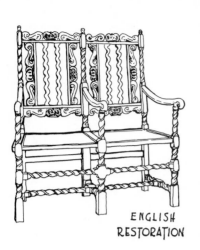

ENGLISH
RESTORATION

1086 AMERICAN CHIPPENDALE, simplified.

1087 ENGLISH c. 1780. Bamboo turnings, marbled, with gilt decorations.

1088 AMERICAN WINDSOR, bamboo turnings.

1088

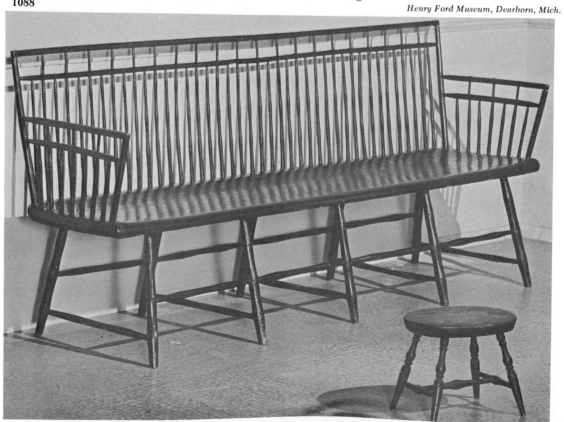

1089 ENGLISH SHERATON, late 18th century, painted.
Israel Sack, Inc.

1090 AMERICAN c. 1820; rush seat, based on the Sheraton "fancy" chair.
Henry Ford Museum, Dearborn, Mich.

1091 NEW YORK, Late Federal, ascribed to Duncan Phyfe.
Ginsburg and Levy

1091

1090

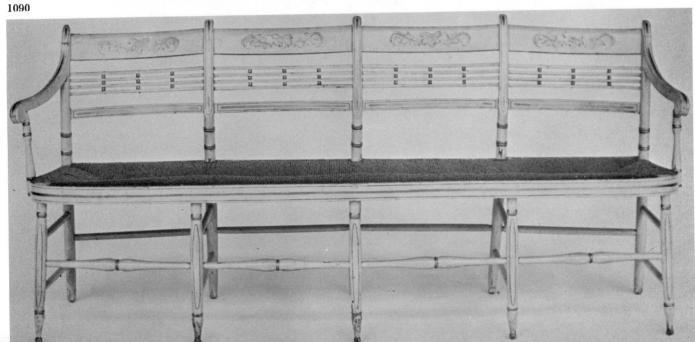

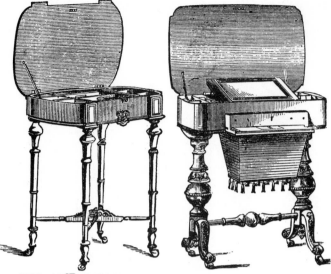

1092 - 1093 ENGLISH VICTORIAN SEWING TABLES.

bases, sometimes with drawer or hinged lid, and elaborately pierced and carved back panel. The style persists, especially in provincial work in all European countries. [217, 707.]

SHADED MARQUETRY. Method of shading or toning marquetry with hot sand.

SHAKER FURNITURE. The Shakers, a religious sect, founded independent communities in the mid-19th century. Chiefly rural and self-sustaining, they produced their own furniture, simple and straightforward in design, soundly constructed and often well proportioned and charming in detail. Almost unornamented and invariably of local woods, such as pine, walnut, maple, and fruitwoods, the Shaker productions are among the best of the rural American types. [1094.]

SEWING TABLE. Small worktable, usually with drawers or lid top, fitted with spool racks, etc., and often with a cloth bag for sewing material. They are mentioned in 17th-century inventories, but are not common until the mid-18th century, after which they appear abundantly. Excellent designs by Sheraton, Hepplewhite, Duncan Phyfe, and others are extant; they are equally common in Louis XVI, Empire and Biedermeier work. See also BAG TABLE; WORKTABLE. [68, 76, 1092.]

SGABELLE. Wooden side chair of the Italian Renaissance based on primitive three-cornered stools. Early types had three legs wedged into solid seat, with board back. Later elaborations had scroll-cut slab

1095 DESKS AND SWIVEL CHAIRS.

1094 BUILT-IN CABINET AND CHEST, TABLE, ROCKING CHAIR and FOOTSTOOL, CANDLESTAND. Note hook strip on wall on which unused chairs hung.

Shaker Furniture

UNAFFECTED AND EXQUISITELY FUNCTIONAL FUR-
NITURE WAS PRODUCED LARGELY BY SELF-TRAINED
CRAFTSMEN, GUIDED BY AN AUSTERE PHILOSOPHY
AND ECONOMY. LITTLE VARIATION APPEARS IN THE
PRODUCT BETWEEN 1800 AND 1900, ALTHOUGH MOST
OF THE REMAINING WORK PROBABLY IS AFTER 1860
FROM COLONIES IN NEW YORK, CONNECTICUT,
MAINE, OHIO, AND KENTUCKY.

*Photographs from "Shaker Furniture" by Edward Deming Andrews and
Faith Andrews, courtesy Dover Publications, Inc., New York*

1097 SHEAF-BACK CHAIR,
Provincial French, end of 18th century.

Museum of the City of New York

1096 SHAVING STAND,
New York, c. 1825.

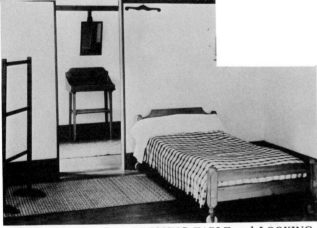

1095A BED with rollers, DRESSING TABLE and LOOKING
GLASS, CLOTHES RACK.

SHAPED WORK. In cabinetmaking all large surface
flatwork made in other than flat planes is known as
shaped work. Such curved swelling or serpentine
planes are made of laminated veneers in forms or cut
out of the solid. The latter requires wide boards,
which are apt to crack.

**SHAVING STAND; SHAVING MIRROR; SHAVING
GLASS; SHAVING TABLE.** Various types of stands
with adjustable mirrors planned as dressing or shaving
stands for men. They appear on the Continent in the
late 17th century, and most versatile forms were developed in Georgian and Victorian England. [1096.]

SHEAF BACK. Typical small chair of France, late
18th and early 19th centuries, having a delicate back
resembling a graceful bundle of rods spreading out in
fan shape. They usually had straw seats. [788, 1097.]

SHEARER, THOMAS. English cabinetmaker and designer, late 18th century. No identified furniture of
his workmanship is known, but his drawings are a
large part of *The Cabinetmaker's London Book of
Prices and Designs* (1788). His style is light and
simple, slightly in the vein of the Brothers Adam. It
undoubtedly influenced Hepplewhite to a great
degree, and subsequently much of the work in America. Shearer appears to be the inventor of the sideboard in one piece with the flanking pedestals; this
type and his ingenious dressing tables were freely
praised by Sheraton. No chair designs are known to
have been made by Shearer.

SHELF CLOCK. Compact clock mechanism in 17th-
and 18th-century England and France, decoratively
fitted with harmonizing bracket or shelf. Eli Terry
of Connecticut first used machinery in clockmaking
and, after 1830, developed unique designs for mass
production. See also BRACKET CLOCK. [1098.]

1098   *French & Co., Inc.*

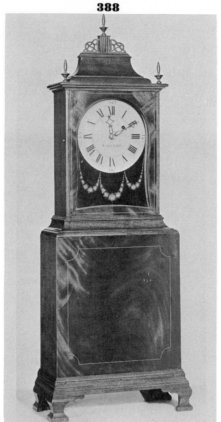

1099

Israel Sack, Inc.

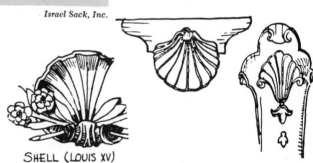

1100 *Wadsworth Atheneum, Hartford, Conn.*

1098 SHELF CLOCKS, ENGLISH ROCOCO, mid-18th century. Ormolu and enamel with matching bracket. **1099** CONCORD, MASSACHUSETTS, c. 1790. Hepplewhite style, mahogany. **1100** BRISTOL, CONNECTICUT c. 1833. Center part mirrored, with glass columns at sides.

SHELL MOTIF. Various shells appear as ornament in all styles, but the scallop-shell (cockleshell) form is most common, especially in Italian and Spanish Renaissance furniture. The Rococo style is actually based in part on the use of the shell ornament. In Queen Anne furniture the shell is typically placed on the knee of cabriole legs; Chippendale used it as a central theme in carving. Rococo shells are perforated; Louis XV style uses pierced shells as a center for two acanthus sprays. In later 18th-century work the conch-shell form is used as an inlay motive. [27, 194, 445, 489, 571, 1032, 1284.]

SHELL TOP. Cupboard of half-round recessed plan, whose round top is a half dome carved with ribs to simulate a shell. Excellent examples in middle-18th-century English work and somewhat later in America. [445.]

SHELLAC. Natural resin soluble in alcohol. The mixture may be brushed on or padded on, and dries quickly, after which it is susceptible to fine satiny polish by rubbing down. The padding produces the high-gloss brittle finish known as French polish. Shellac finishes alone are easily damaged by moisture and heat.

SHELL (LOUIS XV)

SHELVES. They vary from the simplest bracketed shelf for a single object, such as a clock or a figure, to wholly architectural compositions for quantities of books, ornaments, objets d'art. Sometimes enclosed. From delicacy of English Georgian designs [1333] to vigorously ornamental compositions for their own sake covers the evolution from 1750-1800 [724, 1341]. Modern work tends toward functional flexible compositions of architectural intent [1334]. See also BOOK-CASE ; WALL SHELVES; WHATNOT.

SHERATON, THOMAS, 1751-1806. English cabinetmaker, preacher, scholar, his fame rests less on his actual work than on the style that grew from his book *The Cabinetmaker and Upholsterer's Drawing Book,* published in 1790. This was a compendium of all known designs available to Sheraton, and was published more as a catalogue or book of directions for the aid of craftsmen; but the designs in it came to be accepted as Sheraton's own work and the whole style

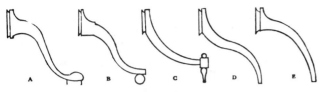

accredited to him. He also published *Designs for Furniture, The Cabinet Dictionary* (1803) and had begun *The Cabinet-Maker, Upholsterer and General Artists' Encyclopedia,* but had only reached the *"C's"* when death overtook him in 1806.

Sheraton's designs are largely in the straight classic manner, after Hepplewhite, Adam, and Shearer. Chairbacks are mostly rectangular; legs are fine tapered squares. Delicacy and grace mark most of his work; he was influenced by the Directoire, and this influence is transmitted to American work through Duncan Phyfe. See also ENGLAND. [44, 303, 500, 1101, 1102.]

Israel Sack, Inc.

1101 AMERICAN SHERATON DROP END TABLE c. 1815.

1102 SHERATON SIDEBOARD c. 1790.

Needham's Antiques, Inc.

SHEVERET. Writing table, late 18th century, France.

SHIELD BACK. Typical chairback form of Hepplewhite, having double curved top rail and a half ellipse below, filled with various openwork designs, such as vase forms, three feathers, swags and ribbon, etc. [47.]

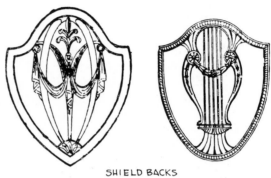

SHIELD BACKS
SHERATON AND HEPPLEWHITE

SHOE. On wooden turnings a small turned disk or fillet under a scroll; also a metal cup terminal for a foot. Brass shoes were favored in 18th-century English work after Chippendale, and often are part of the caster. See also FERRULE; SABOT.

SHOJI. Screen panel of Japanese origin, usually fine lattice effect with paper filler. [1022.]

SHOULDER. Name sometimes applied to the top or thick section of the cabriole leg, also called "knee" or "hip."

SHOW WOOD. The exposed wood parts of an upholstered chair, such as a wood arm, post, frame, apron, or leg.

SHOWCASES. Furniture in cabinet form but usually with glass sides, used to display curios and collections. English showcases after 1685 follow the general shape of cabinets when used for larger objects, such as ship models. The later ones, for smaller objects, resemble more a glass box on a stand.

SIAMOISE. Late-19th-century upholstered sofa or double armchairs, with the seats facing back and front; an S-chair; so named after the Siamese Twins (1811-1874). Also called "tête-à-tête," "vis-à-vis." [1310, 1329.]

Also a fabric popular during the Louis XV and Louis XVI periods for cushions of straw chairs.

SIDE CHAIR. Chair without arms, usually small. Early types were evolved either by adding a back to a stool, called in Italy *sgabelle*, or by omitting the arms of a more important chair. The latter type often appeared in the 16th and the 17th centuries to accommodate the wearers of voluminous skirts, and are variously known as "farthingale" chairs and *caqueteuses*.

SIDE RAILS. The long narrow boards or rails that connect the headboards and footboards of beds.

SIDE TABLES. Tables with fixed tops were used along the walls of dining rooms to assist in the service after 1700. Earlier types, developed from simple frames, had carried chests with linens, silver, liquor, utensils, etc. From these evolved the serving tables, buffets, lowboys, etc., not identical with tables in form.

SIDEBOARD; BUFFET. Originally a literal "side board"—accessory to the large trestle table or board during the service of meals. In Elizabethan England this piece acquired importance, and borrowed from the Italian and French types of credence—sideboards

Anderson Galleries

1103 SIDEBOARD, or *madia*, elevated-chest style. Bologna 16th century.

Sideboards

THE SIDEBOARD-BUFFET APPEARED IN ITALY AS A DEVELOPMENT OF THE CHEST-CREDENZA WALL CABINET, AS ACCESSORY TO CEREMONIAL DINING.

1104 SACRISTY CUPBOARD, Tuscany, 1490-1500.
Metropolitan Museum of Art, Rogers Fund, 1916

SIDEBOARD; BUFFET

IN THE 17TH CENTURY THE SIDE-TABLE IDEA GREW THROUGH THE HUTCH TABLE TO THE LARGE BUFFET.

1105 SPANISH, 17th century. Probably originally fitted with an iron center stretcher.

EARLY AMERICAN

1106 JACOBEAN OAK SIDEBOARD OR DRESSER, 1680-1690. Characteristic molding variety, baluster legs.

SHAKER

1107 OAK SIDEBOARD, West of England or Wales, early 18th century.

1108 CHINESE, polished hardwood.

1109 LORRAINE, sideboard dresser.

Metropolitan Museum of Art, Rogers Fund, 1945

1110 PENNSYLVANIA GERMAN (Manheim, Pennsylvania). Walnut dresser with spoon rack. Early 18th century.

1112 FRENCH, detail of Louis XIII style.

Don Ruseau

1111 ENGLISH, oak, late 18th century, country style.

Anderson Galleries

1113 ADAM SIDEBOARD AND PEDES-TALS WITH URNS.

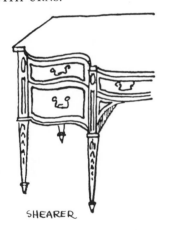

SHEARER

1114 SIDEBOARD. Late-18th-century composition in one piece. Style of the Brothers Adam.

1115 ADAM STYLE c. 1780. Ten-leg sideboard, mahogany with metal mounts.

1116 ENGLISH SHERATON, serpentine form, mahogany inlaid with satinwood.

Needham's Antiques, Inc.

1117 CONNECTICUT c. 1790, Hepplewhite-style cherry sideboard, American-eagle inlay.

Israel Sack, Inc.

—the partial enclosure of doors and drawers. The Italian version, developed from the chest, was a solid cabinet, though a lighter type—*madia* [1103]—resembled the hutch type of Gothic France [169]. The latter contributed to the court cupboard that distinguishes the Jacobean style.

In 17th-century France, the Italian form reached a high state, particularly in the provinces. Great double-bodied cabinets are characteristic. The upper part provided for the display of plates, spoons, tankards, and other vessels [1109] on open shelves. This style spread to rural England, where the dresser (often Welsh dresser) is still current. The American dresser [82] flourished similarly in country houses. [53, 88, 90, 460.]

The true sideboard form of open shelves [1064] was incidental to the court cupboard. Late in the 17th century it took on the typical long narrow shape with

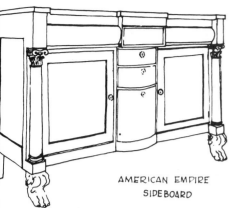

AMERICAN EMPIRE
SIDEBOARD

Metropolitan Museum of Art, Rogers Fund, 1919
1118 EMPIRE, early-19th-century French. Thuja veneers with metal mounts.

IN THE 19TH CENTURY THE SIDEBOARD DEVELOPED INTO A PRETENTIOUS ARCHITECTURAL COMPOSITION FAR BEYOND ITS FUNCTION.

1119 NEW YORK, Empire style.
Henry Ford Museum, Dearborn, Mich.

1120 ENGLISH, carved oak and ebony. Exhibited at the Paris Exposition, 1869.

1121 ENGLISH VICTORIAN c. 1875.

shallower drawers. By the mid-18th century under Adam and Chippendale it was almost a simple table, but an essential part of the sidewall composition was the additional narrow cabinets in which were kept silver, plates, liquor, and often warming devices. Upon these were carried knife boxes. [1113, 1114.]

Shearer was probably the first to combine all these elements into one piece. Hepplewhite, Sheraton, and others of the period designed fine examples of this shape. Sheraton favored a metal back rail, and drew many sideboards suggesting the old three-part grouping. All designers of the period indulged in shaped fronts, the simple bow and serpentine yielding to combinations of curves. Many late-18th-century American sideboards show these traits. [62, 73, 1068.]

In the late 18th century the sideboard produced many offshoots, such as the wine table, the mixing table [1353], and various serving arrangements. [1070, 1239 *et seq.*]

Empire sideboards tended to great bulk and solidity, utilizing the entire available space. In addition there were frequent superstructures for the display of plate and china.

SIDEBOARD PEDESTALS. See PEDESTAL. [1113.]

SILVER. Silver was used in regal furniture in ancient times, and again in the great work of the 17th century in France and England. Louis XIV had small pieces, such as tables, mirror frames, etc., wholly made of silver, exquisitely wrought in the Baroque manner. When the treasury was depleted, most of it was melted down for bullion, disregarding the artistic value. Charles II brought the vogue to England; much woodwork was covered with thin sheets of silver. It was extensively used for handles and mounts through the Early Georgian period.

SILVERWOOD. 18th-century name for English harewood or stained sycamore.

SINGERIES. Rococo decoration of monkeys at play.

SINGLE-ARCH MOLDING. Small astragal or half-round molding around the drawers of chests of the William and Mary period.

SINGLE CHAIR. Old name for side chair.

SINGLE-GATE TABLE. Tuckaway table; one with gate on only one side and one leaf.

SINKAGE. Dropped or set-back surface; set-in panel in post or pilaster or other flat member.

SIRENS. Mythological figures, half woman, half bird, used as a carving motive in Renaissance furniture.

SIX-BACK. American ladder-back chair with six slats, usually slightly arched. Infrequent, but chiefly from the Delaware Valley.

SIX-LEGGED HIGHBOY. The William and Mary type of England and America. See also HIGHBOY.

SKIRT. Apron: part of a piece of furniture. See also CONSTRUCTION.

SKIRT - REGENCE TABLE

SLANT FRONT. Desk or secretary with writing section enclosed by a fall lid that when closed slants back; probably originally to rest a book or writing material upon. See also DESK; SECRETAIRE; SECRETARY. [19, 477.]

SLAT. Crosspiece supported on side rails of bed to carry the spring; horizontal crossbars in chairback to brace uprights and to support back of sitter.

SLAT-BACK CHAIR. Back having horizontal rails or crossbars similar to ladder backs; in Early American work, the slats are characteristically thin and finely shaped.

SLATE. Fine-textured stone, grayish or greenish-black, used for tabletops. [817.]

SLEEPY HOLLOW CHAIR. Comfortable upholstered chair with deeply curved back and hollowed seat and low arms. American type, middle 19th century.

SLEIGH BED. American version of the Empire bed, the scrolled ends slightly reminiscent of sleigh fronts. They are usually used lengthwise to a wall. [122.]

SLIDE, SLIDER. Sliding panel or pull-out shelf, flush framed and fitted between the top drawer and top of a chest of drawers. Also, the pull-out leaves in secretaries, designed to hold candlesticks.

SLIP SEAT. Same as "loose seat"—separate upholstered wood frame, let into the framework of the chair seat.

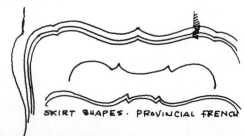
SKIRT SHAPES - PROVINCIAL FRENCH

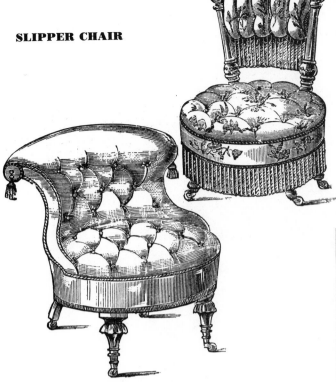

1122 SLIPPER CHAIRS, English Victorian.

SLIPPER CHAIR. Small side chair or armchair with low legs, designed for bedroom use. Generally upholstered. [1122.]

SLIPPER FOOT. Elongated club foot (similar to snake foot) Queen Anne. [567.]

SMITH, GEORGE. English cabinetmaker and designer. In 1808, his book *A Collection of Designs for Household Furniture and Interior Decoration* appeared with comment on the current revolution in taste. This was the Regency taste, with archaeological correctness after the Greek, Roman, and Egyptian models. A later book goes much further toward formulating the 19th-century styles as we know them now. Smith was employed by Thomas Hope and patronized by George IV. The initials G.S. are occasionally found on important pieces of furniture of the period.

SNAKE FOOT. Foot of a tripod table, 18th-century English or American, which suggests a snake shape by its slender, swelling curve.

SNAP TABLE. Tripod table of Chippendale type with hinged tilt top.

SOCKETING. Joining by fitting one piece of wood into a cavity in another, such as chair legs into solid seats.

SOCLE. Plain block used as a plinth or base for a case piece, or as a pedestal of a statue. [988.]

SOFA. Long upholstered seat for two or more persons. The name "sopha" is of Eastern origin and was first used about 1680 to designate a divan-like seat in France; the same type had also been called *canapé.* It had a back and arms at each end, but was distinct from the settee by its greater comfort. Sofas followed the usual evolution of the succeeding styles, varying in ornament, bulk, and comfort through the styles of the 18th and 19th centuries. See also COUCH; REST BEDS; SETTEE; UPHOLSTERING.

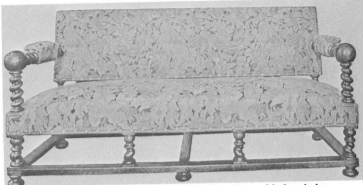

1123 FRENCH, mid-17th century. Heavily padded upholstery on framework of spiral turnings.

SOFA TABLE. Long narrow table with drop leaves at the ends, and drawers. Occurs chiefly in Late Georgian work, in designs by Sheraton and others, but prototypes appear in early-18th-century work. [66.]

SOFFIT. Underside, as of any projecting or ceiling member or the underside of a projecting cornice or wide molding that forms a shelflike projection.

SOMNOE. Night table or bedside table.

SOUPIÉRE. Antique vase form or urn often used in Louis XVI and Empire furniture as the central motive in pedimented tops of beds, chairs, cabinets, etc., and at the intersection of stretchers. [1287.]

LOUIS XIV CONSOLE

SPADE FOOT. A rectangular tapered foot suggesting the outline of a spade; common in Hepplewhite designs. [47, 57, 498.]

SOFAS

French & Co., Inc.

1124 FRENCH OR NORTH ITALIAN, late 17th century.

1125 LOUIS XIV, second half of 17th century. Gilded wood frame upholstered with Beauvais tapestry in the manner of Berain.

Metropolitan Museum of Art, Bequest of Benjamin Altman, 1913

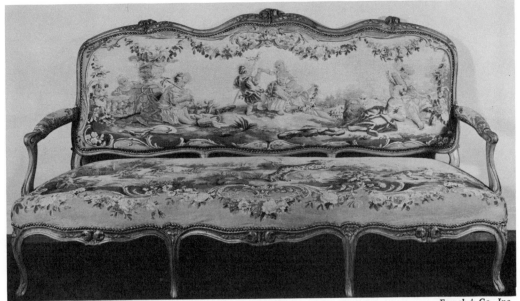

1126 RÉGENCE, transition to Louis XV, canapé. Aubusson tapestry.

1127 EARLY STYLE OF LOUIS XV. Loose cushion.

1128 LOUIS XV CANAPÉ, mid-18th century.

1129 ENGLISH, Mid-Georgian.   *Arthur S. Vernay, Inc.*

1130 ENGLISH, style of Chippendale.   *Arthur S. Vernay, Inc.*

1131 PHILADELPHIA c. 1770. Chippendale.   *Philadelphia Museum of Art*

1132 LOUIS XVI, gilded wood, Aubusson tapestry.   *Symons Galleries, Inc.*

1133 ENGLISH OR IRISH, style of the Adams.
Carved and gilded frame.

French & Co., Inc.

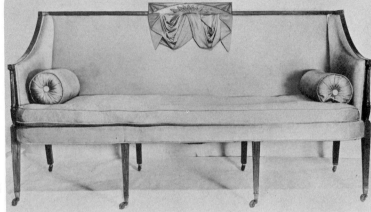

1133

1134 AMERICAN FEDERAL STYLE c. 1800.

John S. Walton, Inc.

1135 AMERICAN, Last quarter 18th century.
Israel Sack, Inc.

1136 NEW ENGLAND c. 1800. Sheraton style,
mahogany with satinwood inlay.

Israel Sack, Inc.

1134

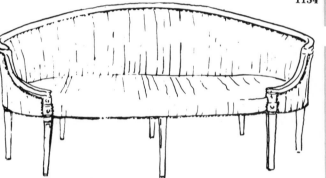

CANAPÉ ENGLISH LATE 18ᵗʰ CENTURY

1135

1136

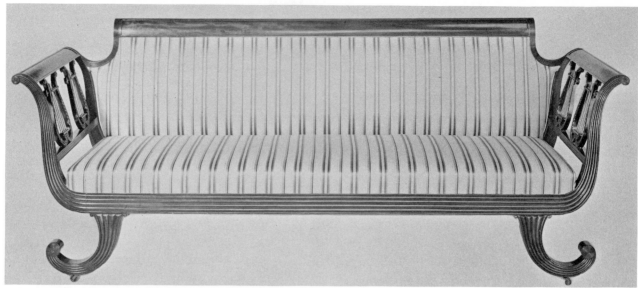

1137 NEW YORK c. 1815, attributed to Duncan Phyfe.

Israel Sack, Inc.

1138 AMERICAN EMPIRE, black mahogany,
black horsehair.   *Calhoun Museum, Clemson College, Clemson, S.C.*

SOFA by THOMAS HOPE

1139 NEW YORK, 1825-1835. Carved and painted black, gilt stencil and freehand decorations. Gold morine upholstery.   *Yale University Art Gallery, Mabel Brady Garvan Collection*

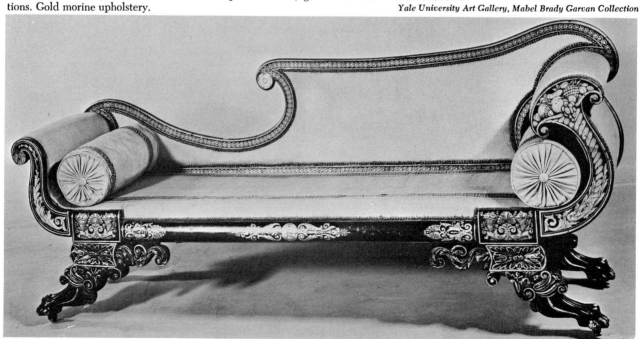

LATER 19TH-CENTURY SOFAS

1141 VICTORIAN ROCOCO frames kept to sinuous lines but failed to achieve the unity of the original Louis XV style.

1140 AMERICAN, 1850-1860. Rosewood, carved.
Metropolitan Museum of Art, Rogers Fund, 1926

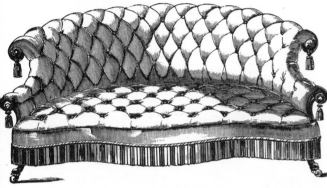

1142 ENGLISH SOFA of the eighties stressed soft tufting to the exclusion of the visible frame.

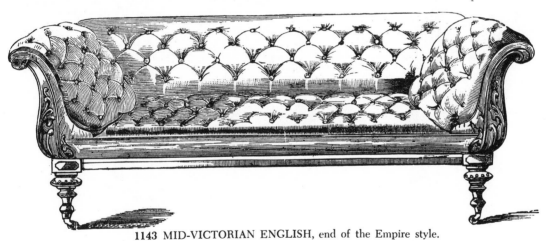

1143 MID-VICTORIAN ENGLISH, end of the Empire style.

SPAIN. The history of Spain after the decline of Rome falls into three major periods:

1. Mohammedan Spain, 700-1400.
2. The rise of Christian Spain to world dominion, 1400-1600.
3. Decline of Spanish world power, 1600-1900.

Spanish culture, following these divisions, is definable into periods:

1. Mudejar; the art of Christianized Moors, 1250-1500.
2. Plateresque: 1500-1556. The Early Renaissance.
3. Herrera, or *Desornamentado*, 1556-1600. Reaction toward severity.
4. Baroque-Rococo, 1600-1700, including the churrigueresque.
5. Cycle of foreign forms, 1700-1900.

Throughout these periods runs one fact: furniture always appears in foreign form, but always rendered in native style. The Spanish interpretation is without exception more vigorous, more masculine, even barbarous, than its foreign prototype.

1144.

MOORISH MOTIFS AND TECHNIQUES PERSIST INTO THE 17TH CENTURY.

1144. GOTHIC CHEST, 15th century, walnut.
1145 MUDEJAR CHEST, 16th century. Walnut, ivory inlay.   1146 "VARGUEÑO," 16th century. Walnut.   1147 CABINET, Indo-Portuguese, 17th century.

Photographs, Hispanic Society of America

1146
1145

1147

Metropolitan Museum of Art, Rogers Fund, 1911

1151 PORTUGUESE ARMCHAIR, 17th century. Embossed leather.

1148 WALNUT CHAIR, 17th century. **1149** 17TH-CENTURY BED, Portuguese(?). **1150** ARMCHAIR, embroidered leather and walnut. Late-16th or early-17th century.

Hispanic Society of America

1152 "VARGUEÑO," walnut and gilded iron.   *Hispanic Society of America*

1149   *French & Co., Inc.*

1150   *Hispanic Society of America*

ITALIAN AND FRENCH INFLUENCE TOOK OVER THE COURT
STYLES OF THE 17TH AND 18TH CENTURIES.

1153 SEDAN CHAIR, Rococo, late 18th century.

1156 BRAZIER, dated 1641. Walnut cased with brass foil.
Brass tray.

All photographs, Hispanic Society of America

1154 CHOIR STALL, second half of 17th century.
Cedar and mahogany. Italian Renaissance influence.

1155 ARMCHAIR, early 18th
century. Painted leather,
beechwood.

1157

18TH CENTURY
SPANISH

1158

1159

1160   *Hispanic Society of America*

1161

**CRUDER PEASANT STYLES
RETAIN A NATIVE QUAL-
ITY UP TO CONTEMPORARY
WORK.**

1157 SCREEN made of old pine
panels.   1158 VENTILATED
STORAGE   CUPBOARD.
1159 SMALL TABLE.   1160
BENCH, 17th century.   1161
SMALL TABLE, iron.

*All photographs except
1160 courtesy of
Lo Mejor de España*

Spanish Colonial

SPAIN WAS A STRONG COLONIAL POWER IN THE 17TH AND 18TH CENTURIES. WEALTH IN THE SOUTH AMERICAN PROVINCES ENCOURAGED AN EXTRAVAGANTLY BAROQUE STYLE, EXCESSIVELY AND OFTEN INCOHERENTLY ORNAMENTAL. THIS MANNER PERSISTS INTO THE TWENTIETH CENTURY IN THE MORE ELEGANT WORK.

Photos, Brooklyn Museum; Latin-American Gallery.

1164

1163

1166

1167

1162

1165

Spanish Colonial

AT THE OTHER END OF THE ECONOMIC SCALE, THE
EUROPEAN INFLUENCE SEEPED DOWN FEEBLY
THROUGH THE MISSIONS TO THE NATIVE PEASANTS.
THEY FOUND NEED FOR A FEW ELEMENTARY AR-
TICLES OF FURNITURE, WHICH THEY DESIGNED
AND ORNAMENTED IN QUAINTLY REMINISCENT
THEMES WITH NATIVE CRAFT.

1170

1168; 1171-1173 PINE FURNITURE OF NEW MEXICO,
early-19th-century influence.

*From "Popular Arts of Colonial New Mexico" by E. Boyd,
courtesy Museum of New Mexico*

1169-1170 TWO CHESTS, southwestern United States.
Scratch-and-gouge carving, 18th-century style.

Wadsworth Atheneum, Hartford, Conn.

1171, 1172, 1173, SPANISH COLONIAL STYLE.

Museum of New Mexico

1168

1169

1172   1173

1171

MUDEJAR: "Moorish inspiration." The Moors were superlative woodworkers, but required little furniture. Seats were merely cushions, tables only low platforms. The Christianizing of Spain, culminating in the expulsion of the Moors in 1492, brought European trends. A magnificent Gothic expression in architecture showed Moorish traces; in furniture the basic forms were handled with Moorish construction technique and ornamentation. Walnut was the best wood; pine, cedar, olive were used. Moorish inlaying with ivory, bone, mother-of-pearl, metals, and woods remained; star patterns and minute abstract interlacing geometrical forms are typical. The term "arabesque" springs from these ornamental bands. Color was brilliant. Leather for seats, chests, etc., was tooled, stamped, embossed, gilded, and painted. [171, 350.]

PLATERESQUE. Spain and Italy were in close touch, particularly through the Pope. The Renaissance came from Italy about 1500. Charles V ruled a vast empire, including Germany, Austria, and the Netherlands; inevitably Flemish and other northern trends were exchanged. The term "plateresque" is from *platero*—silversmith, suggesting the preeminence of the metalwork of the period.

Even the earliest Renaissance work shows no direct copying; the Italian influence was only suggested. Craftsmanship was inferior; heavier proportions resulted from uncertainty, and obvious joinery, even by nails, is visible. Polychrome painting helped cover inferior workmanship. Turned profiles are repetitious or flat, without suave modeling. Structure is supported with metal members. Walnut, pine, oak, chestnut, cedar, and pearwood are commonly used, with metal ornaments, nailheads, inlays, chip or gouge carving used for ornament.

Table forms are distinct; splayed trestles, either of turned, squared, or curved cutout members, are connected by iron stretchers beautifully wrought. Thick plank tops are braced only with cleats; edges are square cut [1220]. Chairs are of simple rectangular form [250]; the upholstery is often stretched across [1151]; nailheads are universally ornamental. The X-type chair was common, a rather topheavy version of Italian form, or a light, Moorish type of repeated slats with inlay. A ladder-back type appeared early, richly painted, rush seated, with the top slat enlarged to accommodate carving. Beds often had iron posts or head panels of decorative iron; the Portuguese influence showed in rows of turned spindles, arches, etc. [1149]. Cabinets were important; the outstanding achievement of the period is the *vargueño*, a desk box with fall front, mounted on a table support. The base often has a pair of double- or triple-turned posts with an arched colonnade between; the upper part contained many small drawers, inlaid or molded, with

some architectural features; the flap had pierced iron mounts with decorative hinges and hasp [1152]. Leather-covered chests and cabinets were studded with nails in outline designs.

HERRERA was architect to Philip II, who succeeded Charles V in 1556. Reactionary to the prevailing richness of the High Renaissance, his style produced harsh, colorless, and bare rooms; furniture was sparse and austere and is known as *Desornamentado*—lacking ornament.

CHURRIGUERA, another architect, gave his name to the churrigueresque style: a robust explosion of Baroque extravagance, under the auspices of the Jesuit Counter Reformation. From about 1600 to 1650, the Italian Baroque style was handled in bizarre Spanish fashion. After that, the French influence dominates. The furnishings of great palaces followed in general form the current styles in Europe: there are Spanish Louis XIV, Spanish Louis XV, Rococo, etc. No clear schools evolved after the 17th century; details were borrowed and assembled. Moorish traits persisted through the 18th century, in inlaying and carving; even the manner of Chippendale and Hepplewhite was so treated. Descending the social scale, the provincial types adhered even longer to the old clichés. [1220.]

Even in the period of Rococo delicacy, the interpretation was vigorous and exaggerated, instead of daintily feminine. Walnut always was favored, but painting was popular, and some mahogany was imported with foreign influences.

The late-18th-century classicism, the Empire and 19th-century eclecticism followed the European trend. Palace furniture had an imported elegance that only the grandees could afford; provincial styles maintained directness and honesty of manner.

1174 SPANISH COLONIAL STYLE.

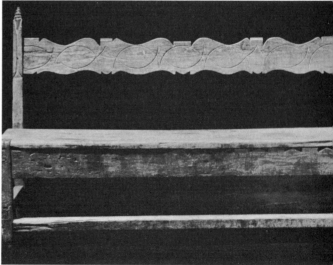

SPAN RAIL. Crosspiece between two uprights, as on a chair, bed frame, etc.

SPANISH CHAIR. English term for a carved high-back chair with upholstered seat and back, introduced into England late in the 16th century.

SPANISH FOOT. Rectangular ribbed foot larger at the base, usually with a weak scroll. [263, 561.]

SPARVER. Tester or canopy.

SPHINX. Mythical winged monster, half woman and half lion. Of Egyptian origin, it occurs in all classical schools of furniture. [86, 1071, 1234, 1346.]

SPICE CUPBOARD. A small cupboard to hold spices, etc., usually hanging. Often miniatures of floor cabinets in the 18th century. [12.]

SPINDLE. A thin turned member, often tapered or molded, used in chairbacks, etc.

SPINET Ca. 1660   SPHINX

SPINET. Early stringed instrument with keyboard similar to but smaller than a harpsichord; ancestor of the piano. Spinet cases of the early 19th century were often converted into shallow writing desks, giving form to the type so named. See also DESK; MUSICAL INSTRUMENTS.

SPINNING WHEEL. Spinning was a genteel occupation for women until the early 19th century; as the spinning wheels often stood in handsomely decorated rooms, they too, were decoratively treated. Late-17th-century wheels in England have ornamental turnings and are made of beech, yew, box, and oak; mahogany examples survive from the 18th century, embellished with inlay and ivory finials. The simple medieval types persisted in country districts and in America.

SPIRAL EVOLUTE. Continuous wavelike scrolls in a band ornament.

SPIRAL TURNING. Twisted turned work, typical of chair and table legs of the 17th century. They were often exercises in technique and were favored in Germany and Flanders. In less robust forms they are found in late-17th-century English work. [560, 631, 654.]

SPLAD; SPLAT. Flat central vertical member in a chairback. Typical developments of splats are important indices of style, such as the Queen Anne scrolled splat, or the pierced splats of Chippendale.

SPLAY. Pitch; rake; cant; outward spread or slant, as of a surface or leg.

SPLINT. Thin splits of hickory or oak woven into chair seats. Early American; persists in rustic types. [6, 1331.]

SPLIT BALUSTER; SPLIT SPINDLE. Turned members cut in half and applied to flat surfaces as decoration, or used in chairbacks as spindles where the projecting turnings might be uncomfortable. The former use is a very common decoration in Jacobean and derivative work. [725.]

SPONGE PAINTING. Primitive decorating texture, 19th-century American. See also PAINTED FURNITURE. [1175.]

1175 PENNSYLVANIA WASHSTAND c. 1830. Sponge painting, yellow and orange. *Henry Ford Museum, Dearborn, Mich.*

SPOOL BED. Most common type of turned work in America, early and middle 19th century.

SPOOL TURNING. Continuously repeated bulbous turning suggesting rows of spools. They appear early in North European work and were much used in Cromwellian and similar chairs. In America in the 19th century it was a favorite turning after the introduction of the machine lathe, and appears in all forms, both free standing and split. Table legs, bed frames, mirrors, etc., were so decorated through the entire middle 19th century. [243.]

SPOON BACK. Queen Anne chairbacks were often curved in profile like a spoon to fit the shape of the body. [270, 566.]

SPOON CASES. Boxes similar to knife boxes, but arranged for spoons.

SPOON RACK. Hanging case for spoons, found principally in country furniture in England and France. See also LEPPEL BORTIE; SIDEBOARD. [1110.]

SPOONED OUT; SPOONING. Hollowed-out surface, such as wooden chair seats of Windsor chairs, etc.

SPRING. Upholstering with coil springs originated in France during the reign of Louis XV, replacing the method of stuffing hair, feathers, etc., over webbed frame covers. They are now also used in cased form to fill cushions and mattresses.

SPRING EDGE. Upholstered edge that is supported by springs rather than by the hardwood frame. Now universally used in good lounge chairs.

SPRUNG MOLDING. Molding applied to a curved surface by springing it into place.

SQUAB. Removable stuffed cushion of chairs; 17th and 18th centuries, originating in France.

SQUARE-BACK CHAIR. The typical Sheraton chairback is square, with variations in the center ornamentation and the crestings.

SQUARE LEG. The Chinese influence gave Chippendale the square leg, which he ornamented either with vertical moldings or with panels of delicate sunken fretwork. The inner surface was usually beveled. Simpler versions, chiefly American, have only a quarter-round bead on the outer edge.

1176 SQUIRREL CAGE TIP TABLE, American, c. 1780.

SQUASH FEET. Flattened ball foot on cabinets, often carved and filleted. [1336.]

SQUIRREL CAGE. Revolving framework on top of the pedestal of a tilt-top table, upon which the top is pivoted. [1176.]

STALL. Ecclesiastical chair for dignitary or choir member. Early chairs were founded on these types. [718, 1154.]

STAND. Any small table, used for holding or displaying objects, such as shaving stands, music stands, candle stands, etc. See also TABLE.

STANDARD. Adjustable or swinging mirrors are carried on uprights called standards. Also the term for a frame that carries a table or case piece.

STANDS

18TH CENT ENGLISH   FRENCH

STANDING SHELF. Small bookcase.

STEEPLE CLOCK. Gothic Revival clock cases popular in 19th-century America. [423.]

STENCIL decoration, important in Gothic work. In American work from 1815-1860 most important as rudimentary mass-production idea. Often in lesser Empire work to simulate appliqués. See also HITCHCOCK; PAINTED FURNITURE. [327, 347, 1139.]

STEPPED CURVE. Broken curve, the parts being interrupted by right angles.

STICK BACK. Chair made up of spindles or small members, as in a Windsor chair.

STILE. Outside vertical member of a cabinet or door, which frames a panel.

STIPO (Italian). Drop-lid cabinet desk, usually tall and highly ornamented. [754].

STOCK. Bed stock, or the framework of a bed that is detached from the canopy-structure in the great beds of the English and French styles. [105.]

STOOLS. Most ancient form of seating, having neither back nor arms. Egyptian stools were X-shaped, usually folding, and having skin or fabric seat; or solid framed with rush or wood seats. The Greeks and Romans used stools extensively except for ceremonial purposes, the forms resembling the ancient Egyptian ones. The curule chair is a developed stool. Throughout the Middle Ages and through the 17th century, stool or form types were proper seating for all but the most important persons; etiquette prescribed who sat on chairs, who on stools of one type and who on another, and who stood. The side chair developed from the stool by the addition of the back. Italian *sgabelli* show the stuck-on appearance of early efforts, and little improvement appears in northern work for another century. Stools and forms were thus slowly pushed down the social scale until they were either completely rustic or, in more elegant surroundings, only for ornamental or lounging purposes. The handsome cabriole-leg types of the Queen Anne period were footstools primarily. Ornamental types were used for dressing tables, window seats, etc., and this use is now most prevalent. See also BENCH. [1177 *et seq.*]

Metropolitan Museum of Art, Rogers Fund, 1918
1179 ITALIAN HIGH RENAISSANCE (Cinquecento).

1180 ENGLISH JOINT STOOL
c. 1625, oak.
Metropolitan Museum of Art,
Gift of Mrs. Russell Sage, 1909

1178 SPANISH, RUSTIC.
Lo Mejor de España

1177 EGYPTIAN.
Metropolitan Museum of Art, Rogers Fund, 1912

STOOLS

1181 ENGLISH, Cromwellian c. 1640, oak.   *Cavallo*

Symons Galleries, Inc.

1184 ENGLISH c. 1800, Directoire influence.

Anderson Galleries

1182 FRENCH, Henri II, oak.

Metropolitan Museum of Art, Rogers Fund, 1922

1187 FRENCH, 1700-1750 (Régence-Louis XV). Part of chaise longue.

1186 CONNECTICUT, 1845-1850, Empire Organ Stool.
Wadsworth Atheneum, Hartford, Conn.

1183 ENGLISH OR FLEMISH, period of Charles II, ebonized.

1185 ENGLISH, Early Georgian.
Arthur S. Vernay, Inc.

1188 ENGLISH c. 1810, gilded. *Symons Galleries, Inc.*

1189 NORTH ITALIAN, late 18th century. *Don Ruseau*

STOPPED CHANNEL FLUTING. Filled fluting: lower part, usually about 1/3 of fluting, filled with a reedlike rounding, sometimes carved like beads. [661, 786.]

STOVE. Heating devices treated as decorative components appear in Gothic times. In Mediterranean regions, braziers [1156] were portable devices after the Moorish practice. In the North the less casual demands for continuous heat brought forth great compositions of masonry and, later, ceramics [708] and iron. Experiments with "heat machines" late in the 18th century resulted in cast-iron stoves [199], which in America especially enjoyed artistic interest.

STRAIGHT FRONT. In chests, secretaries, etc., a flat front, however decorated; differing from the convex, concave, or serpentine front.

STRAIGHT PEDIMENT. Triangular or gable pediment of a cabinet or secretary, unbroken and uninterrupted.

STRAP HINGE. Hinge with long straplike leaves, usually of iron, and common in Gothic work in England and on the Continent. [544.]

STRAPWORK. Carved surface ornament in bands or panels, based on interlacing straplike bands. It is typical of Elizabethan and Jacobean work, and was probably imported with French Renaissance and Italian and Flemish models. It also appears in much German work of the 16th and 17th centuries. [105, 549.]

STRAW CHAIRS. French chairs seated with plaited or woven straw or rush. The framework is generally turned. They originated as rustic types in Europe at an early date, and were designed with a decorative purpose after the 17th century in France. In the 18th century straw chairs were used even in the palaces, and were designed in a charming and decorative manner.

STREAKING. Irregular striping in the grain of wood, broken by mottled or cross-fire figures.

STRETCHER. Crosspieces or rungs connecting legs of chairs, tables, etc. Simple turned stretchers occur in Windsor, ladder-back, and similar chairs, usually arranged like an *H*; other types have diagonal or X-stretchers; box stretchers connect the legs in a continuous line. Greater variety on tables include Y-stretchers, double-H-stretchers, serpentine [1125], arched, and other types, distinct in the various styles.

STRINGING. Narrow inlay band.

STRIPE. Many straight-grain woods exhibit decided striped figure, such as some mahogany, walnut, zebrawood, narra, Orientalwood, and others that grow straight and tall.

STUART. The Stuart kings, James I, Charles I, Charles II, and James II, ruled England from 1603-1688, excepting the period of the Commonwealth, 1649-1660. The epoch is better divided into Early Jacobean, Cromwellian, and Restoration. It covers the transition from oak to walnut, and the subordination of old English structural forms to the incoming Baroque influence. See also ENGLAND.

STUCCO. Plaster-like compound used for molded ornaments by the Brothers Adam. Also used in decorative cabinet panels. See also SCAGLIOLA.

STUDS. Large or fancy upholstery nails used as decoration. [1151.]

STUMP. The lowest part of the tree, in which the grain produces odd figures, curls, shakes, mineral streaks, etc., which may be utilized in cross sections of veneers to make beautiful symmetrical patterns.

STUMP BEDSTEAD. Beds with neither canopy nor posts. [120.]

STYLE. Style signifies the distinctive manner of designing typical of any given time, place, person, or group. In its narrower sense it means fashion, usually a short-lived aspect of taste. Style in reference to art is always given the broader interpretation, synonymous with "school," "period"; as the Gothic style or Elizabethan, Louis XIV, Sheraton, Empire styles. It is more inclusive than the actual name; the style of Sheraton may refer to the work of contemporaries, copyists, or successors who work in a similar manner, Sheraton's designs being sufficiently well known to provide a standard or criterion of the general type. Thus the style may readily be accredited to the compiler of a book formulating its characteristics. In the case of a period name, as Régence or Queen Anne, it is a loose characterization of the style spirit of the era, but it is by no means able to be confined to the exact years of the political designation. Again, a style may be a major movement, such as Renaissance or Rococo, which is in turn treated with individual variation in different countries and times.

SUITE. The suite of furniture is a modern invention, although sets or groups of similar or related chairs were made and sold in England during the late 18th

SUMMER BED. Two single beds placed together and joined by a cornice. An uncommon Sheraton design.

SUNBURST. Figured grain in wood in which crossfire or divergent rays radiate out from a center.

SUNFLOWER. Carved or painted motif in Colonial Connecticut chests. [352.]

Metropolitan Museum of Art, Gift of Mrs. Russell Sage, 1909
1189B SUNFLOWER DETAIL, New England chest, late 17th century.

1189A SUMMER BED. From Sheraton, *The Cabinet-Maker and Upholsterer's Drawing Book* (1790): "The Summer Bed in Two Compartments—These beds are intended for a nobleman or gentleman and his lady to sleep in separately in hot weather. Some beds for this purpose have been made entirely in one, except in bed-clothing, being confined in two drawers, running on rollers, capable of being drawn out on each side by servants in order to make them. But the preference for this design for the purpose, must be obvious to every one in two or three particulars. First the passage up the middle, which is about 22 ins. in width, gives room for the circulation of air, and likewise affords an easy access to the servants when they make the beds."

century. The notion of a single motif in all the furniture of the dining room or bedroom is a pure commercial product. It is unwholesome in that it is seldom possible to stretch the same theme over several distinctive shapes and retain the original quality of the idea. [1324 *et seq.*]

SUNKEN PANEL. Sinkage or set-in panel in posts or other flat parts of furniture.

SWAG. Festoon; swinging or suspended decoration, representing drapery, ribbons, garlands of fruit and flowers, etc. Greek and Roman examples were copied in stone from the practice of decorating altars and temples with such garlands; Renaissance reproductions were both freer and more conventionalized. All styles of classic inspiration use swags, painted, carved, or inlaid in every form on all manner of pieces. Textile [1134], inlaid [1229], carved [1030.]

SWAG

SWAN. Typical motive of Directoire style, especially in Italy. Chairbacks [212], bed and chair posts, and uprights.

SWAN, ABRAHAM. English cabinetmaker, 18th century.

SWAN-NECK. Curved broken pediment of two S-curves, usually ending in paterae; a definitely Baroque concept beautifully treated in 18th-century work. [1030.]

SWEDEN. See SCANDINAVIA.

Swedish Box-Bed
Late 18th Century

SWELL FRONT. Convex curved front, as in a chest or commode or any case piece. [603.]

SWING GLASS. Mirror carried by two uprights or standards on pivots, so as to swing freely; cheval glass. [874.]

SWING LEG. Hinged leg to support a drop leaf; similar to gateleg, but lacking the lower stretcher. [1219.]

SWISS furniture is predominantly Alpine German, a well-to-do peasant style with positive Italian qualities. Native woods alone are used—pine, walnut, birch, and oak. Much carving of good quality and even more painted decoration are typical. Renaissance German influences are most persistent in chests, cabinets, and tables; chairs of three-legged *sgabelle* type are common. [244, 464, 1209.]

SWIVEL CHAIR. Revolving seat on a fixed frame, used for desk chairs, dressing chairs, music stools, etc. [540.]

SYCAMORE. Hard, light, dense wood with maple grain, but distinguishing flakes closely and regularly placed. The American sycamore is prone to warp and check; hence its limitation to interior parts. The English sycamore grain resembles maple; where curly it has more regularly parallel markings. Dyed gray, the English sycamore is known as harewood. It is properly the maple-leaved or London plane tree.

SYNTHETIC MATERIALS. Laboratory products substitute for almost every natural material successfully in varying degrees. In furniture today they are encountered as molded parts, laminates, bonding agents, finishes, hardware, surfacings, upholstery coverings and filling materials.

MOLDED PARTS. Chair shells are compression-molded chiefly of Fiberglas. They are strong, light, colorful, clean, inexpensive. Drawers, small cases and containers, such as radio enclosures, may be molded at a fraction of the cost of fabricating in wood or metal.

LAMINATES AND BONDING AGENTS. Plywood of wood-veneer surfaces may have cores made of wood chips, bonded together with synthetic materials by laboratory processes. The face veneers are bonded to the cores with similar materials. The facings, instead of wood veneer, may be sheet materials with a synthetic face in color or printed effects, designed to withstand impact, abrasion, light, moisture, etc. (laminates). Other bonding agents take the place of animal glues. Such agents intentionally emphasize resistance to

SWEDISH CLASSICISM

moisture or bacteria, or may be designed for more rapid adhesion, or other special qualities. There are contact cements, adhesives made from casein, phenolics, resorcinol.

FINISHES include a range of lacquers, paints, colorings, and surfacings employing synthetic base materials and, for special techniques and equipment, procedures from heat to electronics. Broadly speaking, these have completely supplanted the old varnishes, shellacs, and paints and their time-consuming processes.

HARDWARE. Synthetics like nylon have found use in moving parts for furniture. They may be quieter, reducing friction and wear; stronger than die castings and better than machined metals.

FABRIC coverings are in two groups. The woven fabrics of synthetic yarns like rayon, nylon, Orlon, Acrilon, etc., have versatility and quality that have been firmly established without eliminating silk, wool, cotton, linen, etc. Mixtures of natural and synthetic fibers are currently more common than any single-content fabric. Each material has special properties, and none has so far completely usurped the functions and advantages of any other. The second group is that of the coated fabrics, largely vinyl or rubber-base application to a fabric backing. These are embossed for special textures like leather, with weaves and patterns aspiring to look more or less like the natural material.

UPHOLSTERY FILLERS like polyurethane foam, foam rubber, Dacron, rubberized hair, etc., have come to replace largely the cotton felt, springs, kapok, down and feathers of historic use. No one completely answers every need, and time alone will establish their relative replaceability.

TABERNACLE. Niche or recess in a piece of furniture, such as a cabinet, for a statue or a vase. [457.]

TABLE. Tables have changed since ancient times according to the evolution of social customs, yet the few table forms remaining from Egypt are astonishingly similar to ours. These were four-legged types, the use of which we can only surmise. In Greece and early Rome, tables suggest altars in shape, and probably that was their original use. Later, Rome had bronze pedestal tables and tables with carved slab sides. Both shapes were prototypes for Renaissance styles. Prior to that, Gothic tables were cruder, based on trestle forms; they were really not essential in the Gothic scheme, as dining was done off boards temporarily set on trestles. Other tables of ceremonial or ecclesiastical significance were adapted to general purposes as the need arose. Italian tables of the 15th century are trestle types, elaborated by means of

turning. Long narrow types used in the monasteries have remained to be known as refectory tables. Other specialized types appeared from this time on, as the amenities of living increased.

CONSOLE TABLES are more decorative side tables probably designed originally as architectural compositions. At first symmetrical, they ceased to be decorated on the side against the wall; finally the emphasis was permitted to be entirely on the front. In some cases this necessitated their being fastened to the wall.

DINING TABLES. Expanding types appeared in Italy, France, and England early in the 16th century, the draw top being commonest. Drop-leaf and center-opening tables are known from the 16th century. The ultimate development came in 18th-century England when social usage in general changed so rapidly. Continental Europe took its table forms from England after that.

DRESSING TABLES appeared commonly about the end of the 17th century. The luxury of the period in England and France encouraged their development in many varieties. Men made much of dressing tables in England and France, and for over a century much ingenuity was expended on arrangements of mirrors, lighting, etc. The "Beau Brummels" of England and the *poudreuses* of France are outstanding types.

SIDE TABLES. Tables with fixed tops were used along the walls of dining rooms to assist in the service after 1700. Earlier types, developed from simple frames, had carried chests with linens, silver, liquor, utensils, etc. From these evolved the serving tables, buffets, lowboys, etc., not identical with tables in form.

WORK AND GAME TABLES in various forms appeared with the rise of fads for needlework, painting, etc., late in the 17th century. Whole families of small tables for sewing, tea service, drawing, reading, games, etc., came under this heading. The types are not necessarily distinct, so that few forms have special characteristics, and all types today are adapted, scaled up or down, or revised for any purpose desired.

WRITING TABLES OR FLATTOP DESKS developed from ordinary tables by the addition of drawers under the top. They are also known as library tables.

1190 EGYPTIAN, 1600-1500 B.C., wood.
Metropolitan Museum of Art, Rogers Fund, 1912

Metropolitan Museum of Art, Gift of George Blumenthal, 1941

1191 LATE GOTHIC, northern Europe, 16th century.

Wadsworth Atheneum, Hartford, Conn.

1194 NEW ENGLAND, 1670-1690. Bulbous turning recalls Tudor design. Oak.

1192 ITALIAN TILT-TOP, 16th century, walnut.

Metropolitan Museum of Art, Rogers Fund, 1913

1195 FLEMISH, 17th-century twist turning.

Metropolitan Museum of Art

1193 FRENCH, early 17th century, walnut.   *Don Ruseau*

1196 AMERICAN, 1690-1700. Trumpet-turned, dovetailed corners. Inlaid stone top may be imported.

Metropolitan Museum of Art

TABLE 420 TABLE

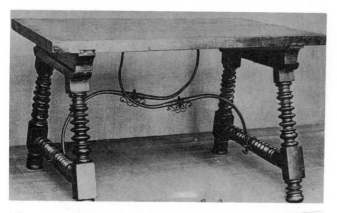

1197 SPANISH, 17th century, walnut. *Hispanic Society of America*

1198 FLORENTINE WALNUT, 16th century.

Metropolitan Museum of Art, Fletcher Fund, 1949

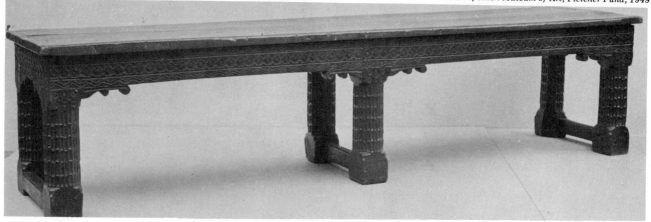

1199 ENGLISH REFECTORY, period of Henry VIII, oak, twelve feet long.

1200 ENGLISH, Italian influence, c. 1660.
Stair and Company, Inc.

1201 TUDOR DRAW TOP.

Metropolitan Museum of Art, Fletcher Fund, 1923

1202 TUSCAN WALNUT REFECTORY, plank top. Early 16th century.

THE TRESTLE FORM FOR DINING PREVAILED IN THE MIDDLE AGES. ORNAMENTAL VARIATIONS LIKE THE SLAB SIDE, SAWBUCK, AND MELON-TURNED PEDESTAL APPEARED AFTER THE 15TH CENTURY THROUGHOUT EUROPE.

1203 ITALIAN, vase-shaped slab side, 16th century.

1204 VENETIAN, 1610-1640. Carved slab.

1205 *Right.* SPANISH, 17th century.

Hispanic Society of America

1206. *Bottom.* ENGLISH, Tudor oak, 17th century.

Stair and Company, Inc.

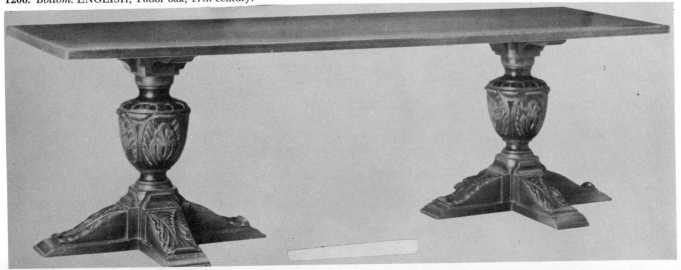

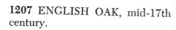

DRAW-TOP TABLES

1207 ENGLISH OAK, mid-17th century.

Stair and Company, Inc.

1208 ENGLISH c. 1600. Tudor with Early Renaissance detail.

Stair and Company, Inc.

1209 SWISS, 17th century. Walnut and applewood.   *Metropolitan Museum of Art, Rogers Fund, 1907*

TABLE   423   TABLE

1210 FRANCE, 16th century, Renaissance. Walnut.   *Philadelphia Museum of Art*

THE DRAW TOP MET THE NEED FOR AN EXPANDING TOP IN THE 16TH CEN-
TURY, DEVELOPED ON THE FOUR-LEGGED OR SLAB-SIDE BASE, WEIGHTED TO
BALANCE INCREASED LEVERAGE. THE WEIGHT FACTOR TENDED TO GET OUT
OF HAND. THIS STYLE REACHED A HIGH POINT IN TUDOR ENGLAND.

1211 DUTCH, 17th century. Oak.   *Metropolitan Museum of Art, Rogers Fund, 1913*

1212 NEW YORK c. 1800. Classical type of two half-round console sections tied with center drop-leaf section. Owned by Robert Fulton.   *Museum of the City of New York*

EXTENSION IDEAS FLOWERED IN THE 19TH CENTURY

1213, 1213A, 1213B

1213, 1213A, 1213B PHILADELPHIA c. 1810. Accordion center supports carried inserted leaves.   *Israel Sack, Inc.*

TABLE

1214

Israel Sack, Inc.

Stair and Company, Inc.

1214 ENGLISH c. 1620. Sawn oak, baluster shape. **1215** ENGLISH, mid-17th century. Oak, turned posts, trestle foot. **1216** PENNSYLVANIA c. 1710. Walnut, classic turned legs as made in England a century earlier.

1217 FRENCH GATELEG TABLE, Louis XIII, mid-17th century. Walnut.

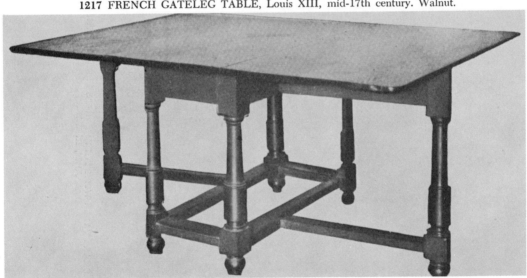

GATELEG TABLES BEGIN WITH THE EARLIEST FOLDING PORTABLE FORMS. AFTER THE 15TH CENTURY A NEED FOR EXPANDING PORTABLE TABLES AROSE AS ROOMS BECAME SMALLER. THE GATELEG REACHED ITS CLIMAX ABOUT 1700 IN VERY LARGE CONSTRUCTIONS WITH TWELVE LEGS. OTHER EXPANSION IDEAS APPEARED IN THE 18TH CENTURY, SUCH AS THE SWING LEG WITH NO STRETCHERS.

1219 NEW YORK c. 1770. Swing leg, Chippendale style.
Metropolitan Museum of Art, Bequest, 1933, in memory of Salem Towne Russell

1218 ENGLISH c. 1810. Oval swing leg, wood hinges, mahogany.

1220 SPANISH, rustic.   *Lo Mejor de España*

1221 SPANISH, 17th century.   *Hispanic Society of America*

1222 FRENCH, Régence. Hoof foot and curvature of legs, fore-shadowing cabriole, and elaborate stretcher indicate softening of Louis XIV lines into transitional Régence.

French & Co., Inc.

1223 ENGLISH c. 1730. Height of French Baroque influence. Developed cabriole shape is still a scroll leg.

Victoria and Albert Museum, Crown Copyright

1224 ENGLISH, George II. Marble top on gilded base.   *French & Co., Inc.*

1225 ENGLISH, Adam. These types served as buffets, often in composition with end cabinets or pedestals.   *French & Co., Inc.*

1226 FRENCH, Louis XVI, attributed to Salembier. Console form.   *French & Co., Inc.*

1230   1227

SMALLER SIDE TABLES FLOURISHED AFTER THE
18TH CENTURY, FUNCTIONING AS SERVERS, WRITING
AND DRESSING TABLES, CONSOLES, OR MERE
DECORATION

1227 LOUIS XIV. Side table sometimes called *desserte*. Marble
top, brass banding.   *French & Co., Inc.*

1229 ENGLISH, decorated Sheraton.   *Symons Galleries, Inc.*

1230 ENGLISH PIER TABLE, end of 18th century. Decorated satinwood, marble and bronze.
        Metropolitan Museum of Art, Gift of Louis J. Boury, 1932

1231 AMERICAN EMPIRE, 1800-1820. Marble top and
columns, ormolu and gilded carved wood.
                     Museum of the City of New York

1232 ENGLISH REGENCY, 1825-1850. Mirror back.
                     Needham's Antiques, Inc.

1229

1232

1231

1234 AMERICAN, Early Empire.
Ginsburg and Levy

1233 ENGLISH c. 1800, Sheraton, with swinging drawer as aid in dressing or writing.
Needham's Antiques, Inc.

1235 MARYLAND c. 1760, Chippendale style. Game or breakfast table, Pembroke type; arched stretcher. **1236** ENGLISH c. 1790. Sheraton, inlaid satinwood. **1237** NEW YORK, end of 18th century. Style of Phyfe. **1238** ENGLISH REGENCY, early. Drop leaf, mahogany banded with rosewood and satinwood.

1236   *Symons Galleries, Inc.*

1238   *French & Co., Inc.*

1235   *Israel Sack, Inc.*

1237   *New-York Historical Society, New York City*

TABLE   430   TABLE

Wine and Drinking Tables

1239, 1239A ENGLISH c. 1790, Hepplewhite style (two views). Hunt table. Brass bottle holder pivoted to serve full circle. Drop leaves on ends. **1240** ENGLISH c. 1800. Lift-out center in top exposes lead-lined containers for ice. **1241** MASSACHUSETTS, 1720-1740. Tile-top mixing table. **1242** ENGLISH c. 1800. Hunt breakfast table with fold-over top leaves carried on gatelegs.

1239   *Symons Galleries, Inc.*   **1239A**

1240   *Symons Galleries, Inc.*

1241 *Henry Ford Museum, Dearborn, Mich.*

1242

*Symons
Galleries,
Inc.*

TABLE   431   TABLE

1243 AMERICAN, 18th-century rustic with a T-base, New England. **1244** TURNED
PARTS. Virginia(?). **1245** AMERICAN JOINT STOOL. **1246** TUSCAN, 17th century.

1243

1244

1245   *Israel Sack, Inc.*   1246

1247 *Lo Mejor de España*   1248   *Don Ruseau*   1249   *Arthur S. Vernay, Inc.*

1247 RUSTIC SPANISH. **1248** RUSTIC FRENCH. **1249** SMALL DRUM TABLE, Late
George III. **1250** AMERICAN SHERATON. **1251** FRENCH c. 1800. Directoire. **1252**
PENNSYLVANIA c. 1850. **1253** EMPIRE, English c. 1815.

1250 *Israel Sack, Inc.*   1251   *Symons*   1252   *Henry Ford Museum*   1253   *Symons Galleries, Inc.*

1258   1257   *Israel Sack, Inc.*

1256
Dalva

1254
Symons

Small Tables

ACCESSORIES TO MINOR COMFORTS OF HOME LIFE, CARRIED A LIGHT OR A BOOK OR A JUG. LATER THEY BECAME MORE SPECIALIZED FOR TEA, SEWING, LAMPS, BOOKS, AS A BEDSIDE TABLE, OR AID IN DRESSING.

1254 ENGLISH REGENCY, 1812. Hinged top over padded tea caddy. **1255** ENGLISH DUMBWAITER c. 1765. **1256** LOUIS XVI, brass-framed marble top. **1257** SALEM c. 1800. Sheraton mahogany and satinwood. **1258** PORTSMOUTH, NEW HAMPSHIRE, c. 1800. Birch end table.

1259 DUNCAN PHYFE TAMBOUR FRONT, 1812(?). **1260** ENGLISH WORKBOX, Sheraton style (stand doubtful). **1261** PHILADELPHIA, 1810-1820.

1255   *Needham's*

1261   *Israel Sack, Inc.*

1260

1259   *Ginsburg and Levy*

1262 GERMAN, late-18th-century Rococo.   *Dalva Brothers, Inc.*

Israel Sack, Inc.

1263 WORKTABLE, American Sheraton.

A SPECIAL DEVELOPMENT OF THE 18TH CENTURY WAS A COMPACT BOUDOIR UTILITY TABLE, EQUIPPED FOR DRESSING, WRITING, OR SEWING.

1264

1264 AMERICAN EMPIRE, label of Charles-Honoré Lannuier.
Ginsburg and Levy

1265 NEW YORK c. 1817.
Museum of the City of New York

1265 *Museum of the City of New York*

BIEDERMEIER

Card and Game Tables

1266 NEW YORK c. 1800. Sheraton cloverleaf, folding top, label of John Dolan.   **1267** TILT TABLE with guinea holes; scroll footed.   **1268** FOLD-ING-TOP TABLE by Lannuier.   **1269** PHILADELPHIA, possibly by Affleck.   **1270** NEW YORK, 1835-1845.   **1271** NEW YORK c. 1760. Early style of Chippendale. Folding top, gateleg.   **1272** SALEM, 1790-1810. Attributed to Samuel McIntire.

1270

1268 *Ginsburg and Levy*

New-York Historical Society, New York City

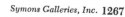

Symons Galleries, Inc. **1267**

1266 *Israel Sack, Inc.*

1274 *Israel Sack, Inc.*

1272 *Henry Ford Museum, Dearborn, Mich.*

1269 *Ginsburg and Levy*

1277 *Symons Galleries, Inc.*

1271 *Henry Ford Museum, Dearborn, Mich.*

TABLE 435

1273 AMERICAN, style of Lannuier. *Israel Sack, Inc.*

1276

Needham's Antiques, Inc.

1274 SALEM c. 1815. Regency style, folding top.

1275 FEDERAL STYLE of Charles-Honoré Lannuier. Gaming table.

1276 ENGLISH c. 1765. Chippendale, mahogany.

1277 *Left* REGENCY "GAMES" TABLE c. 1810. Reversible top; leathered backgammon surface in well.

1278, 1278A PROVINCIAL FRENCH with reversible top as above, showing detail.

1275 *Now in Museum of the City of New York*

1278 *Don Ruseau*

1278A

TABLE   436   **TABLE**

1280 FRENCH, height of the Rococo. Louis XV c. 1750.

Console Tables

CONSOLE TABLES, BASICALLY WALL DECORATIONS,
MAY BE FREE STANDING OR HUNG ON THE WALL. AS
A DECORATIVE FORM THEY SPRANG FROM THE SIDE
TABLE IN LOUIS XIV WALL COMPOSITIONS.

1279 HANGING CONSOLE, French, gilt wood and marble.
Louis XVI period.

1282 ENGLISH CHIPPENDALE, Mid-Georgian.

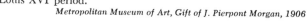

1283 ITALIAN ROCOCO, late 18th century.

1281 FRENCH, 19th-century neo-Rococo.

1285 LOUIS XVI, CLASSIC STYLE.

Metropolitan Museum of Art, Gift of J. Pierpont Morgan, 1906

1284

French & Co., Inc.

Metropolitan Museum of Art,
Rogers Fund, 1921

1286

1284 ITALIAN, 18TH CENTURY. Marble veneer top.

1286 LOUIS XV, 1760-1770. Painted gray.

1287 TUSCAN, 18th century. Walnut and gilt.

1287 *William Rockhill Nelson Gallery of Art, Kansas City, Mo.*

TABLE CHAIR. Armchair or settle with hinged table-top as the back. [3, 879.]

TABLE DORMANT. First type of table to assume permanent stationary form in the Middle Ages, in place of the usual boards set on trestles.

TABLET CHAIR. Armchair with one flat arm wide enough to use as a writing table. Frequent in American Windsor types, 18th century. [319.]

TABOURET; TABORET. Low upholstered footstool, French, 18th century (from *tabour*, a small drum). [643.]

TAILPIECE. A tongue on the back of some Windsor chair seats, designed to receive two spindles that act as a brace for the bow. [321.]

TALLBOY. Highboy or chest-on-chest, a wide low chest carrying a slightly narrower taller chest. The top tier of drawers is often divided into two or three. English and American. See also HIGHBOY.

TAMBOUR. Flexible shutter or door, operating either vertically or horizontally, made of thin strips of wood

1288 TAMBOUR - FRONT SECRETARY, American - Sheraton style, Federal period.

Israel Sack, Inc.

1289 TAVERN TABLE, early 18th century. American.

Israel Sack, Inc.

glued to linen or duck. It runs in a groove and may follow any shape. Favored in Louis XVI work, English work of the Sheraton period and contemporary American work, as in rolltop desks.

TAMO. Japanese ash; light yellowish wood with strong oaklike figure.

TANGUILLE. Red-brown Philippine wood with striped figure and soft texture, sometimes called Philippine mahogany. It is not accepted as mahogany.

TAPER. Diminishing toward a point, characteristic of furniture legs, round or square, of the 18th century. The taper produces the effect of lightness and grace.

TAPESTRY. Fabric of wool with silk or linen, usually pictorial in design. An ancient method of weaving, it came to be used to upholster chairs, etc., in the 17th century. It is therefore an appropriate type of covering for all styles of this time, such as French styles through Louis XV, English work through Queen Anne. William Morris revived tapestry weaving with his neo-Gothic style about 1880. [561, 642.]

TARSIA. Intarsia.

TASTE. In the narrow sense, as applied to furniture, an affectation of historical influence, as, "in the Gothic taste," "in the Chinese taste."

TAVERN TABLE. Low oblong table on simple framework of turned or square members; chiefly American and English, 18th and early 19th centuries. [1289.]

TEA. The introduction of tea into Europe created a fad that was responsible for changes in manners. Tea and its service was so important that it acquired a

Ginsburg and Levy
1290 TEA TABLE c. 1760. By Gilbert Ash, New York.

ritual with many appurtenances, among them a series of small tables for the service. These are known as "tea caddies," "teakettle stands," "teapoys," and "tea tables," a family of graceful, well-designed small stands. [1254, 1290.]

TEAK. Large family of Oriental woods best known for resistance to moisture and decay. They are very heavy, light- to medium-brown in color, with a straight, open grain. Extensively used for furniture in the East, and in contemporary work, especially in Denmark and the United States.

TELAMONES. Atlantes; human figures on a supporting member.

TENON. Tongue or projecting part of wood that is fitted into a corresponding hole or mortise.

TENT BED. Field bed; smaller four-poster resembling a tent, with rather low canopy.

TERM. Pedestal, plinth, or pillar, often carrying a bust or decorative figure, used as accents in decorative compositions.

TERMINAL FIGURES. Ornamental use as a finish motif of the conventionalized human figure, all or part. They are often found mounted in full relief on the pillars of cabinets, etc., particularly in Late Renaissance work of Italy, France, and England.

TERN FEET. Three-scrolled feet, sometimes merely grooved with three lines.

TESTER. Canopy of a four-post or draped bed, either of wood or fabric. [109.]

TÊTE-À-TÊTE. Small two-seat sofa or love seat of the 19th century in which the two seats face in opposite directions, the backs forming an S-curve. Also SIAMOISE. [1310].

TEXTILES. Woven materials were essential to the earliest furniture for upholstery and decoration value. Egyptian stools had seats of stretched fabrics, linen, cotton, wool, and silk, and Roman couches were made comfortable with silk cushions. European textiles of the Middle Ages were largely influenced by the Orient. China and Japan sent silks; Persian, Mohammedan, and Byzantine textiles added color, vivid pattern, and texture to the harsh medieval halls. In the 12th century weaving began in Italy, and silks and damasks and velvets came into European use in the form of hangings for beds and walls, cushions, etc. Lucca, Venice, Florence, and Genoa produced velvets and silks in rich patterns current to this day. Renaissance furniture is usually upholstered in these materials, as well as in the tapestries that were woven in France and the Lowlands, after the 16th century. Tapestry covered chairs of most English periods through the Early Georgian. Needlework and embroidery were universally used through the 17th century. Crewel embroidery is typical of all Late Jacobean work. Beds were draped in costliest velvets and silks of Italian, French, and Spanish workmanship. There were many simple weaves of linen, wool, mohair, and cotton, such as rep and moquette.

Rococo styles everywhere used the most elegant materials: silks, satins, damasks, brocade, brocatelle, taffeta, and velvet of European and Oriental make. Colors were light pastel tones; textures were refined and smooth, and remained so in fine work for almost two centuries. Rococo patterns, while small in scale, were widely spaced or rambling.

The classic revivals—Louis XVI, Adam, etc.—returned to small overall patterns in silks, velvets, and all other fine materials. Smooth surfaces were favored. The printing of material, usually cotton, silk or linen, like the *toiles-de-Jouy* made in France by Oberkampf, spread over Europe, and by 1800 was in general favor for upholstery and hangings. The Empire style reestablished smooth, plain materials in hard colors and finishes. Victorian England and America used haircloth and durable fabrics. Later, the Paris styles brought back the elegancies of the 18th century.

Modern fabrics are less dependent on pattern than on the textural interest of weaves and specialties in yarns. Rayon has added to the list of original fibers, and a new catalogue of textiles includes rayon, cellophane and a host of synthetics—even fibrous glass—woven in both historical and new patterns.

THERM FOOT. Tapered foot of rectangular plan. Spade foot.

THERM LEG. Four-sided or square tapered leg.

THIMBLE TOE. Spade foot, more often turned than square.

THIRTEEN-STATE TRACERY. Geometric tracery pattern found in 18th-century English and American secretaries, based on a Chinese motive. The coincidence of its dividing the space into thirteen divisions has led to the belief that it symbolizes the thirteen original states.

THONET. The Viennese Michael Thonet began to bend wood into chair elements about 1840, perfecting the engineering aspect so practically that his "Vienna bentwood" became one of the earliest mass-production successes. Its utter functionalism and directness of both structural and visual aims produced furniture that is esthetically outstanding. [134, 913, 1003, 1006, 1084.]

THREE-PLY. Plywood or veneered work of three layers, the grain of the two outside layers being across the grain of the center. Not practical in panels over 3/8 inch thick.

THROWN(E) CHAIR. Turned chair: old English. [238 *et seq.*]

THROWN(E) WORK. Turning, from the old name for turning, or throwing. Also "turneyed."

THUJA (THUYA). Wood of the North African arborvitae, used entirely as veneers. Burly grain and a rich brown-red in color, it is one of the most decorative veneers, and has been so recognized since Roman times. [438, 1118.]

THUMB MOLDING. Convex molding shaped in a flattened curve, like the profile of the thumb.

TILES are used principally for tops liable to damage from liquids, heat, or abrasion. They go back to Moorish work and appear early in Mediterranean lands. Portuguese *Azulêjos* are outstanding. The practice

spread to the Netherlands and northern Europe in the 16th century. Here they found new uses in stoves and chimney facings, as well as decorative inserts in cabinetwork. [1241.]

TILL. Drawer or compartment in desks, chests, etc., for money, jewels, etc. They are often made with secret locks or spring.

TILT-TOP TABLE. Tabletop hinged to the base or pedestal so that it may be tipped to a vertical position to save space or to display the decorative features of the top. The idea is found in medieval work but reached its best development in the 18th century. English usage and the customs of tea service inspired the design of many small tables. [1192, 1294.]

TIP-UP (TIP-TOP) TABLE. Table whose top either folds down like a book over the base or tips over the unfolded base. [1291.]

TODDY-TABLE. Small Georgian drinking stand.

TOE. The end or tip of a cabriole foot.

TOILES de JOUY. See JOUY; OBERKAMPF.

TOILET GLASS; TOILET TABLE. Accessories to dressing or the toilet. The use of these articles seeped down from royalty to the nobles and gentry in the 17th century, and became very common in the 18th century when luxury was the keynote of furnishing. See DRESSING TABLE.

TOLE. Painted tin, used for small articles and accessories.

TONGUE AND GROOVE. Wood joint, in which a continuous projecting member fits into a similar rabbet or groove.

TOOTH ORNAMENT. Carved ornamental repeat molding, like dentils. Also called "dogtooth." It occurs in Romanesque, Gothic, and very Early Renaissance work, chiefly in England and northern Europe.

TOP RAIL. Top cross member of the back of a chair, settee, etc.

TORCH. The torch or flambeau occurs as an ornamental motive in Roman architecture; it reappears in Renaissance furniture and again in the classic revivals of the late 18th century. The flaming torch is typical of Louis XVI ornament; Directoire decoration includes a formal torch, while the burning torch is

Tilt-Top Tables

1292 TILT—TOP with patriotic portrait inlay. Probably Albany, New York area c. 1824.

1293 SHERATON c. 1795. Breakfast table.

1294 SHERATON TILT-TOP TABLE, 49 inches by 60, end of 18th century.

1291 SMALL TILT-TOP TEA TABLE.

Ginsburg and Levy

1295 NEWPORT, 1750-1780. Secretary, school of Townsend and Goddard.

common in Empire ornament, usually in bronze appliqué.

TORCHÈRE. Stand for holding lights; developed from the Gothic flambeau, the Early Renaissance types were chiefly iron, delicately wrought. Sixteenth-cen-

tury Italian torchères were either column forms or after the Roman candelabra or *lampadaires.* Baroque types were ornately classical or twisted columns. France had great torchères through Louis XIV's reign, highly ornamented with carving, gilding, Boulle work, etc. Rococo forms were light and graceful, finally coming to be hung entirely on the walls. In England the torchère was important during the early 18th century, borrowing from French sources. Chippendale and the Adams used torchères of large classical types as decorative features, the Adams copying the Roman forms literally. French Empire torchères were likewise large and ornate, closely following antique designs. [770.]

TORTOISESHELL. Small pieces of the shell of the sea turtle used in inlays on furniture in combination with brass strips and wood. Originated by Boulle during the reign of Louis XIV and extensively copied in Germany and elsewhere.

TORUS. Bold convex round molding, usually in circle of 1/2 inch or more, sometimes flattened. See MOLDING.

TOW. Flax fiber used as upholstery stuffing in place of hair in inexpensive furniture.

TOWEL HORSE; TOWEL RAIL. Rack or framework for hanging towels, used in conjunction with a washstand in the 18th and 19th centuries. [1326.]

TOWNSEND, JOHN. Cabinetmaker in Newport, 1760-1770. Worked with cousin John Goddard, father Job, and uncle Christopher in perfecting blockfront with shell in chests and desks. See also GODDARD, JOHN; RHODE ISLAND SCHOOL. [1389.]

TRACERY. Delicate latticelike forms of bars and lines with spaces for glass or openings. These derive from the Gothic windows in which a framework within the large opening was necessary to sustain the glass, which at first was in small sections. The shapes evolved were beautifully designed within the whole opening. The principle was applied to windows, bookcase doors, etc., where large areas of glass appeared impracticable or too bare, and in the 18th and 19th centuries produced interesting variations. Chippendale developed Gothic, Chinese, Rococo, and simple geometric themes for tracery, which, like his fretwork, is the epitome of 18th-century types. Sheraton used metal latticework similarly, and the Biedermeier and other 19th-century styles developed characteristic designs.

Tracery, when it encloses glass, should, properly, actually separate pieces of glass, but modern commercial work merely uses a cutout pattern or filigree *over* a pane of glass. [148.]

TRAY. Shallow drawer, usually with a low front, or the front cut out for handhold; also an additional box placed in the top drawer of a chest for jewelry and small articles.

TRAY TABLE. Folding stand used to support a tray.

TREEN. Small woodenware, such as bowls, trays, boxes, etc., generally with minimum joinery. Archaic.

TREFOIL. Three-cusped or three-arc ornament characteristic of Gothic work. Usually inscribed within a circle. [1144.]

TRELLISWORK. Latticework in chairbacks; decorative galleries, etc. See also FRETWORK.

TRESTLE FOOT. Base, usually on a table, with vertical members or legs ending on a horizontal board on the ground; inverted T shape. [1215.]

TRESTLE TABLE. Originally, all tables were merely loose boards placed upon trestles or horses. In the Middle Ages the "dormant table" was a permanent structure of table with trestles attached; this became the fixed-table type. The trestle form survived, as distinguished from the four-legged or pedestal table, in various arrangements of posts and feet, more or less ornate, in all styles to the present. [10, 1202.]

TRIANGLE SEAT OR CHAIR. Corner chair. One of the early types of chairs of northern Europe, made of turned posts and rungs on a triangular plan. Alpine countries after the 14th century; England after the 16th. See also HARVARD CHAIR. [232, 239.]

TRIGLYPH. Ornament for a frieze, spaced at regular intervals and consisting of a flat raised surface with three grooves, or two whole and two half V-shaped depressions. Derived from Greek temple architecture and used in classical interpretations in furniture.

TRIO TABLES. Nest of three tables.

TRIPOD TABLE. Pedestal table with three out-swinging legs. A favorite shape for small incidental tables in Georgian work, particularly of the Adam and Chippendale schools. [64, 1176, 1296, 1338.]

TRIPTYCH. Three-paneled altarpiece later used decoratively; and mirror frame or decorative unit of a

Dalva Brothers, Inc.

1296 TRIPOD TABLE (guéridon) by Goutier, period of Louis XVI. *Bronze d'oré* and white marble.

center panel with two hinged leaves. Byzantine and Gothic religious triptychs on wood and ivory were among the finest artistic productions of the Middle Ages.

TRIVET. Three-legged metal table or stand used near a fireplace for warming dishes. England, 18th and 19th centuries.

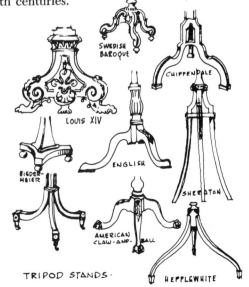

Anderson Galleries

1296A TRUMEAU, Late Louis XIV or Régence. Painted, carved, and gilt moldings.

TROPHIES. Decorative motive popular in Louis XIV and later work, especially Empire, after the classic custom of composing weapons, flags, drums, and other military symbols into a decorative grouping.

TRUCKLE BED. Trundle bed.

TRUMEAU. Overmantel treatment of Louis XV and Louis XVI style, consisting of mirror and painting. Subsequently detached and used as a decorative mirror in composition with a commode or chest, console tables, etc. [859.]

1297 TRUNDLE BED pulls out from under "stump" bedstead. American, 18th century.

Israel Sack, Inc.

TRUMPET TURNING, LEG. Turned leg with flaring profile of a trumpet turned upward. Typical of English work, Restoration period and later, and similar American furniture. See also TURNING. [14, 736, 816, 1196.]

TRUNDLE BED. Low rolling frame fitted as a bed, designed to roll under a larger bed. American and English 18th and early 19th centuries. Also called truckle bed. [1297.]

TRUSS. In furniture, a brace or understructure for tables and chest-stands, or a bracket. Usually ornamentally treated. [10.]

TUB CHAIR. Round large easy chair with wide wings. English, time of Sheraton and later. [289, 1301.]

TUCKAWAY TABLE. Compact folding table with cross-legs which fold together to permit the top leaves to drop close together. Early American modification of a narrow English gateleg table.

TUDOR. English rulers:

Henry VII, 1485-1509
Henry VIII, 1509-1547
Edward VI, 1547-1553
Mary, 1553-1558
Elizabeth, 1558-1603

Their reigns cover the last phases of the Gothic style and the introduction of Renaissance ideas. Furniture is heavy, richly carved oak. See also ENGLAND. [458, 1199.]

TUDOR ARCH. Elliptical arch pointed in the center, representative of the English Tudor style.

TUDOR ROSE. Conventionalized rose used as a symbol of the Tudors; frequently a decorative motif in English carved oak furniture of the 16th and 17th centuries.

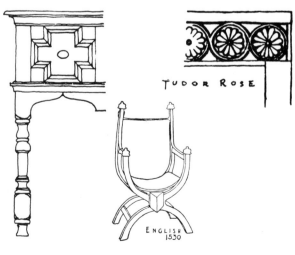

TUDOR ROSE

ENGLISH 1550

TUFFT, THOMAS. Died 1793. Philadelphia cabinet- and chair-maker; his label is known on a lowboy of simple but good style.

TUFTING. In upholstery, the tieing down of an upholstered surface by means of a button sewed through the upholstery. The arrangement of buttons and the resulting folds produce patterns in the upholstering. See also UPHOLSTERY. [1140.]

TULIP. A conventionalized flower pattern suggesting the tulip leaf and flower. It occurs both carved and painted on chests of the Netherlands, South Germany, England and America between the 15th and early 18th centuries. [11, 352.]

TULIPWOOD. Heavy tan wood with red markings, from Central America. Extensively used in Louis XV furniture.

TUPELO. Gumwood, grayish white in color, medium hard and strong, subject to warping unless carefully cut and dried. Used chiefly in lower-priced furniture as posts and face veneer, generally stained to imitate walnut or mahogany.

TURKEY. Furniture of Turkey is based on a different domestic organization and has little parallel in Western work. Beds are chiefly piles of rugs in divan form, whence the interpretation of Turkish divans, Turkish beds, etc., in various periods. Turkish chairs are softly overstuffed, and other so-called Turkish features are simply allusions to the softly cushioned effect associated with Turkish rooms. Turkish woodwork is primitive in outline, depending on complex inlays for decorative effect. It is most significant for its influence on 19th-century European work, particularly the Second Empire emphasis on upholstery.

TURKEYWORK. Embroidery work, popular in the 17th century for upholstery. Many Early American inventories list pieces so covered.

TURKISH ROCKER. Overstuffed easy chair mounted on a spring platform. Late-19th-century American.

TURNING. Turning, one of the most ancient woodworking processes, is done by the application of cutting tools to the rotating surface. The device for rotating or turning the wood is called a lathe. This is the oldest idea in woodworking machinery. Egyptian lathes were operated by a bowstring; later lathes were worked by treadles. In the Middle Ages, a form of spring lathe depended on the elasticity of a wood

lever alternately winding and unwinding a winch. Probably the earliest application of water power and, later, steam power was to the lathe, so that in all ages turning has been a convenient and direct method of treating wood decoratively. Legs, posts, feet, spindles, rungs, stretchers, etc., are most often turned. Turnings are also cut through (split turnings) and applied to flat surfaces as decoration, as in Jacobean work. [238, 538, 992.]

Almost every style has distinctive profiles in its turnings, so that the outline and character of a turning may be a key to the style. Early Italian Renaissance turnings are mostly of the baluster type, with well-proportioned fillets, etc., in the classical manner. Spanish turnings, influenced by the characteristic Moorish style, consist of closely repeated disks and ball forms, deeply and sharply incised. They also used a straight turning with collars and fillets suggesting the column form. Early Spanish and Portuguese legs were also spiral-turned, probably brought from India. Spiral turnings are a feature of Flemish work, whence it came to England as a prime detail of late-17th-century furniture. French 17th-century work shows tremendous

1297A EARLY AMERICAN TURNINGS, from Nye, Colonial Furniture (1895).

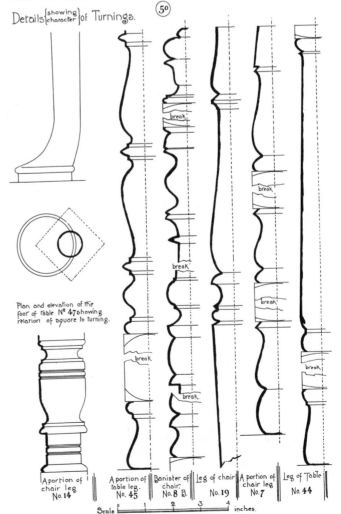

Details {showing character} of Turnings.

Metropolitan Museum of Art, Gift of J. Pierpont Morgan, 1916

1298 TURNER'S CRAFT, highly advanced; Flemish, 17th century.

variety of turnings, particularly combinations of profiles of twisted, column, and baluster forms, deeply cut disks and ball types. The most characteristic turning of northern Europe through the 17th century was the ball or sausage type, a much-repeated simple profile that is familiar in Cromwellian and American work of the 17th century. In England the large melon-bulb turning is an outstanding key to furniture of the Tudor and Stuart periods. Later, the William and Mary turnings were of unique trumpet, inverted cup-and-bell turnings, besides the much-varied spiral and composite types. The practice of carving on turned surfaces, prevalent in Early Jacobean work, reappeared in Early Georgian times, richly ornamented and fluted turned shafts forming the pedestals of tables, etc. Clustered turnings suggested bamboo in the Chinese taste, and a definite imitation called "bamboo turning" appeared in English and American furniture.

SPOOL BEDS

CANADA

UNITED STATES Ca. 1860

Turning, almost absent in Rococo work, reappeared in the Louis XVI style. Legs were invariably a sharply tapered turning with severe fillets and bands, and usually fluted. These were favored by the Adams, Hepplewhite, and Sheraton. There was a typically flared-out turning, one of several eccentric turnings; another was the country turned leg with the spoon or pad foot suggesting a cabriole leg. This appears in American work, along with the simple balusters and the vase turning typical of the Windsor chair. With the advent of power machinery came the spool turning, a monotonous repetition of a simple profile that overflowed America in the 19th century. [815.]

TURTLEBACK. Oval or elliptical boss or half-turned decoration. Common in Jacobean and similar American cabinetwork as applied decoration; also found on some Renaissance work on the Continent.

TUSCAN. Simplest order of Roman architecture. See also ORDERS.

TWIN BED. Uncommon until the 20th century. Sheraton mentions the idea, suggesting a "summer bed" of two narrow units united by an arched canopy. See also SUMMER BED. [1189A.]

TWIST. Spiral or screw turning. [129, 172, 1195.]

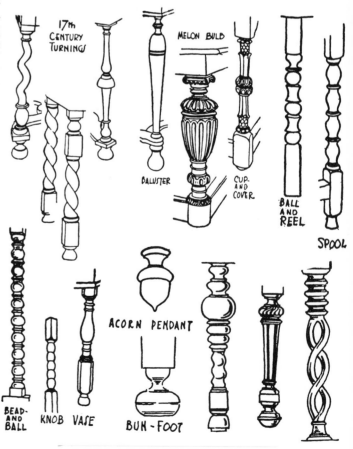

17th CENTURY TURNING

MELON BULB

BALUSTER

CUP AND COVER

BALL AND REEL

SPOOL

BEAD-AND-BALL

KNOB VASE

ACORN PENDANT

BUN-FOOT

TWIST

Hampton and Sons Catalogue, c. 1880

1299-1299A UMBRELLA STANDS, English Victorian, in iron and wood.

UMBRELLA STAND. Chiefly English mid-19th-century development of simple utilitarian receptacle into a conspicuous item of hall furniture. See also COSTUMER; HATRACK. [1299.]

UNDERBRACING. The arrangement of stretchers on chairs, tables, and stands with legs, etc., distinctive to various styles.

UNITED STATES OF AMERICA. See AMERICA.

UPHOLSTERY. Upholstering consists of stretching of textiles or leather across a rigid framework [107]. Elementary upholstering used nothing more; in Egypt and other ancient cultures, as well as in the earliest Renaissance, skins or leather were merely nailed across such a framework. Later, cushions were placed over this; finally, the padding or cushion was sewed together with the covering material. Padding was made still more comfortable by increasing the depth of cushions, filled with down, horsehair, soft feathers, wool, etc.; in the 16th century the upholstering, now thick, was further softened by the use of additional loose cushions or *carreaux*. Springs came into use in the 18th century, and with this improvement modern upholstery begins.

Springs became helical in the mid-19th century, and elaborate methods were developed to make seats more resilient. Much later flat springs came into use. The flat zigzag steel wire requires least thickness for

maximum resiliency. Modern thin-looking work is made possible by substituting for springs elastic tapes of rubberized fabric, resilient cording, and other materials to make a firm, yielding platform.

Spring upholstery requires a deeper wooden frame. Frames are best made of hard nonsplitting woods like ash or birch, securely joined with glued dowels and braced with corner blocks to resist the tension of tied springs. On the bottom the webbing is crisscrossed and stitched together. The springs are arranged over this in rows; they are stitched down and tied together in such a way as to brace them against tension from any direction. Burlap covers the top of the springs; over this is placed hair or felt, then a layer of wadding, then muslin, and finally the finish material. In much modern work loose cushions are placed over the spring seat or platform; these cushions may be filled with down, floss, hair, cotton felt, springs, foam rubber, synthetic spongy material like polyurethane foam, rubberized hair, Dacron fluff, etc. With loose cushions a special roll or stitched edge is sewed on the platform.

Like original simple padding drawn over a board, some advanced work achieves a molded effect with a thin padding of foam rubber cemented to a molding shell, then covered with fabric. In this the seating comfort results more from the shape of the shell than from the resilience of the cushioning; loose cushions of soft material are often added. Combinations of new materials and methods have created a new repertoire of comfortable sitting with great advantages of lightness in weight and appearance, cleanliness and simplicity of covers and their replacement. Comfort varies with molded chairs, since each shape is essentially a one-position design.

Historically, the upholsterer's role in movable furniture was minor until the decline of the Empire in France. The "upholder" of earlier times (French *tapissier*) was concerned with fabrics. He hung drap-

1300 UPHOLSTERER'S CARD, English, c. 1770.
Needham's Antiques, Inc.

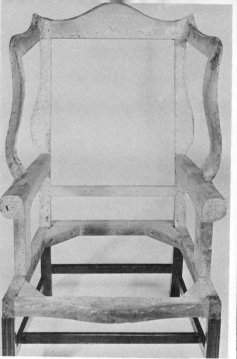

Arthur S. Vernay, Inc.

Israel Sack, Inc.

Sleepy Hollow Restoratio

1301 SHERATON EASY CHAIR c. 1800.
Firm upholstery, comfortable shape.

1302 AMERICAN WING CHAIR c. 1770.
Frame stripped to show construction.

1303 WASHINGTON IRVING'S CHAIR,
style of the French Restoration, c. 1820.
Drawer under seat.

ENGLISH VICTORIAN UPHOLSTERY, 1850-1880

1304, 1305, 1306, 1307
Hampton and Sons Catalogue, c. 1880.
Furniture Collection of the Grand Rapids Public Library

1304

1305

1306

1307

eries and tapestries, applied materials to walls, etc. His work in the 17th century was in draping the great beds. Dozens of named parts made up the ensemble. Rich trimmings—fringes, gimps, galloons, braids—supplemented embroidery [1142]. As the beds declined, chairs and sofas took over the trimmings and the fabrics. At Knole about 1610 there were curule chairs with all wood-frame parts covered with silk damask, layers of soft cushions for seat and back [1081]. The Gobelin factories supplied materials for wall and seat coverings for Louis XIV. The loose cushion became thicker as the lavish informality of the 18th century ascended. New shapes of chairs appeared as sitting manners relaxed. The stiff-backed canapé became a sofa; there were the bergère and the fauteuil, the confessional and the chaise longue, the marquise and the *gondole*, and the *causeuse*—the total expression of an age of lively indolence.

Britain followed the French example as nearly as the national temperament permitted, but the contained shape never was altogether lost in 18th-century seatings.

French interest in the Near East mounted in the period of Louis-Philippe (1830) to a craze for Turkish corners, cushions of heaps of carpets and fabrics, but French orderliness demanded separate, firm pieces. The purveyor of fabrics took over furniture design; he submerged the obvious wood structure, and found ways to make his chairs and sofas all-fabric bulks; lush softness suggested harem scenes, as dramatized by contemporary painters like Delacroix. Springing was perfected so that wire-framed shapes remained firm but yielded luxuriously. Deep tufting helped hold the fillings in place and kept the designed shape whole. Under this influence appeared many new types: the *confortable*, a completely upholstered overstuffed lounge chair; the ottoman, a backless cushion seat (in a small version it may be a hassock); the *pouf*, literally a puffy shape of a stool; the *borne*, a central island in a room, usually circular, with a middle pillar for a backrest; the divan, originally a mere heap of cushions, translated into a bulky low sofa shape with no visible framing.

Upholstery techniques in commercial practice changed little until the 1930's. The rise of synthetics created new springing, new cushioning, new covers. Some of these were developed from transportation seating, a continuous field of experimentation since the mid-19th century. Fine wire coils and mesh sheet springing and wire spring cushioning gave way after 1930 to rubberized hair, latex tapes and cords, foam rubber, and the endless list of laboratory products, more adaptable to mass production than to the old handicraft of upholstery.

The variations in quality of material, labor, and

Journal für Bau-und-Möbel Schreiner, Tapezirer,
Courtesy Cooper Union Museum, New York City

1308, 1309 GERMANY c. 1845. Biedermeier debased by upholstery.

1309

design are infinite and too complex for any but the expert to judge. The practice of advertising one or more features as indicative of quality is often misleading, and a dangerous guide to the amateur judge of values. Legislation has established certain minimums of quality and cleanliness in manufacture, but in the medium and better qualities the purchaser has no better guide than the guarantee of a sufficient price and a reputable manufacturer. [1300 *et seq.*]

URN. Vase-shaped vessel used as a decorative motive in Greco-Roman carving and borrowed in the Renaissance and subsequent styles based on classic styles. In French work it is sometimes referred to as *soupière*. It is used free standing as finials, and at the intersection of crossed stretchers, etc., particularly in the Adam and Louis XVI styles.

URN STAND; URN TABLE. Small table accessory to the tea service, Chippendale school. [585.]

VALANCE. The drapery of the tester or canopy of a bed; later the top or horizontal section of any drapery arrangement.

VANBRUGH, SIR JOHN, 1664-1726. English architect and designer, influential in the development of the Early Georgian style.

VANITY. Modern name for a dressing table.

VARGUEÑO. Spanish cabinet-desk with fall front, most distinguished furniture type of Spain, 16th, 17th and early 18th centuries. See also DESK; SPAIN. [1032, 1146.]

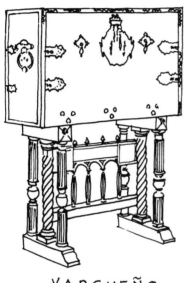

VARGUEÑO
SPANISH · 16TH CENT

VARNISH. Wood-finishing material of gum dissolved in linseed oil, applied in films or skins, by brush or spray, to protect and beautify wood surfaces. It appears to have been known to the ancients, but the secret was lost to medieval workers, who used only oil and wax which was absorbed into the wood. True brushing varnishes, using dammar or copal in oil, were probably the basis of the *vernis Martin*, but no reliable records indicate that varnish was made before 1848. Spirit varnishes or gums like shellac in alcohol, ·chiefly padded on the wood, had been known in Europe since the 17th century. At first, varnishes presented a sticky, overglossy look, but rubbing and improved quality today produces a fine satiny gloss. Varnishes for special purposes are made with tung oil or synthetic bases, like cellulose derivatives.

VASE. Ornamental vase or urn shapes after the classic sources are used extensively in Adam, Louis XVI, and similar work. Carved or painted, it is often the source of freely scrolled foliage designs. Free standing it is used as finials or decorative accents.

VASE SPLAT. Chairback suggesting vase form common in most Renaissance types; most highly developed in Queen Anne chairs.

VASE TURNING. Profile in turnery that suggests a vase with bulbous base and tapering neck. Commonly found in the leg turning of Windsor chairs.

VEILLEUSE. French type of chaise longue. Period of Louis XV.

VELOUR. Velvet or plush, often of wool or mohair.

VELVET. Fabric with soft close pile, usually of silk or rayon: velveteen is of cotton.

VENEER. The art of utilizing fine woods decoratively for their color and markings appears in earliest history [26]. Simultaneously it was realized that such use is not always consistent with the best structural advantages. The device of gluing a thin layer of decorative wood to a thicker backing for substance—the

1309A MATCHED ROSEWOOD VENEERS laid up diagonally in diamond-matched pattern in screen of Louis XV style.
Symons Galleries, Inc.

essence of veneering—goes back to ancient Egypt and Rome. It virtually disappears until the Renaissance, reappearing as inlaying, intarsia, etc., in the 16th century wherever the Renaissance influence touched. Not until the 17th century was veneering of whole surfaces practiced extensively; the invention of a finer saw permitted slicing the wood into thin sections.

When large enough sections of the wood could be successfully cut and glued, the style of veneering changed from excessive marquetry to plain surface designs. In England this transition is noted at the end of the 17th century. The William and Mary style had favored "seaweed marquetry" and "oystering." The Queen Anne style displayed the actual pattern of the wood grain in its own beauty.

In the 19th century the technique of wood veneering was improved by new methods of cutting and applying veneers, and later by the study of better adhesives, but not enough to avoid giving veneers a bad name. Until recent years there was an unfortunate literary allusion to "thin veneers" and "cheap veneers" that left a prejudice in many minds. Actually, the advantages of veneering are manifold:

1. It is the only way to utilize the beauty of the wood in repeated surfaces or to make patterns by matching the lines of the grain.

2. It permits the use of fragile woods or of cuts that sacrifice strength to beauty, as burls and crotches by backing them with a sturdy wood of no special beauty or value.

3. It reduces the cost of rare woods by yielding many surfaces per inch of thickness.

4. It provides a method of increasing the strength of wood many times, since the process of laminating veneers in successive layers at right angles offsets the cross-grain weakness of wood.

5. Shaped work, such as curved sections, when cut out of the solid are apt to split owing to uneven internal stresses; when built up of veneers these inequalities are avoided.

Modern veneering, utilizing specific glues, with equipment for proper drying and testing of wood, applying great and equal pressure, precise preparation of surfaces and joints, yields a fabricated product superior in strength and beauty to the solid wood.

Veneers are sawn, sliced, or shaved, or peeled by rotary cutting on a sort of lathe. Each method produces a different grain.

The whole log, cut into veneers, is called a "flitch." The sheets are applied in a variety of ways to produce different wood patterns—book-matched, diamond, butted, side- or end-matched, etc. See WOOD.

VENICE. Control of sea trade in the Middle Ages brought great wealth and cosmopolitanism to Venice; prior to the Renaissance her art was of mixed origins and secular splendor. Early Renaissance Venetian work shows mixtures of Eastern and European forms Her cultivated social life created furniture styles of rich individuality; with the decline of commerce came social decadence and extravagant living. Venetian furniture of the 18th century is highly ornamental, fancifully painted, and theatrical in outline. The whole school of North Italian Settecento Rococo is sometimes called Venetian. See also ITALY; PAINTED FURNITURE. [116, 300, 342, 867, 1043, 1055, 1204.]

VERNIS MARTIN. Varnish process invented by the Martin brothers in France during the period of Louis XIV. It had great brilliancy and depth, and the process was widely used. It proved to be less durable than the Oriental lacquering that inspired it. See FRANCE.

VICTORIAN. General term for English and American furniture, 1840-1900. In England, Early Victorian, 1830-1850, may include the Late Sheraton-Empire-Regency, the end of classicism; the neo-Gothic, more or less continuously after 1830 through Eastlake and Morris. Mid-Victorian, 1850-1880, covers French revivals of Louis Quatorze and Louis Seize, better or worse copying down to outright bastardization of ornamental themes; free choice motif selection from the Italian and French Renaissance, as used contemporaneously in the France of Louis-Philippe and the Second Empire; sporadic waves of nostalgia for Elizabethan and Jacobean. Currently there was also much copying of Georgian and pre-Georgian. Late Victorian, 1880-1905, takes in the neo-Renaissance and some revivals of English 17th-century work as well as Empire, and includes the reform movements begun by Eastlake and Morris. See also NINETEENTH CENTURY. [94, 124, 166, 338, 616, 877.]

The name "Victorian" is used even more sweepingly in reference to the United States, although the inspiration was more often from France than from England. The designer or artisan-designer lost identification in the process of mechanization. The great bulk of commercial output was innocent of the influence of trained designers or architects. Inspiration was freely and uncritically drawn from all sources. Divisions by period are similar to the English.

EARLY VICTORIAN emerged from the Late Empire and neoclassical styles of Phyfe, debased Sheraton "fancy" chairs, with considerable Gothic detail; mahogany favored, some walnut and maple [728, 891].

MID-VICTORIAN consistently showed a Rococo-Louis

right-hand page

1313 REST BED, duchesse type.
1314 ROCKING CHAIR. **1315** EASY CHAIR. **1316** SOFA, Rococo manner. **1317** FOUR-PIECE AS-SEMBLAGE for center group. **1318** CORNER CHAIR. **1319** UTILITY TABLE for sewing, games, etc. **1320, 1321, 1321A** VERSIONS OF BAL-LOON-CHAIR EVOLUTION.

Metropolitan Museum of Art, Gift of Mrs. Charles Reginald Leonard, 1957, in memory of Edgar Welch Leonard, Robert Jarvis Leonard, and Charles Reginald Leonard
1310 AMERICAN MIDCENTURY LOVE SEAT (Vis-à-Vis).

BRITISH VICTORIAN BEDSTEADS
1850-1880

1311 Renaissance derivative.

1312 Iron or brass, Gothic detail in tubing and stamped parts.

1313

1314

1315

1316

1317

1318

1320

1321

1321A

1319

1322 BREAKFRONT CABINET, 1860-1880.

XV basis, exaggerated scale and curvature, heavy carving of fruit and flowers, principally in walnut with some rosewood and mahogany; new shapes and types like those of the French Second Empire, with complicated seatings and lush upholstery. Machine work appeared in fancy shaping, molding, turning, veneering, and carving, applied heavily and often meaninglessly. Marble tops and fancy hardware of metal, carved wood, porcelain, etc., were featured. Black horsehair upholstery covering was a hallmark. Provincial work was simpler, some in quaint good taste, like the spool-turning beds, simple commodes, and some distinctive chairs. Elliptical shapes were more common than round.

LATE VICTORIAN began with rectilinear shapes and Renaissance details after 1870 and the Philadelphia Exposition of 1876, this phase spanning the Columbian Exposition of 1893. Superficially influenced by Eastlake, whose doctrine of simplicity was overwhelmed by machined details inexpertly combined with Oriental suggestions in incised carving, applied brackets, panels, turnings, etc., some of it was suggested by the Gothic, some of Tudor origin. Oak came into extensive use in the 1880's, eventually in the yellow varnish finish of the "Golden Oak" period. Design was almost universally a factory product, the professional designer unknown. This was the heyday of patent furniture, combinations of functions, more or less rationally, like bed-wardrobe, desk-bookcase, table-chest; mechanistic devices to save space or multiply utility.

1323 BUFFET CABINET c. 1880. Metal mounts, suggestion of Berain design.

1324 CHAIR.
1325 WASHSTAND, marble top.
1326 TOWEL HORSE.
1327 CHEST OF DRAWERS.
1328 DESK OR DRESSING TABLE.

VICTORIAN PAINTED BEDROOM "SUITE," COTTAGE STYLE, c. 1880

Catalogue of Hampton & Sons,
Furniture Collection,
Grand Rapids Public Library

1326

1327

1324

1325

In the 1890's came waves of inexpert eclectic styles: faulty essays in American Colonial, Empire, machined Louis XV, unscaled Renaissance from all sources; Japanese themes rendered in bamboo, real and imitated. There were also echoes of William Morris in simple cottage furniture that ended in the Mission style.

VIGNOLA, GIACOMA DA, 1507-1573. Italian architect who classified the orders of architecture after the standardized proportions of Vitruvius.

VINE MOTIF
(GOTHIC)

VINE MOTIVE. Conventional rhythmic band ornament. Occurs as carved decoration chiefly in Gothic style; painted bands appear in classic English and French work of the 18th century, in imitation of its use on Greek and Roman vases. [349.]

VIOLETWOOD. Amaranth or purpleheart.

VIS-A-VIS. Tête-à-tête or Siamoise sofa, in which two sitters face in opposite directions. [1310, 1329.]

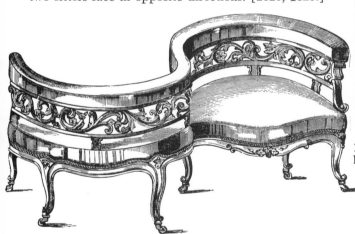

1329 VIS-À-VIS, English Victorian, 1865-1880.

VITRINE. Cabinet with clear glass door, sometimes glass sides and top, for the storage and display of china, curios, etc. [181, 1330.]

VITRUVIAN SCROLL. Wavelike series of scrolls in band ornament, carved, inlaid or painted. Also called "running dog."

VITRUVIUS. Roman writer on architecture, used as source by Renaissance designers.

Needham's Antiques, Inc.

1330 VITRINE, English Regency, c. 1810. Black-and-gold lacquer.

1331 WAGON SEAT, Pennsylvania, c. 1780. Poplar, splint seat.

Metropolitan Museum of Art, Gift of Mrs. Robert W. de Forest, 1933

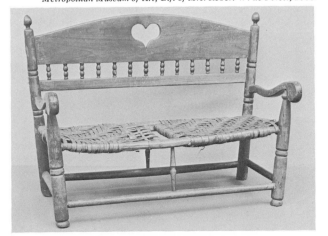

VOLUTE. Spiral scroll. Its earliest form is in the capital of the Greek Ionic order, after which it is found extensively in Roman work and all later classic styles. A Gothic form is based on plant life, naturalistic leaves curling inward. See also SCROLL.

WAGON SEAT. Crude Early American double seat on a frame, used both in a wagon or in the house. Some had splint or rush seats, but most were merely wood. [25, 1331.]

WAINSCOT. Panelwork not covering the wall all the way to the ceiling.

WAINSCOT CHAIR. Paneled chairs of French and English type, 16th and 17th centuries. American types follow the English examples. They were probably developed from the detachment of a piece of wall paneling with a seat-board attached. [8, 225, 551, 624.]

WALL FURNITURE. The classification of all pieces of furniture intended for use against the wall: cabinets, buffets, chests, cupboards, bookcases, hanging cabinets, etc.

WALNUT. Since ancient times walnut, the genus *Juglans,* has been a leading furniture wood because of its prevalence wherever civilizations have flourished, as well as its excellence and wide adaptability. Walnut has great strength without excessive weight, is hard enough to withstand much shock, yet cuts well, carves handily, and takes a fine polish. It is durable and able to resist much internal stress from moisture changes, as well as the ravages of many insects. As solid lumber and veneer it has the greatest variety of colors, textures, and figures; there are stripes, burls, crotches, mottles, curls and wavy figures, butts, etc., as well as a variety of freaks and cuts that produce interesting patterns. Like mahogany and

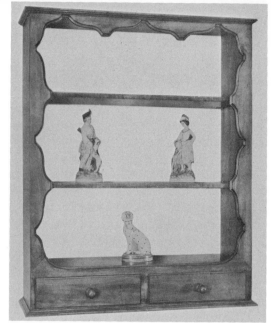

1332 WALL SHELF, American, maple.

maple, walnut has been injudiciously finished in the past; the unfortunate connotation of black walnut grows from the malpractice of dark staining in Victorian America.

The characteristic American walnut is the black walnut, one of the best in the world; moderately dark, gray-brown with a simple figure. American butternut or white walnut, lighter in color, is not quite the equal of black walnut, but a beautiful and serviceable wood. English, French, Italian, and Spanish walnuts are lighter in color, finer in texture, but otherwise the equal of American black walnut. The Circassian or Caucasian walnut is a gnarly tree whose wood shows contorted grain-markings in vividly contrasting light and dark browns. Other walnuts—Persian, Russian, Turkish, Bolivian, Brazilian (Imbuya), and Japanese —have varying characteristics.

African and Australian, Oriental or Queensland walnuts are not true walnuts, the latter being of the laurel family.

In historic times walnut occurs in furniture of the entire Italian and Spanish Renaissance. In France it displaced oak as soon as Renaissance forces came in;

1334 DANISH, 1952. Panel wall system designed by Finn Juhl.   *Frederick Lunning, Inc.*

1333 HANGING CUPBOARD, Georgian, satinwood.

Wall Shelves

SHELVES FOR DISPLAY AND UTILITY AP-
PEAR IN EARLIEST WORK, AND THEY BE-
COME ORNAMENTAL IN EVERY PERIOD.
GOTHIC AND RENAISSANCE RELICS SHOW
VARIED USES AND TREATMENT. THEIR
HIGHEST DECORATIVE DEVELOPMENT AP-
PEARED IN 18TH-CENTURY ENGLAND.
MODERN WORK UTILIZES SHELVES AND
WALL FURNITURE FOR SPACE ECONOMY
AND ENRICHMENT OF WALL SURFACE.
SPRING TENSION POLES ARE USED AS SUP-
PORTS, AS ARE CANTILEVER BRACKETS
CARRIED ON METAL STRIPS.

1335 ENGLAND c. 1860. MAHOGANY WARD-
ROBE with drawers, shelves and hanging space.
Furniture Collection, Grand Rapids Public Library

Museum of the City of New York

1336 AMERICAN WARDROBE c. 1833. Mahogany, stencil decorations.
Gothic arch panels, "squash" carved feet.

similarly it was accepted in Flanders and the Low
Countries and South Germany with the earliest Renaissance influences. In England walnut had only slight
acceptance until the Restoration. Then all manner
of craftsmen were imported, and brought with them
the preference for the wood in which they had been
trained. The reign of Queen Anne is the Age of Walnut, and walnut held sway until fashion turned to
mahogany about 1730. In America walnut was used
wherever found, particularly in Pennsylvania. [1044.]

WARDROBE. Large cabinet or cupboard for hanging
clothes. In Europe, where clothes closets are not commonly provided in the plan of the room, such wardrobes are extensively used. They are often planned
in the proportion of the old armoire. See also ARMOIRE.
[804, 1335.]

1337

1338 *Metropolitan Museum of Art*

1339 *Anderson Galleries*

Henry Ford Museum, Dearborn, Mich.
1340

1337 ENGLISH c. 1840. **1338** "ATHÉNIENNE." French Neoclassic. **1339** SHERATON, corner basin stand c. 1790. **1340** AMERICAN c. 1830. Painted and stenciled.

Washstands

WARP. Twisting or bulging of wood boards resulting from changes of moisture content within the fibers. All wood absorbs and throws off moisture, but if unevenly restrained or improperly protected it may curve or twist as the moisture causes the uneven swelling or drying of the fibers.

Also, the lengthwise threads in fabric.

WASHSTAND. Small table or cabinet holding a basin and the accessories for washing, developed during the 18th century in many forms by all designers in England, America, and on the Continent. [1325, 1337.]

WATER BENCH. American, 19th-century rustic, usually found on the back porch for the ablutions of farmhands; usually homemade of available materials, sometimes with a zinc basin, a lower cupboard for pitchers, an upper shelf. See also RUSTIC FURNITURE.

WATER LEAF. Ornamental detail based on the elongated laurel leaf. Its simple delicate form is typical of

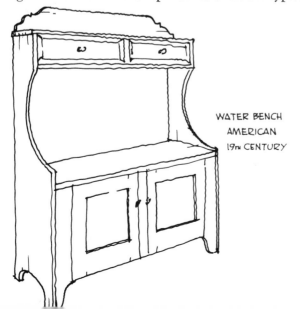

WATER BENCH
AMERICAN
19TH CENTURY

Hepplewhite, Sheraton, Adam, Louis XVI, and contemporary American work.

WATER GILDING. Thin deposit of gold and mercury on ormolu mounts.

WAVE SCROLL. Continuous spiral band decoration, also called Vitruvian scroll or "running dog."

WAX INLAYING. Wax filled into cutout patterns in wood.

WEBBING. Linen or jute bands from 2-1/2 to 4 inches wide, used in upholstery as a base for springs or stuffing like hair. The bands are tacked at the ends to the wood frame and woven across, and are then stitched together. See also UPHOLSTERY.

WEBFOOT. Grooved or carved foot of a cabriole leg suggesting the webbed feet of animals.

WEDGWOOD. English pottery ware of fine hard texture. The Wedgwoods were interested in the Classic Revival in the 18th century, and duplicated many of the antique vase forms under the direction of Robert Adam. They also made plaques that were used as inserts in the same manner as Sèvres plaques were applied in France. See also CERAMIC.

WEISWEILER, ADAM. Cabinetmaker, latter part 18th century, of German origin, who worked in France during the Louis XVI period and early stages of the Empire. [659.]

WELSH DRESSER. Cabinet with drawers and door compartments below, the receding upper part having

Arthur S. Vernay, Inc.
1342 ENGLISH ÉTAGÉRE
c. 1780.

1341, 1341A VICTORIAN WHATNOTS, 1860-1875.

open shelves for the display of china. See also SIDE-BOARD. [1111.]

WELTING. Narrow fabric edging or border of round section sewed into the seams of upholstery for finish and accent.

WHATNOT. French *étagère*. Tier of shelves supported by turned posts, used for the display of curios, etc. English 18th century and later. See also ÉTAGÉRE. [124, 1341.]

WHEAT-EAR. Carved ornament of several ears of wheat used in chairbacks, mirror frames, etc., by Hepplewhite and in America by McIntire and others.

WHEEL-BACK. Round or oval chairback with radiating spindles or bars resembling the spokes of a wheel, found mostly in later 18th-century English chairs.

WHITEWOOD. Woodworker's name for yellow poplar, although the name sometimes includes basswood and magnolia. Light yellowish color with satiny sheen; sometimes called canary wood in England. It holds paint well, and is moderately firm in structural use. Has a faint grain and does not polish well.

WHORL. Spiral scroll decoration.

WICKER. General term for furniture woven of various natural or synthetic materials, such as willow, reed, rattan, or spirally twisted paper. Particularly used in summer and outdoor furniture.

WIG STAND. Small stand, tripod, or turned pedestal fitted with drawers for materials for wig dressing, sometimes a dummy head to carry the wig. English 18th century.

WILLARD. Massachusetts family of clockmakers active 1743-1848. Benjamin established a factory in Grafton, Mass., about 1765; Simon, working in Roxbury, invented the banjo clock about 1800. Aaron worked in Boston after 1790.

WILLIAM AND MARY. Ruled England 1689-1702. Of Dutch origin, William brought a complete style to replace the deteriorating Late Jacobean. This period is marked as the Age of Walnut. Its furniture is more domestic in scale, more elegantly designed and finished, and is characterized by innovations like the cabriole leg, seaweed marquetry, the highboy, and flat serpentine stretchers. See also AMERICA; ENGLAND. [12, 14, 735, 815.]

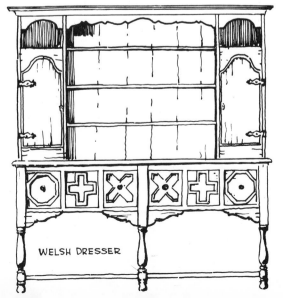

WELSH DRESSER

WINDOW SEAT. Bench with two ends, as arms, or a small backless settee used in the embrasure of a window. Fine types in 18th-century English work; also found in French and Italian styles after 1750. The deep reveal of early buildings provided an inviting place to sit; particularly true in northern countries where the walls were thick and the windows small; Gothic and Renaissance window seats were functional and much used. Fine types are found in 18th-century England, France, Italy, and America, after 1750. [1343.]

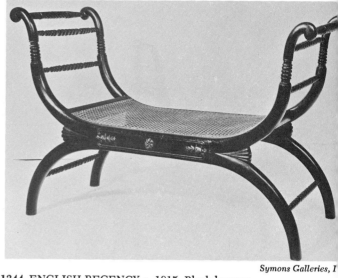

Symons Galleries, I

1344 ENGLISH REGENCY c. 1815. Black lacquer.

1345 REGENCY MAHOGANY c. 1805.   Symons Galleries, I

1343 ENGLISH, "French taste," c. 1775.   Needham's Antiques, Inc.

1346 By LANNUIER c. 1815. Mahogany, black and gold
Maryland Historical Society

WINDSOR. Style of chair using bentwood back frame and wood seat with the legs pegged directly into the seat instead of being framed with aprons. The type seems to have originated around Windsor Castle in England between 1700 and 1725, and appears always to have been made by wheelwrights or turners rather than by cabinetmakers. It is likely that they attempted to imitate the finer Queen Anne chairs with rustic attempts at round backs and splats; the English Windsor usually has a pierced slat flanked by turned spindles suggesting wheel spokes. The legs were invariably splayed, as often cabriole as turned [528, 1347]. The American colonists carried the Windsor to its ultimate development, producing a chair of the utmost strength, comfort, lightness, and ease of manufacture. The first Windsors appeared around Philadelphia after 1725; by 1760 they were the predominant chairs for common use. They appeared in infinite variations of comb back, fan, hoop, and bow backs, made in combinations of woods. The saddle-shaped seat was generally of thick pine, sometimes of soft birch. The bent members were beech, hickory, ash, or birch, and the turned parts were maple, ash, birch, oak, or beech. They were often painted or left in the raw wood. The notion was later extended to settees [17, 1088, 1350]; beds, tables, etc. [314 *et seq.*] Windsors are now found occasionally with upholstered seats, and there is evidence that this was the pristine condition. Normally the saddle-shape modeling of the thick seat (elm in England, pine in America) is a vital point of a good Windsor. When the seat is quite flat with straight sides and there are signs of tack marks, authorities conclude that padding was applied. [1349.]

Needham's Antiques, Inc.

1348 ENGLISH, late 18th century. Bent stretcher.

1349, 1349A AMERICAN c. 1770(?) One-piece back and arms. Detail: upholstery over unshaped seat.

Collection of Mrs. Samuel Schwartz

1347 ENGLISH, walnut, Early Georgian. Seat shaping significant.

Arthur S. Vernay, Inc.

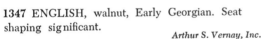

AMERICAN WINDSOR TURNINGS

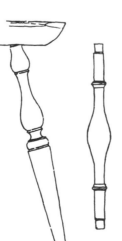

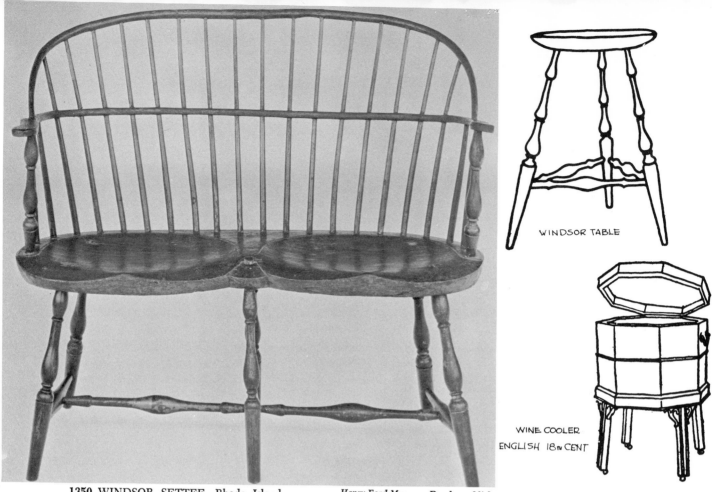

WINDSOR TABLE

WINE COOLER
ENGLISH 18th CENT

1350 WINDSOR SETTEE, Rhode Island,
1750-1800.

Henry Ford Museum, Dearborn, Mich.

The basic Windsor idea of legs stuck into a wood seat persisted in country work in England and America throughout the 19th century. In the United States particularly, it then evolved into the simplest form of everyday chair with only the two front legs so treated, the back legs and upper back being a mixture of every known theme. [81, 334, 335, 530.]

WINE COOLER. Metal-lined tub for wine service, decoratively treated in the 18th-century English styles. [1351, 1352.]

1351

Metropolitan Museum of Art, Rogers Fund, 1924

1352 WINE COOLER, English, Adam style, 1770-1780. Mahogany.

1351 NEW YORK c. 1820. Mahogany wine cooler.
Museum of the City of New York

WINE SIDEBOARD. Cabinet fitted to hold wines for imminent use. [1353, 1354.]

WINE TABLE. Horseshoe-shaped table for the serving of wine. English after 1750. See also HUNT TABLE. [1239.]

WING. Projecting side of a piece of furniture.

WING BOOKCASE. Breakfront, the receding side portions suggesting the wing form.

WING CHAIR. Comfortable large chair with side pieces, usually overstuffed. The general type existed in France as the "confessional," but the usual implication is the type evolved in England and America after 1750. [261, 1302.]

WINGED CLAW. Heavy couch foot used in Empire sofas and other heavy pieces. [542.]

WINTHROP. Slant-top desks are colloquially called Governor Winthrop secretaries, for no good reason. See also DESK.

1354 WINE SIDEBOARD, French, c. 1760. Crotch mahogany grain in exquisitely proportioned panels.

THE AMENITIES OF WINE SERVICE BROUGHT INTO BEING SOME UNIQUE FURNITURE DESIGNS—SIDEBOARDS, SERVERS, COOLERS, TABLES, CABINETS, ETC.—AT A TIME WHEN THE WHOLE LEVEL OF FURNITURE REACHED HEIGHTS OF SOPHISTICATED ELEGANCE.

1353 ENGLISH c. 1780. Serpentine front wine sideboard.
Arthur S. Vernay, Inc.

1354A

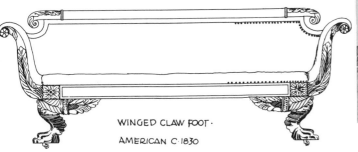

WINGED CLAW FOOT·
AMERICAN C·1830

1355 THE PARTS OF THE TREE, AND CUTTING METHODS.

WOOD. Wood has always been the basic material for furniture; it has in fact never had a serious rival. Its preeminence is the result of many virtues:

1. Various woods are readily available wherever conditions have favored human living.
2. It is among the strongest of organic materials, and stronger for its weight than other materials. It offers a variety of strengths and weights for different structural and decorative uses.
3. It is easily worked; it grows in convenient sizes; it cuts easily with simple tools; it can be agreeably surfaced with no great labor.
4. It can be joined together in many ways: nailed, glued, joined, etc. (see JOINERY).
5. It is agreeable to the touch; it feels good. Being a poor conductor of heat, its temperature is less startling than that of other materials.
6. It produces less noise under impact than other materials of equivalent strength.
7. It is relatively light in weight.
8. It may be easily repaired when broken or injured.
9. It possesses intrinsic beauty in infinite variety of color, texture, and pattern; it can be worked in many ways to exploit and enhance this beauty.

Selection of woods and grains; matchings of veneers and other methods of accentuating the grain; various methods of finishing, polishing, etc., to bring out and preserve these qualities, offer a range of beautiful effects unique to wood and to wood alone.

The disadvantages of wood are largely the result of its organic nature.

1. The fibers of wood are capable of absorbing and losing moisture according to the humidity of the surrounding air. This causes cracking, swelling and shrinking, warping or twisting, checking or surface cracking. The remedy lies in: (*a*) the careful growth and selection of grains for various uses; (*b*) proper drying, both by air and applied heat in kilns; (*c*) the protection of the wood from too sudden changes of temperature and humidity, by coating with a resistant film like varnish, lacquer, etc. (see FINISH); (*d*) fabrication of wood into plywood (see PLYWOOD).
2. It is inflammable. Wood can be chemically treated to resist fire, but the process is costly and used only rarely.
3. It is subject to attack by worms and insects. Various treatments and finishes afford more or less protection.

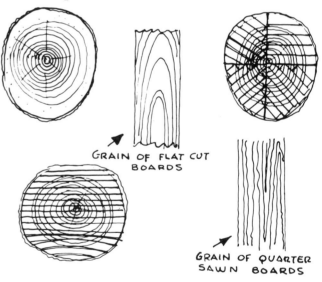

GRAIN OF FLAT CUT BOARDS

GRAIN OF QUARTER SAWN BOARDS

The grain of wood is exhibited by cutting cross sections in various ways through the fibers, the arrangement of which is different and distinctive in every wood, as well as in different logs of the same wood, and different parts of the same tree. Thus, woods present different appearances according to: (*a*) botanical variety, (*b*) method of cutting the log, (*c*) part of the tree from which it is cut.

The typical structure of wood consists of long fibers, differently placed in different woods, but always in concentric rings out from the center of the tree. These rings are the results of alternate growth and dormant periods in the seasons; they are called "annual rings," and indicate the age of the tree. There are also radial lines—"medullary" or "pith rays"—that cross the annual rings. The combinations of these rings, as well as the size and arrangement of the fibers, are infinitely complex and variable, but assume definite character in the different woods, by which the woods are identified. Oak, for example, has a coarse, open-grained texture; the pores are large and the pith rays so distinct as to be known as flakes. In maple, on the other hand, the fibers are so fine and close that the surface of the wood is silky smooth. Straight grains or comb grains are common to some varieties, while other figures are known as curly grain, mottled, fiddleback, blister, bird's-eye, etc.; more specialized are beeswings, rope figures, quilted, roe, raindrop, plum pudding, broken stripes, swirls, etc. Color is likewise a distinguishing factor of the species. The pigment may be evenly distributed, as in mahogany, or may be strikingly contrasting between the heartwood and the sapwood, as in birch; it may also be arranged contrastingly in the annual rings, causing a strong stripe figure, as in zebrawood. Pigment may also be deposited irregularly by stains from decay or injury that produce an erratic interesting pattern when cut through.

There are several ways of cutting the log that produce various figures. A board cut through the middle of the whole log will show straight comb stripes on the outer sides while the midsection will appear as a more irregular figure. Such a board is called "plain sawed." When the log is first cut into quarters, then sawed into boards at approximately right angles to the concentric rings, it is called "quarter sawed." Each method produces its distinct grain, with separate properties and uses.

In cutting veneers there are many processes that produce highly varied figures. The oldest method of *slicing* veneers yields a grain similar to the long grain; it can be cut at any angle between the flat grain and the quarter. *Sawed* veneers show the same tendencies. *Peeled* or *rotary-cut* veneers are literally unrolled from the log by rotating the log against a long knife. The grain appears very actively figured. Cross sections of small limbs used whole in veneering are known as "oystering"; these odd designs of concentric circles were favored in late-17th-century English work. Knots are utilized as a decorative feature, particularly in cedar and pine.

The part of the tree from which the wood is cut is readily classified. The *long grain* is the best and commonest all-purpose wood; the fibers being straightest, the wood is strongest. Decorative grains are cut

from other parts. The *crotch*, where the tree forks into two limbs, produces a vivid irregular V-shaped grain, sometimes with markings described as plumes or feathers, cross fire, etc. The *swirl*, or the outside of the crotch-block, is very irregular, but lacks the V-shape of the crotch figure. The *butt* or *stump* figure, cut from the base of the log where it spreads horizontally toward the roots, is also a slightly V-shaped figure, often with smaller cross rays, curls, etc. The *burl* is a tumor or wart, an erratic wild growth anywhere on the tree, which shows a finely pitted or gnarly figure in cross section of most woods. *Bird's-eye*, an erratic, spotty figure occuring chiefly in maple, is formed by the growth of buds too deep to break through the bark. *Curly* or *wavy* figures are an unexplained phenomenon in which more or less fine cross stripes appear at right angles to the long grain; they may be partially the result of the swaying of the tree. Different in fineness of the curl are the fiddleback, roll, and blister figures.

The selection of woods best suited to structural or decorative uses is a matter of expert knowledge as well as of choice. The distinction between softwood and hardwood is not always correctly used; many properly called softwoods are physically harder than some hardwoods. Actually, the term "softwood" may be applied only to evergreen or nondeciduous trees, such as pine, hemlock, fir, spruce, etc. All deciduous or leaf-shedding trees are hardwood whether the wood is as soft as basswood and poplar or as hard as maple or oak. The leading American woods of general structural value in furniture are walnut, oak, maple, birch, cherry, gumwood, pine; less used except for specialized purposes are beech, chestnut, poplar, basswood, ash, fir, elm, magnolia, butternut, cottonwood, redwood, spruce, cedar, sycamore, cypress. These are used both as veneers and as solid lumber. Of the imported woods, mahogany is by far the best and most commonly used, its vast range of hardness and strengths, color and figure lending it to almost every purpose. Others frequently used both as lumber and veneers are rosewood, primavera, avodire, European and tropical walnuts, holly, ebony, sycamore, satinwood, eucalyptus, pear, teak, tulip, zebra, amaranth, koa, vermilion. Almost exclusively used as veneers are amboyna, snakewood, yew, thuja, olive, kingwood, myrtle, acacia, laurel, cocobolo, box, sandalwood, laburnum, and a vast list of more or less similar varieties. There is considerable confusion and obscurantism in the nomenclature of these woods, resulting from confusion of identification, local or foreign names, the ambiguity of trade promotions, and the effort to disguise a familiar wood with its botanical or literary name, etc.

1356 WEST INDIAN MAHOGANY, flat cut.   1357 ZEBRAWOOD.   1358 BRAZILIAN ROSEWOOD.

CHARACTERISTIC WOOD GRAINS

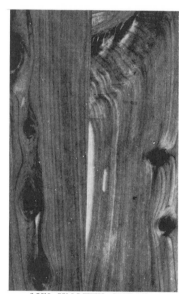

1359 KNOTTY CEDAR.   1360 MAPLE, bird's-eye figure.

1361 CUBAN MAHOGANY, plum-pudding figure.   1362 MAHOGANY, fiddleback figure.   1363 MAHOGANY, broken stripe.   1364 MAHOGANY, rope figure.   1365 MAHOGANY, mottle figure.

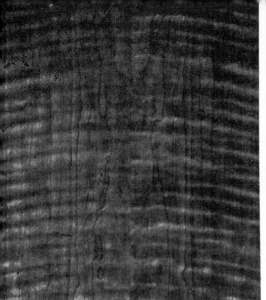

1366 CHERRY, curly figure.

1367 WALNUT, sliced, pin knotty.

1368 WALNUT, narrow heart, sliced.

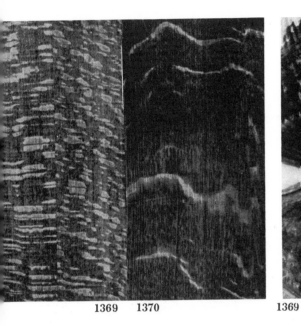

1369 LACEWOOD figure due to prominent pith rays or flakes, as in oak.

1370 WHITE OAK, flake figure.

1371 WALNUT, four-piece match butt.

1369   1370

1369

1372 WALNUT, crotch swirl.

1373 WALNUT, feather crotch.

1373A WALNUT, stumpwood (butt).

Writing Tables

ALMOST ANY TABLE CAN FUNCTION AS A
DESK OR WRITING TABLE. IT BECOMES
SPECIALIZED BY THE ADDITION OF
DRAWERS OR RACKS. THE FRENCH *BU-
REAU PLAT* AND ENGLISH LIBRARY TABLE
TEND TO BE LARGE ENOUGH TO USE FOR
LARGE FOLIOS, PRINTS, AND ENGRAVINGS.

1374 SPANISH, early 17th century. Walnut;
drawers faced with red velvet. *Anderson Galleries*

1375 FRENCH, 1650-1680. Writing table by
Boulle. *Victoria and Albert Museum, Crown Copyright*

1376 "BUREAU PLAT,"
Louis XIV. Inlaid wood,
ormolu mounts.

Dalva Brothers, Inc.

1377 LOUIS XV.
Dalva Brothers, Inc.

1378 "BUREAU PLAT" with cartonnière;
Louis XIV–Régence.
*Metropolitan Museum of Art, Gift of J. Pierpont Morgan,
1906*

Frick Collection

1379 LOUIS XVI.

From "Chinese Household Furniture" by George N. Kates, courtesy Dover Publications

1381 *Top right.* CHINESE, brass and copper mounts on polished dark wood.

1383 HEPPLEWHITE SERPENTINE FRONT c. 1780.   *Needham's Antiques, Inc.*

Brunovan, Inc.

1380 *Top left.* Italian Directoire c. 1800. Drop front, writing drawer.

Writing Tables

1382 "CARLTON HOUSE" DESK, English, 1780-1790.

Frank Partridge, Inc.

Needham's Antiques, Inc.

1384 *Top left.* SHERATON DRUM TABLE c. 1790.

1385 *Top right.* CHIPPENDALE RENT TABLE c. 1770.

Needham's Antiques, Inc.

1386 *Center.* KNEEHOLE DESK c. 1780. Nest of pigeonholes drops to flush top. Maker's label, "Seddons." *Needham's Antiques, Inc.*

1387 OVAL DESK with slides, Hepplewhite design. Label, "Wright & Mansfield." *Symons Galleries, Inc.*

1389 BLOCKFRONT KNEEHOLE DESK, attributed to John Townsend, Newport, Rhode Island, c. 1770.

1388 RHODE ISLAND BLOCKFRONT c. 1770.

1390 CHIPPENDALE SCHOOL c. 1755. "Four-way" pedestal writing table, black leather top.

Symons Galleries, Inc.

1392 REGENCY, 1810-1820. Rosewood inlay, unusually shaped drop-leaf.

1391 ENGLISH c. 1780. Kidney-shaped kneehole writing table.

Symons Galleries, Inc.

1393 NEW YORK, Sheraton style. Probably by Major Pierre L'Enfant for the first Congress of the United States in Federal Hall, 1789.

New-York Historical Society, New York City

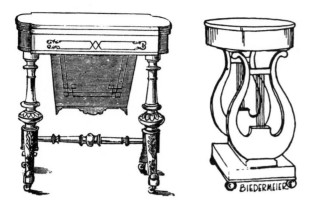

BIEDERMEIER

WORKTABLES in various forms appeared with the rise of fads for needlework, painting, etc., late in the 17th century. Whole families of small tables for sewing, tea service, drawing, reading, games, etc., came under this heading. The types are not necessarily distinct, so that few forms have special characteristics and all types today are adapted, scaled up or down, or revised for any purpose desired. See also BAG TABLE; DAVENPORT; READING STAND; SEWING TABLE; TABLE.

WREATH. A classical motive, chiefly Roman, which recurs in the Renaissance and all later revivals of the classical style. Early Renaissance wreaths were severely round and firm in outline; later, they grew richer and ornate. These were painted, carved, or appliquéd, often in conjunction with coats-of-arms or monograms. In the Empire style they were commonly bronze appliqués, using laurel leaves or other austere shapes.

WREN, SIR CHRISTOPHER, 1632-1723. English architect largely responsible for the Restoration style, following the classic manner of Palladio. He directed the reconstruction of much of London after the Great Fire. While he is known to have designed little mobile furniture, his general direction influenced the school of woodcarving of which Grinling Gibbons was pre-eminent.

WRITING ARM. Tablet arm; wide board arm suitable for a writing tablet, as in Windsor chairs. [319.]

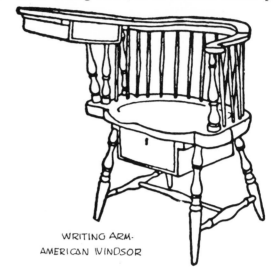

WRITING ARM.
AMERICAN WINDSOR

WRITING DESK; WRITING TABLE. Flattop desk or any table type of proper size for writing, usually fitted with drawers or desk compartments. Original desk or "bureau" was merely a table with cloth called *bure*. See also DESK; ESCRITOIRE; LIBRARY TABLE; TABLE. [319, 1374.]

WROUGHT IRON. Forged iron in furniture is bent, beaten, cut, or otherwise shaped when hot, as differing from cast iron, which is molded. In earliest work iron bindings were the principal means of holding wood boards together [544]. As joinery developed, the iron became merely adjunct or bracing and finally only decorative as appliqués or as working hardware, such as hinges, locks, handles. [1152.]

WROUGHT IRON

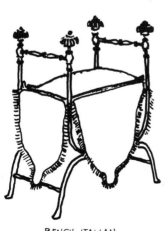

BENCH ITALIAN

TABLE ITALIAN

BED SPANISH

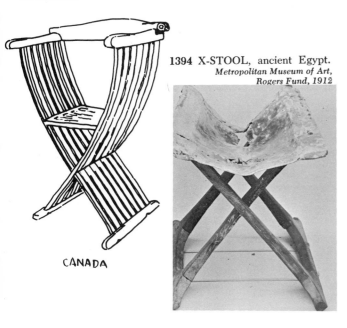

1394 X-STOOL, ancient Egypt.
*Metropolitan Museum of Art,
Rogers Fund, 1912*

CANADA

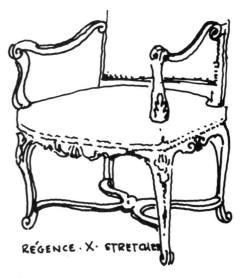

REGENCE · X · STRETCHER

X-CHAIR. Ancient type of chair based on the folding chair. It was known in Egypt and Rome, and appears in the Middle Ages.

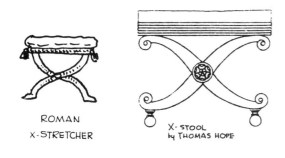

ROMAN
X-STRETCHER

X-STOOL
by THOMAS HOPE

X-STOOL. The simplest form of folding stool, found in ancient Egyptian remains and most subsequent types. Earliest forms had leather or skin seats. Renaissance stools were solid, often having the crossed members carved. This was the curule chair of the Romans, and is particularly characteristic of the Empire style.

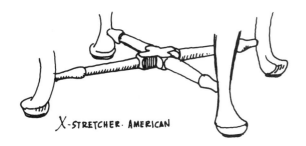

X-STRETCHER · AMERICAN

X-STRETCHER. Crossed stretchers on chairs or tables, etc. [246, 257, 260, 264, 317, 476.]

YEW. Hard, close-grained red-brown wood, resistant to wear and decay. Takes a high polish; used on furniture chiefly for decorative veneered effects and inlaying since 17th century, although it was also so used by the ancients.

YORKSHIRE CHAIR. English carved side chair of the 17th century, peculiar to Yorkshire. It stems from the panel or wainscot chair, and is invariably of oak with turned front legs and stretchers. [237.]

X · STRETCHER

YORKSHIRE
CHAIR

YORKSHIRE DRESSER. Dresser or dish cupboard with a low back. It originates in Yorkshire, and is usually of oak or deal.

YUBA. Tasmanian oak; has dense texture and regular curly figure.

ZEBRAWOOD. Hard decorative wood from British Guiana; named for its vigorous stripings of dark reddish-brown on creamy ground. Used chiefly for inlays and bandings, but more extensively on large surfaces in modern work.

ZUCCHI, ANTONIO, 1726-1795. Italian decorative painter who worked in England, often under the direction of Robert Adam, painting medallions and wall designs and probably furniture decorations. Husband of Angelica Kauffmann.

BIBLIOGRAPHY

AMERICAN

Andrews, E. D., and Andrews, F., *Shaker Furniture* (1962).
Bjerkoe, E. H., and Arthur, B. J., *The Cabinetmakers of America* (1957).
Brazer, E. S., *Early American Decoration* (Springfield, Mass., 1940).
Burroughs, P. H., *Southern Antiques* (Richmond, Va., 1931).
Christensen, E. O., *Early American Wood Carving* (1952).
————, *The Index of American Design* (1950).
Comstock, H., ed., *The Concise Encyclopedia of American Antiques* (1958).
Cornelius, C. O., *Early American Furniture* (1932).
————, *Furniture Masterpieces of Duncan Phyfe* (1922).
Dow, G. F., *The Arts and Crafts of New England, 1704-1775* (1927).
°Downing A. J., *Architecture of Country Houses* (1861).
Downs, J., *American Furniture, Queen Anne and Chippendale Periods in . . . Winterthur Museum* (1952).
Drepperd, C. W., *A Dictionary of American Antiques* (1952).
————, *Handbook of Antique Chairs* (1948).
Dyer, W., *Early American Craftsmen* (1915).
Elwell, H. W., *Colonial Furniture and Interiors* (Boston, 1896).
French, L., *Colonial Interiors* (1923).
Halsey, R. T. H., and Cornelius, C. O., *Handbook of the American Wing of the Metropolitan Museum* (1928).
Halsey, R. T. H., and Tower, E., *The Homes of Our Ancestors* (1936).
Hamlin, T., *Greek Revival Architecture in America* (London, 1944).
Hipkiss, E. J., *Eighteenth Century American Arts* (Boston, 1941).
Holloway, E. S., *American Furniture and Decoration, Colonial and Federal* (1928).
Hornor, W. M., *The Blue Book of Philadelphia Furniture, William Penn to George Washington* (Philadelphia, 1935).
Kelemen, P., *Baroque and Rococo in Latin America* (1951).
Kettell, R. H., ed., *Early American Rooms* (Portland, Me., 1936).
————, *The Pine Furniture of Early New England* (1929).
Lea, Z. R., ed., *The Ornamented Chair: Its Development in America* (Rutland, Vt., 1960).
Lewis, E., *The White House* (1937).
Lockwood, L. V., *Colonial Furniture in America* (1902).
Luther, C. F., *The Hadley Chest* (Hartford, Conn., 1935).
Lyon, J. W., *Colonial Furniture of New England* (Boston, 1891).
McClelland, N., *Duncan Phyfe and the English Regency* (1939).
Marsh, Moreton, *The Easy Expert in Collecting and Restoring American Antiques* (1959).
Melcher, M., *The Shaker Adventure* (1960).
Metropolitan Museum of Art, *The Greek Revival in the United States* (1943).
Millar, D., *Colonial Furniture* (1925).
Miller, E. G., *American Antique Furniture* (Baltimore, 1937).
Moore, M. R., "Hitchcock Chairs" (pamphlet, 1933).
Newark Museum, *Classical America, 1815-1845* (Newark, 1963).
Nutting, W., *Furniture of the Pilgrim Century* (1921).
————, *Furniture Treasury*, 3 vols. (1928-1933).
————, *A Windsor Handbook* (1917).
Nye, A., *Colonial Furniture* (1895).
Ormsbee, T. H., *Collecting Antiques in America* (c. 1940).
————, *Early American Furniture Makers* (1930).
————, *Field Guide to American Victorian Furniture* (Boston, 1964).
————, *The Story of American Furniture* (1934).

°*Indicates a source book of the period.*

Palardy, J., *Les Meubles Anciens du Canada Français* (c. 1960).
Pickering, E., *The Homes of America* (1951).
Rogers, M. R., *American Interior Design* (1947).
Sack, A., *Fine Points of Furniture (Early American)* (1950).
Singleton, E., *Furniture of Our Forefathers* (1901).
Stoneman, V. C., *John and Thomas Seymour, Cabinetmakers in Boston, 1794-1816* (Boston, 1959).
Taylor, H. H., *Knowing, Collecting and Restoring Early American Furniture* (Philadelphia, 1930).
Yates, R., and Yates, M., *A Guide to Victorian Antiques* (1949).

ANCIENT

Richter, G. M. A., *Ancient Furniture* (1926).
Robsjohn-Gibbings, T. H., and Pullin, C. W., *Furniture of Classical Greece* (1964).

ANTIQUES AND COLLECTING

Bles, A. de, *Genuine Antique Furniture* (1929).
Cescinsky, H., *The Gentle Art of Faking Furniture* (London, 1931).
Drepperd, C. W., *First Reader for Antique Collectors* (1954).
————, *A Dictionary of American Antiques* (1952).
Guild, L. Van A., *The Geography of American Antiques* (1927).
Harper, G. W., *Antique Collector's Guide and Reference Handbook* (1939).
Hinckley, F. L., *A Directory of Antique Furniture* (1953).
Kinney, R. P., *The Complete Book of Furniture Repair and Refinishing* (1950).
Lee, R. W., *Antique Fakes and Reproductions* (Northborough, Mass., 1950).
Litchfield, F., *Antiques, Genuine and Spurious* (1921).
Lockwood, L. V., *The Furniture Collector's Glossary* (1913).
Lockwood, S. M., *Antiques* (1926).
Lucas., A., *Antiques, Their Restoration and Preservation* (1932).
Minns, E. W., *The Art of Restoring and Refinishing Antique Furniture* (Newburgh, N.Y., 1939).
Rodd, J., *The Repair and Restoration of Furniture* (London, 1954).
Savage, G., *The Art and Antique Restorer's Handbook* (London, 1954).
Wenham, E., *Old Furniture in Modern Rooms* (1939).
Winchester, A., *Living with Antiques* (1941).
Yates, R., *Antique Fakes and Their Detection* (1950).

EASTERN EUROPEAN

Czarnecka, I., *Folk Art in Poland* (Warsaw, 1957).
Lukomski, G. K., *L'Art Décoratif Russe* (Paris, 1928).
————, *Mobilier et Décoration des Anciens Palais Impériaux Russes* (Paris, 1928).
————, *Zarskoje Sselo* (Berlin, 1924).
Roche, D., *Le Mobilier Français en Russie* (1902).

ENGLISH

Adam, R., and Adam, J., *The Architecture, Decoration and Furniture of Robert and James Adam. Selected from Works in Architecture* (1778-1822) (London, 1880).
Aslin, E., *Nineteenth Century English Furniture* (1962).
Bell, J. M., ed., *The Furniture Designs of Chippendale, Hepplewhite and Sheraton* (1938).
Bell, J. M., and Hayden, A., *The Furniture of George Hepplewhite* (1910).
Benn, H. P., and Shapland, H., *The Nation's Treasures* (1910).

Beveridge, T. J., *English Renaissance Woodwork, 1660-1730* (1921).

Binstead, H. E., *English Chairs* (1923).

Blake, J. P., and Reveirs-Hopkins, A. E., *Little Books About Old Furniture*, 4 vols. (1930).

Bolton, A. T., *The Architecture of Robert and James Adam* (1922).

Bracket, O., *An Encyclopedia of English Furniture* (1927).

————, *English Furniture Illustrated* (1950).

————, *Georgian Art, 1760-1820* (London, 1929).

————, *Thomas Chippendale: A Study of His Life, Work and Influence* (1924).

Cescinsky, H., *English Furniture of the Eighteenth Century* (1911).

————, *English Furniture from Gothic to Sheraton* (1929).

————, and Gribble, E. R., *Early English Furniture and Woodwork* (1922).

°Chippendale, T., *Designs of Interior Decorations in the Old French and Antique Styles* (1800).

°————, *The Gentleman and Cabinet-Maker's Director* (1754).

°————, *Household Furniture in Genteel Taste* (1760).

Clouston, R. S., *English Furniture and Furniture Makers of the 18th Century* (1906).

Crow, G. H., *William Morris, Designer* (1934).

Davies, L. T., and Lloyd-Johnes, H. J., *Welsh Furniture* (Cardiff, 1950).

Eastlake, C. L., Jr., *Hints on Household Taste in Furniture* (1872).

Edwards, R., *Georgian Cabinetmakers, c. 1700-1800* (1955).

Ellwood, L. M., *English Furniture and Decoration, 1680-1800* (Stuttgart, 1933).

Fastnedge, R., *English Furniture Styles* (1961).

————, *Sheraton Furniture* (1961).

Fenn, F., and Wyllie, B., *Old English Furniture* (1920).

Forman, R., *Nursery Furnishing and Decoration* (1950).

Gloag J., *Georgian Grace: A Social History of Design from 1660-1830* (1956).

————, *The Englishman's Chair* (1964).

Harris, J., *Regency Furniture Designs from Contemporary Pattern-books (1803-1826)* (1961).

Harris, M., and Sons, *The English Chair, Its History and Evolution* (1937).

Hayden, A., *Chats on Cottage and Farmhouse Furniture* (1912).

————, *Chats on Old Furniture* (17th ed., 1950).

————, *Old Furniture* (1930).

Hayward, C. H., *English Period Furniture* (London, 1936).

Heal, A., *The London Furniture Makers from the Restoration to the Victorian Era* (1953).

Heaton, J. A., *Furniture and Decoration in England During the 18th Century* (1889-1892).

°Hepplewhite, A., *The Cabinet Maker and Upholsterer's Guide* (1794).

°Hope, T., *Household Furniture and Interior Decoration* (1807).

Hughes, T., *Old English Furniture* (1964).

Hurrell, J. W., *Measured Drawings of Old Oak English Furniture* (1902).

°Ince, W., and Mayhew, T., *The Universal System of Household Furniture* (1762).

Jackson, P. J. W., *English Furniture of the 18th Century* (Victoria and Albert Museum) (1957).

Jourdain, M., *Decoration and Furniture During the Later 18th Century (1760-1820)* (1922).

————, *Decoration and Furniture in England During the Early Renaissance, 1500-1640* (1924).

————, *Regency Furniture, 1795-1820* (1948).

————, *The Work of William Kent* (1948).

Lenygon, F., *Furniture in England from 1660-1760* (1924).

MacQuoid, P., *A History of English Furniture*, 4 vols. (1904-1908).

————, and Edwards, H., *The Dictionary of English Furniture* (1924).

°Manwaring, R., *The Cabinet and Chair Maker's Real Friend and Companion* (1765).

————, *Chair Maker's Guide* (1766).

Marx and Taylor, *Measured Drawings of English Furniture* (Oak period) (1931).

Nickerson, David, *English Furniture of the 18th Century* (1964).

Ormsbee, T. H., See under Symonds.

Percival, M., *The Oak Collector* (1925).

————, *The Walnut Collector* (1927).

Roe, G. F., *English Cottage Furniture* (1949).

————, *Victorian Furniture* (1952).

————, *Windsor Chairs* (1953).

Rogers, J. C., *English Furniture* (1950).

Rubira, J. C., *Muebles de Estilo Ingles* (Barcelona, 1946).

Sayer, R., *The Ladies [sic] Amusement or The Whole Art of Japanning Made Easy* (London, 1762; reprinted 1959).

°Shearer, T., *The Cabinet Maker's London Book of Prices and Designs* (1788).

°Sheraton, T., *The Cabinet Dictionary* (1803).

°————, *The Cabinet Maker and Upholsterer's Drawing-Book* (1791-1793).

°————, *Designs for Household Furniture* (1801).

Singleton, E., *French and English Furniture* (1904).

°Smith, G., *The Cabinet Maker and Upholsterer's Guide* (1826).

°————, *A Collection of Designs for Household Furniture and Interior Decoration* (1808).

Smith, H. C., *Buckingham Palace, Its Furniture, Decoration and History* (1931).

Strange, T. A., *English Furniture, Woodwork and Decoration* (detail drawings) (1903).

Symonds, R. W., *English Furniture from Charles II to George II* (1929).

————, *Furniture Makers in 17th-18th Century England* (1954).

————, *Old English Walnut and Lacquer Furniture* (1923).

————, *The Present State of Old English Furniture* (1927).

————, and Ormsby, T. H., *English Furniture of the Walnut Period* (1947).

Tanner, H., *English Interior Woodwork of the XVIth, XVIIth, and XVIIIth Centuries* (1902).

Victoria and Albert Museum, *Catalogue of English Furniture and Woodwork* (1930).

————, *Georgian (English) Furniture* (1951).

————, *A History of the English Chair* (1951).

————, *A History of English Furniture* (1955).

Wheeler, G. O., *Old English Furniture* (1924).

FRENCH

Adams, L., *Décorations Intérieures et Meubles des Époques Louis XIII et XIV* (Paris, 1865).

Amott, J., and Wilson, J., *The Petit Trianon, Versailles* (1908).

Androuet du Cerceau, J., *Collection de Meubles* (Paris, 1890?).

Bajot, É., *Art Nouveau* (Paris, 1898).

————, *Motifs Louis XVI* (Paris, 1900).

Bayard, E., *Les Meubles Rustiques Régionaux de la France* (1925).

Berain, J., *Son Oeuvre Complète* (the style of Louis XIV) (Paris, 1882).

————, *Les Meubles du XVIIIe Siècle* (Paris, 1922).

Collection de l'Art Régional en France (Survey of French Provincial Furniture in 12 vols.): Vol. 1—Algoud, *Mobilier Provençal*, Vol. 2—Leclerc, *Mobilier Normand*. Vol. 3—Colas, *Mobilier Basque*. Vol. 4—Gelis, *Mobilier Alsacien*. Vol. 5—Gauthier, *Mobilier Vendéen*. Vol. 6—Gauthier, *Mobilier Auvergnat*. Vol. 7—Germain, *Mobilier Bressan*. Vol. 8—Champier, *Mobilier Flamand*. Vol. 9—Banéat, *Mobilier Breton*. Vol. 10—Sadoul, *Mobilier Lorrain*. Vol. 11—Gauthier, *Mobilier Bas-Breton*. Vol. 12—Janton, *Mobilier Bourguignon*.

Contet, F., ed., *Intérieurs Directoire et Empire* (Paris, 1932).

Costantino, R. T., *How to Know French Antiques* (1961).

Dilke, E. F. S., *French Decoration and Furniture in the XVIIIth Century* (London, 1901).

Dreyfus, C., *Le Mobilier Français*, 2 vols. (Paris, 1921): Vol. 1—*Époques de Louis XIV et XV*. Vol. 2—*Époque de Louis XVI*.

Dumonthier, E., *Le Mobilier Louis XVI* (Paris, 1922).

————, *Les Sièges de Georges Jacob* (Paris, 1922).

————, *Les Sièges de Jacob Frères* (Paris, 1921).

————, *Les Tables* (Louis XVI et Premier Empire) (Paris, 1924).

Félice, R. de, *Little Illustrated Books on Old French Furniture,* 4 volumes: Vol. 1—*Middle Ages and Louis XIII.* Vol. 2—*Louis XIV.* Vol. 3—*Louis XV.* Vol. 4—*Louis XVI and Empire* (1920-1923).

Funck-Brentano, F., *L'Ameublement Français sous la Renaissance* (Paris, 1913).

Gauthier, J., *La Connaissance des Styles dans le Mobilier* (Paris, 1933).

————, *Décoration et Ameublement Directoire et Empire* (Paris, 1930).

————, *Le Mobilier des Vielles Provinces Françaises* (Paris, 1935).

Hessling, E., *Empire Möbel* (Leipzig, 1914).

————, and Hessling, W., *Möbel im Directorstil* (Berlin, 1914).

Janneau, G., *Les Beaux Meubles Français Anciens,* 5 vols.: Vol. 1—*Les Commodes.* Vol. 2—*Les Petits Meubles.* Vol. 3—*Les Grands Meubles.* Vol. 4—*Lits de Repos et Lits.* Vol. 5 —*Les Sièges* (Paris, 1929).

Ledoux-Lebard, D., *Les Ébénistes Parisiens (1795-1850)* (Paris, 1951).

Longnon, H. A., and Huard, F. W., *French Provincial Furniture* (London, 1927).

Maillard, E., *Old French Furniture and Its Surroundings (1610-1815)* (1925).

Molinier, E., *La Collection Wallace* (Paris, 1902).

————, *Le Mobilier Royal Français au XVIIe et au XVIIIe Siècles* (Paris, 1902).

Mottheau, J., *Meubles Usuels. Directoire et Empire* (Paris, 1952).

————, *Meubles Usuels. Louis XIV* (Paris, 1952).

————, *Meubles Usuels. Régence et Louis XV* (Paris, 1952).

Museum of Decorative Arts, Paris, *Grand Ébénistes et Menuisiers Parisiens (1740-1790)* (Paris, 1956).

°Nicolay, J., *L'Art et la Manière des Maîtres Ébénistes Français au XVIIIe Siècle* (1956).

Oglesby, C., *French Provincial Decorative Art* (London, New York, 1951).

Packer, C., *Paris Furniture by the Master Ébénistes* (Newport, England, 1955).

°Percier, C., and Fontaine, P., *Recueil de Décorations Intérieures, Meubles, Bronzes, Etc.* (Paris, 1801).

Planat, P., *Le Style Louis XVI* (Paris, 1907).

Ricci, S. de, *Louis XIV and Regency* (1929).

————, *Louis XVI Furniture* (1913).

Ruemler, E., *Le Style Louis XV* (Paris, 1914).

Salverte, C. de, *Les Ébénistes du XVIIIe Siècle* (Paris, 1937).

Seguy, E., *Petits Meubles Anciens* (Paris, 1910).

————, *Sièges Anciens* (Paris, 1910).

Strange, A., *French Interiors, Furniture, Woodwork* (London, 1900).

————, *An Historical Guide to French Interiors* (1907).

Vacquier, J., *Les Vieux Hôtels de Paris,* 13 vols. (Paris, 1913-1921).

Verlet, P., *Le Mobilier Royal Français* (1956).

Viollet-le-Duc, E., *Dictionnaire du Mobilier Français,* 6 vols. (Paris, 1872-1875).

Watson, F. J. B., *French Furniture in the Wallace Collection* (1956).

————, *Louis XVI Furniture* (1950).

GENERAL

American Institute of Interior Designers, *Interior Design and Decoration: A Bibliography* (1961).

Aronson, J., *Book of Furniture and Decoration: Period and Modern* (1952).

Bajot, É., *Encyclopédie du Meuble* (1900).

Bayard, É., *L'Art de Reconnaître les Styles* (Paris, 1913; 1925).

Boger, L. A., *The Complete Guide to Furniture Styles* (1959).

Clark, K., *The Gothic Revival* (1950).

Clifford, C. R., *Period Furnishings* (1949).

The Connoisseur, ed. *The Concise Encyclopedia of Antiques,* 3 vols. (London, 1954-1957).

Cotchett, L. E., *The Evolution of Furniture* (1939).

Dutton, R., *The Victorian Home* (London, 1954).

Eberlein, H. D., and McClure, E. A., *Practical Book of Period Furniture* (Philadelphia, 1914).

Feulner, A., *Kunstgeschichte des Möbels* (Berlin, 1927).

Foley, E., *Decorative Furniture, Its Form, Colour and History,* 2 vols. (1925).

Giedion, S., *Mechanization Takes Command* (New York, 1948).

Gloag, J., *A Short Dictionary of Furniture* (London, 1952).

Hackett, W. H., *Decorative Furniture* (1902).

Harvard, H., *Dictionnaire de l'Ameublement et de la Décoration* (1887-1890).

Hoffman, H., ed., *Sitzmöbel aus Sechs Jahrhunderten* (Stuttgart, 1938).

Hunter, G. L., *Decorative Furniture* (Grand Rapids, Mich., 1923).

Kahle, K. M., *An Outline of Period Furniture* (1929).

Kimball, S. F., *The Creation of the Rococo* (Philadelphia, 1943).

Lessing, J., *Gotische Möbel* (Berlin, 1889).

Lichten, F., *Decorative Art of Victoria's Era* (1950).

Litchfield, F., *Illustrated History of Furniture* (1922).

Lock, M., *Original Designs for Furniture, 1740-1765* (1863).

°————, and Copeland, H., *A New Book of Ornaments* (1768).

Lynes, R., *The Tastemakers* (1954).

McBride R. M., *A Treasury of Antiques* (1946).

Mould, R. G., *Refinishing and Decorating Furniture and Other Home Accessories* (1953).

°Nicholson, P., and Angelo, M., *The Practical Cabinetmaker, Upholsterer and Complete Decorator* (London, 1826).

°Pugin, A., *Designs for Gothic Furniture* (Neo-Gothic) (London, 1835).

Reeves, D., *Furniture, an Explanatory History* (1947).

Roche, S., *Mirrors* (1957).

Salomonsky, V. C., *Masterpieces of Furniture Design* (Grand Rapids, Mich., 1931).

————, *Masterpieces of Furniture in Photographs and Measured Drawings* (1953).

Schmitz, H., *The Encyclopedia of Furniture* (1926).

Sigworth, O., *The Four Styles of a Decade* (1960).

Truman, N., *Historic Furnishing* (1950).

Vandan, C., *Great Styles of Furniture* (English, Italian, French, Dutch, Spanish) (1963).

Whiton, S., *Elements of Interior Design and Decoration.* (1960).

Winchester, A., ed., *The Antiques Treasury* (1959).

GERMAN, DUTCH, AND AUSTRIAN

Arens, F., *Meisterrisse und Möbel der Mainzer Schreiner* (Mainz, 1955).

Arps-Aubert, R. von, *Sächsische Barockmöbel, 1700-1770* (Berlin, 1939).

Baaren, H., and Schublad, E. G. C., *Het Meubel en Het Interieur* (Deventer, 1950).

Baer, C. H., *Deutsche Wohn- und Festräume aus Sechs Jahrhunderten* (Stuttgart, 1912).

Bromberg, P., *Decorative Arts in the Netherlands* (1944).

Falke, O. von, and Schmitz, H., eds., *Deutsche Möbel* (Stuttgart, 1923-1924).

Feulner, A., *Bayerisches Rokoko* (Munich, 1923).

Folnesics, J., ed., *Innenräume und Hausrat der Empire und Biedermeierzeit, in Österreich-Ungarn* (Vienna, 1922).

Hahm, K., *Deutsche Bauernmöbel* (Jena, 1939).

Holme, C., ed., *Peasant Art in Austria and Hungary* (London, 1911).

Luthmer, F. and Schmidt, R., *Empire-und Biedermeier-Möbel* (Frankfurt, 1922).

Lux, J. A., *Empire und Biedermeier* (Stuttgart, 1930).

Ritz, J. M., *Alte Bemalte Bauernmöbel* (Munich, 1938).

Sauerlandt, M., *Norddeutsche Barockmöbel* (1922).

Schmitz, H., *Deutsche Möbel:* V. 2, *Barock und Rokoko* (Stuttgart, 1923); V. 3, *Klassizismus* (Louis XVI, Empire, Biedermeier) (Stuttgart, 1923).

————, *Vor Hundert Jahren. Festräume und Wohnzimmer des Deutschen Klassizismus und Biedermeier* (Berlin, 1920).

Singleton, E., *Dutch and Flemish Furniture* (1907).

Zweig, M., ed., *Wiener Bürgermöbel* (Vienna, 1921).
————, *Zweites Rokoko Innenräume und Hausrat in Wien um 1830-1860* (Vienna, 1924).

MEDITERRANEAN: ITALIAN AND SPANISH

Arte Italiana—Arte Italiana Decorativa e Industriale, 4 vols. (Venice, 1890-1891).
Arte y Decoración en España (1920-1928).
Bode, W. von, *Italian Renaissance Furniture* (1921).
Bottomley, W. L., *Spanish Details* (1924).
Burr, G. H., *Hispanic Furniture* (1941).
Byne, A., and Stapley, M., *Spanish Interiors and Furniture* (1921).
————, *Spanish Ironwork* (1915).
Colección el Meuble en España, 6 vols. (Madrid, 1949-1951).
Domenech, R., and Bueno, L. P., *Meubles Antiguos Españoles* (1914).
Eberlein, H. D., *Interiors, Fireplaces, and Furniture of the Italian Renaissance* (1927, reprint).
Eberlein, H. D., and Ramsdell, R. W., *The Practical Book of Italian, Spanish and Portuguese Furniture* (1915).
————, *Spanish Interiors, Furniture and Details* (1925).
Ferrari, G., *Il Legno e la Mobilia Nell'arte Italiana* (1925).
Helburn, W., Inc., pub., *Italian Renaissance Interiors and Furniture* (1916).
Holme C., *Peasant Art in Italy* (1913).
Hunter, G. L., *Italian Furniture and Interiors* (1920).
Lessing, J., *Italienische Möbel, XVI Jahrhundert* (Berlin, 1893).
————, *Italienische Truhen, XV-XVI Jahrhundert* (Berlin, 1891).
Marangoni, G., *Enciclopedia delle Moderne Art Decorative Italiane* (Milan, 1925).
Morazzoni, G., *Italian Furniture of the Neo-Classic Period (1760-1820)* (1955).
————, *Il Mobile Genovese* (Milan, 1949).
————, *Mobili Veneziani Laccati* (Milan, 1959).
Odom, W. M., *A History of Italian Furniture* (1918-1919).
Pedrini, A., *L'Ambiente, il Mobilio e le Decorazioni del Rinascimento in Italia* (Turin, 1925).
Schottmueller, F., *Furniture and Interior Decoration of the Italian Renaissance* (New York, 1921).
Schubring, P., *Cassoni, Truhen und Truhenbilder der Italienischen Fruehrenaissance* (Leipzig, 1923).
Taullard, A., *El Mueble Colonial Sudamericano* (1944).
Tinti, M., *Il Mobilio Fiorentino* (Milan, 1929?).
Williams, L., *The Arts and Crafts of Older Spain* (London, 1907).

MODERN

Aloi, R., *L'Arredamento Moderno* (Italy, 1934).
————, *Esempi di Arredamento Moderno di Tuto li Mondo* (Milan, 1950).
Chareau, P., *Meubles* (Paris, 1928).
Decorative Art—The Studio Yearbook of Furnishing and Decoration (London, 1903-date).
Dieckmann E., *Möbelbau in Holz, Rohr und Stahl* (Stuttgart, 1931).
Ditzel, N., and Ditzel, J., *Danske Stols—Danish Chairs* (Copenhagen, 1954).
Dorp. E. van, *Moderne Eenvoudige Meubels* (Amsterdam) (1928).
Fabbro, M. dal, *Furniture for Modern Interiors* (1954).
————, *Modern Furniture* (1949).
Greber, J., *Paris Exposition, 1937. Décoration Intérieure* (Paris, 1937).
Griesser, P., *Das Neue Möbel* (Stuttgart, 1932).
Groneman, C. H., *Bent Tubular Furniture* (Milwaukee, 1941).
Haard, U., *Modern Scandinavian Furniture* (1964).
Havelaar, J., *Het Moderne Meubel* (Modern Dutch) (Rotterdam, 1924).
Hennessey, W. J., *Complete Book of Built-ins* (1950).
————, *Modern Furnishings for the Home* (1952).
Hoffmann, H., *Modern Interiors* (1930).
Holme, G., *Industrial Design and the Future* (1934).
Hooper, J. and R., *Modern Furniture and Fittings* (1948).
Huldt, A. H., and Benedicks, E., eds., *Design in Sweden Today* (1948).

Joel, D., *The Adventure of British Furniture* (London, 1953).
Kahle, K. M., *Modern French Decoration* (1930).
Koch, A., *Bett und Couch* (Stuttgart, 1950).
————, *Einzelmöbel und Neuzeitliche Raumkunst* (Darmstadt, 1930).
Laszlo, P., *Interiors and Exteriors* (1947).
Leoni, P., *La Construzione del Mobile Moderno*, Part 2 (1946).
Logie, G., *Furniture from Machines* (London, 1947).
Malmsten, C., *Schwedische Möbel* (Basel, 1954).
Museum of Modern Art, *Twentieth Century Design* (1959).
Nelson, G., ed., *Chairs* (1953).
New Furniture (G. Hatje, ed.) (1952 to date; annual).
Olmer, P., *Le Mobilier Français d'Aujourd'hui* (Paris, 1910-1925).
Retera, W., *Het Moderne Interieur* (Amsterdam, 1937).
Schneck, A. G., *Das Möbel als Gebrauchsgegenstand*, 4 vols. (1937-1951).
Schuster, F., *Ein Möbelbuch* (Modern Simple Furniture) (Stuttgart, 1933).
Seeger, M., *Gute Möbel, Schöne Räume* (Stuttgart, 1953).
Todd, D., and Mortimer, R., *The New Interior Decoration* (1929).
Witzemann, H. M., *Deutsche Möbel Heute* (Stuttgart, 1954).

ORIENTAL

Cescinsky, H., *Chinese Furniture* (London, 1922).
Dupont, M., *Les Meubles de la Chine* (1926).
Ecke, G., *Chinese Domestic Furniture* (Rutland, Vt., 1962).
Guérin, J., *La Chinoiserie en Europe au XVIIIᵉ Siècle* (1911).
Ishimoto, K. E. T., *The Japanese House, Interior and Exterior* (1964).
Kates, G. N., *Chinese Household Furniture* (1962).
Lancaster, C., *The Japanese Influence in America* (1963).
Nakamura, K., *Tokonoma* (Alcoves) (Tokyo, 1958).
Roche, O., *Les Meubles de la Chine* (Paris, 1926).
Strange, E. F., *Chinese Lacquer* (London, 1926).
Yoshida, T., *Das Japanische Wohnhaus* (Berlin, 1935).

SCANDINAVIAN

Fischer, E., *Svenska Möbler i Bild*, 2 vols. (Stockholm, 1950).
Hellner, B., *Svenska Möbler* (Stockholm, 1947).
Hopstock, C., *Norwegian Design, Viking Age to Industrial Revolution* (Norway, 1961).
Lagerquist, M., *Rokokomöbler* (Stockholm, 1949).
Plath, J., *The Decorative Arts of Sweden* (1948).
Wettergren, E., *Modern Decorative Arts of Sweden* (**1926**).
Wollin, N., *Modern and Swedish Decorative Art* (**1931**).

WOODS, WOODWORKING, AND FURNITURE CRAFTS

Constantine, A., *Know Your Woods* (1959).
Hinckley, F. L., *Directory of the Historic Cabinet Woods* (1960).
Howard, A. L., *Timbers of the World* (1951).
Jackson, F. H., *Intarsia and Marquetry* (1903).
Johnson and Sironen, *Manual of the Furniture Arts and Crafts* (1928).
Margon, L., *Construction of American Furniture Treasures* (1949).
Pattou, A. B., and Vaughn, C. L., *Furniture Finishing, Decoration and Patching* (Chicago, 1927).
Pinto, E. H., *Treen, or Small Woodware Through the Ages* (1949).
Rowe, E., *Practical Woodcarving* (1930).
Rudd, J. H., *Practical Cabinet Making and Drafting* (1912).
Simmonds, T., *Wood Carving* (1930).
Steinmetz, R. C., and Rice, C. S., *Vanishing Crafts and Their Craftsmen* (New Brunswick, N.J., 1959).
U.S. Department of Agriculture, Forest Products Laboratory, *The Identification of Furniture Woods* (Madison, Wis.).
————, *Wood . . . Colors and Kinds* (Washington, D.C., 1956).
Vanderwalker, F. N., *Wood Finishing, Plain and Decorative* (Chicago, 1944).
Wells, P. A., and Hooper, J., *Modern Cabinetwork* (London, 1909).
Wheeler, C. G., *A Manual of Woodworking* (1924).

A GLOSSARY OF DESIGNERS AND CRAFTSMEN

Aalto, Alvar, contemporary Finnish architect and furniture designer.

*Adam Brothers, English architects: John, 1721-1792; Robert, 1728-1792; James, 1730-1794; William, 1739-1822.

*Affleck, Thomas, Philadelphia, Pa. Died 1763.

Albertolli, Giocono, Italy, Directoire period. See under Nineteenth Century.

Allen, Josiah, Charleston, S.C He appears in the city directory between 1809-1813.

*Allison, Michael, New York City. Active at the beginning of the 19th century.

Ancellet, Denis-Louis, France. JMÉ 1766. Court furniture for Louis XVI.

Appleton, Nathaniel, Salem, Mass. Early 19th century.

Ash, Gilbert, New York City, 1717-1785.

Ash, Thomas, New York City. Died 1813.

Asinelis, Antonio, Italy, 16th century.

Atlee, William, Philadelphia, Pa., 18th century.

Aubiche, Jacques d', France, 18th century.

Axton, Thomas, England, 17th century.

Axton, William, Jr., Charleston, S.C. Died 1800.

Bachelier of Toulouse, France, 16th century.

Bachman, John, Lancaster County, Pa., late 18th century.

Badlam, Stephen, Dorchester, Mass., 1751-1815.

Baerze, Jacques de, Flanders, 14th century.

Baillie-Scott, M. H., Scotland. Born 1865. Architect.

Barry, Sir Charles, England, 19th century. Architect.

Barry, Joseph B., Philadelphia, circa 1810.

Baumgartner, Ulrich, Germany, 17th century.

Beck, Sebald, Germany, 16th century.

Belchier, John, England. Died 1753.

Bell, Philip, England, 18th century.

Belli, Andrea Alessandro, Italy, 16th century.

Belli, Giovanni, Italy, 16th century.

*Belter, John Henry, New York City. Died 1865.

Beman, Reuben, Jr., Connecticut, active 1785-1800.

*Beneman, Guillaume, France. JMÉ 1785.

Bennett, Samuel, England, late 17th century.

*Berain, Claude, France, 17th and 18th centuries.

*Berain, Jean (the elder), France, 1638-1711.

*Berain, Jean (the younger), France, 1678-1726.

Bergamo, Fra Damiano da, Italy, 1490-1550?

Bertoiia, Harry, contemporary American designer.

Bertolina, B. J., Italy, 16th century.

Blake, S., England, 19th century.

Bland, Charles, England, 17th century.

Bolte, Adrian, England, 17th century.

Borgona, Felipe, Spain, 16th century.

*Boulle, André-Charles, France, 1642-1732.

Boulle, Pierre, France, 17th century.

Boulton, Matthew, England, 18th century.

Bourdin, Michel, France, 16th century.

Bouvier, Michael, Philadelphia, Pa., active 1819-1859.

Bradburn, John, England, 18th century.

Bradshaw, William, England, 18th century.

Brettingham, Matthew, England, 1699-1769. Architect. Pupil of William Kent.

Breuer, Marcel, contemporary American architect.

Breuhaus, Fritz A., Germany, early 20th century.

Brinner, John, New York City, 18th century.

Brizard, Sulpice, France, 1735?-1798. JMÉ 1763.

Brodstock, William, England, 17th century.

Brookshaw, George, England. Cabinetmaker circa 1783.

Bulfinch, Charles, New England, 1763-1844. Architect.

Burnham, Benjamin, Philadelphia, 18th century.

Burroughs, John, England. Fl. 1662-1690.

*Caffieri, Jacques, France, 1678-1755.

Calder, Alexander, Charleston, S.C., active 1796-1807.

Callow, Stephen, New York City, 18th century.

Campbell and Sons, England, 18th century.

Canabas, Joseph (Gegenbach), France, 1715?-1797. JMÉ 1766.

Carlin, Martin, France. Died 1785.

Carpenter, Thomas, England, 18th century.

Carter, John, England, 18th century. Architect.

Casbert, John, England, 17th century.

Challen, William, New York City, 18th century.

Fl.=Flourished.
JMÉ=Maître Ébéniste.
*=See Text.

480

*Chambers, Sir William, England, 1726-1796. Architect, published *Designs of Chinese Buildings, Furniture, etc.*

Chapin, Aaron, active in Connecticut in 1780's.

Chapin, Eliphalet, Connecticut, 1741-1807.

Cheney, Silas E., Litchfield, Conn., active 1799-1821.

Chippendale, John, England, 18th century.

*Chippendale, Thomas, Sr., England, 1718-1779.

Chippendale, Thomas, Jr., England, 1749-1822.

*Cipriani, Giovanni Battista, 1727-1785. In England from 1755.

Claude, Charles S., France, 18th century.

Cobb, John, England. Partner of William Vile. Died 1778.

Cogswell, John, Boston, Mass., active 1769-1782.

Cole, Cornelius, England, 17th century.

Collman, L. W., England, 19th century. Decorator.

Connelly, Henry, Philadelphia, Pa., 1770-1826.

Copeland, H., England, 18th century.

Corbusier, Le (Charles Jeanneret), France, 1887-1965.

Cotte, Jules Robert de, France, 18th century.

Cotte, Robert de, France, 1656-1735. Architect.

Couet, L. Jacques, France, 18th century.

Courtnay, Hercules, Philadelphia, Pa., active about 1762.

*Cox, Joseph, New York City, 18th century.

Coxed, G., and Wosilk, T., England, 17th century.

Cramer, M. G., France, 18th century.

*Cressent, Charles, France, 1685-1768.

Criaerd or Criard, André (1689-1776) and Mathieu (older brother), France. Worked for Oeben.

Crunden, John, England, last half of 18th century.

Cucci, Domenico (Italian), France, 17th century.

Daley, John, Baltimore, Md.

*Darly, Matthias, England, 18th century.

*David (David Roentgen), France, 1743-1807.

Davies, John, Boston, Mass., after 1635.

Delorme, François, 1691-1768. JMÉ 1735. Chinoiserie.

Delorme, Philibert. See L'Orme, Philibert de.

Denizot, France, 18th century.

Dennis, Thomas, Ipswich, Mass., 17th century.

Derignee, Robert, England, 17th century.

Deskey, Donald, America, active in the modern movement.

Desmalter family. See Jacob.

Dester, Godefroy, France. JMÉ 1774.

De Vries. See Vries, Vredeman de.

Disbrowe, Nicholas, Hartford, 1612-1683.

Downing, Andrew Jackson, 1815-1852. American designer and writer.

*Dunlap, Samuel, 2nd, member of New Hampshire joiners, late 18th century.

Du Quesnoy, F. H., and J., Flanders, 17th century.

Eames, Charles, contemporary American designer.

Eastlake, Charles Locke, 1833-1906.

Egerton, Matthew, Brunswick, N.J., 1739-1802.

Elfe, Thomas, Charleston, S.C., active 1747-1776.

Elliott, Charles, England, 18th century.

Elliott, John, Philadelphia, Pa., Died 1791.

Essex, Joseph, Boston, 18th century.

Étienne, Avril, France, 18th century.

Farmborough, William, England. Worked with Burroughs, 1672-1690.

Fitzcook, H., England, 19th century.

Flaxman, John, England, 1755-1826. Artist.

Flötner, Peter, Germany, 16th century.

Fontaine, Pierre-François, France, 1762-1853. Empire period, with Charles Percier, 1764-1838.

France, William, England, 18th century.

France and Beckwith, England, circa 1770.

Frankl, Paul, American designer. Died 1958.

Frothingham, Benjamin, Charleston, S.C., about 1756-1809.

Gabler, Matthias, Germany, 17th century.

Gaines, John, Portsmouth, N.H., active 1724-1743.

Gale, Cornelius, England, late 17th century.

Galletti, Giovanni, Italy, 18th century.

Garnier, P., France, 18th century.

Gaudreau, Antoine Robert, France. Died 1751.

Gautier, Andrew, New York City, 18th century.

Germain, Thomas, France, 18th century.

Gettich or Gottlieb, Paulus, Germany, 17th century.

Geuser, Marx, Germany, 17th century.

Gheel, Francis van, Flanders, 18th century.

*Gibbons, Grinling, England, 1648-1720. Carver.

Gibbs, James, England, 1674-1754. Architect.

Gilbert, John, England, 19th century.

Gillet, Louis, France, 18th century.

*Gillingham, James, Philadelphia, Pa., 18th century.

Gillow, Richard, England, 18th century.

Gillow, Robert, England, 17th and 18th centuries.

Gimson, Ernest, English designer, 1864-1919.

Giovanni, Fra, Italy, 16th century.

*Goddard, John, Newport, R.I., 1723-1785.

Golle, Peter (Dutch), France, 17th century.

Goodison, Benjamin, England, 18th century.

*Gostelowe, Jonathan, Philadelphia, circa 1744-1795.

Goujon, Jean, France, 16th century.

*Gouthière, Pierre, France, 1740-1806.

Grendey, Giles, England, early 18th century.

Grene, William, England. Coffermakers to the Crown, 16th century.

Griffiths, Edward, England, 18th century.

Gropius, Walter, contemporary American architect.

Gumley, John, England, 18th century. Cabinetmaker to George I.

Haeghen, Vander, Flanders, 18th century.

Haig, Thomas, England, 18th century. Partner of Chippendale.

Haines, Ephraim, Philadelphia, Pa. Worked with Henry Connelly.

Hains, Adam, Philadelphia, Pa. Born 1768, and active until circa 1815.

*Halfpenny, William and J., England,

18th century. Architects, authors of *New Designs for Chinese Temples* (1750).

Hallet, William, England, 17th or 18th century.

Hampton & Sons, London, mid- and late-19th century.

Heal & Son, England, cabinetmakers after 1840.

Heinhofer, Philip, Germany, 16th and 17th centuries.

Helmont, Van, Flanders, 18th century.

*Hepplewhite, George, England. Died 1786. His widow, Alice H., published *The Cabinet Maker and Upholsterer's Guide* (1788).

Hernández, Gregorio, Spain, circa 1576-1636. Architect, sculptor.

Hitchcock, Lambert, Hitchcockville, Conn. (working after 1818).

Hoffman, Josef, Austria, 1870-1923 (Wiener Werkstätte).

Holbein, Hans, England, early 16th century.

Holland, Henry, England, 1746-1806. Architect.

Holmes, W., England, 19th-century designer.

Holthausen, H. J., France, 18th century.

*Hope, Thomas, England and Flanders, 1769-1831.

Hopkins, Gerrard, Philadelphia, Pa., 18th century.

Hosmer, Joseph, Concord, Mass.

*Ince, William, England, 18th century. Ince and Mayhew published *The Universal System of Household Furniture.*

*Jacob, Georges, France, 1735-1814. JMÉ 1765.

Jacob-Desmalter (François Honoré Georges), France, 1770-1841.

Jacob-Desmalter (Georges Alphonse), France, 1799-1870.

Jacobsen, Arne, contemporary Swedish architect.

Jennens and Bettridge, England. Manufacturers of papier-mâché furniture, 19th century.

Jensen, Gerriet, England, 17th century. Cabinetmaker to the Crown.

Johnson, Thomas, England, 18th century. Carver; author of *Twelve Girandoles* (1755) and *One Hundred and Fifty New Designs.*

*Jones, Inigo, England, 1573-1652. Architect.

Jones, William, England, 18th century. Designer; author of *The Gentleman's and Builders' Companion.*

Juhl, Finn, Danish contemporary.

*Kauffmann, Angelica, England, 1741-1807. Painter.

Keller, Johann Heinrich, Switzerland. Early Baroque.

*Kent, William, England, 1684-1748. Architect-designer.

Kiskner, Ulrich, Germany, 17th century.

Klenze, Franz Karl Leo von, 1784-1864. German architect.

Kolding, Peter Jensen, Copenhagen, Denmark, about 1600.

Kraft, J. C., England, 18th century.

Lacroix, Roger Van Der Cruse, France, 1728-1799. JMÉ 1755. Signed R.V.L.C.

Ladetto, Francesco, Italy, 18th century.

Lalonde, Richard de, France, late 18th century. Designer.

*Langley, Batty and Thomas, England, 18th century. Architects; authors of *The City and Country Builder's Workman's Treasury of Designs* (1740).

Langlois, Peter, England. Born 1738. Cabinetmaker in the manner of Boulle.

*Lannier, Charles-Honoré, New York City. Active 1805-1819.

Lardant, Jacques, France, 16th century.

Laszlo, Paul, contemporary American.

Lawton, Robert, Jr., Newport, R.I. Working 1794.

*Le Brun, Charles, France, 1619-1690.

Le Corbusier. *See* Corbusier, Le.

Le Moyne, Jean-France, 1645-1718.

Le Roux, J. B., France, 18th century.

Lehman, Benjamin, Philadelphia, Pa., late 18th century.

Leleu, Jean François, France, 1728-1807. Worked with Oeben.

Lemon, William, Salem, Mass., active around 1796.

Lepautre, Jean, France, 1617-1682.

Levasseur, Étienne, France. Born in 1721. Worked in the manner of Boulle. The family continued in the tradition through the 19th century.

Linnell, J., England, 18th century.

*Lock, Matthias, England, 18th century. Carver and designer. Published *A New Book of Ornaments* (1768).

Loos, Adolph, Austria, late 19th century. Sezession.

L'Orme, Philibert de, France, 16th century.

*McIntyre, Samuel, Salem, Mass., 1757-1811. Carver.

Mackintosh, Charles Rennie, Scotland. Born 1868.

Marc, Jean, France, 17th century.

Majano, Giuliano de, Italy, 1432-1490.

Malmsten, Carl, Swedish contemporary.

*Manwaring, Robert, England, 18th century. Cabinet- and chairmaker. Published *The Cabinet and Chair Maker's Real Friend and Companion* (1765); *The Chair-Maker's Guide* (1766).

Marchand, Nicolas-Jean, France. Born 1697. JMÉ 1738.

Margaritone of Arezzo, Italy, 1236-1313.

*Marot, Daniel, France, 1650-1712. Architect and designer.

Marot, Gérard, France, 17th century.

Marot, Jean (son of Gérard Marot), France, 1625-1679. Architect.

*Martin, Guillaume, Simon, Étienne, Julien, and Robert, France, 18th century. *See also* Vernis Martin.

*Mayhew, Thomas. *See also* Ince and Mayhew, England.

McCobb, Paul, contemporary American.

*Meissonnier, Juste-Aurèle, France, 1693-1750.

Mills and Deming, New York City, active around 1790.

Molitor, Bernard, France under Louis XVI. JMÉ 1787.

Montigny, Philippe Claude, France, 1734-1800. JMÉ 1766.

Moore, James, England. Died 1726. Cabinetmaker to the Crown.

Moore, James, the Younger, England. Died 1734.

*Morris, William, England, 1834-1896.

Moser, Koloman, Austria, Sezession.

Nelson, George, contemporary American.

Norman, Samuel, England, 18th century. Partner of Goodison.

*Oeben, Jean François, France. Born circa 1720, died 1763. Developed Gobelin factory.

Oppenord, Alexandre Jean (Dutch), France, 17th century.

*Oppenord, Gilles-Marie, France, 1672-1742.

*Oudry, Jean-Baptiste, France, 18th century. Artist.

*Palladio, Andrea, Italy, 1518-1580. Architect.

Panturmo, J. di, Italy, 1492-1556.

Parran, Benjamin, England, 18th century. Partner of Goodison.

Parzinger, Tommi, contemporary American.

Passe, Crispin de, France, 17th century.

Paudevine, John, England. Upholsterer in the Restoration period.

Paul, Bruno, Germany, early 20th century.

*Percier, Charles, France, 1764-1838. Architect and designer.

*Pergolesi, Michel Angelo (Italian), England, 18th century. Decorator employed by the Adam brothers. Published *Original Designs*.

Philippon, Adam, France, 16th century.

Phill, Thomas, England. Upholsterer, reigns of Anne and George I. Died 1728.

*Phyfe, Duncan, New York City, 1768-1854.

Piffetti, A. Pietro, Italy, 1700-1777.

Pillement, Jean Baptiste, France, 1713-1789.

Pillon, Germain, France, late 16th century. Designer.

Pimm, John, Boston, Mass., circa 1740.

Ponti, Gio, contemporary, Italian.

Porfirio, Bernardino di, Italy, 16th century.

Price, Richard, England. Joiner and chairmarker to Charles II. Died before 1686.

Quervelle, Anthony Gabriel, Philadelphia, Pa. Active 1820?

Randolph, Benjamin, Philadelphia, Pa., circa 1762-1792.

Rennie, James, England. Partner of Thomas Chippendale. Died 1766.

Revitt, N., England, 18th century. Architect.

Rheydt, Melchior, Cologne, Germany, after 1600.

Riesen Burg, Bernard Van, France, early 18th century. Signed BVRB.

Riesener, Henri-François, France, 18th century.

Riesener, Jean-Henri, France, 1734-1806.

Rietveld, Gerrit, Holland. Born 1888 (De Stijl).

Roberts, Richard, England. "Chairmaker to His Majesty," 1728.

Roberts, Thomas, England. Joiner-chairmaker, reigns of William and Mary, and Anne.

Rodwell, James, England. Cabinetmaker, reign of George II.

*Roentgen, David 'better known as David), France, 1743-1807.

Rogers, Harry, England, 19th century. Designer.

Rohde, Gilbert, American designer. Died 1944.

Rohe, Mies Van Der, contemporary American architect.

Roller, Alfred, Austria, early-20th-century Sezession.

Rossi, Properzia de, Italy, 15th and 16th centuries.

Ruhlmann, Jacques Emile, France. Died 1933.

Rukers, Thomas, Augsburg, 16th century.

Russell, Gordon, England. Contemporary.

Saarinen, Eero, American, 1911-1961.

*Sambin, Hugues, France, 16th century. Designer.

Sanderson, Elijah, Salem, Mass., active 1771-1825.

Sass, Jacob, Charleston, S.C., active 1774 to about 1828.

*Saunier, Claude Charles, France, era of Louis XVI.

*Savery, William, Philadelphia, Pa., active from 1740's to 1787.

Schinkel, Karl Friedrich, Berlin, 1781-1841. Architect.

Schmieg, Carl, contemporary American.

Schoen, Eugene, 20th-century American, architect-designer.

*Seddon, George, England, 1727-1801.

*Seddon, Thomas, England, 19th century.

Sené Family: Claude, 1724-1792; JMÉ 1742; Claude II, Le Jeune; JMÉ 1769.

Sené, Jean Baptiste, France, born 1748. Furnisher to the Crown, 1785.

Serlius, Sebastian, France, 16th century. Designer.

Seymour, John, Boston, Mass., active 1790-1810.

Shackleton, Thomas, England. Partner of Seddon.

Shaw, John, Annapolis, Md., active 1773-1794.

*Shearer, Thomas, England, 18th century. Cabinetmaker and designer. *The Cabinetmaker's London Book of Prices and Designs* (1788).

*Sheraton, Thomas, England, 1751-1806. Cabinetmaker and designer.

Short, Joseph, Newburyport, Mass., active 1771-1819.

Skillin, John, and Simeon, Boston, Mass. Carvers, late 18th century.

Slocombe, P., England, 19th century. Designer.

*Smith, George, England. Cabinetmaker and designer. Published *A Collection of Designs for Household Furniture and Interior Decoration* (1808).

Soli, Guiseppi, Italy, Empire period.

Stewart, James, England, 18th century. Architect.

Stickley, Gustave, Grand Rapids, Mich., late 19th century, early 20th.

Stitcher and Clemens, Baltimore, Md., circa 1804.

Street, Sir George, Royal Academy, England, 1824-1881.

Swan, Abraham, England, 18th century.

Tasso, Giovanni Battista, Italy, 15 and 16th centuries.

Tatham, Thomas, England, 1763-1818.

Taylor, John, New York City, 18th century.

Terry, Eli, 1772-1852. Connecticut clockmaker.

*Thomire, Pierre Phillippe, France, 1751-1843.

Thonet, Michael, Vienna, after 1846.

Tiffany, Louis Comfort, American designer, 1848-1933.

Tilliard, Jean Baptiste, France, 1685-1766.

Tolfo, G., Italy, 16th century.

Toms and Luscombe, England, 19th century.

Topino, Charles, France. JMÉ 1773.

Toppan, Abner, Newbury, Mass., 1764-1836.

Tosi, Francesco Marie, Italian architect. Died 1859.

Town and Emmanuel, England, 19th century.

*Townsend family, Rhode Island, for about a century before 1750 to the middle of the 19th century.

*Townsend, Edmund, Rhode Island, 1736-1811.

*Townsend, Job, Rhode Island, 1699-1765.

Townsend, Stephen, Charleston, S.C., between 1763 and 1768.

Trevigi, Girolama Da, England, 1503-1544.

*Tufft, Thomas, Philadelphia, late 18th century.

Turing, William, England, early 18th century. A partner of John Gumley in the 1720's.

Uccello, Paolo, Italy, 1397-1479.

Ugliengo, Carlo, Italy, 18th century.

Van de Velde, Henri, Belgium. Born 1863. Art Nouveau.

Van der Rohe, Mies, contemporary American architect.

*Vanbrugh, Sir John, England, 1664-1726. Architect.

Venasco, Giovanni Paolo, Italy, 18th century.

Verbruggen, Peter (the younger), Flanders, 1660-1724.

Verhaeghen, Theodore, Flanders, 18th century.

Vile, William, England. Died 1767.

Viollet-Le-Duc, Eugène Emmanuel, France, 1814-1879. Gothic Revival.

Voysey, C. F. A., England, 1857-1941. William Morris group.

Vries, Jan Vredeman de (Flemish), France, 1527-1606. Published *Différents Pourtraicts de Menuiserie.*

Wagner, Otto, Austria, 1841-1918. Architect.

Walker, Robert, Charleston, S.C., active 1799-1833.

Ware, Isaac, England, 18th century. Architect.

Wayne, Jacob, Philadelphia, Pa., active after 1785.

Weaver, Holmes, Newport, R.I., 1769-1848.

Webb, Isaac, Boston, Mass., 18th century.

Webb, Philip, English architect of the Ruskin group, 1830-1915.

Webster, John, Pennsylvania, 18th century.

Wedgwood, Josiah, England, 1730-1795.

Wegner, Hans J., Danish contemporary.

*Weisweiler, Adam (German), France, 18th century.

Wenman, Richard, New York City, 18th century.

Wertheimer, Samson, England, 19th century.

White, Stanford, New York City, 1853-1906. Architect.

Willard, Simon, 19th-century Connecticut clockmaker.

Willet, Marinus, New York City, 1740-1830.

Williams, John, Newcastle, Del.

Wolfender, John, Boston, last quarter of the 17th century.

Wormley, Edward, contemporary American.

*Wren, Sir Christopher, England, 1632-1723. Architect and designer.

Wright, Frank Lloyd, 1869-1959, American architect.

Wright, Russel, contemporary American.

Wright and Mansfield, England, 19th century.

Zabello, Francesco, Italy, 16th century.

*Zucchi, Antonio Pietro, England, 1726-1795. Painter; husband of Angelica Kauffmann.